Contents

iii

iv   Contents

PREFACE

○

This book began as a second edition of *Working Canadians*. We quickly realized that a thorough overhaul was needed to capture the phenomenal rate and scope of change that has transformed Canadian workplaces and labour markets since *Working Canadians* was published in 1984. A measure of this change is the fact that we have retained only three of the original forty-seven articles. Equally important, we designed *Working Canadians* as a stand-alone teaching resource at a time when there were few texts of any kind in the area. Now we find ourselves shaping the content of this reader to mesh with the themes and debates in the revised second edition of our text, *Work, Industry, and Canadian Society*. In short, this collection of articles is a completely new book which, we hope, captures some of the most significant changes that have occurred both within the workplace and the classroom since the early 1980s.

The forty articles in this new collection attempt to strike a balance between, on the one hand, scholarly perspectives, and, on the other, more popular discussions of the leading trends defining work in the 1990s. *Work in Canada* seeks to document and analyze the diversity of real-life experiences of Canadians in the world of work. Despite the growing scholarly literature on work (not only by sociologists but also by researchers in labour history, industrial relations, organizational analysis, and other disciplines), the rapid pace of change in labour markets and workplaces inevitably means that scholarship lags somewhat behind. Thus, we have integrated scholarly literature with articles written by journalists, trade unionists, managers, consultants, and policy analysts. The result is intended to encourage readers to reflect upon and debate the various options available to Canada for work and employment at this crucial juncture in our history.

Used on its own, *Work in Canada* offers a lively introduction to anyone interested in the current debates, trends, and issues—and their sociohistorical context—that are reshaping work. But primarily we designed *Work in Canada* as a supplementary reader for use in tandem with the revised second edition of our text, *Work, Industry, and Canadian Society*. Each section is issue-oriented, providing examples and case studies that flesh out the theoretical perspectives and empirically-based trends presented in the text. Used as a pair, *Work in Canada* and *Work, Industry, and Canadian Society* will, we believe, fully meet the teaching and learning needs of college and university instructors and their students in the sociology of work, labour studies, human resource management, and related areas.

The nine sections of this reader do not precisely correspond to the ten chapters in *Work, Industry, and Canadian Society*. This is largely due to the fact that the topics covered in the reader often address themes that crop up in various text chapters. But generally instructors will find a good fit between the reader and the text, one that allows them flexibility in assigning issue-

CHART P.1   Chapter Guide to Using *Work in Canada* with *Work, Industry, and Canadian Society*

Work in Canada	Work, Industry, and Canadian Society
1) Industrialization in Canada	Chapter 1: Industrialization and the Rise of Capitalism
2) Contemporary Work Trends	Chapters 2 and 3: Industrial Capitalism, Post-Industrial Society and Social Theory; Canadian Labour Force Trends
3) Canadian Workers and the New Global Economy	Chapters 2 and 3
4) Labour Markets and Inequality	Chapter 4: The Sociology of Labour Markets
5) Women's Employment	Chapter 5: Women's Employment
6) Organizing and Managing Work in the New Economy	Chapter 6: The Organization and Management of Work
7) Unions and Industrial Relations	Chapter 7: Unions and Industrial Relations
8) Power and Control at Work	Chapter 8: Power, Control, Resistance and Conflict: Critical Perspectives on Work
9) Experiencing Work	Chapters 9 and 10: The Meaning of Work; Job Satisfaction and the Quality of Work

oriented readings. Chart P.1 outlines our attempt to link the two books, although we expect that some instructors will prefer to organize the material differently.

Briefly, the highlights of the topics covered in each of the reader's nine sections are as follows. Part 1 (Industrialization in Canada) provides three contrasting vantage points for understanding the historical dynamics of the industrialization process: skilled male craftsmen of early 20th-century Hamilton; women in late 19th-century Ontario's agrarian economy; and the transformation of offices in the first three decades of this century. Part 2 (Contemporary Work Trends) elaborates several central issues in the sociological analysis of labour markets. These range from the quality of jobs in the service economy, the dilemmas of part-time work, and participation in informal or unpaid work, to the impact of population aging on work organizations and retirement policy.

Part 3 (Canadian Workers and the New Global Economy) picks up several crucial public policy and theoretical issues, namely, productivity, worker training, free trade, and Canada's location in a postindustrial global economy. Part 4 (Labour Markets and Inequality) offers case studies that explore the labour market barriers historically faced by disadvantaged groups—visible minorities, persons with disabilities, and native Canadians. Part 5 (Women's Employment) amplifies key themes in the contemporary feminist analysis of work. The section underscores the gendered structure of work, and the resulting problems and inequalities, through articles on sexual harassment, immigrant women garment workers, women engineers, and an analysis of the challenges of pay equity.

Part 6 (Organizing and Managing Work in the New Economy) parallels the chapter in *Work, Industry, and Canadian Society* with a similar title. This is achieved by a thematic focus on new human resource management practices, corporate downsizing, Japanese management applied in Canada, and union-management cooperation to achieve work reforms. Part 7 (Unions and Industrial Relations) again mirrors the discussion in the text, elaborating several pivotal issues. These include the future of the Canadian labour movement, the state's erosion of public sector collective bargaining, the sources of militancy in the Canadian Auto Workers Union, and the question of women in union leadership positions.

Power and Control at Work, as discussed in the textbook, offers a critical perspective to counterbalance the management-initiated strategies outlined in the section on the organization and management of work. A worker-centred view of quality-of-working-life programs, technological change, and workplace health and safety is articulated in this section. Part 9 (Experiencing Work) adopts a micro-analysis of work experiences. The issues discussed include job satisfaction and work values, the working conditions in the low end of the service sector, problems of balancing work and family, and the personal impact of unemployment.

We acknowledge that many topical issues have necessarily been excluded, largely due to the constraints of page space and the availability of good Canadian material. While the articles in this volume are focused on specific problems or issues, we believe that they will be sufficiently provocative so that readers will look beyond the specifics of each case. In order to provide a theoretical perspective, we have, in the section introductions, attempted to identify relevant theories and debates. After each set of readings, we present some discussion questions and additional readings that will encourage further analytic thinking.

To conclude, we owe a huge vote of thanks to several graduate students, who combed the library in search of relevant material for this reader. In particular, Barbara Heather, Ahmet Oncu, and Deborah Neale were very able research assistants. Nelson Canada also made a major contribution to the final shape of the book, soliciting detailed, helpful reviews from several reviewers, including Craig McKie of Carleton University and David Lewis of McMaster University. To Charlotte Forbes, Bob Kohlmeier, Nicole Gnutzman, and their colleagues at Nelson, we want to express our appreciation for their flexible view of deadlines and the encouragement they provided. Finally, the support and understanding of our families was indispensable to this project (and many others).

Graham S. Lowe and Harvey J. Krahn
Edmonton, October 1992

Industrialization in

Canada

EDITORS' INTRODUCTION

o

In 1850, a few decades before Confederation, eastern and central Canada were primarily agricultural societies, although in some regions other natural resource-based industries (fishing and forestry, for example) also provided employment. Aboriginal peoples were the main inhabitants of western and northern Canada, their hunting and gathering societies still largely unchanged by European influence. By 1900, however, European immigrants had begun to shape an agricultural economy in the Prairie provinces, and the process of industrialization was well underway in central Canada. A look back to this era provides valuable insights about how typical patterns of work changed with the advent of factory-based mechanized production. Equipped with this historical understanding, we are better able to assess changes occurring in the workplace of the 1990s.

Compared to the United States and western European nations, the shift from an agricultural to an industrial economy took a different course and occurred somewhat later in Canada. Nevertheless, in a general sense, the process of industrialization in Canada resembled the social and economic changes observed elsewhere: wage labour became the dominant form of employment relationship; mechanized production systems largely replaced craftwork; large bureaucratized workplaces became more common; white-collar occupations grew in size and importance; and there emerged a class of professional managers intent on making management a "science."

Craig Heron provides a detailed historical account of the power struggle between foundry owners and skilled (male) metal workers in Hamilton at the turn of the century. Employers were able to gain much greater control over production, at the expense of craftworkers, through the introduction of

1

new technology that made many workers' skills obsolete. The adoption of "modern" management techniques that systematized and routinized work also aided these industrial capitalists in their struggle with the craft unions that had traditionally played a central role in most aspects of heavy metal manufacturing. In fact, some of the technological and managerial changes introduced by employers had as much to do with combatting unions as with increasing production. Heron's discussion of labour–management conflict, changing skill requirements, and the social impact of new technologies and management strategies in early industrial Canada is highly relevant today. As we shall see in following sections, the same issues are once again being hotly debated as Canada moves into a post-industrial era at the end of the 20th century.

Most accounts of industrialization have had a very male-oriented focus, an imbalance addressed by Marjorie Cohen, who describes changes in women's work as industrialization proceeded. One of the most important consequences for women's employment, at least in Europe, was the increasing segregation of women into a limited number of occupational settings. In pre-industrial economies in which the household was the centre of productive activity, a greater integration of women's and men's work roles had been observed. But with industrialization, men became more responsible for securing the family income (in factories and other workplaces), while women were most often left with the domestic responsibilities. Women who participated in the paid labour force found their roles restricted to a limited number of low-status occupations (domestic servants, for example).

However, Cohen makes an important distinction between the Canadian and the European experience. In pre-industrial Canada, where most production involved the extraction and export of raw materials, home-based production was never as widespread as it had been in Europe. Consequently, as Canada industrialized, women did not really move out of production activities and back into domestic roles; rather they basically stayed in the latter. In other words, a distinct gender-based system of occupational segregation already existed.

The third reading examines the "administrative revolution" that paralleled the evolution of the industrial capitalist economy. Graham Lowe describes how the consolidation of business enterprises and the rapid growth of government bureaucracies early in this century created huge challenges for management. The need to organize vast amounts of information, and to coordinate the work of large numbers of employees, led to a rationalization of office work, the introduction of "modern" management schemes, and significant growth in managerial occupations. The emerging administrative systems also required a growing army of workers in routine clerical jobs to process, file, and communicate vital information. As in the manufacturing workplaces described by Heron, new office-management strategies were used not just to increase efficiency but also to gain more control over the labour of employees. Lowe goes on to document how, as office work became a "female" occupational enclave, the status of clerical (office) work also declined.

The three articles in Part 1 describe some of the central features of Canada's industrialization experience. They also introduce a number of central themes around which subsequent sets of readings are organized, including: power and control in the workplace; gender-based occupational segregation; the motivations and assumptions underlying different management approaches; and labour–management conflicts.

DISCUSSION QUESTIONS

○

1. What are the central defining characteristics of (a) "industrialization," (b) "industrial capitalism," and (c) the "administrative revolution"?
2. To what extent did Canada's industrialization experience resemble (or diverge from) the pattern of social and economic change observed in Europe and the United States?
3. What is meant by the "U-shaped curve" explanation of female labour force participation? How well does it describe the Canadian experience?
4. Was "scientific management" a response to, or a cause of, labour–management conflicts?
5. Is the term "crisis" appropriate to describe the changing work experiences of skilled craftsmen during Canada's period of industrialization?
6. What do managers do? Has their role changed over the past century?

SUGGESTED READINGS

○

Chandler, Jr., Alfred D. *The Visible Hand: The Managerial Revolution in American Business.* Cambridge, Mass.: Harvard University Press, 1977.

Heron, Craig. *Working in Steel: The Early Years in Canada, 1883–1935.* Toronto: McClelland & Stewart, 1988.

Laxer, Gordon. *Open For Business: The Roots of Foreign Ownership in Canada.* Toronto: Oxford University Press, 1989.

Parr, Joy. *The Gender of Breadwinners: Women, Men and Change in Two Industrial Towns, 1880–1950.* Toronto: University of Toronto Press, 1990.

Pentland, H. Clare. *Labour and Capital in Canada: 1650–1860.* Toronto: James Lorimer, 1981.

The Crisis of the Craftsman: Hamilton's Metal Workers in the Early Twentieth Century[*]

Craig Heron

I

o

.... In recent years labour historians have been increasingly fascinated with the lively history of the skilled stratum of the nineteenth-century working class, the artisans. Often colourful, articulate, tough-minded men, these craftsmen were not only leading actors in the emergence of a working class in the early years of the century; when they gave up their self-employed status and entered the "manufactory" to practise their craft under one employer's roof, they brought with them the accumulated traditions, values, and institutions of the pre-industrial era. A vibrant artisanal culture therefore continued to thrive in late nineteenth-century industry, where the skills of these men were indispensable to many sectors of production.

Artisanal culture had much broader dimensions than life in the workshops where the craftsmen toiled. They were confident of the social worth their skills bestowed upon them and expected to lead dignified, respectable lives. Central to their outlook on the world was a gritty spirit of independence and determination to resist subordination. In the workshops, and in society generally, they demanded for all men and women the maximum of personal liberty and freedom from coercion and patronage, and politically they became the staunchest proponents of egalitarian democracy. From employers they expected no interference with their traditional craft practices, which controlled the form and pace of production. Their "manhood,"

[*] Abridged from Craig Heron, "The Crisis of the Craftsman: Hamilton's Metal Workers in the Early Twentieth Century," *Labour/Le Travailleur* 6 (Autumn 1980): 7–48. Reprinted in Graham S. Lowe and Harvey J. Krahn, eds., *Working Canadians: Readings in the Sociology of Work and Industry* (Toronto: Methuen, 1984), pp., 34–45 [reprinted by Nelson Canada in 1991]. Reprinted by permission of the author and the publisher.

they insisted, demanded such treatment. The principal institutions of collective self-help which promoted and defended this artisanal life were, of course, their craft unions.

All of these social and ideological phenomena, however, rested on the craftsmen's continuing shop-floor power, and by the end of the nineteenth century that power was being challenged by employers who saw these men and their mode of work as serious obstacles to larger corporate strategies....

I I
o

Metal-working shops, especially foundries, machine shops, and agricultural implement works, had predominated in Hamilton's industrial structure since the mid-nineteenth century. According to one study, 50 metal-working firms employed 2,634 workers, or 38 per cent of the city's workforce, in 1891.[1] Particularly important were the stove-manufacturing shops, whose size and production made the city a national leader in the industry. The leading stove foundry, the Gurney-Tilden Company, was described in 1892 as "the largest industry of their kind in the Dominion."[2] It was in this industrial setting that Hamilton's artisans worked the metal into the wide range of products that won for Hamilton the epithet "The Birmingham of Canada."

Of the two most prominent groups of craftsmen in the city, the moulders could lay claim to the deepest roots in pre-industrial society. In fact, moulders liked to trace their ancient traditions to the biblical figure Tubal Cain. From their skilled hands came metal castings as diverse as stoves, machinery casings, and ornamental iron and brass work. Technological change had almost completely bypassed the foundry, which remained down to the end of the nineteenth century a classic "manufactory" of highly skilled craftsmen working in one employer's shop. A turn-of-the-century article in *Iron Age* emphasized that the craft "is learned almost entirely by the sense of feeling, a sense that cannot be transferred to paper. It is something that must be acquired by actual practice. A sense of touch plays such an important part in the construction of a mold that without it it is impossible to construct a mold with any reasonable expectation of success."[3] This sense was what craftsmen liked to call the "mystery" of their trade. With a few tools and the knowledge under his cap, the moulder prepared the moulds to receive the molten iron or brass. A mould began with a "pattern," usually wooden, in the shape of the finished casting, which was embedded in sand. Preparing and "ramming" the sand (that is, pounding it firmly with iron-shod poles) required great care and precision so that when the pattern was drawn out a perfect mould remained to hold the molten metal. If a cast product was to have a hollow space, the moulder inserted a "core," a lump of specially prepared sand that had been carefully shaped and baked hard at the coremaker's bench (originally moulders made their own cores, but gradually a division of labour emerged). Once cool, the casting was shaken out of the sand and cleaned, to be ready for any finishing processes. The size of the objects to be cast ranged so widely that the moulder might work on a bench or prepare his moulds in great stretches of sand on the foundry floor.[4] "The jobs he undertook," recalled one observer of Canadian foundries, "were varied in the extreme, a single job sometimes entailing days of careful labor, and the work being given a finish in which the maker took pride."[5]...

I I I
o

The 1890s marked a turning point in the work world of moulders and machinists. Over the next 30 years a transformation within metal-working factories swept away the artisanal culture of these workers which had flourished in the preceding decades. Technological and managerial innovations undermined and ultimately destroyed a work environment in which skilled craftsmen with indispensable expertise had resided over the pace and organization of the labour process.

The driving force behind this process of change sprang from the new shape of economic life in Canada. By the 1890s Hamilton's industrial life was being integrated into national and international markets which involved stiffer competition for the city's firms and the rise of increasingly large corporate enterprises. Hamilton not only participated in the Canadian merger movement in the pre-war decade, with the creation of such firms as the Steel Company of Canada and the Canadian Iron Corporation; it also opened its floodgates to branch plants of American giants like International Harvester and Canadian Westinghouse. These developments certainly increased both the scale of the average workplace in the city and the economic clout of employers and, perhaps more important, generated a sharpened concern about protecting profits against more powerful competition. Some of the city's oldest metal shops, especially the stove foundries, were particularly hard pressed in this new environment.

With their eyes fixed on profit margins, corporate managers in Hamilton attacked labour costs on two fronts. The first, aggressive anti-unionism, was ultimately the prerequisite for the second, the restructuring of the work process. The shop-floor power of craftsmen that was consolidated in their unions was a constant threat to corporate planning of production. Before 1900 individual employers, and occasionally groups of them, challenged unions in the city with varying degrees of success, but after the turn of the century anti-unionism became a cornerstone of labour relations for the largest Hamilton firms. The city's two largest employers of skilled metalworkers, in particular, had well-established reputations as union-busters before their arrival in Hamilton. International Harvester's predecessor companies had such an anti-labour record, dating from the 1880s, that the Hamilton labour movement mounted a vigorous and ultimately successful campaign to prevent the city fathers from granting the Deering company a bonus to locate in Hamilton.[6] Similarly in 1903 George Westinghouse, president of both the Canadian and American companies, engaged in a much publicized exchange with the American Federation of Labor President Samuel Gompers over the question of unionizing his staff; he made it quite clear that this was one corporation which would tolerate no workers' organizations in its plants.[7] The Westinghouse management in Hamilton never departed from that position....

I V
o

Employers were not simply attempting to eliminate unions in order to push their workers harder; they were equally concerned about having the flexibility to re-organize the work process in order to rid themselves of their reliance on testy, independent-minded craftsmen whose union regulations kept the supply of new men and the pace of work strictly under control. After 1900 Hamilton employers' strategies fit into an emerging consensus about factory management in Canada. During the decade before World War I Canadian companies succumbed to the North American mania for more "system" in industrial organization.[8] At first the emphasis was on precise cost accounting as a means of determining the actual production cost of an item and of isolating areas in the entire manufacturing operation where costs needed to be reduced. "Broadly speaking," wrote accountant H.L.C. Hall in *Industrial Canada*, organ of the Canadian Manufacturers' Association, "factory economy means the production of your output for less money...." He suggested a two-fold purpose for a costing system: "First to induce economy by elimination of waste and second to induce economy by intensifying production." The manager could expect the "system" to tell him "the efficiency of every man and every machine per labour hour and machine hour," as well as informing him of "all delays and the reasons for the failure to arrive at the maximum." Often tied to these new cost-accounting plans were special wage-incentive schemes which encouraged each worker to attempt to increase his output in return for a bonus or premium in addition to his regular wages.[9]

The fascination with "systematic" management began to reach full flower in Canada after 1911, when American writers, notably Frederick W. Taylor and his school of "scientific management," were catching great public attention. These new management specialists advocated complex procedures for establishing "scientific" norms for the speed of work based on stop-watch measurement, along with incentive wage payment systems that both rewarded the fast worker and punished the laggard. A key tenet of the Taylor system was the centralization of all control over the production process in the hands of the managers through planning, routing, scheduling, and standardization.[10] The Canadian business press generally applauded these new plans. *Canadian Machinery*, metal-trades journal of the Maclean publishing empire, declared that, "The principles are general in their application and where applied, valuable results will be obtained," and *Industrial Canada* concluded in 1914: "The experience of manufacturers seems to be that scientific management decreases a staff while it increases its efficiency.... Reports from firms on this continent show that scientific management has become practical."[11] Clearly new ideas were in the air about how to run a factory.

Managers in Hamilton's metalworking industries used three related tactics to pursue their goals of tightening their grip on the labour process, speeding up production, and reducing labour costs. Wherever possible the chief elements in a re-organization of production in the city's foundries and machine shops became narrowing the work of the skilled, upgrading labourers to become "handymen" who specialized in only one fragment of the process, and introducing new machinery. "If skilled labour is necessary," argued one foundry expert, "means must be used to apply the skill only to those operations in which it is needed, subdivision of labour and the use of mechanical appliances and power being applied wherever this can be profitably done."[12] As the subdivision of labour and co-ordination of production progressed, primitive notions of assembly-line production began to appear. A Hamilton *Herald* reporter spotted this trend on a tour through the new Westinghouse plant in 1905:

> The thing that strikes the notice of the observer before all else is the manner in which everything is planned out so that everything that is being made makes a direct progression through the works. Economy is seen everywhere. The raw materials are delivered to the spot where they will be used.... And the machines are situated so that each piece passes right down the line to where the parts are assembled and put together ready for testing and shipping. Nothing is handled twice.... Everything works like clock-work, and all are truly "parts of one stupendous whole."[13]

.... Moulding machines were introduced into Canada relatively slowly. Canadian trade journals were passionate promoters of the new equipment and criticized Canadian foundrymen for their backwardness. The editor of the *Canadian Engineer* argued in 1906 that

> the moulding machine is destined to revolutionize the foundry business, for when ... a simple power machine, operated by one laborer, another shovelling sand, and one to carry out the flask, can turn out one mould per minute; or on a union rule of seven hours moulding, pouring 140 moulds per man; being twice as much as a union moulder can do by hand, then no enlightened owner of a foundry will submit to the primitive hand moulding methods of making duplicate castings, which we find in so many foundries in Canada today.[14]

In April 1908 *Canadian Machinery* was able to announce that "during the last one or two years Canadian foundrymen have been realizing the value of molding machines and several installations have been made, which are doing good work"; and in June it published a detailed analysis of moulding machine practice in an unidentified Canadian machinery foundry, where the installation of the machines and the use of handymen had cut production costs considerably. The same month, at the American Foundrymen's Association's first convention in Toronto, the new machinery was exhibited and discussed extensively. Canadian membership in the association immediately leaped from 17 to 57.[15]

Hamilton's foundries were not slow to adapt. The two biggest, International Harvester and Canadian Westinghouse, were, in fact, pioneers in the field. Henry Pridmore, a leading manufacturer of moulding machines, had begun his experiments in 1886 in the McCormick Harvester works in Chicago where the company introduced the new machinery in a successful attempt to drive out the local moulders' union. A company executive later boasted: "Their great foundries and their novel molding machinery were the admiration of the iron world." Not surprisingly then, a visitor to the new Hamilton Harvester plant's foundry in 1904 discovered moulding machinery in each moulder's stall.[16] The Canadian Westinghouse plant was similarly in the vanguard of managerial innovation. The superintendent of its foundry was David Reid, "one of the most prominent foundrymen of America." His extensive American experience had included managing a foundry where he had been responsible for some major restructuring of the work process: "By introducing modern methods here, such as molding machines, and dividing labor, whereby the molder practised the art of molding and nothing else, the melt was increased for 12 or 15 tons daily to between 50 and 60 tons."[17] Reid's influence, however, was not restricted to the Westinghouse foundry; in 1905 he became the president of the Associated Foundry Foremen of America, a scion of the American Foundrymen's Association, and launched a Hamilton branch. The purpose of the organization was "education" for better foremanship, and its meetings were devoted to discussions of more efficient foundry practice.[18]...

Mechanization did not sweep relentlessly over the whole industry; in 1916, for example, the NFA's committee on foundry methods found that not more than 25 per cent of its North American membership had taken advantage of the available mechanical appliances. But it was in the larger foundries, such as those that dominated the industrial landscape in Hamilton, that innovation was most advanced. By the 1920s most of the city's foundries had introduced a full range of mechanical devices. The machinery at the Hamilton Stove and Heater Company so impressed a foundry trade journalist in 1920 that he burbled, "Verily, the molding machine only requires to be taught to talk, when it will be perfect." By 1928 the *Canadian Foundryman* could gloat over the sweeping changes since the pre-war years:

> Twenty years ago an unskilled man in the foundry would not have been permitted to handle even a slick, being only allowed to assist in the ramming of big jobs perhaps, lifting or similar work. Now unskilled labour can step into

an up-to-date foundry and within a few days perform a task equal to that of the skilled molder, due to present day equipment.[19]

.... By the 1920s, therefore, the role of the artisan in the foundry had been reduced to only those few tasks which could not be turned over to machines and handymen. Skilled workers had certainly not been banished from the industry, and their union survived down to the end of World War I on the basis of their continuing importance in the production process, however much that may have been eroded and confined. But they no longer wielded their artisanal control mechanisms for setting the pace of production as they had 30 years before. As early as 1909, Josiah Beare, a young union moulder in Hamilton, told a workmate: "Jim, I have worked too hard in my time; the pace is set too fast for the average man to keep up, and I am a nervous wreck"; he died six weeks later of "heart trouble." Half a century later Joe Davidson, future leader of Canada's postal workers, arrived in Hamilton as an experienced Scottish moulder and discovered "the more intense style of working" at Canada Iron Foundries; in nearby Dundas, he found, "The motto was 'produce or else' and every day was a mad race, the men working like beasts."[20]

V

Twenty years ago a molder was at home with his slick and trowel, but place the good mechanic of those years in the modern foundry and he would feel like a "fish out of water."[21]

In 1928 most observers would have agreed with this Canadian business journalist that the heyday of the craft worker in Canada's metalworking industries had passed. A new, rationalized, more highly mechanized mode of work had emerged to confine the skilled metal worker to small, unspecialized shops on the periphery of modern industry or to a sharply limited role in the process of mass production. On the one hand, in the case of both the moulders and the machinists, the craftsmen found large areas of their traditional work mechanized and divided up among less skilled labourers. On the other, a few "well-rounded mechanics" survived inside large-scale industry, but these craftsmen found their work narrowed, circumscribed, and intensified. In this new role in production there was increased pressure on the skilled men to apply themselves strictly to work that required their technical know-how. The old artisanal sense of working a product through all or most of its stages of production to completion was lost. And the pace of work, formerly so carefully regulated by custom and entrenched in union regulations was now set by corporate administrators.[22] The skilled metal workers who hung on in the context of mass production became simply a part of a complex continuum of industrial workers under the detailed supervision of efficiency-conscious managers. The artisan of the 1890s gave way to the skilled production worker whose overall status in the workplace had undoubtedly declined.

If some craftsmen survived in the workplace, artisanal *culture* did not. The mode of work in the foundries and machine shops of the late nineteenth century had involved a commanding role for the artisans in determining the rhythms of the total production process. These men had nurtured an intense craft pride that fed on their indispensability to industry. Structurally the craftsmen's trade unions had been the repositories of both the mechanisms of job control and the ideology of craft superiority. Thirty years of conflict with employers who saw the manifestation of this culture in their factories as an obstacle to their larger corporate strategies, however, resulted in final defeat for the craft unions and all they represented by the early 1920s....

NOTES
o

1. R.D. Roberts, "The Changing Patterns in Distribution and Composition of Manufacturing Activity in Hamilton Between 1861 and 1921," MA thesis, McMaster University, 1964, 78.

2. *Hamilton: The Birmingham of Canada* (Hamilton 1892), n.p. The E.C. Gurney Company became Gurney-Tilden during the 1890s when John H. Tilden moved into control. The Toronto branch of the firm became independent and retained the Gurney name. Stoves were Canada's most important foundry products at the turn of the century; in 1902 there were 297 stove foundries in Canada out of a total of 527. Clyde A. Saunders and Dudley C. Gould, *History Cast in Metal: The Founders of North America* (n.p. 1976), 15. On the growth of industry in Hamilton see, in particular, Marjorie Freeman Campbell, *A Mountain and a City: The Story of Hamilton* (Toronto 1966); C.M. Johnston, *The Head of the Lake: A History of Wentworth County* (rev. ed., Hamilton 1967); Bryan Douglas Palmer, "Most Uncommon Common Men: Craft, Culture and Conflict in a Canadian Community, 1860–1914," Ph.D. thesis, State University of New York at Binghampton, 1977; Roberts, "Manufacturing Activity"; Robert H. Storey, "Industrialization in Canada: The Emergence of the Hamilton Working Class, 1850–1970s," MA thesis, Dalhousie University, 1975.

3. John Sadlier, "The Problem of the Molder," *Iron Age* 6 June 1901, 26b.

4. Benjamin Brooks, "The Molders," reprinted from *Scribner's* in *Iron Molders' Journal* (hereafter *IMJ*), XLII, no. 11 (November 1906), 801–8; Margaret Loomis Stecker, "The Founders, the Molders, and the Molding Machine," in J.R. Commons, ed., *Trade Unionism and Labor Problems* (2nd ed., Boston 1921), 343–45.

5. *Canadian Foundryman* (hereafter *CF*), XIX, no. 5 (May 1928), 39.

6. Hamilton Public Library, Hamilton Collection, International Harvester Scrapbook, 1.

7. *Pittsburgh Dispatch*, 3 May 1903 (clipping in Westinghouse Canada Archives, P.J. Myler Scrapbook).

8. On the growing interest in "systematic" business management in the late nine-teenth century, see Joseph A. Litterer, "Systematic Management: The Search for Order and Integration," *Business History Review*, 35 (1961), 461–76; Daniel Nelson, *Managers and Workers: Origins of the New Factory System in the United States 1880–1920* (Madison, Wisc. 1975), 48–54. Canadian business journals directed their readers' attention to various management theories and experiments in North America. In 1905 the *Canadian Engineer* began a two-year series of articles by one A.J. Lavoie on system in business operation. The outpouring from other publications included: G.C. Keith, "The General Scheme of Cost Keeping," *CM*, I, no. 4 (April 1905), 131–32; "Systematic Works Management," *ibid.*, I, no. 10 (October 1905), 403; G.C. Keith, "Is Piecework a Necessity?" *ibid.*, III, no. 4 (April 1907, 122–23; D.B. Swinton, "Day Work vs. Piecework," *ibid.*, II, no. 12 (December 1906), 453; "The Art of Handling Men," *ibid.*, III, no. 9 (September 1907), 27–29; "Machine Shop Time and Cost System," *ibid.*, 32–34. Also H.C.L. Hall, "Economy in Manufacturing," *Industrial Canada* (hereafter *IC*), VI, no. 7 (February 1906), 430–31; no. 11 (June 1906), 732–35; VII, no. 2 (September 1906), 103–5; "The Model Factory," *ibid.*, VII, no. 7 (February 1907), 586–88; no. 9 (April 1907), 723–35; C.R. Stevenson, "System Applied to Factories," *ibid.*, no. 5 (December 1907), 420; L.E. Bowerman, "What a Cost System Will Accomplish," *ibid.*, VIII, no. 10 (May 1908), 774–75; Kenneth Falconer, "Cost Finding in the Factory," *ibid.*, VIII, no. 8 (March 1908), 639–40.

9. Hall, "Economy in Manufacturing," 420, 430, 732–33. The increasing use of time-clocks in Canadian factories facilitated the computation of precise labour-time. See my "Punching the Clock," *Canadian Dimension*, 14 (December 1979), 26–29.

10. Harry Braverman, *Labor and Monopoly Capital: The Degradation of Work in the Twentieth Century* (New York 1974), 85–138; Bryan Palmer, "Class, Conception and Conflict: The Thrust for Efficiency, Managerial Views of Labor and the Working Class Rebellion, 1903–22," *Review of Radical Political Economics*, 7 (1975), 31–49; Nelson, *Managers and Workers*, 55–78; Samuel Haber, *Efficiency and Uplift: Scientific Management in the Progressive Era, 1890–1920* (Chicago 1964), 52–55; Heron and Palmer, "Through the Prism of the Strike," 430–34; Graham S. Lowe, "The Rise of Modern Management in Canada," *Canadian Dimension*, 14 (December 1979), 32–38.

11. *CM*, VII, no. 2 (February 1911), 58; *IC*, XIV, no. 4 (November 1913), 423.

12. Arthur Smith, "Methods of Solving the Problem of Foundry Help," *CF*, V, no. 5 (May 1914), 85.

13. *Herald*, 14 October 1905 (clipping in Westinghouse Canada Archives, P.J. Myler Scrapbook).

14. "The Coming of the Molding Machine," *Canadian Engineering* (hereafter *CE*), XIII, no. 7 (July 1906), 265. The journal urged foundrymen to attend the annual convention of the American Foundrymen 's Association to learn more about the new machinery. Among the few Canadians who did attend were Hamiltonians David Reid of Canadian Westinghouse and A.H. Tallman of Tallman Brass, *CM*, III, no. 6 (June 1907), 36–37.

15. "Molding Machines: Principles Involved in their Operation," *CM*, IV, no. 4 (April 1908), 53–56; "Molding Machine Practice in a Canadian Machine Foundry," *ibid.*, IV, no. 6 (June 1908), 65–66; no. 7 (July 1908), 46–48, 52; *IC*, VIII,

(July 1908), 1108. *Canadian Machinery* carried numerous descriptive articles and advertisements for the machinery, as did the *Canadian Foundrymen* when it was launched in 1910.

16. "Stripping Plate Machine: Inception and Development," *CF*, IX, no. 6 (June 1918), 123; Robert Ozanne, *A Century of Labor-Management Relations at McCormick and International Harvester* (Madison 1967), 20–28; Cyrus McCormick, *The Century of the Reaper: An Account of Cyrus Hall McCormick, the Inventor of the Reaper: of the McCormick Harvesting Machine Company, the Business He Created; and of the International Harvester Company, his Heir and chief Memorial* (Boston 1931), 131–250; *Iron Age*, 1 September 1904, 3. This must have been one of the first installations of moulding equipment in Canada.

17. *CM*, II, no. 4 (April 1906), 145–46.

18. *Ibid.*, 145–46; *LG*, V, no. 9 (April 1905), 1047; *CE*, XIII, no. 8 (August 1906), 303. The foundry foremen's association became the subject of considerable controversy in 1906, since the moulders' journal was convinced the new organization was yet another union-crushing apparatus of the foundrymen. David Reid vigorously denied the charge, but in some North American cities it did conform to the union's expectations. See National Founders' Association, *Review*, February 1906, 17–18; *IMJ*, XL, no. 8 (August 1904), 608–9; XLII, no. 2 (February 1906), 98; no. 3 (March 1906), 181–84; no. 5 (May 1906), 358–60; no. 7 (July 1906), 505–6; no. 9 (September 1906), 670.

19. Stecker, "Founders, Molders, and Molding Machines," 435; *CF*, X, no. 3 (March 1919), 58–59; XI, no. 4 (April 1920), 115, XIV, no. 10 (October 1923), 30; XVIII, no. 5 (May 1927), 6–9; no. 7 (July 1927), 6; no. 10 (October 1927), 8–10; XIX, no. 5 (May 1928), 17–18, 39.

20. *IMJ*, XLV, no. 9 ('September 1909), 647; Joe Davidson and John Deverell, *Joe Davidson* (Toronto 1978), 39–40.

21. *CF*, XIX, no. 5 (May 1928), 39.

22. Of course, while formal trade union controls disappeared, we should not ignore informal techniques that workers used to regulate the pace of work in North American industry for years to come. See Stanley B. Mathewson, *Restriction of Output Among Unorganized Workers* (New York 1931); Donald Roy, "Quota Restriction and Goldbricking in a Machine Shop," *American Journal of Sociology* 57 (March 1952), 427–42; Bill Watson, "Counter-Planning on the Shop Floor," *Radical America* 5(May–June 1971), 78–85.

Capitalist Development, Industrialization, and Women's Work✠

Marjorie Griffin Cohen

EARLY PERSPECTIVES ON INDUSTRIALIZATION

o

Over time, the understanding of the effect of industrialization on women's work, based primarily on the British experience, has undergone considerable change. It has shifted from a perspective which saw the process as one that would bring women's work from the margins to the centre of productive activity, to one which sees industrialization as essentially restricting the nature of women's work.

The tendency in the nineteenth century was to see the impact of industrialization on women as a dramatic one which greatly changed the nature of the household and the nature of women's work.[1] During industrialization, in particular the transformation from cottage industrial production to factory production in Britain, the most noticeable change in female employment was the extent to which women were leaving the home to work. At the time this appeared to be a general feature of the industrializing process that would undermine the position of male labour and the family as industrialization progressed. In the words of one observer, the factory process was having disastrous consequences because of the 'gradual displacement of male by substitution of female labour in a large proportion of the industrial occupation of the country.... This evil ... is spreading rapidly and extensively ... desolating like a torrent, the peace, the economy, and the virtue of the mighty masses of the manufacturing districts. Domestic life and domes-

✠ Abridged from Marjorie Griffin Cohen, *Women's Work, Markets, and Economic Development in Nineteenth-Century Ontario* (Toronto: University of Toronto Press, 1988), chapter 2, "Capitalist Development, Industrialization, and Women's Work." Reprinted by permission of the publisher and the author.

tic discipline must soon be at an end.'[2] Marx and Engels also stressed the tendency for male labour to be displaced by female labour as industrialization progressed: 'the more modern industry becomes developed, the more is the labour of men superseded by that of women. Differences of age and sex have no longer any distinctive social validity for the working class.'[3]

In hindsight this perspective appears to have greatly exaggerated the true state of things. But however melodramatic the prediction appears now, it was not based on an unfounded perception of what seemed to be occurring at the time. The critical industry in Britain's industrialization process was the textile industry, and the changes occurring in it appeared to contemporary observers to offer insights into the likely effects of industrialization as industry after industry was drawn into the factory. There is substantial evidence to show that in the early stages of factory work, workers in the textile industries were primarily women and children.[4]

The expansion of women's work outside the home in the first industries to become industrialized quite naturally led contemporary observers to assume that a revolution was taking place in work for women. This was almost universally assumed to be bad for the entire family—not because women were working, for women had certainly worked in the family economy, but because this work was taking women away from the home, where they had combined paid employment with domestic responsibilities.[5]...

In short, the industrialization process was seen by contemporaries as drastically changing women's work as a whole by removing their paid work from the home to the factory and by radically reducing their ability to perform traditional household duties. To those who expected factory work to increase dramatically, it appeared that the tendency for women to become wage-earners could only accelerate.

TWENTIETH-CENTURY PERSPECTIVES ON INDUSTRIAL CAPITALISM: A PARADIGM

o

.... Throughout this century there has been considerable disagreement about whether the changes brought by capitalist industry resulted in a deterioration or an improvement in women's position, but the restrictive effect of the nature of women's labour has been widely accepted.[6] This emphasis on the narrowing of women's labour sphere has become basic to current analyses of the transition from pre-industrial economies to industrial capitalism. In fact, a general paradigm of the effect of industrialization on women's labour has developed, based on the British and Western European experience. While there is not, of course, total agreement about the details, and while various aspects of the paradigm have been questioned and modified over time, its principal outlines are generally clear. What is more, they are frequently accepted as typical characteristics of the development of capitalist industry wherever it occurs.

The changes in women's labour associated with capitalist industrialization occurred primarily because the home was separated from the workplace. As industry moved out of the household, the home was no longer a place of production and the family's function as a productive unit disappeared.[7] This significantly narrowed women's ability to contribute to the family economy. When production occurred within the household, women's labour was an integral part of how the family earned its living. While the distinctions between male and female work in the pre-industrial family economy are acknowledged, and are understood to be a function of women's responsibility for children and housework, the relatively more integrated nature of the family's work is stressed.[8] Men and women did much the same type of work, even if the actual tasks they performed were different. In agriculture, women were as much a part of the productive process as men. While male labour was more likely to involve field work and women's labour was more likely to be centred around the immediate environs of the dwelling-place, the family's livelihood was dependent on the labour of both. In cottage and craft production the whole family would be engaged in the work process—the income of the family was critically dependent on the complementary nature of the tasks performed by males and females in the production of commodities. There are different opinions about whether women's labour in the pre-industrial household was valued by the family as being equal to that of males. Some stress that the complementary nature of the labour meant that women's labour was not subservient to men's.[9] But for the most part women's labour is considered to have been subservient to male labour, even when this labour was critical to how the family earned its income.[10]

The separation of production from the household greatly increased the differentiation in the division of labour by gender.[11] As the physical location of production separated male and female labour, both occupational and industrial segregation by gender became more pronounced. Through their productive activities outside the home, males became increasingly responsible for securing the family income.[12] Since waged labour forced males to be absent for long periods of time, male involvement in domestic affairs became negligible. The correlative of this situation was that housework and child care became more and more the primary responsibility of women. While women had certainly been more involved with these tasks than men in the pre-industrial household, the ability to combine domestic tasks with the general productive work of the family meant that domestic activities did not consume the whole of women's labour. In fact, it is frequently maintained that child care and housework were considerably subordinate to female labour in the family enterprise in the pre-industrial period.[13] With the removal of the main source of the family's income from the home, the married woman's ability to combine income-producing labour with domestic labour was seriously curtailed. Initially this affected married middle-class women and the wives of wealthy farmers, changing their lives from intimate involvement in the family enterprise to essentially lives of leisure.[14] Eventually this retreat of women into the domestic sphere became characteristic of working-class women too. The difficulties of combining domestic work with waged labour when waged labour involved excessively long hours and when there were few substitutes for women's domestic labour meant that, increasingly, only those families on the margins of economic existence would continue to rely on the labour of the married woman outside the home.

The rise of the housewife, then, as the 'dominant mature feminine role' is perceived to have emerged with the development of industrial capitalism.[15] Whether this was a positive or a negative development is a subject of considerable debate. To some, the loss of income-earning activity increased the married woman's dependence and adversely affected women's status in society.[16] To others, the change in the basis of marriage from an economic partnership to one of economic dependence for the wife had a more positive impact because it improved the standard of living for the average family, in particular because the mother and wife had more time to devote to the well-being of her family and its domestic circumstances.[17] Nevertheless, there is general agreement that the labour sphere of the married woman was considerably restricted as her duties became more centred on child care and housework. She became dependent on her husband economically and became more isolated as her work assumed a less collective nature.

The increased rigidity in the division of labour by gender also affected the labour of women who worked outside the home. Waged work for women may have increased through the industrial transformation process, but rather than expanding the occupational diversity for women, as was initially anticipated, women's paid work was increasingly restricted to a small range of jobs.[18] In the manufacturing sector, women's paid employment was confined almost exclusively to those industries which were industrialized first. As industrialization spread, women did not move into new areas of work. Rather, 'the rise of the factory girl was an exceptional and atypical development in the industrializing economy.'[19] As crafts and trades were taken outside the household and developed along capitalistic lines, women's ability to participate decreased. Daughters and wives were excluded from production as waged-labour became more significant to the larger-scale organization of these industries, and as industries in which women had once been dominant required greater amounts of capital. Structural changes in the economy reduced the significance of agriculture as an employer of labour altogether, so women's agricultural occupations, which had employed the greatest proportion of females in the pre-industrial period, declined rapidly.[20] The decline in female employment, as cottage industries were transformed by industrialization, was partially offset by the feminine nature of the early factory work-force, but the expansion of factory jobs did not fully replace the loss of female employment in cottage production. Ivy Pinchbeck maintains, for example, that the proportion of males in the textile industry was greater under factory production than it had been under the domestic system, where the estimates are as high as eight women and children to every man employed.[21]

The striking feature of industrialization's impact on women's paid labour throughout the nineteenth century was the increased concentration of women in one area of employment which clearly was expanding for them—domestic service.[22] Early studies of women's labour during industrialization tended to ignore the effect of the development process on this type of work, assuming either that it remained relatively unchanged until late in the nineteenth century or that the rise of factory labour for women meant that single women became less dependent on domestic service for employment.[23] Recently there has been much more attention paid to the rise of domestic service as a typical pattern, cross-culturally, for female employment during the industrializing process. In Britain this type of work absorbed an increasing proportion of the total labour force in the second half of the nineteenth century, rising from 13 per cent of the total labour force in 1851 to 16 per cent by 1891, while at the same time it became more feminized and more characterized as temporary employment.[24] Women tended increasingly to find work in domestic employment as the demand for this type of work expanded while opportunities in other areas of employment were decreasing.[25]...

The separation of the home from the workplace clearly had significant implications for the increased rigidity in the division of labour by gender. But as significant as its effect on reducing occupational diversity for women was its effect on reducing women's overall ability to participate directly in how the family earned its income. That is, not only were the types of income-earning jobs women could perform being restricted, but so too was the number of income-earning opportunities, relative to the size of the female population.[26]

The participation of women in the income-earning areas of economic activity is now widely accepted as having reached its peak in the pre-industrial period, and as having declined during the initial phases of industrialization only to recover the previous high degree of participation over the very long run. In fact, it is now posited that there has been, historically, a high correlation between the household mode of production and female work-force participation, a correlation further evidenced by the analysis of women's labour experience in Third World countries today as capitalist industry transforms certain sectors of the economy.[27] In Britain, women's participation experience is described as a U-shaped curve, with the low point in activity occurring in the third quarter of the nineteenth century.[28] The recovery to pre-industrial levels is seen as occurring only in the second half of the twentieth century, when married women's participation in wage-earning occupations increased rapidly.

This general paradigm of social development and its effect on female labour through the capitalist industrialization process can be summarized as positing three major changes. First, industrialization separated the home and the workplace. In the pre-industrial period the household was the productive unit, with the family working together in the production process. As industry moved out of the household, the home was no longer a place of production and the family's function as a production unit disappeared. Second, this process brought about an increased differentiation in the division of labour by gender. As the physical location of production separated male and female labour, occupational and industrial segregation by gender became more pronounced. The rise of waged labour meant that males became increasingly responsible for securing the family income. At the same time, the division of labour in the family, in which women had always been more responsible for child care and housework than males, became more pronounced as women's opportunities to combine income-earning labour with household activities decreased. Married women's labour in the home became characterized by maintenance activities for the family: reproduction, child-care activities, and housework became their primary work roles. While unmarried women's work was likely to be associated with market activity, it was occupationally and industrially segregated from the work of males and for the most part was temporary. The third major change associated with capitalist industrialization—a change integral to the separation of the household from income-producing activities, married women's retreat into the home, and the restricted nature of women's paid work—was the progressive polarization of the public and private spheres of life, with men increasingly associated with public life and women relegated to the private sphere.[29] In the pre-industrial household, work was integrated with other types of household activities, so the distinction between the public and private functions of specific individuals within the household was largely insignificant. But, as income-earning activities were withdrawn from the household, a sharper distinction was made between the private sphere of the home and the public sphere of economic life. As women were confined to the household, their world and work became increasingly privatized and isolated, and the new ideology that women's rightful place was in the home gained currency.[30]...

THE CANADIAN EXPERIENCE

...[T]he colonial, export-oriented market economy of pre-industrial Ontario relied on a distinct form of production within the family and a method of organizing labour that placed different emphasis on the division of labour by gender from that in pre-industrial Britain. The underdeveloped nature of the economy, the limited supply of labour, and the primary orientation of market activity toward the export market tended to produce a much sharper division of labour in the household economy between production for the market and that for household consumption. In the early stages of development, female labour was centred on production for the household while male labour was focused on production for the market. In this respect one cannot point to a *withdrawal* of females from market production as the economy was transformed to industrial capitalism. Rather, economic growth brought women's production efforts increasingly into the market's sphere, both through production for the market within the household and through waged labour. Similarly, it is not possible to see the transformation in Ontario as resulting in a major split in the public and private spheres of life, and a sharper differentiation in the division of labour by gender. The private nature of production, the isolation of female labour, and a rigid division of labour by gender were common features of the pre-industrial period.

The changes in women's labour which occurred as local markets developed and the economy industrialized were complex and uneven. Even by the end of the period under consideration most female labour was not directed toward the market. But ultimately there was neither an overall decline in the proportion of women active in production for the market nor a restriction in the number of occupations available to women. Specifically, the pattern of women's market-oriented activity did not assume the U-shape of the English experience. It may be more appropriately characterized as a pattern of slow and steady increase in participation, but one which affected women in different sectors in different ways....

NOTES

o

1. For examples of early perspectives on industrialization and women see J.F.C. Harrison, *The Early Victorians 1832–51* (New York: Praeger 1971), 74–7; Neil J. Smelser, *Social Change in the Industrial Revolution: An Application of Theory to the British Cotton Industry* (Chicago: University of Chicago Press 1959), 281ff.; Ivy Pinchbeck, *Women Workers and the Industrial Revolution 1750–1850* (London: Virago Press 1981 [1930]), 196–201.

2. Lord Ashley, *Answer to the Address of the Central Short-Time Committee*, cited in Pinchbeck, *Women Workers and the Industrial Revolution*, 197.

3. Karl Marx and Friedrich Engels, *Manifesto of the Communist Party*, in *The Marx-Engels Reader*, ed. Robert C. Tucker (New York: W.W. Norton 1972), 341.

4. For information on the significance of the textile industry in the industrialization process see Phyllis Deane, *The First Industrial Revolution* (Cambridge: Cambridge University Press 1967), 84; David S. Landes, *The Unbound Prometheus: Technological Change and Industrial Development in Western Europe from 1750 to the Present* (New York: Macmillan 1955), 42, 89; Smelser, *Social Change in the Industrial Revolution*, 202; Frances Collier, *The Family Economy of the Working Classes in the Cotton Industry 1784–1833* (Manchester: Manchester University Press 1964), 3. Pinchbeck, for example, shows that in 1844 women represented 56 percent of the

workers in cotton mills, 69 percent of workers in woollen mills, and 70 percent of workers in silk and flax mills (Pinchbeck, *Women Workers and the Industrial Revolution*, 197).

5. Estimates for the percentage of married women working in cotton factories by mid-century range from 25 to 30 percent (Harrison, *The Early Victorians*, 75; Catherine Hall, 'The Home Turned Upside Down?: The Working-Class Family in Cotton Textiles 1780–1850,' in *The Changing Experience of Women*, ed. Elizabeth Whitelegg et al. [Oxford: Martin Robinson 1982], 25.) The census of 1851 indicated that 25 percent of all married women and two-thirds of all widows had an 'extraneous occupation' (Viola Klein, *Britain's Married Women Workers* [London: Routledge & Kegan Paul 1965], 12).

6. Some see the rise of the capitalist market economy as dramatically reducing women's position in society. See, for example, Alice Clark, *Working Life of Women in the Seventeenth Century* (London: Routledge & Kegan Paul 1982 [1919] and Roberta Hamilton, *The Liberation of Women: A Study of Patriarchy and Capitalism* (London: George Allen & Unwin 1978). Others stress that the transition to industrial capitalism did little to improve women's status (Louise Tilly and Joan Scott, *Women, Work, & Family* [New York: Holt, Rinehart and Winston 1978]), or that it improved women's position only in the very long run (Richards, 'Women in the British Economy'; Ann Oakley, *Woman's Work: The Housewife Past and Present* [New York: Vintage 1976]). For examples of various positions which hold that industrialization improved women's position in society see: John Burnett, *Useful Toil: Autobiographies of Working People from the 1820s to the 1930s* (London: Allen Lane 1974), 135; Harrison, *The Early Victorians*, 77–8; Klein, *Britain's Married Women Workers*, 2; Wanda F. Neff, *Victorian Working Women* (London: Frank Cass & Co. 1966 [1929], 248, 252; Pinchbeck, *Women Workers in the Industrial Revolution*, 306, 313; Edward Shorter, *The Making of the Modern Family* (New York: Basic Books 1975), passim; Harold Perkin, *The Origins of Modern English Society 1780–1880* (London: Routledge & Kegan Paul 1969), 157–8.

7. Tilly and Scott, *Women, Work, & Family*, 228; Oakley, *Woman's Work*, 33; Rowbotham, *Hidden from History: 300 Years of Women's Oppression and the Fight against It* (London: Pluto, 3rd ed. 1977), Ch. 5; Pinchbeck, *Women Workers and the Industrial Revolution*, 306; Catherine Hall, 'The Butcher, the Baker, the Candlestickmaker: The Shop and the Family in the Industrial Revolution,' in *The Changing Experience of Women*, ed. Whitelegg et al., 5; Wally Seccombe, 'Domestic Labour and the Working-Class Household,' in *Hidden in the Household: Women's Domestic Labour under Capitalism*, ed. Bonnie Fox (London: Women's Press 1980), 76–7; Lee Holcombe, *Victorian Ladies at Work: Middle-Class Working Women in England and Wales 1850–1914* (Hamden, CT: Archon 1973), 4.

8. Oakley, *Woman's Work*, 11, Lawrence Stone, *The Family, Sex and Marriage in England 1500–1800* (Middlesex: Penguin 1979), 139; Seccombe, 'Domestic Labour and the Working-Class Household,' 77; Tilley and Scott, *Women, Work, & Family*, 43.

9. Oakley, *Woman's Work*, 27; Hans Medick, 'The Proto-Industrial Family Economy: The Structural Function of Household and Family during the Transition from Peasant Society to Industrial Capitalism,' *Social History* 3 (Oct. 1976), 313.

10. See, for example, Chayton and Lewis, introduction to Clark, *Working Life of Women in the Seventeenth Century*, xxxv; Sally Alexander, 'Women's Work in Nineteenth-Century London: A Study of the Years 1820–50,' in *The Rights and Wrongs of Women*, ed. Juliet Mitchell and Ann Oakley (New York: Penguin 1976), 78; Peter Lastlett, *The World We Have Lost*, 2nd ed. (New York: Charles Scribner's Sons 1973), 2; Shorter, *The Making of the Modern Family*, 67.

11. Alexander, 'Women's Work in Nineteenth-Century London,' 75; Rowbotham, *Hidden from History*, 2; Lise Vogel, 'The Contested Domain: A Note on the Family in the Transition to Capitalism,' *Marxist Perspectives* 1 (1978), 66; Shorter, *The Making of the Modern Family*, 264; Tilly and Scott, *Women, Work, & Family*, 231; Oakley, *Woman's Work*, 34.

12. Pinchbeck, *Women Workers and the Industrial Revolution*, 112, 312–13; Clark, *Working Life of Women in the Seventeenth Century*, 12–13. For discussions of the issues surrounding the concept of the individual male providing the income for the entire family, see Michele Barrett and Mary Mcintosh, 'The "Family Wage",' in *The Changing Experience of Women*, ed. Whitelegg et al., 71–87; Wally Seccombe, 'Patriarchy Stabilized: The Construction of the Male Breadwinner Wage Norm in Nineteenth-Century Britain,' *Social History* (Jan. 1986), 53–76.

13. Tilly and Scott, *Women, Work, & Family*, 58–9; Shorter, *The Making of the Modern Family*, 264; Oakley, *Woman's Work*, Ch. 2.

14. Tilly and Scott, *Women, Work, & Family*, 74; Pinchbeck, *Women Workers and the Industrial Revolution*, 28; Klein, *Britain's Married Women Workers*, 9; Burnett, *Useful Toil*, 165; Clark, *Working Life of Women in the Seventeenth Century*, 38; Holcombe, *Victorian Ladies at Work*, 4. The fact that servants were increasingly hired by the wealthy farming or middle-class households is seen as evidence that the females of this class were becoming leisured ladies. But recently this reasoning has been challenged. Chris Middleton claims that 'if prosperous yeomen employed several women servants … it was not so that their wives and daughters could enjoy more ease and leisure; it was rather because there was too much work for them to cope alone' (Chris Middleton, 'Patriarchal Exploitation and the Rise of English Capitalism,' in *Gender, Class & Work*, ed. Eva Gamarnikow, David Morgan, June Purvis, Daphne Taylorson [London: Heinemann 1983], 21). Patricia Branca points out that the increased time devoted to child care did not leave the middle-class woman idle time during the nineteenth century. What is more, though domestic help was common in middle-class households, most hired only one worker and, with the increased demands on household labour, having only one servant meant that the housewife continued to exert considerable labour within the household (Patricia Branca, *Silent Sisterhood: Middle Class Women in the Victorian Home* [London: Croom Helm 1975], 53–7).

15. Oakley, *Woman's Work*, 32. See also Eli Zaretsky, *Capitalism, the Family, and Personal Life* (New York: Harper & Row 1976), 64; Clark, *Working Life of Women in the Seventeenth Century*, 11.

16. Richards, 'Women in the British Economy,' 356; Oakley, *Woman's Work*, 59; Clark, *Working Life of Women in the Seventeenth Century*.

17. Pinchbeck, *Women Workers and the Industrial Revolution*, 312–13; Bruce Curtis, 'Capital, the State and the Origins of the Working-Class Household,' in *Hidden*

in the Household, ed. Fox, 131; Shorter, *The Making of the Modern Family,* xiii, 264; Branca, *Silent Sisterhood,* passim.

18. The extent of the increase in women's wage work is inconclusive. Pinchbeck maintains that with industrialization, wage-earning occupations for women became more numerous (Pinchbeck, *Women Workers and the Industrial Revolution,* 1) and Tilly and Scott claim that as a daughter a woman would usually be a wage-earner (Tilly and Scott, *Women, Work, & Family,* 228). However, Richards maintains that the possibility that waged labour increased in the early transitional decades is a *bare* possibility, but that it most certainly decreased after 1820 (Richards, 'Women in the British Economy,' 346).

19. *Ibid.,* 345. Pinchbeck also maintains that 'women were relegated to certain occupations, the number of which tended to be reduced as capitalist organization developed,' and although factory work was an expanding field of employment for women, all other opportunities for wage work had declined (Pinchbeck, *Women Workers and the Industrial Revolution,* 121, 306).

20. Richards, 'Women in the British Economy,' 349. For an examination of the changes in the employment conditions of women in agriculture during the eighteenth and nineteenth centuries, see Pinchbeck, *Women Workers and the Industrial Revolution,* Part I. Patricia Branca points out that agriculture labour remained the major type of employment for women up until 1850 (Branca, *Women In Europe since 1750,* 25).

21. Pinchbeck, *Women Workers and the Industrial Revolution,* 124. See also Richards, 'Women in the British Economy,' 345.

22. McBride, *The Domestic Revolution,* passim; Tilly and Scott, *Women, Work, & Family,* 68–9; Burnett, *Useful Toil,* 137.

23. Pinchbeck, *Women Workers and the Industrial Revolution,* 4; B.L. Hutchins, *Women in Modern Industry* (East Ardsley: EP Publishing 1978 [1915], 73.

24. McBride, *The Domestic Revolution,* Table 2.2. The author says the pattern is similar in Europe, the United States, and Latin American countries.

25. For an example of the perspective that considers expanding work for servants as a function of the increased leisure of women in the home see Burnett, *Useful Toil,* 144. He maintains that 'domestic help was necessary to the Victorian middle and upper classes partly because wives and daughters had become virtually functionless ...' and because people accumulated more things.

26. For information on the impact of demographic changes, especially the effect of a surplus female population on labour opportunities, see Richards, 'Women in the British Economy,' 349; Tilly and Scott, *Women, Work, & Family,* Ch. 5; Louise A. Tilly, Joan W. Scott, and Miriam Cohen, 'Women's Work and European Fertility Patterns,' *Journal of Interdisciplinary History* VI (Winter 1976), 447–76.

27. Richards, 'Women in the British Economy,' 337; Ester Boserup, *Woman's Role in Economic Development* (London: George Allen and Unwin 1970), passim; Barbara Rogers, *The Domestication of Women* (London: Tavistock 1980), passim.

28. Richards, 'Women in the British Economy,' 337; Oakley, *Woman's Work,* 34ff.; Tilly and Scott, *Women, Work, & Family,* 229; Scott and Tilly, 'Woman's Work and the Family in Nineteenth Century Europe,' in *The Family in History,* ed. Charles E. Rosenberg (Philadelphia: University of Pennsylvania Press 1975), 147;

Thompson, 'Women and Nineteenth-Century Radical Politics,' 115; Sheila Lewenhak, *Women and Work* (Glasgow: Fontana 1980), 172.

29. Melissa Clark, "The Status of Women in Relation to Transitions in the Mode of Production,' in *Occasional Papers of the McMaster University Sociology of Women Programme* 1 (Spring 1977), 152; Hall, 'The Shop and the Family in the Industrial Revolution,' 15; Seecombe, 'Domestic Labour and the Working-Class Household,' 80–1; Alice Clark, *Working Life of Women in the Seventeenth Century*, 286; Oakley, *Woman's Work*, 59.

30. Barrett and Mcintosh, 'The "Family Wage",' 74; Pinchbeck, *Women Workers and the Industrial Revolution*, 312–13; Oakley, *Woman's Work*, 43–56.

Corporate Capitalism and the Administrative Revolution⌖

Graham S. Lowe

.... Administrative systems and office personnel were an integral part of the new economic era that dawned throughout North America and Western Europe around the turn of the century. Information became a highly valued resource for the professional managers who took the reigns of corporate capitalism. Central offices thus became organizational nerve centres. They collected, processed, stored and communicated mountains of facts and figures indispensable for managerial decision-making.[1]

The most striking feature of the administrative revolution was the replacement of the small, informal nineteenth-century counting house run by a handful of male clerks by sprawling twentieth-century offices, where masses of women performed more routinized and narrowly focused clerical tasks as if on a paper-processing assembly line. C. Wright Mills's image of the modern office as an enormous high-rise file, spreading its regulatory tentacles throughout the economy, could not be more appropriate. 'The office,' Mills concludes, 'is the Unseen Hand become visible as a row of clerks and a set of IBM equipment, a pool of dictaphone transcribers, and sixty receptionists confronting the elevators, one above the other, on each floor.'[2]

The unifying theme of this chapter is, in a word, control. Control was the driving force behind the administrative revolution. The office as 'unseen hand' permitted managers to manipulate more carefully not only market forces, but also the entire production process including human labour. Administrative control exercised through the office increasingly demanded

⌖ Abridged from Graham S. Lowe, *Women in the Administrative Revolution* (Toronto: University of Toronto Press, 1987), chapter 2, "Corporate Capitalism and the Administrative Revolution." Reprinted by permission of the publisher and the author.

that the same principles of co-ordination, integration and rationalization be applied to clerical work....

The impetus for the administrative revolution can be found in three dynamics of economic development. The first incorporates the ascendancy of corporate capitalism, mainly due to the expansion of manufacturing and service industries. The second dynamic is organizational, embodied in the growth of huge public and private sector bureaucracies. The third dynamic, integrally connected to the first two, is the rise of a new professional class of managers whose quest for efficiency wrought far-reaching rationalizations in work processes, first in factories then later in offices. These three dynamics laid down the broad parameters for far-reaching industrial, organizational and occupational changes in Western capitalist societies from the late nineteenth century onward.

The details of how these trends were played out differed, of course, within each national context. At a very general level, however, the rise of modern capitalist economies rested on the twin pillars of thriving manufacturing and services sectors. Centralized bureaucracies became the standard form of work organizations. The blue-collar proletariat, prominent actors in the nineteenth-century industrialization process, eventually were overshadowed by expanding white-collar occupations. Foremost among these were office clerks and managers. These developments surfaced in Canada somewhat after their appearance in the United States, Britain or Germany. But once unleashed their dramatic effects soon became evident. Looking beyond the specifics of each national case, there can be little doubt that the interweaving of these changes produced the fabric of modern administration.

A corporate headquarters or the sprawling office complex of a government department is, from the outside, tangible evidence of the new-style office which gradually replaced the old, one-room counting house of pre-industrial capitalism. But behind the façades of these bureaucracies lie the most fundamental characteristics of the administrative revolution: a profusion of fairly routine clerical tasks; the accelerating rationalization of office procedures; a shift in recruitment from males to females; and a diminished social status for clerical occupations as a result. Indeed, the internal restructuring of the office which gathered pace after 1900 is most graphically illustrated in the feminization of its labour force. These dramatic alterations in the social character of the office workforce signalled deep-seated changes in the very substance of administration.

How, though, is clerical feminization directly connected to the rise of corporate capitalism? The crucial link is to be found in the new roles into which clerks were cast as the office assumed ever greater responsibility for exercising administrative control. Elaborate recording, communicating, filing, analysing and accounting procedures, so essential to the growing scale and complexity of business and government operations, formed the basis of modern clerical activities. Regulation of external market forces and control over internal work processes are what make the office inseparable from the functions of contemporary management. Indeed, with the rise of the modern corporation a widening array of detailed managerial functions were parcelled into specific tasks and delegated to clerical underlings. Without an extensive and efficient army of clerks, top management would be hamstrung. To invoke a physiological analogy: 'Management, the brain of the organization, conveys its impulses through the clerical system which constitutes the nervous mechanism of the company.'[3]

Internal changes in administrative structures and processes affected office working conditions, technology and job content. The generalist male bookkeeper no longer fitted into the more fragmented and standardized division of labour. These internal developments in administration coalesced with larger social trends which increased the availability of women for paid employment. Hence by the end of the 1920s, the female office clerk formed a prominent new social group in many of the leading Western capitalist societies.

Centralized bureaucratic organizations, the development of coherent managerial philosophies and practices, and the rapid growth of a pool of female clerical workers are, in short, the hallmarks of the administrative revolution. But as David Lockwood would be quick to remind us, 'there is no sharp dividing line between the counting house and the modern office.'[4] True enough, the evidence that I present shows that the transition was gradual in Canada, the United States and Britain. And there are no compelling reasons not to believe that this probably is the case in other advanced capitalist countries which I have not examined in this study. Certainly in Canada the essential features of modern administration were plainly evident in major manufacturing and service organizations by 1930. Small-scale offices run by a couple of male general clerks and bookkeepers were becoming relics of an earlier phase of capitalism. In other words, the onslaught of corporate capitalism from roughly 1900 heralded the beginnings of a revolution in the means of administration. I now turn to consider the specific details of this in one country, Canada.

THE DEVELOPMENT OF CORPORATE CAPITALISM IN CANADA

o

Canada embarked on the road to industrialization later than Britain or the United States. The nation's colonial legacy as a staple producing hinterland exerted a strong influence on the timing and character of its economic growth.[5] Canada was a late industrializer. Early signs of industrialization were evident by the 1870s, even earlier by some accounts, with the emergence of the factory system of production. But progress was slow; not until the opening years of the twentieth century did industrialization surge forward. By the end of the First World War the economic importance of

industry surpassed that of agriculture.[6] By then the small-scale local enterprises of the post-confederation era had given way to huge corporations in
key manufacturing and service industries. The present distribution of the
gross national product was firmly established.[7] In short, Canada was cata-
pulted into a trajectory of wholesale economic and social change that also
set in motion a revolution in administration....

THE RISE OF LARGE-SCALE ORGANIZATIONS

o

The centralized bureaucracy was the organizational form most compatible
with an expanding industrial economy. Workplaces in late nineteenth-century Canada tended to be small, rudimentary in their organization and lacking any coherent management strategy. As late as 1890, four out of five manufacturing firms employed fewer than 75 people.[8] Sun Life Insurance
Company, later to dominate the insurance world, then had a head office
staff of 20.[9] More typical would have been the office of Imperial Oil's Winnipeg branch, which looked like this in 1883: 'A single room (upstairs) size
about 14' x 18', one roll top desk for the manager, a high desk and stool for
the writer, a table, sofa, box-stove, a half cord of wood piled up in the corner
and as a final touch—one pair of hip-length boots.'[10]

The forces of industrialization unleashed around 1900 dramatically
altered the organizational framework of business and government. Fundamental to the administrative revolution was the ascendancy of large corporate and government bureaucracies. The centralization of planning, co-ordination and information processing in offices can be traced back to the early
twentieth century. As in most other advancing industrial nations, by the
1920s big business and big government—organized hierarchically and regulated by elaborate systems of administrative controls presided over by
professional managers—dominated the Canadian economy. There were,
however, important organizational differences cross-nationally. For
instance, managerial hierarchies arose in Germany and America during the
1880s and 1890s, in Britain during the 1920s and in France not until after the
Second World War. Canada followed just behind the United States in this
respect, being more advanced than Britain and most of Europe.[11]...

Perhaps the record of Sun Life's astounding growth best exemplifies the
way bureaucracy inevitably spawned huge central offices populated by
numerous clerks. Sun aggressively swallowed up competitors on its way to
conquering international life insurance markets. By 1930, after 124 acquisitions in the preceding four decades, Sun Life's Montreal headquarters
employed 2,856.[12] It only seems fitting that we turn to T.B. Macaulay, President of Sun Life in 1905, for insights regarding what propelled organizational change during this era:

Institutional success is but another name for growth, and corporate growth implies expansion—the absorption and concentration of wealth—and wealth, as we all know, is the power that rules and controls men and relations.... To life insurance, concentration of wealth is an absolute necessity. A life insurance company should be a perpetuity, and its wealth should accumulate with the increase of the amount at risk.'[13]...

THE NEW SCIENCE OF MANAGEMENT

o

A key ingredient in the transition from entrepreneurial to corporate capitalism was the ascendant power of the salaried manager. The rise of large-scale organization was synonymous with centralized managerial hierarchies. The nature of management authority, and how it is exercised, has been at the core of organizational theory since Max Weber proposed his model of bureaucracy.

Research by business historian Alfred D. Chandler Jr., provides the most penetrating account of how, after 1870, professional managers became the 'visible hand' of American business, replacing elusive market mechanisms. Chandler argues that a centralized, departmentally based structure was the institutional response to technological progress and expanding consumer markets in the United States after 1850.[14] The traditional 'rule of thumb' approach to management was replaced by 'scientific' administrative systems. Higher productivity and profits, lower costs, and reduced decision-making uncertainty could be more effectively achieved through careful managerial co-ordination. Rapid industrialization in the United States after 1870 brought together two trends: the development of large, increasingly complex factories and the entry of trained engineers into management positions.[15] This convergence initiated a drive for more methodical approaches to management. Observing the British case, Sidney Pollard traces the root of modern management even further back, to the early industrial revolution:

Basically, the range of the problems of management was the same in all industries that had to deal with them for the first time during the industrial revolution: labour recruitment and training, discipline, control over production, accountancy and accountability were the ingredients of a science which varied only in detailed application not in principle, as between different sectors of the economy.[16]

The new breed of managers who took command of corporate capitalism enlarged the scope of managerial concerns beyond technology to include the manipulation of social and organizational aspects of production. Around the turn of the century the relative pace of technological change slowed. Employers therefore had to search for other means of maximizing their firm's potential. The pioneers of factory management were often engineers who had been promoted into positions of authority. They laid the groundwork for the rigorous scientific management of Frederick W. Taylor. Time study methods, piece rate payment schemes, and closely regulated tasks largely devoid of skills and responsibilities reduced growing numbers of blue-collar workers to automatons. Employees were viewed as mere cogs in the productive machinery, motivated solely by economic self-interest.

A contrasting approach was advocated by industrial reformers, early personnel 'experts', and other forerunners of the human relations movement. This managerial orientation emphasized the importance of the 'human' factor in the production process. Yet no single strategy dominated. Rather, employers often combined elements of both approaches to suit their particular needs. The common thread was a quest for greater efficiency, higher productivity and a more compliant and co-operative labour force.[17] While the finer strategic details varied from industry to industry and organization to organization, by the 1920s the foundation of contemporary management was solidly established on the guiding principles of efficiency, co-ordination and control....

THE RISE OF MODERN MANAGEMENT IN CANADA

o

Despite the obviously indispensable role of managers in the industrialization process, the exact nature of their goals and strategies has received little attention in Canada. The administrative revolution, and the attendant growth of a female clerical workforce, are organically connected to new forms of organization and management. The ferment of post-1900 economic change in Canada helped to shape a consensus among an increasingly self-conscious group of professional managers regarding solutions to the most urgent organizational, production and labour problems. By the 1920s management had become institutionalized through professional associations, employer groups, business journals and specialized staff functions in public and private sector organizations. The ideological beacon of the management movement rested on a common understanding of the need to implement 'progressive reforms' to increase production efficiency, reduce costs and regulate how workers perform their jobs. An underlying motivation was the achievement of a harmonious partnership between capital and labour. By the early twentieth century a repertoire of solutions to the problems of factory and shop management were readily available. During the 1920s these same principles found their way into the offices of Canada's leading corporations and government bureaucracies.

The sweeping rationalization of production launched at the end of the nineteenth century in the United States spilled over into Canada. Closer economic links with the American industrial system meant that Canadian managers, when faced with standard problems of co-ordination, inefficiency and labour, naturally turned an eye southward. Paul Craven argues that 'the reliance on imported techniques characteristic of the staples economy extended to techniques of business organization as well. Canada's managerial revolution, in a word, was imported from the United States.'[18] Craven explains that there were three conduits through which Canadian managers acquired the latest American administrative practices: direct foreign investment when management policies were dictated by American head offices; the hiring of American managers or 'efficiency experts'; and trade organizations and journals. Increasingly after 1900, influential national business publications such as the *Monetary Times* and *Industrial Canada* began to articulate a coherent view of the major challenges facing management. In addition to scientific management, the various solutions discussed in editorials and articles incorporated cost accounting, welfare work and vocational training. Publications aimed at specific industries, such as the *Journal of the Canadian Bankers' Association*, the *Canadian Textile Journal* and *Canadian Railway and Marine World* carried similar features....

The economic boom ushered in with the twentieth century presented Canadian businessmen with a welter of perplexing managerial problems. Many of these problems were common to large, complex organizations. Initial solutions centred around the reorganization of factory production. Industrialists were counselled to emulate the 'model factories' which began appearing during the first decade of the century.[19] *Industrial Canada* advocated 'economy in production', advising manufacturers to introduce labour-saving devices.[20] And as early as 1907, discussions of the model factory underlined the office's administrative role. A well-organized office, divided into executive, recording and sales branches, and employing accountants, bookkeepers and, of course, clerks to record and analyse all costs would, it was argued, facilitate efficient production.[21]

Taylor's brand of scientific management had developed a clientele in Canadian industry by the start of the First World War. The Lumen Bearing Company of Toronto had adopted the Taylor system by 1911. As an official of the firm explained, 'efficiency management is the biggest problem in manufacturing today.'[22] The company's rationalization programme included time-study by experts in order to determine piece work rates and the elimination of job planning by mechanics. The results no doubt attracted considerable attention from other employers when casting production jumped from 28 to 65 units per day. The Canadian Pacific Railway scored one of the more notable successes in the application of Taylorism.[23] H.L. Gantt, a close associate of Taylor, was hired in June 1909 to reorganize locomotive repair work at the railway's Angus Shops in Montreal scientifically. Gantt's reforms included a piece work payment system, job routines set down on instruction sheets, standardized tools, an elaborate scheduling method for repair work, and the physical reorganization of the shop.[24]

Tangible increases in output and control over labour gained wide publicity for scientific management. In 1911, H.L. Gantt told Canadian manufacturers about 'the straight line to profit'. Preaching that 'scientific management is the new gospel of industrial progress', he urged business-men to slash unnecessary costs rather than raise prices. This was a funda-mental axiom of the Taylor system. Gantt then struck a keynote in modern management theory: 'To eliminate this blind by-play with chance and sub-stitute methods based on technical inquiry and proved [sic] results, is the task of scientific management. Every element in a business should come under this searching inquiry, from shop to office. And whenever it strikes, it means the elimination of waste time, waste energy, waste materials.[25]

If manufacturers and other businessmen harboured lingering doubts about these new approaches, they may well have been won over by the three articles F. W. Taylor himself published in *Industrial Canada* during 1913. Beyond Taylor's job redesign formulas lay a new vista of harmonious labour relations in which an enlarged economic pie could yield bigger pieces for all. Scientific management, asserted Taylor, demanded a 'com-plete mental revolution' among workers and employers alike. He explained:

> The new outlook that comes to both sides under scientific management is that both sides may soon realize that if they stop pulling apart and both push together as hard as possible in the same direction, they can make that sur-plus so large that there is no occasion for any quarrel over its subdivision. Labour gets an immense increase in wages, and still leaves a large share for capital.[26]

In short the 'labour problem' would be solved once and for all.

As in the United States and elsewhere, Canadian manufacturers pre-ferred to remedy organizational and labour inefficiencies through a battery of reforms rather than wholesale adoption of the unwieldy Taylor scheme. Piece work payment systems were especially popular. These allowed man-agement to control production output, to relocate decision-making regard-ing production from the factory floor to the front office, and to reduce labour costs.[27] In 1921 the *Labour Gazette* reported on commonly used meth-ods of wage payment.[28] Many of the incentive systems discussed had been devised by Taylor, Gantt or Emerson, the three foremost American scientific management experts.

Part and parcel of quantifying labour time and calculating wage costs was the introduction of mechanical time recording devices. Employee time recorders were introduced into Canada in 1902 as an accurate way to mea-sure labour costs and worker productivity.[29] By 1915 the International Time Recording Company of Canada, the major distributor of these clocks and a predecessor to IBM, listed 50 large Canadian organizations among its cus-tomers. After the First World War IBM successfully marketed this equip-ment in offices. The firm's sales pitch argued that 'office help is expensive: and one of the largest overhead items. [It] should be measured and checked as carefully as light, heat, power, rent, etc.'[30]

Reducing labour costs was a top priority for businessmen, and time recorders were but one weapon in management's cost cutting arsenal. As the *Monetary Times* elaborates: 'Cost systems are an essential part of modern scientific business management. For the capital invested in a business proves just as efficient as are the brains employed to handle it; and the best guide for brains is analysis. That is the function of a cost system to give the manufacturer a detailed knowledge of his business—and to give him this detailed information regularly and automatically.'[31] Canadian managers became well aware that 'the secret of efficiency, after all, is costs.'[32] Cost accounting arose out of the attention given to the subject of costs by early British and American industrial engineers seeking more skillful management techniques. An early textbook on the topic claims that 'organization, management and cost accounting are so intimately related that it is almost impossible to consider them separately.'[33] Cost accounting records all manufacturing, marketing, distribution, administration and other costs. Analysis of these data allows management to regulate what each component of the production process contributes to final profits.

The spread of cost accounting in Canada paralleled post-1900 industrial growth. Extolling the 'practical value' of cost accounting, *Industrial Canada* argued in 1903 that the new science provided overall managerial control in addition to reducing expenses.[34] General economic prosperity and expanding national markets heightened competition among corporations. Cost accounting thus offered two main advantages: accurate cost estimates of planned production; and a critical appraisal of the effectiveness of managerial techniques, production methods and labour efficiency. Cost accounting was readily integrated with other rationalization strategies. After the First World War cost accounting became an established part of Canadian administrative practice. Indeed, banks often made the implementation of a cost system a condition for extending credit. Observing this trend, the *Monetary Times* concluded that 'soon the concern will be rare which does not use a cost system of some kind or other.'[35]

Welfare work, or industrial betterment, was a complementary technique for grappling with the 'labour problem'. The welfare work movement's concern with human factors in production makes it a forerunner to the human relations approach, which has dominated personnel management in the post-Second World War period. As such, it embodied quite different assumptions about worker motivation and employee relations than the utilitarian rationality of scientific management. Turn-of-the-century welfare work schemes gave way to modern personnel management during the twenties.[36] The human element in this approach was especially important in offices, where the efficiency measures of the Taylorites were only partly applicable. An insurance executive, speaking in 1927, expanded on this point:

Personnel management has made great strides in the field of training workers. There is a great opportunity and responsibility for each [insurance] company to train and develop its clerical workers by carefully thought-out
methods of instruction. A number of years ago the outstanding figure in
business in general was the industrial engineer whose entire time was occupied in developing new machinery and new systems. The present day business is not so much in need of new machinery and new systems as it is in the
development of 'Human Beings'.[37]

The Canadian welfare work movement derived much of its inspiration
from the American experience. The publicity John H. Patterson attracted
when he introduced a model welfare scheme in National Cash Register's
Dayton, Ohio plant did not escape Canadian businessmen. Americans were
leading the way in the field and by the end of the First World War the 'welfare secretary' of Patterson's era had been established as a new profession—
the personnel manager.[38] In one of the first public discussions of welfare
work in Canada, *Industrial Canada* argued that 'pleasant surroundings are
conducive to the economical production of good work, while at the same
time they attract a much better class of working people.'[39]

Welfare work had a strong ideological affinity with the ideas of the
urban reformers and other middle-class progressives of the time. Attractive
looking factories with well-manicured lawns and healthful working conditions were thought to induce higher moral standards among workers and
hence reduce class tensions. Pension plans, employee share ownership
plans, company newspapers, cafeterias serving subsidized meals, athletic
facilities, educational programmes, and medical departments were tangible
results of the welfare work movement. Profit-minded employers justified
these expenses on both moral and pragmatic grounds. The real advantage
of the plans, however, lay in reducing overt employee discontent which
detracted from productivity. *Industrial Canada*, for example, 'found that care
for the physical, intellectual and moral welfare of ... employees had a direct
return in increased output and better work'.[40] Here the goals of welfare
work and the various other forms of modern management converged.
Indeed, at Williams, Green and Rome, an Ontario manufacturer of shirts,
collars and cuffs, humanitarian features aimed at achieving industrial harmony through improved conditions of work were part of a comprehensive
scientific management system.[41]

Usually the 'welfare secretary' who ran the company welfare plans was
a counterbalance to the stop-watch wielding efficiency expert. By 1910 firms
at the vanguard of the movement had established welfare departments
headed by these new specialists.[42] Welfare work and scientific management
may be thus viewed as complementary programmes. In management circles a consensus emerged, defining both as useful measures for countering
labour and organizational problems....

Using broad brush strokes, I have painted the backdrop to the administrative revolution which transformed the office landscape between 1900 and 1930. Three themes dominate the canvas: the creation of a twentieth-century industrial economy founded on the twin pillars of manufacturing and services; the growing dominance of large, centralized bureaucracies as work organizations; and the ascendancy of a new breed of professionals, the modern manager, with a mission to rationalize organizational life. These interacting trends surfaced with considerable impact in Canada in the early twentieth century. In addition to the stimulus of expanding markets and rising demand for a greater variety and sophistication of goods and services, Canada's administrative revolution was energized by two other sources. One was the already well-developed service infrastructure built around the commerce and finance of colonial staple industries. The other was the importation of U.S. manufacturing systems, organizational forms and managerial policies. The interweaving of these economic, organizational and managerial forces gave rise to modern administration....

NOTES
o

1. D.W. Birchall and V.J. Hammond, *Tomorrow's Office: Managing Technological Change* (London, Business Books, 1981), p. 15.

2. C. Wright Mills, *White Collar: The American Middle Classes* (New York, Oxford University Press, 1956), p. 189.

3. Allan A. Murdoch and J. Rodney Dale, *The Clerical Function* (London, Sir Isaac Pitman, 1961), p. 2.

4. David Lockwood, *The Blackcoated Worker: A Study in Class Consciousness* (London, George Allen and Unwin, 1958), p. 36.

5. There is an extensive literature examining the impact of staples production on Canadian economic development. Perhaps the best summary of the staple thesis is found in Harold Innis, *The Fur Trade in Canada* (Toronto, University of Toronto Press, 1970), pp. 383–402. For general overviews of Canadian economic development from a staple perspective see Richard E. Caves and Richard H. Holton, *The Canadian Economy: Prospect and Retrospect* (Cambridge, Mass., Harvard University Press, 1961); W.T. Easterbrook and Hugh G.J. Aitken, *Canadian Economic History* (Toronto, Macmillan, 1956). The new political economy, synthesizing Innis and Marx, is outlined in Mel Watkins, 'The staple theory revisited', *Journal of Canadian Studies*, 12 (1977), pp. 83–95; Daniel Drache, 'Harold Innis and Canadian capitalist development', *Canadian Journal of Political and Social Theory*, 6 (1982), pp. 35–60. However, the staple theory is increasingly under dispute. For recent interpretations see William L. Marr and Donald G. Paterson, *Canada: An Economic History* (Toronto, Macmillan, 1980). Richard Pomfret, *The Economic Development of Canada* (Toronto, Methuen, 1980) offers a well-documented rejection of the staples model.

6. For an excellent discussion of Canada as a late industrializing nation, see Gordon Laxer, 'Foreign ownership and myths about Canadian development', *Canadian Review of Sociology and Anthropology*, 22 (1985), pp. 311–45.

7. O.J. Firestone, 'Canada's economic development, 1867–1952', paper prepared for the Third Conference of the International Association for Research in Income and Wealth, Castelgandolfo, Italy, September 1953, p. 178.

8. Firestone, 'Development of Canada's economy', p. 230.

9. 'Personnel File No. 2', Sun Life Archives, Montreal.

10. *Imperial Oil Review*, August 1922, p. 9.

11. See Alfred D. Chandler, Jr. and Herman Daems (eds), *Managerial Hierarchies: Corporate Perspectives on the Rise of the Modern Industrial Enterprise* (Cambridge, Mass., Harvard University Press, 1980), for comparative perspectives on the development of the modern firm in the U.S. and Western Europe (Canada is not covered in the volume), p. 3.

12. As of 31 December. 'Personnel File No. 2', Sun Life Archives, Montreal. Neufeld (*Financial System*, p. 257) describes Sun Life's expansion up to 1930 as 'The most remarkable of any financial intermediary in Canada's history'.

13. *Sunshine* (Sun Life's employee magazine), January, 1905, p. 12.

14. Alfred D. Chandler Jr., *The Visible Hand: The Managerial Revolution in American Business* (Cambridge, Mass., Harvard University Press, 1977), p. 8.

15. See Daniel Nelson, *Managers and Workers: Origins of the New Factory System in the United States, 1880–1920* (Madison, University of Wisconsin Press, 1975), chapter 1.

16. Sidney Pollard, *The Genesis of Modern Management* (Harmondworth, Penguin, 1968), p. 78.

17. Bryan Palmer refers to this eclectic reform programme as the 'broad thrust for efficiency'. See his 'Class, conception and conflict: the thrust for efficiency, managerial views of labour and the working class rebellion', *Review of Radical Political Economics*, 7 (1975), p. 32. Leland H. Jenks views the work management movement in the United States and Britain as spawning professional managers through a two-stage process. During the first stage, firms in various industries communicated their managerial experiences to one another. This forged a consensus regarding which problems should be subjected to systematic managerial inquiry. Standards for effective solutions were collectively established. As these ideas spread, a second phase was entered, in which the movement became institutionalized in newly formed professional management associations. Jenks's concept of consensus and institutionalization guides my discussion of the evolution of modern management in Canada. See his 'Early phases of the management movement', *Administrative Science Quarterly*, 5 (1960), pp. 421–47.

18. Paul Craven, *'An Impartial Umpire': Industrial Relations and the Canadian State* (Toronto, University of Toronto Press, 1980), p. 94. Documentation of the application of scientific management in Canada is limited. See Bryan D. Palmer, *A Culture in Conflict: Skilled Workers and Industrial Capitalism in Hamilton, Ontario, 1860–1914* (Montreal, McGill-Queen's University Press, 1979), pp. 216–22; Craig Heron and Bryan D. Palmer, 'Through the prism of the strike: industrial conflict in southern Ontario, 1901–14', *Canadian Historical Review*, 58 (1977), pp. 423–58.

19. In 1907 *Industrial Canada* (hereafter *IC*) ran a series of three articles by H.L.C. Hall, a Fellow of the International Accountant's Society, on the 'model factory'.

20. *IC*, February 1907, p. 586.

21. Ibid, p. 588.

22. *IC*, May 1911, p. 1073.

23. Daniel Nelson, *Frederick W. Taylor and the Rise of Scientific Management*, (Madison, University of Wisconsin Press, 1980), p. 149.

24. *Railway and Marine World*, January 1912, pp. 1–3.

25. H.L. Gantt, 'The straight line to profit', *IC*, March 1911, p. 837.

26. *IC*, April 1913, pp. 124–5. Also see F.W. Taylor, 'Principles of scientific management', *IC*, March 1913, pp. 1105–6; 'How scientific management works', *IC*, May 1913, pp. 1349–50.

27. See e.g. 'A tight check on piece work', *IC*, January 1916, p. 693.

28. *Labour Gazette* (hereafter *LG*), August 1921, pp. 1019–25.

29. *IC*, 1 May 1902, p, 337.

30. IBM Canadian Sales Record, 10 February 1921 (IBM Archives, Toronto). Such an advertisement appeared in *IC*, September 1921, p. 81. The advertisement computed that if an office staff of 40 loses 15 minutes each day, then the annual loss to the company would be $1,500.

31. *Monetary Times (hereafter MT)*, September 1919, p. 30.

32. *MT*, 6 October 1916, p. 9.

33. John P. Jordon and Gould L. Harris, *Cost Accounting: Principles and Practice*, 2nd edn (New York, Ronald Press, 1925), p. 19.

34. *IC*, August 1903, p. 26.

35. *MT*, 26 September 1919, p. 30; also see 5 December 1919, p. 23.

36. See *LG*, April 1925, pp. 358–69. There has been little research on welfare work in Canada. The most thorough treatment is in Robert Storey, 'Unionization versus corporate welfare: the "Dofasco Way"', *Labour/Le Travailleur*, 12 (1983), pp. 7–42. For the United States see Nelson, *Managers and Workers*, chapter 6.

37. *Life Office Management Association, Proceedings of the 1927 Annual Conference*, p. 75.

38. National Cash Register Co. in Dayton, Ohio, pioneered welfare work in the late 1890s under the direction of John H. Patterson, its president. The modern personnel department dates from the 1901 NCR strike (Nelson, *Managers and Workers*, p. 148). Also see Samuel Crowther, *John H. Patterson: Pioneer in Industrial Welfare* (Garden City, NJ, Doubleday, 1924). The National Association of Employment Managers was launched in the United States in 1919 and the following year began publishing the journal *Personnel*.

39. *IC*, 2 June 1902, p. 432.

40. *IC*, January 1907, p. 506.

41. For discussions of the Williams, Green and Rome scheme see *LG*, February 1907, pp. 892–4; *IC*, February 1910, pp. 693–6; *IC*, March 1910, pp. 786–7.

42. *IC*, March 1910, p. 787; *LG*, April 1911, pp. 1138–9.

- 630-1852 cell
- 657-3844

email: mgureoh6@nuwose.com

Contemporary Work

Trends

EDITORS' INTRODUCTION

As the readings in Part 1 reveal, manufacturing had come to play a central role in the Canadian economy by the beginning of the 20th century. However, in the same way that agriculture gave way to manufacturing, the service industries slowly expanded to overtake both the resource-based industries and manufacturing. By 1991, over 70 percent of employed Canadians worked in the service industries. This significant labour market trend has prompted a great deal of debate about the quality of work in the "service economy." Some writers comment on the new and challenging employment opportunities in a more competitive, information-based, and computer-driven economy. Others lament the growing number of low-pay, low-skill jobs in the increasingly insecure service sector labour market. Which perspective is correct?

Based on a detailed analysis of data from the 1989 General Social Survey (a Statistics Canada survey of roughly 6,000 employed Canadians aged 15 to 64), Harvey Krahn concludes that neither the overly positive nor the completely negative assessments tell the complete story. Instead, it is apparent that the service sector provides both rewarding and less desirable employment opportunities. The important question is whether one type is expanding faster than the other. Krahn distinguishes between "upper-tier" service industries (e.g., health, education, banking, legal services, transportation) and "lower-tier" service industries (e.g., retail sales, and food and beverage services). The survey data show that, on average, jobs in the upper-tier services require more skills, are better paid, provide more benefits, and tend to be more secure.

Krahn also comments on the trend toward more nonstandard jobs, noting that almost one in four employed working-age Canadians are working in part-time, part-year, or temporary positions. Such nonstandard jobs are more common in the lower-tier services, but are also observed in some segments of the upper tier. In his concluding comments, Krahn reflects on a number of themes discussed in more detail in some of the readings that follow: the polarization of the Canadian labour force; the overrepresentation of women and youth in the lower-tier services and in nonstandard jobs; training and underemployment; the labour market implications of an aging population; and opportunities for immigrant workers in the Canadian labour market.

Part-time work, the most common form of nonstandard work, accounted for only 4 percent of all employment at mid-century. By 1991, the national part-time employment rate was 16.5 percent, representing over two million workers, 70 percent of whom were women. In an extract from their book on the same topic, Ann Duffy and Norene Pupo discuss why so many women work part-time. While some women would prefer full-time work, many choose to work part-time since this arrangement allows them to maintain their domestic and child-care responsibilities. But Duffy and Pupo question the meaning of this individual "choice," noting that it is made within a set of structural constraints. In other words, given that they remain responsible for housework and child care, and given the shortage of affordable, quality child care in Canada, the choice women face is rather limited.

While part-time work offers the potential for a more balanced family–work life (for both women and men), and could be a response to high rates of unemployment (sharing work among a larger number of people), most part-time jobs today pay little, provide few benefits, and offer only limited career opportunities for women. Duffy and Pupo ask a critical question: what can employers, unions, and legislators do to change this situation, so that some of the potential benefits of part-time work can be realized?

The third reading in this section reminds us that "work" includes not only those activities that translate into a paycheque or financial profit, but all human activity that produces a socially valued product or service. Thus, unpaid housework, child care, care for other dependants, volunteer work, and many unpaid tasks performed in the "irregular" or "underground" economy all constitute work, although they are frequently ignored in discussions that are restricted to paid employment or self-employment. It should be obvious from this short list that women are much more likely to be performing such unpaid and unrecognized work. It is also possible that, with the exception of unpaid housework and child care, some forms of unpaid work may be more or less common in different regions of the country.

In their study of a number of small communities in rural Newfoundland, Lawrence Felt and Peter Sinclair discuss three types of unpaid productive work (home construction, other subsistence work contributing to the welfare of the household, and unpaid work arrangements between households). Their assessment of the extent of such unpaid work ("Everyone does it"), and of the types of people most likely to engage in it, provides us with a very clear picture of the interaction between the formal and informal economies. Felt and Sinclair conclude that these unpaid work arrangements allow many residents of the region to maintain a reasonable standard of living despite the limited opportunities for well-paid employment.

Two long-term demographic trends —low fertility rates and increased life expectancy—mean that Canada's population is slowly aging. The last two articles in this section discuss some of the labour force implications of this phenomenon. David Foot and Rosemary Venne discuss the potential career blockages ("plateauing") faced by many members of the very large "baby boom" generation employed in large, hierarchical work organizations. The mismatch between labour force characteristics and organizational structure will require innovative responses on the part of employers and managers if they wish to keep their employees challenged and productive. Flatter organizational structures that encourage and reward lateral rather than vertical career movements may be part of the solution.

Ellen Gee and Susan McDaniel reflect on retirement and pension issues. As the Canadian work force slowly ages, we are also observing that more people want to retire early (especially men). However, given the fiscal crises faced by governments, attempts have been made to reduce old age security benefits. At the same time, employment security is decreasing, as other articles in this reader document. Consequently, plans for early retirement may not translate into reality for many younger and middle-aged members of today's work force. Gee and McDaniel suggest that, in the future, Canadians will have to choose between earlier retirement and a reduced income level. They also discuss a number of other related concerns, including mandatory retirement policies, the impact of higher levels of immigration on future retirement scenarios, and the relationship between a gendered division of labour and the higher levels of poverty among elderly women.

DISCUSSION QUESTIONS

1. What are the critical defining characteristics of the new service economy? Has the shift from a manufacturing-based economy to a service economy altered patterns of social inequality in Canada?

2. Given that unpaid work provides socially useful goods and services, should we, as a society, seek ways to transform some or most of this activity into paid work?

3. Part-time work is the answer to both the problems of employers trying to remain competitive and employees trying to balance their work and family commitments. Discuss.

4. Since most women in part-time jobs "choose" such jobs for personal or family reasons, why should we be concerned about the overrepresentation of women in such jobs? What about students in part-time jobs?

5. Discuss the advantages and disadvantages of a policy of mandatory retirement from the perspective of individuals, workplaces, and society as a whole.

6. Flatter (less hierarchical) organizational structures have been proposed as a solution to the mismatch between the age structure of the Canadian work force and the career opportunities available in most contemporary workplaces. Is this a feasible solution? Would it benefit all or most working Canadians? Are there any disadvantages?

SUGGESTED READINGS

o

Economic Council of Canada. *Good Jobs, Bad Jobs: Employment in the Service Economy.* Ottawa: Supply and Services Canada, 1990.

Harding, Phillip, and Richard Jenkins. *The Myth of the Hidden Economy: Towards a New Understanding of Informal Economic Activity.* Milton Keynes: Open University Press, 1989.

McDonald, P.L., and R.A. Wanner. *Retirement in Canada.* Toronto: Butterworths, 1990.

Myles, John. "The Expanding Middle: Some Canadian Evidence on the Deskilling Debate." *Canadian Review of Sociology and Anthropology,* 25: no. 3 (1988): 335–64.

Warme, Barbara D., K.L.P. Lundy, and L.A. Lundy, eds. *Working Part-time: Risks and Opportunities.* New York: Praeger, 1992.

Wigdor, Blossom T., and David K. Foot. *The Over-Forty Society: Issues for Canada's Aging Population.* Toronto: James Lorimer, 1988.

Quality of Work in the Service Sector*

Harvey Krahn

INTRODUCTION

o

A century ago (1891), the service industries accounted for less than one-third (31%) of employment in Canada. The primary industries (agriculture and natural resource-based industries) still employed almost half (49%) of the Canadian labour force, with 20% in the secondary sector (manufacturing and construction). By mid-twentieth century (1951), almost half of all employed Canadians (47%) were working in the service industries. The primary industries had declined significantly, employing only 22% of the labour force, while the secondary sector had expanded to account for 31% of all employment. Service sector employment has continued to grow steadily since then, while both the primary and secondary sectors have contracted further (in relative terms). Today, with 70% of employed Canadians working in the service industries, the term *service economy* is an accurate description.[1-3] The economies of other western industrialized countries have evolved similarly, but Canada has moved further than most in terms of service sector employment.[4-6]

Various service industries have expanded in different eras. During the 1950s and 1960s, the fastest growth was observed in the public services (education, health and welfare, and public administration). In the decades following, the commercial services expanded somewhat more rapidly. Thus, looking back over the past two decades, the service industries accounted for 79% of total employment growth in Canada between 1970 and 1979, and 94% between 1980 and 1989.[7-8]

* Abridged from Harvey Krahn, *Quality of Work in the Service Sector*, General Social Survey Analysis Series, no. 6 (Ottawa: Statistics Canada, 1992), chapter 1 and conclusion. Reprinted by permission of the publisher and the author.

Long before the evolution of the modern service economy, Adam Smith dismissed service sector work as "unproductive of any value", when commenting on the contributions of "menial servants", as well as "churchmen, lawyers, physicians, men of letters of all kinds" along with "players, buffoons, musicians, opera singers" and others who did not work in the primary or secondary sectors where goods with real value were produced.[9] Such traditional prejudices have slowly weakened as new service industries have evolved, and as the service sector has come to dominate western economies. Today, economists recognize that the service industries, like the goods-producing industries, can be a driving force in the economy and can contribute significantly to international competitiveness. [10-12] . . .

A   TYPOLOGY   OF   THE   SERVICE INDUSTRIES

o

Although debates continue about the definition of a service, and the classification of service industries and occupations, [13-14] the simplest approach is to define a service as the exchange of a commodity that has no tangible form.[15] The traditional distinction between *goods-producing* primary industries, manufacturing and construction) and *service* sectors (all other industries) reflects this basis definition. . . .

The 10-category classification system used in this GSS report closely resembles the industrial typology used in a recent study of shifts in the Canadian wage distribution between 1981 and 1986.[16] Agriculture is distinguished from other natural resource-based industries (forestry, fishing, mining, petroleum and utilities). These two sectors, along with manufacturing and construction, comprise the goods-producing sector. The service sector is then subdivided into six categories: distributive services; business services; the education, health and welfare sector; public administration; retail trade; and other consumer services. Thus, this typology is also very similar to the classification system developed in the recent Economic Council of Canada discussions of employment in the service economy.[17] The Economic Council distinguished "dynamic services" (distributive and business services) from "traditional services" (retail trade and personal services) and "non-market services" (education, health and welfare, and public administration).

In anticipation of some of the findings from this study, retail trade and other consumer services are labelled *lower-tier* services to distinguish them from the other four *upper-tier* service sectors where work rewards and skill requirements are more extensive. [18-19] A further potentially useful distinction within the upper-tier services separates *non-market* (public administration and the education, health and welfare group) from *market-based* services (distributive and business).

THE SERVICE ECONOMY: GOOD JOBS OR BAD?

o

Evaluations of the quality of work in the service economy have tended to be either very positive or very negative, with popularized accounts typically taking the more extreme positions. For example, one critic of the "leisure society" describes the "mind-numbing ennui of the service sector, that sprawling, institutionalized servitude for which the young are being prepared by means of unemployment and inactivity to be grateful".[20] Alternatively, a best-selling account of "post-industrial society" extols the benefits of employment in the service industries, arguing that skilled information workers enjoy much more satisfying and rewarding work.[21-22] However, neither of these writers relies heavily on relevant data to support these broad generalizations.

Nevertheless, several recent Canadian studies do allow some more informed (but less sweeping) generalizations about the quality of work in the service sector. It is clear that there is a great deal of diversity in jobs across the service industries. The expansion of the service sector over the past several decades, and the relative decline of the blue-collar primary and secondary sectors, has involved growth in both low-skill, low-status jobs, as well as in high-skill, well-paying positions. This observation has fuelled the debate about whether a polarization of incomes and occupational structure has led to a decline of the traditional middle class. [23-24]

An extensive analysis of shifts in the Canadian income distribution reveals that most of the jobs created in the first half of the 1980s were either very low-paying or in the middle-to-upper income brackets.[25] Since the service sector accounted for virtually all of the new jobs appearing in the past decade, this study suggests a parallel growth of good and bad jobs in the service industries. A similar conclusion emerges from studies of changing occupational skill demands. Canadian workers' self-reports of the skill demands of their jobs, as well as independent estimates of skill requirements across occupational categories, show a distinct polarization between high-skilled service jobs in the public sector and business services and low-skill jobs in retail trade and the consumer services.[26-27] . . .

NON-STANDARD WORK: EVEN MORE BAD JOBS?

o

While most employees, including those in the service industries, have a full-time, year-round, permanent paid job, such traditional employment relationships may be declining. Part-time work has clearly increased since the middle of the century when it was largely non-existent, particularly in the past two decades. But other alternative employment relationships, such as limited term contract positions, employment in temporary help agencies, self-employment, and multiple-job holding are also becoming more prevalent in Canada and in other western industrialized economies.[28]

These alternative types of employment have been called "atypical work situations", "contingent work", and "non-standard forms of work".[29-32] Debates over this emerging trend have questioned whether such alternative employment relationships are, for some workers, a response to a difficult labour market.[33-36] In other words, do some workers create their own jobs because other jobs are not available, or do they choose temporary work when permanent jobs are scarce? Others have debated the extent to which "flexible firms", relying heavily on part-time, temporary or sub-contracted workers (in order to reduce their costs and commitment to employees), have emerged in the economic restructuring of the 1980s.[37-43] Whatever their origin, these non-standard forms of work typically provide less job security which, for most workers, is an important consideration. Thus, to the extent that these types of employment are increasing, employment may become less secure for many labour force participants.[44-47]...

CONCLUSIONS AND IMPLICATIONS

o

.... Like other recent national surveys, the 1989 GSS reveals that over 70% of employed Canadians have jobs in the service industries. About one in three of these service workers are employed in the lower-tier services. Alternatively, two-thirds are working in the upper-tier services where jobs tend to be more rewarding, reminding us of the dangers of overgeneralizing about *bad jobs in the service sector.* Nevertheless, nearly one in four (almost three million) Canadian workers are employed in retail trade and other consumer services.

Not all of these individuals are in *bad jobs,* but then, not all of the jobs in the upper-tier services and goods-producing sector are *good jobs.* However, on average, it is clear that Canadians employed in the lower-tier services receive fewer intrinsic and extrinsic work rewards. Thus, while overgeneralizations about job ghettos in the service sector must be questioned, it is also important to recognize that almost one-quarter of employed Canadians are working in industries where high quality jobs may be the exception, rather than the norm. . . .

As a society, Canadians have become accustomed to cheaply-priced and convenient services, the most obvious being fast food restaurants and round-the-clock shopping. It is unlikely that we will be willing to give up these services. Hence, the demand for workers in lower-tier service industries will probably remain high. . . .

The data analyses in this report have consistently shown that women and youth are much more likely to work in less rewarding jobs in the lower-tier services. Calls for the removal of barriers, which keep women out of better jobs are becoming commonplace, but must be repeated. It is evident that the higher incidence of poverty among working women (compared with employed men) in Canada is due to their over-representation in lower-paying and otherwise less rewarding jobs.[48]

As for young workers, many are still students, working part-time as they complete their education. For these workers, less rewarding jobs may not be very problematic. Students can view these jobs as temporary, to be replaced (following graduation) by better jobs in upper-tier services and the goods-producing sector. However, there is also some evidence that many young people who have left school completely (including some with higher education credentials) have trouble moving out of the *student labour market* in the lower-tier services into more rewarding jobs in other sectors.[49-50] To some extent, such career blockages may be a result of an unusually large baby-boom cohort moving through the education system and into a labour market with an insufficient number of *good jobs.*[51] These career barriers may also be the result of "downsizing" in both the private and public sectors, and the resulting decline in entry level positions for young, better-educated workers. Whatever the reason, it is clear that some young workers are employed in lower-tier services, not by choice, but because better employment opportunities are not available. . . .

Considering own-account self-employment, multiple-job holding, part-time, part-year and temporary work, the 1989 GSS reveals that over 30% of employed Canadians are in non-standard jobs. If a more restricted definition including only part-time, part-year and temporary jobs is used, then 2.8 million (22%) workers are in non-standard jobs. The majority are part-time workers, but part-time jobs are also often seasonal and/or temporary jobs.

A cross-sectional survey, such as the GSS, cannot inform us about trends over time, but other data sources suggest that there has been an increase in non-standard work over the past decade in Canada. This trend clearly needs to be monitored. While such employment relationships may be advantageous to employers desiring greater labour force flexibility,[52] they frequently represent a precarious work situation for employees.[53] For many working Canadians, non-standard jobs mean a lower than average income and an insecure standard of living. No doubt some workers prefer such jobs for a variety of different reasons. But whatever the motivations of non-standard workers, questions about the quality of non-standard jobs are still legitimate and important. . . .

Generalizations about *low pay in the service sector* are obviously too broad, but more specific conclusions about well-paid jobs in upper-tier services and much lower pay in the lower-tier, especially in non-standard jobs, are clearly substantiated. In addition, the GSS reveals that the ratio of clerical, sales and service incomes to managerial and professional incomes is lower in retail trade and other consumer services. In other words, there is a greater income inequality across occupational groups within the lower-tier services.

Furthermore, lower-tier service workers must remain in their jobs for a longer time before seniority translates into higher income. Given that women are over-represented in the lower-tier services and in non-standard jobs within them, the nature of the relationship between gender and labour market poverty can begin to be seen more clearly. Continued cutbacks in the upper-tier services, particularly in the unionized public sector, where women have had somewhat better employment opportunities in the past few decades, could lead to a worsening of Canadian women's employment situation.[54]

The distribution of fringe benefits (medical, dental and pension plans, and paid maternity leave) accents income differences across industries. Upper-tier service workers, and people employed in some of the goods-producing industries, are more likely than others to receive these types of benefits. Alternatively, Canadians employed in retail trade and other consumer services, particularly those in non-standard jobs, are less likely to enjoy such benefits.

This polarization of benefits will have an even greater impact on the quality of life of Canadians in the future. As the *baby boomers* in the work force move closer to retirement age, more workers will have an immediate need for additional health care coverage and adequate pensions. Again, because larger proportions of women than of men are working in lower-tier services, women will be most likely to be negatively affected. Obviously, any successful attempts to aid female entry into better jobs would have an impact on this future scenario. In addition, successful union organizing efforts in lower-tier services would, no doubt, be followed by collective bargaining for more employment benefits. Finally, legislation regarding minimum wages, pensions, and termination benefits, for example, would make some of the upper-tier service benefits available to a wider range of Canadian workers.[55]. . .

It is noteworthy that a significant minority of Canadian workers state that their job requires limited skills, that it is unrelated to their education, and that they are overqualified for their job. Some of these individuals are students working in part-time positions outside of their area of training until they graduate. Others have no higher educational credentials. However, a substantial number of these overqualified workers with underutilized skills are well-educated and would prefer more challenging work, if they could find it.

This underutilization of human resources is seldom recognized in current discussions of the fit between Canadian workers' skills and future labour market requirements. For example, a recent policy paper stated that: ". . . the economy and the labour force appear to be developing along divergent paths, creating a potential gap between the flexibility and skills of workers, and the skills our economy will demand." [56] It may well be that the current match between skill levels and job requirements is not particularly good. However, the tone of recent policy papers suggests that, in general, Canadians are underqualified and incapable of participating successfully in a high-technology, global economy. Such conclusions ignore the fact that many Canadians are currently employed in jobs that do not utilize their skills and for which they are overqualified. Furthermore, these jobs are not likely to disappear even if the demand for highly-skilled workers increases.

This last observation brings us to a final comment about future employment patterns in Canada's service economy. Until recently, the expansion of lower-tier services (and non-standard jobs) was fuelled, in part, by a growing supply of young workers as the baby-boom generation moved through the education system. In addition, part-time work by students increased dramatically over the past two decades.[57] However, this source of cheap and willing labour has begun to shrink rapidly. The 15 to 24 age group is expected to make up 17% of the labour force in the year 2000, down from 26% in 1971. Only about 180,000 people will enter the labour force annually during the 1990s, compared with 300,000 annually in the 1970s.[58]

Who will fill the vacant jobs in retail sales and other consumer services? Some futurists have pointed optimistically to the growing number of retirees, seeking ways of filling time. However, it is unlikely that many will wish to trade their leisure time for part-time, low-skill, low-paying jobs. Many women have worked, and continue to work, in these types of jobs alongside young students. But since the majority of women are already in the paid labour force, and given their growing demands for access to better jobs, it is unlikely that women will fill the labour market gap created by the shrinking youth cohort.[59]

The most obvious candidates are the growing number of immigrants being allowed into Canada as legislators recognize the implications of the steady aging of the Canadian population.[60] As Canada moves toward the year 2000, its population will become much more racially and ethnically diverse. The degree to which *good jobs and bad jobs* come to be distributed between immigrants and the native-born, and along racial and ethnic lines, is a trend to be monitored. . . .

NOTES

o

1. Matthews, R.A. *Structural Change and Industrial Policy: Redeployment of Canadian Manufacturing, 1960-80.* (Ottawa: Supply and Services Canada, 1985), p.36.

2. Picot, W.G. "The changing industrial mix of employment, 1951-1985." *Canadian Social Trends.* (Ottawa: Statistics Canada, Spring, 1987), p. 11.

3. Lindsay, C. "The service sector in the 1980s." *Canadian Social Trends.* (Ottawa: Statistics Canada, Spring, 1989), p. 20.

4. International Labour Office. *World Labour Report, 1-2.* (Oxford: Oxford University Press, 1987), p. 41.

5. Price, D.G. and A.M. Blair. *The Changing Geography of the Service Sector.* (London: Belhaven, 1989), p. 11-13.

6. Plunkert, L.M. "The 1980s: a decade of job growth and industry shifts." *Monthly Labor Review,* (September, 1990), p. 3-16.

7. Picot, W.G., T. Wannell and D. Lynd. *The Changing Labour Market for Postsecondary Graduates.* (Ottawa: Statistics Canada, 1987), p. 7-8.

8. Côté, M. "The labour force: into the '90s." *Perspectives on Labour and Income.* (Ottawa: Statistics Canada, Spring, 1990), p. 13.

9. Smith, A. *An Inquiry into the Nature and Causes of the Wealth of Nations.* (Chicago: University of Chicago Press, 1976 (1776)), Book 2, Chapter 3, p. 352.

10. Economic Council of Canada. *Good Jobs, Bad Jobs: Employment in the Service Economy.* (Ottawa: Supply and Services Canada, 1990).

11. Economic Council of Canada. *Employment in the Service Economy.* (Ottawa: Supply and Services Canada, 1991).

12. Also see reports from the Service Sector Project completed by the Institute for Research on Public Policy, the Fraser Institute, and Statistics Canada, reviewed in *Canadian Public Policy.* 1990. vol. 16: p. 114-19.

13. See, for example, Gershuny, J.I. and I.D. Miles. *The New Service Economy: The Transformation of Employment in Industrial Societies.* (London: Frances Pinter, 1983), p. 3-4.

14. Price and Blair, op cit, p. 1-6.

15. Price and Blair, op cit, p. 2.

16. Myles, J., G. Picot and T. Wannell. "The changing wage distribution of jobs, 1981-1986." *The Labour Force,* (Ottawa: Statistics Canada, October, 1988), p. 131. These researchers used only eight categories, since they combined retail trade and other consumer services, and omitted agriculture from their analysis. However, this GSS analysis follows their lead in including services to mining with natural resource industries and services to construction in the construction category.

17. Economic Council of Canada, 1991, op cit, p. 9.

18. See Myles, J. and G. Fawcett. "Job skills and the service economy." (Ottawa: Economic Council of Canada, Working Paper No. 4, 1990) who use a very similar typology (they combine public administration with the education, health and welfare sector), and note the low-skill requirements in retail trade and other consumer services.

19. Krahn, H. and G.S. Lowe. "Young workers in the service economy." (Ottawa: Economic Council of Canada, Working Paper No. 14, 1990) use the original Myles et al., op cit, classification scheme and report limited work rewards in the consumer services (including retail trade).

20. Seabrook, J. *The Leisure Society.* (Oxford: Basil Blackwell, 1988), p. 19.

21. Naisbitt, R. *Megatrends: Ten New Directions Transforming our Lives.* (New York: Warner, 1982). Naisbett acknowledges his obvious intellectual debt to Daniel Bell who first developed the "post-industrial society" thesis.

22. See Bell, D. *The Coming of Post-Industrial Society*. (New York: Basic Books, 1973).

23. See, for example: Leckie, N. "The declining middle and technological change: trends in the distribution of employment income in Canada, 1971-84." (Ottawa: Economic Council of Canada, 1988), Discussion Paper No. 342.

24. See Beach, C.M. "The 'vanishing' middle class?: evidence and explanations." (Kingston: Queen's University, School of Industrial Relations, 1988).

25. Myles et al, 1988, op cit.

26. Myles and Fawcett, op cit.

27. Myles, J. "The expanding middle: some Canadian evidence on the deskilling debate." *Canadian Review of Sociology and Anthropology* 25, (1988), p. 335-364.

28. International Labour Office, op cit, p. 41-2.

29. Piotet, F. *The Changing Face of Work: Researching and Debating the Issues*. (Dublin: European Foundation for the Improvement of Living and Working Conditions, 1987).

30. Polivka, A.E. and T. Nardone. "On the definition of 'contingent work'." *Monthly Labor Review*, 112, 12, (1989), p. 9-16.

31. Economic Council of Canada, 1990, op cit, p. 12.

32. Rubery, J. "Employers and the labour market," in D. Gallie (ed.) *Employment in Britain*. (Oxford: Basil Blackwell, 1988), p. 264.

33. Organization for Economic Cooperation and Development (OECD). *OECD Employment Outlook*. (Paris: OECD, 1986), p. 60.

34. Hakim, C. "Self-employment in Britain: recent trends and current issues." *Work, Employment and Society*, 2 (1988), p. 421-450.

35. Dale, A. and C. Bamford. "Temporary workers: cause for concern or complacency?" *Work, Employment and Society*, 2 (1988), p. 191-209.

36. Davies, K. and J. Esseveld. "Factory women redundancy and the search for work: toward a reconceptualization of employment and unemployment." *The Sociological Review*, 37 (1989), p. 219-252.

37. Rubery, op cit.

38. Pollert, A. "The 'flexible firm' : fixation or fact?" *Work, Employment and Society*, 2 (1988), p. 281-316.

39. Lane, C. "Industrial change in Europe: the pursuit of flexible specialisation in Britain and West Germany." *Work, Employment and Society*, 2 (1988), p. 141-168.

40. Lane, C. "From 'welfare capitalism' to 'market capitalism': a comparative review of trends toward employment flexibility in the labour markets of three major European societies." *Sociology*, 23 (1989), p. 583-610.

41. Polivka and Nardone, op cit.

42. Maguire, M. "British labour market trends," in D. Ashton and G. Lowe (eds.) *Making Their Way: Education, Training and the Labour Market in Canada and Britain*. (Milton Keynes: Open University Press, 1991), p. 55-57.

43. Tilly, C. "Reasons for the continuing growth of part-time employment." *Monthly Labor Review*, 114, 3 (1991), p. 10-18.

44. Piotet, op cit, p. 23.

45. Lane, 1989, op cit, p. 605.
46. Maguire, 1991, op cit.
47. Economic Council of Canada, 1990, op cit, p. 13.
48. Gunderson, M., L. Muszynki and J. Keck. *Women and Labour Market Poverty.* (Ottawa: Canadian Advisory Council on the Status of Women, 1990).
49. Krahn, H. and G.S. Lowe, op cit.
50. See also Ontario Ministry of Skills Development. *Out of School Youth in Ontario: Their Labour Market Experience.* (Toronto: Ontario Manpower Commission, 1987).
51. Foot, D.K. and R.A. Venne. "Population, pyramids and promotional prospects." *Canadian Public Policy,* 16 (1990), p. 387-398.
52. Tilly, op cit, p. 10-18.
53. Economic Council of Canada, 1991, op cit.
54. Gunderson et al., op cit, p. 124.
55. Gunderson et al., ibid, p. 44.
56. Employment and Immigration Canada. *Success in the Works: A Profile of Canada's Emerging Workforce.* (Ottawa: Canadian Employment and Immigration, 1989), op cit, p. 1.
57. Cohen, G.L. "Youth for hire." *Perspectives on Labour and Income,* (Ottawa: Statistics Canada, Summer, 1989), p. 7-14.
58. Employment and Immigration Canada, (1989), op cit, p. 13-14.
59. Gunderson et al., op cit, p. 127.
60. Logan, R. "Immigration during the 1980s." *Canadian Social Trends.* (Ottawa: Statistics Canada, Spring, 1991), p. 10-13.

Part-time Paradox: Connecting Gender, Work, and Family*

Ann Duffy and Norene Pupo

Since the 1950s Canada has experienced a dramatic expansion in part-time employment. Currently about one in seven Canadian workers is a part-timer and over 70 per cent of these part-time workers are women. One in every four employed women is working part-time. This proliferation of part-time employment, particularly among women, is not peculiar to Canada. Although there are significant national differences, part-time jobs have boomed in a number of different countries. Analysing the implications of these developments is complicated by conflicting definitions of part-time employment and by differences between part-timers. Notably, distinctions must be made between multiple job-holding, temporary or permanent, and voluntary or involuntary part-timers. With these complexities noted, the part-time paradox remains. Does the expansion of part-time work signal a step toward the increased liberation of women, particularly married women with children who seek manageable forms of paid employment? Or does the growth in part-time employment reflect the entrapment of more and more women in ghettoized, poorly paid, and dead-end jobs as they are forced to accept unsatisfactory solutions to the double day or as they confront an economy creating too few full-time jobs?

For many women, paid employment has meant working part-time. In 1989, 1.4 million Canadian women were employed part-time and one in four (24.5 per cent) worked part-time. As apparent at any fast-food outlet or retail store, men also work part-time (7.7 per cent of male workers are part-timers), but women make up almost three-quarters (72 per cent) of the burgeoning part-time work force. Further, unlike men (and women) who tend

* Abridged from Ann Duffy and Norene Pupo, *Part-time Paradox: Connecting Gender, Work, and Family* (Toronto: McClelland & Steward, 1992), chapters 2 and 7. Reprinted by permission of the publisher and the authors.

to work part-time when they are young (between fifteen and twenty-four years old) and probably juggling education with a part-time job, women work part-time during their prime working years. Sixty-one per cent of employed married women with children under eighteen work part-time (Economic Council of Canada, 1991:74).

For many women the move into paid employment has meant working part-time as a bank teller, cashier, waitress, or clerical worker. Since the movement of women into part-time employment has been "the single fastest growing component of the employed Canadian labour force in the last decade," part-time work is likely to remain an important and growing aspect of women's role in paid employment (Parliament, 1989:5; Burke, 1986:10). . . .

For many analysts this proliferation of part-time employment signals a major crisis. Part-time work is expected to continue to expand at the expense of secure full-time employment. In the future, workers will be increasingly forced to accept insecure, temporary, and peripheral employment. The work force will be split between the minority of workers who are fortunate to obtain permanent full-time work and the majority who must compete for irregular and part-time openings. The prognosis is particularly grim for women, who are already subject to occupational ghettoization, pay inequities, and economic discrimination. Part-time employment is seen as a "circular trap" that locks women into juggling inferior, dead-end, poorly paid jobs along with primary responsibility for child-rearing and housework (Smith, 1983).

Perhaps surprisingly, other analysts enthusiastically embrace part-time employment as the solution to unemployment, as the key to a more leisurely, balanced lifestyle, and as an enormous opportunity for women (and men) with familial responsibilities. From this perspective the expansion of part-time employment offers workers greater freedom in their working lives and more control over the place of work in their lives, and at the same time it offers employment to a larger number of workers. In this scenario, future employers enjoy the benefits of a flexible work force that can respond rapidly to peaks and troughs in production demands and employees are much freer to combine work with education, retraining, leisure, or family activities.

Whether the growth of part-time work signals increased exploitation or expanded opportunities for workers is a puzzle that may be solved in the next decade. In the interim the evidence is decidedly mixed. Today, disgruntled workers who have been forced to accept (involuntary) part-time employment (along with low wages and few benefits) because of the paucity of full-time opportunities work side-by-side with part-timers who are happy to find a way to combine paid employment with educational or familial constraints. Which of these two groups predominates in the future depends not only on the economic well-being of the country but also on the actions of legislators, union leaders, workers, and employers in the next few years. . . .

FULL-TIME, PART-TIME, OR AT HOME?

○

Given that one in four of employed Canadian women is working part-time, that nearly three-quarters (72 per cent) of the almost 2 million Canadians who work part-time are women, and that one in every three employed women with children and a spouse works part-time, it is important to examine how, on a personal level, this movement to part-time employment occurs (Statistics Canada, 1990: 75-76, 85).

A complex interplay of factors—notably financial pressure, family considerations, access to child care, the availability of work, and personal needs—enters into the process that ultimately results in women working full-time, part-time, or remaining full-time in the home. Further, the significance of these various elements changes through the course of women's lives as well as in response to a wide variety of personal, societal, and economic pressures, ranging from ill-health and divorce to layoffs and recession. The result is not only considerable variation among women in terms of their current status but also in terms of the patterns of employment that characterize their lives (Jones, Marsden, Tepperman, 1990). Our interviews suggest that it is not uncommon for women to move back and forth between employment and homemaking and to make several shifts between full- and part-time employment as they accommodate the changing needs of their families and respond to their own personal needs.

The complexity and variety of women's employment patterns are reflected, for example, both in the various forms that part-time employment may take and in the location of part-time work in women's employment histories. In the traditional pattern, women work full-time prior to marriage and motherhood. They then interrupt their paid employment for some period of time. Later (months or years), they return to part-time employment. Once their child-rearing responsibilities are greatly diminished, they often take full-time employment until retiring from the labour force. Individual women's employment histories may, of course, include many variations on this basic approach.

Internationally, two general patterns of part-time employment are apparent. In Britain, the general pattern of interrupted labour force activity (full-time homemaking) followed months or years later by part-time employment typifies the female part-time labour force (Main, 1988; Dex and Shaw, 1986). In short, married women tend to move from full-time employment (prior to child-rearing) to full-time homemaking (early child-rearing) to part-time employment (later or at the end of child-rearing). In contrast, in Sweden women work full-time prior to motherhood, remain members of the labour force while on maternity leave, return to their previous employment on a part-time work schedule, and at some later point return to full-time employment (Hoem and Hoem, 1988; Sunderstrom, 1987). The nature and quality of national policies on maternity and parental leave clearly affect the nature of women's part-time work experience.

Presently, though most Canadian women (58 per cent) still drop out of the labour force for at least a year, Canadian and American women appear to be gravitating toward the Swedish model with its continuous employment pattern (Robinson, 1986:8). The differences between the British and Swedish paths may significantly affect the experience of part-time employment since in one instance the worker moves from being a full-time homemaker to a part-time employee while in the other she shifts from full-time to part-time employee with a hiatus for maternity leave. The contrast in life circumstances (homemaker to part-time worker versus full-time to part-time worker) may be directly responsible for variations in women's responses to part-time employment.

Many of the women we interviewed have followed the traditional path and moved from full-time homemaker to part-time employee (although there are many individual variations in this pattern). Almost all explain this decision in terms of their role in the family and, in particular, their responsibilities for young children at home. Many other elements, however, also enter into the complex and dynamic process that results in women's part-time employment.

Once they are members of the part-time labour force, women react in a variety of ways to their employment situation, often depending on whether they are willing part-timers, whether they compare their present situation to being employed full-time or to being full-time in the home, whether part-time work is seen as a short-term or long-term commitment, and, ultimately, whether time or money is the greatest issue in their day-to-day lives.

Also, often directly affecting the feelings of married part-timers are the attitudes and actions of other family members. If husbands and children are supportive and happy about the mother's work and if it produces a greater sharing of responsibilities (particularly of domestic work and child care) along with an overall increase in marital equality, women's reactions to employment are likely to be more generally positive. Ultimately, whether the part-time solution provides the best or worst of both worlds does not depend solely on the interplay within the family. The quality and conditions of the work itself are the crucial other half of the equation.

THE ISSUE OF CHOICE

Many women part-timers, whether they are students employed evenings at a fast-food restaurant or mothers who work three days a week for the local bank branch, would say that they have chosen to work a part-time schedule.

When asked, they would then explain the particular concerns and needs that entered into their individual decision-making process—more time with the children, time to go to classes, more money for family finances, and so on. The difficulty with this voluntaristic, personalized approach to part-time work is that, particularly for women who are "willing" part-timers, it tends to downplay the many external factors that may, in a sense, "force" some women at certain points in their lives to work part-time, others to stay home full-time, and still others to become full-time employees.

While it is useful to understand how women explain their part-time status to themselves and others, it is important to keep in mind that even for women who describe themselves as having "decided" to work part-time and being satisfied with part-time employment, various social, structural, economic, and political elements may have compelled this particular choice. For example, more British women than American women "choose" part-time employment. Dex and Shaw suggest that the tax relief for day care expenses that American but not British women workers receive and the absence of free health care in the United States but not in Britain create a social context in which American women are encouraged to work full-time (to receive health benefits) while British women are pushed toward part-time employment (1986:39, 126).

Similarly, class differences among workers may condition any decisions about women's paid employment (Lowe and Krahn, 1985). Higher-income families are more likely to be able to afford day care and are more likely to live in an area where day-care facilities are available. Women living in such well-to-do circumstances may be in a much better position to choose freely to stay home or to work full- or part-time. For the lower-income family, with limited or non-existent resources for child care and with one family car, the mother's "decision" to take employment may hinge on the availability of flexible employment, a grandmother or neighbour willing to watch the children, access to public transit, and so forth.

Finally, idiosyncratic individual factors may tip the scale one way or another. For example, a twenty-seven-year-old mother of one who wanted to be employed explains that since her husband works rotating shifts and also has a part-time job (where he makes more money than she could), she feels she has to stay home full-time (Duffy, Mandell, and Pupo, 1989). For many other women, the lack of accessible, affordable, quality day care shuts the door on any possibility of taking paid employment:

> If I were to seek employment, there are no day-care facilities in our area, there are none! There is one day-care centre and they are backlogged. One woman I was just speaking to, she was on the waiting list and had to wait maybe a year and a half and that's all they had. You have to go to the private sector and there are hardly any advertised and you're taking the risk of going with people who maybe don't have references.

As a result, when women say they are working part-time in order to have more time at home or, conversely, to get out of the house, their statements must be located within the larger socio-economic context that conditions the range of their choices. Considerable evidence suggests that many workers would choose to alter their working arrangements, if this were a possibility. This includes not only the more than one woman in five who is working part-time because she could not find full-time employment but also the 57 per cent of working Canadians who would like to change their working arrangements (Benimadhu, 1987: vii; see also, Del Boca, 1983; Nock and Kingston, 1984). In all, 40 per cent of women workers aged 25-34 would be willing to sacrifice income in order to reduce their worktime (Benimadhu, 1987: 12). Some part-timers would, if money were not an issue, like to be full-time at home. Others are waiting till their children are older so they can move into full-time employment. Because of a complex interplay of social and economic structures and personal factors, many workers are not in a position to make actual choices between real alternatives.

This distinction between personal choices and structural constraints is important because if we accept women's choices as an explanation for their part-time employment, then the conflicts and dissatisfactions that women part-timers encounter are their responsibility—after all, they chose it. This personalization of employment decision-making is "oppressive." It encourages women and others in their lives to blame women themselves for their "poor" choices rather than seeing that these choices are rigidly defined by economic and societal structures (Currie, 1988:251). Viewed from a more structural perspective, the politicians who fail to support child-care legislation, the employers who resist increased flexibility in women's and men's employment, and the teachers who continue to encourage girls to train for traditional occupations all deny women the possibility of other choices. . . .

R E F E R E N C E S
o

Benimadhu, Prem.
    1987. "Hours of Work: Trends and Attitudes in Canada." Conference Board of
    Canada Report, January.
Burke, Mary Anne.
    1986. "The Growth of Part-time Work," *Canadian Social Trends* (Autumn): 9-14.
Currie, Dawn.
    1988. "Re-thinking What We Do and How We Do It: A Study of Reproductive
    Decisions," *Canadian Review of Sociology and Anthropology*, 25,2:231-53.
Del Boca, Daniela.
    1988. "Women in a Changing Workplace," in Jane Jenson, Elisabeth Hagen, and
    Ceallaigh Reddy, eds., *Feminization of the Labor Force: Paradoxes and Promises*. New
    York: Oxford University Press.

Dex, Shirley, and Lois B. Shaw.
    1986. *British and American Women at Work*. London: Macmillan.
Duffy, Ann Doris, Nancy Mandell, and Norene Pupo.
    1989. *Few Choices: Women, Work and Family*. Toronto, Garamond Press.
Economic Council of Canada.
    1991. *Employment in the Service Economy*. Ottawa: Minister of Supply and Services.
Hoem, Britta, and Jan M. Hoem.
    1988. "The Swedish Family: Aspects of Contemporary Developments," *Journal of Family* Issues, 9,3 (Sept.): 397-424.
Jones, Charles, Lorna Marsden, and Lorne Tepperman.
    1990. *Lives of Their Own: The Individualization of Women's Lives*. Toronto: Oxford University Press.
Lowe, Graham, S., and Harvey Krahn.
    1985. "Where Wives Work: The Relative Effects of Situational and Attitudinal Factors," *Canadian Journal of Sociology*, 10, (Winter): 1–22.
Main, Brian G.M.
    1988. "The Lifetime Attachment of Women to the Labour Market," in Audrey
    Hung, ed., *Women and Paid Work: Issues of Equality*. New York: St. Martin's Press.
Nock, Steven L., and Paul William Kingston.
    1984. "The Family Work Day," *Journal of Marriage and the Family* (May): 333-43.
Parliament, Jo-Anne B.
    1989. "Women Employed Outside the Home," *Canadian Social Trends* (Summer): 2-6.
Robinson, Patricia.
    1986. *Women's Work Interruptions: Results from the 1984 Family History Survey*.
    Ottawa: Minister of Supply and Services.
Statistics Canada.
    1990. *Women in Canada: A Statistical Profile*. Second Edition. Ottawa: Minister of Supply and Services.
Sundstrom, Marianne.
    1987. "A Study in the Growth of Part-time Work in Sweden." Doctoral dissertation, University of Stockholm.

"Everyone Does It": Unpaid Work in a Rural Peripheral Region*

Lawrence F. Felt and Peter R. Sinclair

.... Considering how inferior the Great Northern Peninsula appears in Canada's official statistics on incomes, unemployment and education (Statistics Canada 1988), a visitor might expect to find villages of ramshackle houses filled with people desperate to get away to Toronto and points west. In fact, most people live in modern, well maintained homes and are satisfied with life in the area. Indeed, approximately 35 per cent are return migrants. We believe that they are relatively satisfied because they know that, with their limited education and occupational qualifications, they can live better on the Peninsula, surrounded by family, friends and open spaces, than in high cost, urban environments (Felt and Sinclair 1991). A vibrant informal economic sector makes it possible to live where they are in acceptable conditions.

THEORETICAL PERSPECTIVE

○

In studies of many third world societies, the distinction between a formal and an informal economy or sector has been made frequently (Clark 1988; Fyle 1987; Hosier 1987; Moser 1984; Nattrass 1987; Trager 1987). Rather than informal economy, we prefer the term informal *sector*, because it does not imply a separate, independent economy. Admittedly, the range of definitions is so wide that we have some sympathy with Peattie's (1987) view that the informal sector lumps together so many diverse activities that it should be abandoned, but Skolka (1985:61) offers some distinctions that help with this problem of terminological confusion:

* Abridged from Lawrence F. Felt and Peter R. Sinclair, "Everyone Does it": Unpaid Work in a Rural Peripheral Region," *Work, Employment & Society* 6 no. 1 (1992): 43–64. Reprinted by permission of the publisher and the authors.

The output of the hidden paid work missing in the gross domestic product is the product of the *'hidden economy'.* . . The output of the unpaid productive work is the output of the *'informal economy'.*

Taken together, Skolka calls these sectors the parallel economy. His separation of the hidden and informal economies corresponds to Rose's (1985) distinction between unofficial and domestic economies, as well as to Gershuny's (1988) reference to underground economy and household or communal economy. Our research deals only with what we prefer to call the informal sector of unpaid work.[1]

Most of the literature on the informal sector is concerned with documenting its existence, measuring its importance to social life, and clarifying how it differs from the formal economy. Most authors do not try to explain variations in the degree of participation or even why the informal sector should exist in the first place. An exception is that some earlier researchers suggested that the informal economy served a compensatory function in that it helped increase living standards for lower income households by augmenting their resources and consumption (Mingioni 1983; Pahl 1984: 317-319). As such, it made some contribution towards reducing inequality. More recently, however, Pahl (1988) has proposed that quite the opposite might result since participation in such informal practices may vary positively with income; i.e. the higher the household income, the more informal economic strategies are utilized. Thus, his recent research has led him to believe (Pahl 1988:251) that the informal economy flourishes among the better off, middle mass of households, particularly in those 'work-rich' households of multiple earners who have the resources and the need to do more for themselves:

> Those already in employment are in the best position to help other members of their family find employment and, with their multi-earner affluence are more likely to own their own homes, own cars, boats, holiday homes and so forth. The more goods and property they own, the more extra work can and needs to be done.

Pahl's view in this statement might be contrasted with the implication of the neo-Marxist theory that unpaid labour makes it possible to maintain a semi-proletarian reserve of workers (see, for Atlantic Canada, Fairly *et al.* 1990; Sacouman 1980). Unpaid labour helps capitalist business in the periphery to survive, despite disadvantages of location, because wages, on an annual basis, need not cover all costs of subsistence at culturally acceptable standards. The low wages associated with low demand labour markets and the seasonal nature of much employment are, in a sense, subsidized by unpaid work (as well as by state transfer payments). None of this is to suggest that unpaid labour is insignificant in urban areas or core regions, but we suspect that it is particularly important to the reproduction of life on the periphery (Smith 1984). Moreover, we should expect to find that the unemployed and those with low incomes would be most likely to participate in the informal economy because of their inability to extract the necessary living resources from wage labour. An unstated implication of the labour reserve theory is that people would prefer to substitute purchased goods and services for self-provisioning.

We propose to show that neither view is adequate, at least not in areas like the Great Northern Peninsula. We believe that informal, subsistence production substitutes for what some people cannot afford to purchase— provided that they have the minimum income from other sources to buy the necessary capital inputs, i.e. the tools, gasoline or building materials, that make subsistence work possible. Since the development of the Canadian welfare state with its system of transfer payments from government to individuals, this should not be an insurmountable problem for most households[2] in our area. This is what the labour reserve theory implies; but we also expect households with more substantial incomes to provide for themselves and other households. We suggest this will occur in isolated rural areas partly because skilled trades workers may not be readily available, even if people wanted to purchase their services. Moreover, as Pahl also reports, many people will provide for themselves regardless of personal or household income because of the satisfaction they get from doing their own work or procuring their own supplies. It is not simply a matter of cost. People also do things for other households not because they expect any return to themselves, but because they feel obliged to help out; and through such help they enhance their status within the community (Sider 1986). Our finding that two-thirds of respondents did not expect any specific repayment for their assistance is consistent with Sider's suggestion that offering and/or receiving assistance need not result in any specific 'credit' or 'debt' being acknowledged. Lack of alternatives and a culture of self-help should make informal economic activity attractive across social boundaries. While we agree with Pahl that low incomes do not lead people to undertake more unpaid work as a compensation, we do not expect to find a strong relationship between unpaid work and middle or high incomes either. Thus, we suggest that *the degree of participation in the informal sector is independent of socio-economic status.*

From earlier research on rural Newfoundland (Faris 1972; Firestone 1967; Porter 1983) and our own knowledge of the area, we expected to find a sexual division of labour based on traditional conceptions of men's and women's work. No other dimension of social location appeared as likely a basis to predict what people do. Thus we hypothesized that *participation by individuals in particular unpaid work activities is best predicted by gender.* Beyond gender we did anticipate that marital status would have some impact on informal economic activity. Marriage brings expectations of a separate household in which the married persons will have the prime responsibility for its continuity. *In contrast with single persons, we expected married people to be more involved in the informal sector, particularly in home construction.*

The informal sector is more than the work that members of households do for themselves; it also involves unpaid work for other households. We presumed that this type of participation would be more likely on the part of people with resources to bring to their tasks and who, in other respects, exhibited commitment to the welfare of the area in which they lived. For most unpaid work the principle resource is time, although tools and access to a vehicle are required in such activities as house repairs and giving lifts. People who are not employed probably have more 'free' time and thus we expected that *the longer a person was employed, the less would s/he contribute unpaid labour for others*. Organizational members participate in formal groups outside their household, often with an explicit objective of improving the welfare of others. Thus we predicted that *the number of organizational memberships held by a person would be positively related to unpaid work for others*. Whom do people work for in other households and who does work for them? Given the centrality of kinship to both social relationships and economic activity in Newfoundland fishing settlements (Faris 1972; Firestone 1967), we hypothesized that *inter-household informal tasks are undertaken by and for kin rather than friends or acquaintances*.

Following a brief introduction to the Great Northern Peninsula and the survey data, we examine these hypotheses in three areas: home construction; other types of subsistence work for one's own household; and the unpaid labour contributed to other households. In conclusion, we consider the social meaning and implications of the informal sector we have identified in relation to the general theoretical issues previously introduced.

THE GREAT NORTHERN PENINSULA OF NEWFOUNDLAND

o

Newfoundland and Labrador is Canada's most recent and poorest province. Most of its people live along the coast of the rocky, almost barren island of Newfoundland, long known for its fishing grounds. Among the most isolated are the 26,000 inhabitants of the Great Northern Peninsula, which stretches northeast from Bonne Bay for 300 kilometres. The Peninsula suffers from a harsh climate, with long snowy winters and harbours closed for months by ice. The growing season is short and soils are poor. Marine resources, especially cod and shrimp, are the main basis of the regional economy. The population is scattered among more than 60 coastal settlements of which the largest is St Anthony, a service centre and fishing port with slightly more than 3,000 people. Although a few permanent residents have been traced back to the late eighteenth century, settlers were discouraged as long as France exercised treaty rights that gave French fisherman exclusive access to the region's fish. By 1911, there were still only 10,481 inhabitants on the whole Peninsula. It is thus an area of recent settlement and one that remains sparsely populated.

The Great Northern Peninsula is characterized by numerous indicators of marginality, such as low incomes, high dependence on welfare and unemployment insurance, a weak labour market, low levels of education, loss of youth who migrate in search of work opportunities, and minimal access to social services. In most respects, the Peninsula is one of the least privileged areas in Canada.

...[U]nemployment is painfully high—more than three times the national rate in 1986, although the labour force participation rate was higher than for the province and about the same as the national average. Reflecting the importance of the small boat fishing sector of the economy is the relatively high percentage of men who are self-employed (13.5 per cent compared with 4.8 per cent for Newfoundland). The service sector is less well developed, whereas relatively more people are found in primary industry (mainly fishing) and manufacturing (almost exclusively fish processing). Incomes are low even by Newfoundland standards and, relative to Canada, male incomes are especially depressed. The 1986 median income for men was $11,489 (58 per cent of the Canadian median) and for women it was $6,957 (72.9 per cent of the Canadian median). Finally, the dependence on transfer payments in our research area is particularly high with 32.2 per cent of total income coming from this source compared with 21.2 per cent in Newfoundland and only 11.1 per cent in Canada.

M E T H O D O L O G Y

o

Our research is based on structured interviews with all persons 18 years or older in 250 Peninsula households. The census clusters the households into 36 communities and unincorporated districts. We first sampled ten of these communities and districts, with the probability of inclusion being proportionate to the unit's population, and then randomly selected 25 households in each centre such that each household on the Peninsula had an equal probability of appearing in the sample. The communities chosen were Rocky Harbour, Parson's Pond, Port au Choix, Flower's Cove, Cook's Harbour, St Anthony, Main Brook, Englee, Roddickton, and Census Subdivision D on the northern tip of the Peninsula. After extensive investigation we decided that the best sampling frame of households was provided by the 1988 telephone directory up-dated to August 1988 where possible. There are hardly any unlisted numbers on the Peninsula, but we recognize that a small percentage of households with no telephone are excluded.

The interviews were conducted by six persons familiar with the communities concerned. Three had previous experience as survey interviewers, but all were thoroughly prepared by the researchers prior to conducting the interviews, which lasted from one to one and a half hours. If no response could be obtained from any person in a selected household, interviewers were asked to substitute from our randomly selected list. Only 12 households were substituted in this way. Once permission was obtained to interview one adult in the household, that household became part of the sample. Of course, other adults in the household might be impossible to contact or refuse to take part. It appears that the interviewers failed to complete 39 interviews at this stage,[3] giving a response rate of 93.4 per cent. Because the same questions were being asked of different household members, we stressed that each interview should be conducted in private. In total, 554 interviews were completed between late August and early December 1988. We shall now use this information to analyse the informal sector of unpaid work.

HOME CONSTRUCTION

o

Home construction and repair is the largest project of self-provisioning in which the people of the area are likely to take part. Thus we asked all respondents if they had helped to build their dwelling. Those who reported that they had taken part in construction were then asked whether they had worked alone or with relatives and friends on 13 specific tasks that we considered important. They also had an opportunity to add any further activities.

An exceptionally high 95.1 per cent of respondents reported living in a dwelling owned by one or more members of their household, despite the economic marginality of the area. This paradox is easily explained. House prices are low, but more significantly a large percentage of adults build their own homes—64.4 per cent of households in our sample contain at least one person who took part in constructing the dwelling. In the Peninsula's smallest villages (represented in our sample by the five with a population of 600 or less), the incidence of home construction reached 72.8 per cent of households compared with 56 per cent in the larger villages or small towns where the market in houses seems somewhat more developed.

Who is likely to build? As a preliminary test of our main hypothesis that individual participation in the informal sector is independent of socio-economic status, we examined home building in relation to personal income with a control for gender. For women, there is no hint of a connection between home construction and personal income; for men, the per cent who help build their homes increases with income as Pahl's theory implies, but the relationship is not statistically significant. We also failed to find any relationship when occupational categories were introduced as a predictor variable (data not reported here). Thus our hypothesis of independence holds up so far.

In the prevailing culture, married people are more likely than single persons to feel the need for a separate dwelling. Given the scarcity of rental accommodation and of older houses for sale, they are likely to build a new house and in many cases to contribute their own labour to the project. This expectation is confirmed as 54.1 per cent of married persons compared with only 14.3 per cent of single persons have contributed to building their current home. Most house construction tasks (with the exception of interior finishing) have typically been considered as men's work. Thus it is no surprise to find that married men are more often involved in home construction than married women—68.6 per cent compared with 40.2 per cent, although the participation of wives is still substantial. . . .

SUBSISTENCE PRODUCTION
o

In addition to home construction, we examined other types of subsistence production, although in less detail. All respondents were asked who usually performed 23 different household tasks. Many of these tasks centred on child care and routine housework, but we do not examine these activities here (Sinclair and Felt forthcoming); rather we focus on the provision of other goods and services. We look first at the extent to which households are involved in subsistence production and subsequently at the characteristics of individuals who perform these groups of tasks.

We believe that the extent of self-provisioning is high in that most households can count on members who undertake minor house and car repairs and who supply a wide range of consumption goods—clothes, berries, jam, vegetables, wood for home heating, and wildlife for food. On the nine items examined, an average of 71.9 per cent of households usually supplied themselves. Other research has shown a similar high degree of involvement in subsistence production in two Peninsula villages of contrasting economic conditions—Anchor Point and Bird's Cove (House *et al.* 1989: 57). Hill's earlier Newfoundland sample included several similar activities, but in no instance did the percentage of households participating reach 50 per cent (Hill 1983: 235).[4] On the Great Northern Peninsula, hunting, which is usually undertaken to provide food, is remarkably widespread. Supplying wood is important in an area where much of the winter heating comes from wood stoves. Picking berries (84.4 per cent of households) and making jam (85.2 per cent) is much more common than growing vegetables (47.6 per cent). This may reflect the difficulties of gardening due to poor soils and the short growing season in some parts of the Peninsula, but many people like to grow their own potatoes and vegetables and are prepared to go to considerable effort when the area around their home is unsuitable. Thus, in the north it is common to see people working on roadside plots far from the nearest village. An unfortunate omission from our data is information on self-provisioning with fish, which we would expect to be common, as it was in Hill's research (Hill 1983: 235).

To get a better sense of how important home production is to households on the Peninsula, we created a simple index based on the nine items. Thus the range for each household was from zero to nine according to the number of activities reported for the household. (The alpha co-efficient for reliability was 0.72). We found that 62.8 per cent of households score seven or higher, which indicates an extensive informal sector that involves most people in the region.

We have argued that socio-economic status is unassociated with participation in the informal sector. We now examine this hypothesis at the household level by correlating the participation index with other household variables. Although the index is positively related to total household income (r=0.25; p=<0.001), this relationship disappears when other variables are taken into account. Households with larger incomes usually contain more adults, who are both potential earners and subsistence production workers. In a regression analysis of the index of self-provision with household income, average personal income of adult residents and the number of adults as independent variables, only the number of adult residents proved significant. Although the number of adults and household income are correlated as expected (r=0.40; p=<0.001), there is no independent impact of either personal or household income on involvement in subsistence production. We conclude that the most important determinant is the labour capacity of the household. The more labour power is available, the more likely it is that many subsistence tasks will be undertaken.

We expected to see strong gender differences for most subsistence production tasks and we also anticipated that involvement would vary with marital status. For these analyses, in addition to the subsistence production previously discussed, we have included shopping, banking and completing tax returns as three examples of services. Because there were only 38 widowed, separated or divorced individuals in the sample, these cases were excluded. . . . It is immediately obvious that married people are much more likely to contribute goods and services to the household than are single persons. This is true for both women and men. . . . Men pick berries about as often as women, but seldom make jam—presumably because that is kitchen work. Single men (usually young) are most likely to contribute through cutting wood or hunting, while single women do the shopping more than any other task. Both are likely to bank, but it is unclear whether this banking is for themselves alone or for other household members. The tax return item was notable as the only one in which most people reported that a paid worker usually did it, which is why so few claim to perform this work.

UNPAID WORK BETWEEN HOUSEHOLDS

o

The third component of the informal sector that we investigate is unpaid work that connects different households.[5] To do things for members of other households for no monetary return is clearly part of the culture of this area. Asked what people would do for each other without expecting pay, almost 85 per cent (86.5 per cent of men and 82.5 per cent of women) could name at least one such activity, the most common being house repairs and babysitting. Three or more activities were volunteered by 47.8 per cent. Once more, gender differences are extreme as women and men tend to think of quite different activities. It is interesting that most respondents do not consider working without pay to be part of a system of reciprocal exchange. Only 33.6 per cent claimed that any kind of return would be expected.

But do people actually do such jobs, even if they recognize that others might? Most people claim so—66.8 per cent said they had worked without pay at least once in the last year and 81.9 per cent of households were linked to others through having at least one member so engaged. Building or repairing homes is the main activity for the men, but substantial numbers saw wood, haul boats, and do mechanical work. Women babysit, knit, sew, clean house, cook for others and give lifts.[6] . . .

We had thought that inter-household assistance networks would be rooted in kinship in this relatively isolated rural area of Newfoundland. This prediction is supported only for the women in our sample. In the unpaid activities we investigated, women are more likely than men to help out relatives (47.8 per cent compared with 32.8 per cent) and men are more likely than women to help friends. 51.1 per cent of the men report that they worked exclusively for their friends compared with only 25.9 per cent of the women. Compared with those who work for others, slightly fewer people, 56.5 per cent, report that they received help of an informal nature in the past year, but this still involved 70 per cent of the households. Babysitting was the most common assistance reported by women (16.7 per cent) followed by sewing/knitting and house cleaning. Women are helped most by their relatives and men more often by their friends. We conclude that women, especially married women, are involved in informal networks through which they provide and receive assistance with child care and housework, while men's informal activity is more directly involved with the creation of home equity and traditionally male tasks.

C O N C L U S I O N
o

In this paper we have documented important aspects of the informal sector of an isolated, peripheral area in Canada. Our central hypothesis was that the amount of participation by individuals and households was independent of socio-economic status. With respect to home construction, we showed that participation is not significantly related to other structural variables such as employment and income, although it is significantly related to education. We did find a small positive correlation between household income and other types of self-provisioning, but the relationship was not significant in a regression analysis that included the number of adults in the household. We concluded that labour supply was more critical than income; however, we acknowledge that informal economic activity requires goods that have to be purchased. It is possible that households more impoverished than one finds on the Great Northern Peninsula would be unable to undertake the more expensive activities.

In conclusion, we shall consider the underlying meaning and broader implications of this analysis. Although we have provided evidence that challenges Pahl's (1984; 1988) analyses in some respects, this research was conducted in an isolated rural area that may well differ from patterns established in more heavily urbanized areas. The type of informal sector in rural areas like the Great Northern Peninsula should not be treated the same as most urban counterparts for several reasons. First, much of it does not involve cash transactions to avoid taxation; it is unpaid labour. Second, in most cases, we are not dealing with the kind of situation that Gershuny (1983) describes in which services once purchased (domestic work, entertainment, transportation, etc.) are now being replaced by relatively cheaper home production. According to Gershuny, technological innovation creates and cheapens the goods, such as household appliances and automobiles, that make it possible and financially advantageous for households to take over the provision of services. However much sense this makes in urban industrial areas, it does not apply in rural contexts where purchased services were rare and even basic consumer goods were in short supply or could not be purchased because people were too poor. The Great Northern Peninsula is much closer to this latter category. It has always exhibited a relatively important informal sector, albeit one that adjusts to new needs and circumstances.

Does it then follow that unpaid work takes place in order to maintain a cheap labour reserve for capitalism? In other words, does unpaid work cheapen the costs of reproducing labour? In a sense this is a valid argument because unpaid work does have this consequence, but it is not an argument that explains either the origin of unpaid work or the variation in the extent to which people undertake it. Instead, we believe that unpaid labour is not somehow put into action by the imperatives of capitalism, but is a constructive, conscious response by people to their circumstances.

The widespread informal sector in the Great Northern Peninsula and, presumably, in other similar areas, is best understood as a constructive reaction to the environment, isolation, small population, and poor local economy. The small population and low density of settlements in an area physically isolated from large centres has meant that people must often provide services and repairs for themselves. The low incomes generated from the fishing economy discourage the development of an extensive network of commercial services and trades. The residents copy by building and repairing their own homes, making clothes, and using the resources of their local environment for food and fuel. Yet the informal sector is more extensive than it need be, if getting by were the only motivation for participation. We have seen that household income, for example, does not determine involvement, which appears to be culturally as well as structurally conditioned. That is, many activities are undertaken because they are socially valued. Thus, in our research, there is no evidence that respondents substitute market for domestic or communal services as soon as they are able to do so. In this report, we are unable to support Warde's (1990: 511) recent conclusion based on a sample of 'middle aged', relatively affluent households in northwest England:

> in our sample there was no positive relationship between market and domestic involvement. Our sample appeared to be substituting market for domestic services when they could afford to.

In part, the different results may reflect the relatively small number of high income individuals in our sample. Perhaps there is a threshold after which people begin to substitute market purchases for self-provisioning. In part, the results may reflect differences in cultural values. On the Great Northern Peninsula, to provide for one's self and, when necessary, for others brings generalized respect. This interpretation is consistent with Sider's (1980) recent analysis of exchange and reciprocity in rural Newfoundland communities. Providing assistance must also be understood as a social occasion. For example, many families own or have access to cabins in the woods to which they retreat for days at a time in autumn and winter in order to hunt, cut wood and party.

Although the informal sector does not produce greater equality among households of this region than would otherwise exist, we feel that it does have socially positive impacts when we consider the region as a whole. For example, the extent of the informal sector in our research area suggests that living standards are higher than income data imply, and to that extent the informal sector may reduce regional disparities in Canada. Casual observation of housing standards and material possessions certainly supports this conclusion. However, we have no comparative data from urban areas that would allow us to assess with confidence the relative importance of the informal sector in isolated rural areas. Even if we are correct, the existence of a flourishing informal sector is insufficient reason for avoiding the special problems of such areas and no excuse for neglecting the needs of the poor because of a mistaken belief that they are the prime beneficiaries of unpaid labour.

NOTES

o

1. It is important to note that this view of the informal economy differs from most researchers on developing areas for whom small scale, commercial production and trade is usually the central component.

2. Without assuming democratic arrangements in households, we think it important to treat the household as a group among whom important resources and consumption items are shared.

3. We compared the number of adults reported by respondents with the number of interviews actually completed. The uncertainty is caused by the fact that occasional discrepancies appeared because household members sometimes disagreed on the number of residents. Apart from recording errors, this could well arise as a result of disagreement over whether a family member working or studying away was still part of the household.

4. In part, the lower figures in the Newfoundland study may reflect different wording of the questions and the fact that information was collected from only one member of each household. However, we would expect less self-provisioning in Hill's sample because it included the major urban areas.

5. Only 8.7 per cent reported doing 'odd jobs' for pay.

6. Glatzer and Berger (1988: 521) report that German social networks support house repairs and babysitting, but rarely routine housework.

REFERENCES

Clark, G. (ed.) (1988) *Traders Versus the State: Anthropological Approaches to Unofficial Economies*, Boulder: Westview.

Fairly, B., Leys, C. & Sacouman, J. (eds.)
(1990) *Restructuring and Resistance: Perspectives from Atlantic Canada*, Toronto: Garamond.

Faris, J.
(1972) *Cat Harbour: A Newfoundland Fishing Settlement*, St. John's: Institute of Social and Economic Research.

Felt, L.F. & Sinclair, P.R.
(1991) 'Home, sweet home: dimensions and determinants of life satisfaction in a marginal region', *Canadian Journal of Sociology*, 16, 1-21.

Firestone, M.M.
(1967) *Brothers and Rivals: Patrilocality in Savage Cove*, St John's: Institute of Social and Economic Research.

Fyle, C.M.
(1987) 'Culture, technology and policy in the informal sector: attention to endogenous development', *Africa*, 57, 498-509.

Gershuny, J.
(1983) *Social Innovation and the Division of Labour*, Oxford: Oxford University Press.

Gershuny, J.
(1988) 'Time, technology and the informal economy', in Pahl, R.E. (ed.) *On Work*, Oxford: Blackwell.

Glatzer, W. & Berger, R.
(1988) 'Household composition, social networks and household production in Germany', in Pahl, R.E. (ed.), *On Work*, Oxford: Blackwell.

Hill, R.H.
(1983) *The Meaning of Work and Unemployment*, St. John's: Community Services Council.

House, J.D. with White, S.M. & Ripley, P.
(1989) *Going Away . . . And Coming Back: Economic Life and Migration in Small Canadian Communities*, St. John's: Institute of Social and Economic Research, report no. 2.

Hosier, R.H.
(1987) 'The informal sector in Kenya: spatial variation and development alternatives', *Journal of Developing Areas*, 21, 383-402.

Mingioni, E.
(1983) 'Informalization, restructuring and the survival strategies of the working class', *International Journal of Urban and Regional Research*, 7, 311-339.

Moser, C.O.N.
(1984) 'The informal sector reworked: viability and vulnerability in urban development', *Regional Development Dialogue*, 5, 135-178.

Nattrass, N.J.
(1987) 'Street trading in Transkei—a struggle against poverty, persecution, and prosecution', *World Development*, 15, 861-875.

Pahl, R.E.
(1984) *Divisions of Labour*, Oxford: Blackwell.

Pahl, R.E.
(1988) 'Some remarks on informal work, social polarization and the social structure', *International Journal of Urban and Regional Research*, 12, 247-267.

Peattie, L. (1987) 'An idea in good currency and how it grew: the informal sector', *World Development*, 15, 851-860.

Porter, M.
(1983) "Women and old boats: the sexual division of labour in a Newfoundland outport', in Garmanikow, E. (ed.) *Public and Private: Gender and Society*, London: Heinemann and BSA.

Rose, R.
(1985) 'Getting by in three economies: the resources of the official, unofficial and domestic economies', in Lane, J. (ed.) *State and Market*, London: Sage.

Sacouman, J.
(1980) 'Semi-proletarianization and rural underdevelopment in the Maritimes', *Canadian Review of Sociology and Anthropology*, 17, 232-245.

Sider, G.M.
(1986) *Culture and Class in Anthropology and History*, Cambridge: Cambridge University Press.

Sinclair, P. R. & Felt, L.F.
(forthcoming) 'Gender, work and household reproduction: married men and women in an isolated fishing region', *Canadian Review of Sociology and Anthropology*.

Skolka, J.
(1985) 'The parallel economy in Austria', in Alessandrini, S. & Dallago, B. (eds.), *The Unofficial Economy: Consequences and Perspectives in Different Economic Systems*, Aldershot: Gower.

Smith, J.
(1984) 'Nonwage labor and subsistence', in Smith, J. *et al.* (eds.), *Households and the World Economy*, Berkeley Hills: Sage.

Statistics Canada
(1988) *Population and Dwelling Characteristics—Census Divisions and Subdivisions. Profiles. Newfoundland: Part 2*, Cat. 94-102, Ottawa: Supply and Services Canada.

Trager, L.

(1987) 'A re-examination of the urban informal sector in West Africa', *Canadian Journal of African Studies*, 21, 238-255.

Warde, A.

(1990) 'Household work strategies and forms of labour: conceptual and empirical issues', *Work, Employment & Society*, 4, 495-515.

Population, Pyramids and Promotional Prospects*

David K. Foot and Rosemary A. Venne

I INTRODUCTION

o

The baby boom generation has been the subject of considerable attention. Because of its sheer size in North America, it is easy to document historically the enormous impact the baby boom has had on society and its institutions, which have often been stretched to their limits to accommodate its requirements. Some would say the baby boom generation has changed the shape of these institutions. Jones (1980) views this generation as a tidal wave effecting massive changes in society's institutions as it ages, causing disruption, for example, in schools and the labour force. Similarly, Russell (1987) documents the myriad of institutions that will be affected by the baby boom over the next half century.

The baby boom generation in Canada is defined as those born during the high fertility period from post World War II to the mid-1960s (1947-1966). Following this period, fertility rates declined to below replacement levels resulting in a subsequent 'baby bust' generation (1967-1980). During the 1960s and 1970s labour force growth in Canada reached unprecedented levels (over 3 per cent per annum) due in large part to the baby boom entering the labour force (see Foot, 1987). No other country in the Western World approached these rates of labour force growth.[1] Over the 1980s, with the baby bust generation entering the Canadian labour force, average annual growth has slowed considerably, despite an economic boom that has characterized much of this period.[2] These new trends can be expected to con-

* Abridged from David K. Foot and Rosemary A. Venne, "Population, Pyramids and Promotional Prospects," *Canadian Public Policy* 16, no. 4 (1990): 387–98. Reprinted by permission of the publisher and the authors.

tinue as the much smaller baby bust generation continues to enter the labour force over the 1990s.

Corporate hierarchical structures with a broad base of entry level positions were well designed to accommodate wave after wave of new labour market entrants over the postwar period, and especially over the 1960s and 1970s. However, over the 1980s they are gradually becoming less appropriate as shortages of entry level workers gradually become more widespread in the economy. Over the 1990s it is likely that, unless modified, these structures will prove to be inadequate for the new labour force environment. This emerging 'mismatching' between organization structures and the labour force is the foundation for recent concern over the promotional prospects for the large baby boom generation. . . .

I I   T H E O R Y

o

. . . .The relationship between individual promotional opportunities and organization structures has only recently received attention in the literature. Jones (1980), notes that 'the baby boom will find that just as there once was not enough room for all of them to climb onto the occupational ladder, there later will not be enough room at the top. As each person tries to climb up the business and professional hierarchies, he or she will find other baby boom competitors blocking the way . . . crowded on the first steps of management [they] will be forced to stay right there'. He then goes on to explore some of the implications: for example, longer climbs to the top will become commonplace, frustration will become acute, the mid-career job switch could become a way of life, and emphasis will be increasingly placed on job rotations, and the 'psychic benefits' of work.

Morgan's (1981; 1985) case study actually documents the problem of blocked career paths for the decision-making group of the Canadian federal public service. For approximately a decade (1965-1975) this organization experienced rapid expansion during which time there was considerable career advancement, with promotions according to seniority being the norm. This rapid expansion was followed by a period of slow growth. Having been recruited at entry levels over the previous decade, the bulge of baby boomers advanced to middle management positions and, subsequently found that there was, in Morgan's terminology, 'nowhere to go'.

Bardwick (1986) refers to this phenomenon as the 'plateauing trap'. She notes that the fundamental factors determining overall rates of promotion are impersonal; they have nothing to do with individual competence and they cannot be changed by any individual. While plateauing is inevitable for most employees, it is occurring sooner for the baby boomers due to the large size of their cohort group. As a result of these promotional blockages, employee frustration and a serious problem with morale emerges. Possible solutions to this problem are outlined, including psychological counselling for employees and changes in organization culture, such as retraining and lateral transfers.

Implicit in these analyses are the dual assumptions of linear individual career paths and pyramidal organization hierarchies. Driver (1979; 1985) argues that these two concepts are linked. He points out that there are alternative career paths and associated organizational structures and cultures. He presents a classification of four individual career concepts linked uniquely with four organizational structures (and, ultimately, cultures). (See Table 1.)[3]

Table 1   Career paths and associated characteristics

Career Path	Direction of Job Movement	Number of Occupations	Organizational Structure	Reward Systems
Steady state	None	One	Rectangular	Tenure,fringe benefits
Linear	Upward	Two	Tall pyramid	Promotion, power
Spiral	Lateral/ upward	Five (?)	Flat pyramid	Reeducation, retraining
Transitory	Lateral	Many	Temporary teams	Variety, time off

SOURCE: Adapted by the authors from Driver (1985).

The first two career paths are the most familiar. Briefly, the steady state career represents a lifelong career path where an employee is committed to an occupation for life (for example, a minster of religion or a professor). Since there are many employees at the same level, the associated organization structure is almost flat with an accompanying culture that emphasizes tenure, seniority and fringe benefits. The linear career path is perhaps most pervasive in North America today. Here the employee seeks upward movement towards the top of a tall, increasingly narrow pyramid structure with numerous salary levels. Changes in occupation are infrequent, with promotions and accompanying salary increases and bonuses the main measures of career success.

The next two career paths may be less familiar. The spiral career, which combines mainly lateral moves with a few vertical moves, is associated with a moderate number of changes in occupation over a lifetime. The supporting organization structure is a flat pyramid with a few, broad levels. Here the emphasis is on occupational flexibility with liberal opportunities for lifelong re-education and retraining. Last, the transitory career is characterized by a 'consistent pattern of inconsistency,' with frequent occupational change and lateral mobility. The associated organization structure consists of temporary teams and the organization culture revolves around variety and possible breaks between assignments. . . .

III MEASURING THE 'MISMATCH'

o

Concerns with the way organizations are structured in modern society are not new. Recently, however, several writers have identified the hierarchy as the major focus for criticism. Kochan and Barocci (1985) discuss the traditional system of work organization that arrays jobs into a hierarchy of distinct classifications. Naisbitt (1982), after pointing out that hierarchical structures dominate current industry, argues that they are out of step with, and no longer workable in, the new information economy. He presents hierarchies as rigid structures that slow down the information flow in an organization. Other writers (Crocker, Charney and Chiu, 1984; and Walton and Lawrence, 1985) also characterize North American industry as hierarchical in structure and question its value for the organizations of today.

A possible relationship between this structure and the structures of the labour force has been largely ignored. Recently, Foot (1987) proposed that 'the very nature of the pyramidal organizational structure may be dependent on a pyramidal labour force to support it'. He notes that up to 1980 the postwar Canadian labour force largely displayed a pyramidal age structure that could support the pyramidal organization hierarchy and accompanying linear career concept. He suggests that while these concepts have been appropriate for the 1960s and 1970s they are becoming increasingly under pressure over the 1980s and that this trend will continue into the 1990s as the aging of the large baby boom generation and the entry of the much smaller baby bust generation radically change the shape of the labour force age structure.

Under the linear career concept, there is a close positive association between age and level in the hierarchy. Widespread promotion on the basis of seniority—a common feature of most labour-management agreements (see Morgan, 1981; and Freeman and Medoff, 1984)—secures this relationship. Alternatively, following Cantrell and Clark (1982), the relationship can be viewed as discrete manifestations of the continuous lifecycle earnings process which produces age-earning profiles that rise over most of one's career. Consequently, the comparison of the age structure of the labour force with the pyramidal hierarchical structure of the modern organization can provide an indication of the coincidence or conflict between career paths reinforced by hierarchical organization structures and those actually experienced by individual employees. . . .

IV RESULTS

o

. . . The years when there was the closest coincidence between the labour force distribution and the representative organization hierarchy occurred over the late 1970s . . . . [O]ver the 1960s and 1970s, a gradually improved match between the labour force and organization hierarchy emerged as wave after wave of baby boomers entered the labour force, thus filling out the lower levels of organization hierarchies and reducing the index of mismatching. By 1976 the peak of the baby boom born in 1960 reached the minimum labour force age of 16 years and by 1982 the last of the baby boomers born in 1966 reached this age.

Over the 1980s the trend has been dramatically reversed as the aging early baby boomers experienced mismatching in the middle career levels and the smaller baby bust generation began entering the lower levels of the organization hierarchies. Therefore, over the 1980s mismatching takes two dominant forms. First, there is a scarcity of younger employees at the bottom career levels. The emergence of 'Help Wanted' signs in retail establishments where younger workers often start their careers (often in part-time positions) is evidence of this form. Second, there is a surplus of middle-aged employees in the middle career levels, which explains the recent concerns with career blocking and plateauing. By 1986 these calculations suggest that the mismatching is already worse than it has been throughout much of this historical period. Moreover, this trend is projected to continue through the 1990s and into the next century, when the degree of mismatching will be at unprecedented levels.[4] In essence, the mismatching problem that is emerging over the 1980s represents a reversal of the trend of the previous two decades, and can be expected to intensify over the 1990s and into the next century. It is important to remember that the baby boom cohort in Canada encompasses a 20 year span. Since most people work for approximately 40 to 45 years, the baby boom generation from beginning to end impacts on the labour force for a span of at least 60 years. Hence the mismatch and associated career blockage problems are likely to persist for a long time unless corrective action is taken.

V   I M P L I C A T I O N S

These conclusions . . . verify not only the theoretical results of Keyfitz (1973), Cantrell and Clark (1982) and Denton and Spencer (1982; 1987), but also the more case-based works of Jones (1980), Morgan (1981; 1985) and Bardwick (1986). By the early 1980s, the entire baby boom generation had become of labour force age. The more slowly growing labour force over the 1980s, due in large part to the labour force entry of the following smaller baby bust generation, began intensifying the problems of slower promotional opportunities and increasing ages of promotion at each level in organization hierarchies. This led to blocked career paths, or the plateauing of the baby boom generation. And the situation is not going to improve. In fact, over the 1990s with continuing slower labour force growth, the problem can be expected to intensify as baby boomers continue to accumulate in the middle career levels with 'nowhere to go'.

These findings also provide dramatic verification of Driver's (1985) contention that currently 'organizations are geared to reinforce precisely the wrong career concept—the linear concept—from a societal point of view'. While it is likely that some organizations will continue to maintain structures and cultures that foster the linear career path, many linear oriented organizations will adapt to this new reality by flattening their tall pyramidal organizational structures. A motivation may be to reduce the importance of promotions by reducing the number of hierarchical levels (Bardwick, 1986). When there are fewer levels, less upward movement is possible and much of the employee's attention is directed laterally rather than vertically; in other words, employees are encouraged to move from the linear career path towards the spiral career path.

The likely resurgence of the spiral career path in North America, where the pressures from the baby boom generation are the most intense, will intensify education as a lifelong process and likely see the emergence of the 'generalist'. The employee with a solid training in basic skills and a variety of experiences who can be flexible and move laterally into new positions, is likely to be the most challenged and productive to his or her employer. Lateral swaps or exchanges are likely to become much more common. For example, employees plateaued as Directors of Marketing, Communications and Human Resources may well be rotated to provide new challenges for each employee. In this way, lateral moves are both a solution to an individual employee's plateauing problem, as well as to the entire cohort of employees at that particular organizational level.

And, of course, the 'sensible' employer will recognize these employee contributions and reward the employee appropriately even though no promotion to the next hierarchical level has taken place. In other words, employers who wish to keep their potentially plateaued employees challenged and productive will make sure that lateral as well as vertical moves are reflected in the financial rewards of the employees. With fewer levels in the hierarchy, each level will carry a much broader compensation range. Consequently, the broader pay level as a result of hierarchical flattening will provide the opportunity for monetary rewards to be provided even though there has been no elevation of the employee in the corporate structure.

Other changes for both employers and employees will also be necessary. Employers will likely have to provide more information and support services to assist employees in establishing career 'paths' (as distinct from career 'ladders') as they adapt to the new work environment. In addition, it will be increasingly necessary for employers to provide and purchase more training and education services to facilitate preparation for occupation changes associated with lateral moves. Employees for their part will find it advantageous to encourage and use these services rather than to resist their introduction.

On the human resource planning side, far more attention will need to be paid to programs designed to encourage lateral movement. Information bases will need to be expanded to include data on employees' 'other' skills and interests; policies to encourage the use of educational and training opportunities outside of the employee's current responsibilities will need to be developed; exchange programs must be designed so that employees are encouraged to seek out other employees and positions that may be of interest for lateral moves; and salary structures that position employees in the organization hierarchy may have to be abandoned because an employee who has been rewarded for three lateral moves may well have a higher salary than the 'boss' who may be in the higher level position as a result of one vertical (or promotional) move.

Other changes within organizations are likely to be more subtle. Success in the workplace is likely to be redefined to include the variety of positions held as well as their level in the organization hierarchy. Reducing hierarchical levels may reduce formality, make leaders more accessible, improve communication and information flows, and lead to a more participatory style of management. See Naisbitt (1982); Naisbitt and Aburdene, (1985); and Walton and Lawrence (1985) for an elaboration of these arguments. Increased concern for team work and 'followership' rather than leadership is likely to emerge. Emphasis will need to be on the opportunities for increasingly independent and challenging work—embracing challenge and mastering it will have to be rewarded. Extended study leaves or sabbaticals may become necessary to achieve these goals, as may employee access to improved health and recreation facilities.

This is only a representative and by no means exhaustive list of the changes that can be expected. The key ingredient, however, is the likely transformation of the corporate hierarchy and the workplace in North America over the 1990s and beyond from tall pyramids and linear career paths to flatter pyramids and spiral career paths. This transformation is likely to be accompanied by a much greater emphasis within organizations on human resource management issues than in the past.

Changes are also likely outside of individual organizations. Several public policy issues dealing with the baby boom in the labour force will need to be addressed. To facilitate the spiral career path it will be increasingly necessary for educational institutions, especially post-secondary institutions, to offer timely and relevant courses. Naisbitt and Aburdene (1985) predict a boom in adult education as the new information society transforms people into 'lifelong learners'. This boom will be fuelled to a large extent by the baby boomers as would-be career changers, by people upgrading in fast-changing fields and as a preparation for lateral career moves. Courses will need to be scheduled at times that do not conflict with work (for example, on evenings and weekends) and redesigned into compact, modular courses that can be completed during a short-term leave (for example, three weeks). Teaching methods will also have to change, as the older student often has different 'expectations' than the younger student. Not only do they have more life and work experiences to draw on, they also are more likely to face and recognize a higher opportunity cost on their time (especially if the workload continues to pile up back at the office). In addition, since employers are likely to be willing to pay the fees for these students, educational institutions will be provided with an opportunity to broaden (and increase) their funding bases. The myriad of possible effects on educational policies deserves careful consideration and cannot be adequately explored here.

In the case study of the federal public sector, Morgan (1981; 1985) recommends early retirement as one measure to ease the career blockage problem. Early retirement incentives and flexible retirement policies, such as easing the employee into retirement by allowing employees to become part-time mentors or consultants, are becoming more common. Bardwick (1986) refers to the latter as 'transitional retirement' policies and recommends that these part-time employees should receive a proportionate fraction of their salary and benefits. Of course, the removal of mandatory retirement provisions and the introduction of various flexible retirement policies, such as has been recently introduced into the Canada/Quebec Pension Plan, could work in the opposite direction by allowing employees to remain longer in the senior levels of the organizational hierarchies.

Another public policy that can potentially impact on the promotional prospects of the baby boomers is immigration. Immigration policy in Canada has often been influenced by labour market considerations, and, more recently, has been presented as a solution to population aging and low fertility. However, Foot (1986) has pointed out that because people are most geographically mobile in their early working lives, currently more than half of the immigrants are approximately the same age as the baby boomers. The similar age distribution of these two groups is potentially intensifying the career blockage problems for the baby boom generation. As a way of ameliorating this situation, Foot (1986) recommends an 'age-directed' component be added to Canada's immigration program that would be directed at younger age groups, corresponding to the age range of the baby bust generation.[5] Moreover, bringing in a larger share of younger immigrants would have the benefit of alleviating the shortage of entry level workers and, consequently, would contribute to a lessening of the mismatch at the lower end of the hierarchy. . . .

NOTES

○

1. See, for example, Bean, Layard and Nickell (1986) who document labour force growth rates for OECD countries. Their numbers indicate that over the 1960s the only other country to exceed 2 1/2% average annual growth was Australia, while over the 1970s the closest country with annual growth still 1/2% below that of Canada was the US. These are the two other countries in the world with a baby boom generation comparable in relative size to that of Canada.

2. Macroeconomic booms are usually characterized by an increase in participation rates and hence labour force growth.

3. For an analysis of the personality traits and values associated with these career concepts in Canada, see Bourgeois and Wils (1987).

4. The 'flattening' of the index in the first decade of the 21st century reflects the entry of the children of the baby boomers—the so-called baby boom 'echo' generation—which provides some relief at the entry levels of the 'representative' hierarchy at that time. Beyond the end of this projection period, the baby boom generation will begin reaching retirement age (that is, those born in 1947 reach age 65 in 2012), which will also contribute to some flattening of the index.

5. Consequently, this 'age-directed' component could have an automatic 'sunset' provision when the children of the baby boomers reach the labour market in the first decade of the 20th century.

R E F E R E N C E S

o

Bardwick, J.
  (1986) *The Plateauing Trap* (New York: Amacom).
Bean, C.R., P.R.G. Layard and S.J. Nickell
  (1986) 'The Rise in Unemployment: A Multi-Country Study,' *Economica*, 53:210: S1-22.
Bourgeois, R.-P and T. Wils
  (1987) 'Career Concepts, Personality and Values of Some Canadian Workers,' *Relations Industrielles*, 42:2:528-43.
Cantrell, R.S. and R.L. Clark
  (1982) 'Individual Mobility, Population Growth and Labour Force Participation,' *Demography*, 19:2:147-59.
Crocker, O.C., C. Charney and J. Chiu
  (1984) *Quality Circles: A Guide to Participation and Productivity* (Toronto: Methuen).
Denton, F. and B. Spencer
  (1982) *Population Aging, Labour Force Change and Promotion Prospects*, QSEP Research Report No. 30 (Hamilton: Faculty of Social Sciences, McMaster University).
_____ (1987) *Age Structure and Rate of Promotion in the Canadian Working Population*, QSEP Research Report No. 210 (Hamilton: Faculty of Social Sciences, McMaster University).
Driver, M.J.
  (1979) 'Career Concepts and Career Management in Organizations.' Pp. 79-139 in C.L. Cooper (ed.), *Behavioral Problems in Organizations* (Englewood Cliffs: Prentice-Hall Inc.).
_____ (1985) 'Demographic and Societal Factors Affecting the Linear Career Crisis,' *Canadian Journal of Administrative Studies*, 2:2:245-63.
Foot, D.K.
  (1986) *Population Aging and Immigration Policy in Canada: Implications and Prescriptions*, Population Working Paper No. 1 (Ottawa: Employment and Immigration Canada).

———— (1987) *Population Aging and the Canadian Labour Force,* IRPP Discussion Paper No. 87.A.5 (Ottawa: The Institute for Research on Public Policy).

Freeman, R.B. and J.L. Medoff

(1984) *What do Unions do?* (New York: Basic Books Inc.).

Jones, L.Y.

(1980) *Great Expectations: America and the Baby Boom Generation* (New York: Ballantine Books).

Keyfitz, N.

(1973) 'Individual Mobility in a Stationary Population,' *Population Studies,* 27:2:335-52.

Kochan, T.A. and T.A. Barocci

(1985) *Human Resource Management and Industrial Relations* (Boston: Little Brown & Company).

Morgan, N.

(1981) *Nowhere to Go? Possible Consequences of the Demographic Imbalance in Decision Making Groups of the Federal Public Services* (Montreal: Institute for Research on Public Policy).

———— (1985) *Implosion: An Analysis of the Growth of the Federal Public Service in Canada (1945-1985)* (Montreal: Institute for Research on Public Policy).

Naisbitt, J.

(1982) *Megatrends: Ten New Directions Transforming our Lives* (New York: Warner Books).

———— and P. Aburdene (1985) *Re-Inventing the Corporation* (New York: Warner Books).

Russell, C. (1987) *One Hundred Predictions for the Baby Boom: The Next 50 Years* (New York: Plenum Press).

Walton, R. and P. Lawrence (eds.)

(1985) *Human Resource Management: Trends and Challenges* (Boston: Harvard Business School Review Press).

2.5 Pension Politics and Challenges: Retirement Policy Implications[*]

Ellen M. Gee and Susan A. McDaniel

INTRODUCTION

As the Canadian population ages, greater policy attention will be focussed on retirement and pension issues at all levels of government, as well as in the private sector. Research in these areas has burgeoned, but there are still many unanswered questions. Our goal is to focus upon four retirement policy implications of recent pension politics and challenges—age at retirement, mandatory retirement, income inequalities, and implications for women. These implications are interrelated in complex ways, but the general thrust appears to be that recent pension politics and challenges could have negative effects—lowering income levels in retirement, increasing income disparities, and constraining choices in later life.

It is curious that recent pension politics/challenges and their implications have been so little explored, not only with respect to retirement policy but also to a whole range of social policy issues. Wanner and McDonald (1989:13) characterize this inattention as 'inexplicable'. In a climate of increasing concern about population aging, a consideration of the consequences for retirement of recent pension politics is noticeably absent.

It is acknowledged that retirement is a complex phenomenon, related to political, economic, demographic, and social factors (McDonald and Wanner, 1990) and that our exploration touches on only some aspects of a complicated and multi-faceted issue. Our purpose is to be broad, contemporary, and speculative, in the hope of sparking future research and thinking on retirement and pension policy in Canada. . . .

[*] Abridged from Ellen M. Gee and Susan A. McDaniel, "Pension Politics and Challenges: Retirement Policy Implications," *Canadian Public Policy* 17, no. 4 (1991): 456–72. Reprinted by permission of the publisher and the authors.

IMPLICATIONS FOR AGE AT RETIREMENT

o

As life expectancy increases and as quality of life (i.e. life free from major health problems or disabilities) is extended, it might be predicted that the additional healthy years would be divided between work and retirement. Such has not been the case. As Keyfitz (1989:4) states, '. . . retirement is coming to be earlier not only as a fraction of life, but absolutely'.

In other words, the trend in recent years has been towards earlier retirement. Of Canadian men aged 65 and over in 1971, nearly one-quarter were working; by 1987, this figure had declined to 5 per cent (Keyfitz, 1989). A 1984 Gallup Survey found that 47 per cent of workers wanted to retire before the age of 65 (McDonald and Wanner, 1990). A 1989 study conducted in Alberta found that 56 per cent of those interviewed planned to retire before the age of 65 (Population Research Laboratory, University of Alberta, 1989). The strength of the preference to retire early is such that people do not wait for eligibility for public pensions, but increasingly, as US data have shown, use their own savings as a bridge between leaving their last job and the age of 62 when Social Security eligibility begins (Packard and Reno, 1989). Parallelling this preference for early retirement, Pampel and Weiss (1983) reported, in a longitudinal study of 18 developed countries, that all were easing workers out of the labour force by making retirement more attractive.

Potential retirement income is one of the key predictors of age at retirement; higher retirement income is associated with younger age at retirement. Knowing this, we can ask what are the implications of recent pension politics/challenges for age at retirement? The claw-back[1] will mean de-indexation of pensions, even if in a de facto way. In future, the longer in retirement, the less pension income will be pegged to the cost of living. While at first only well-off seniors will be affected, it will be relatively few years before middle and lower-income seniors are affected as well (National Council of Welfare, 1990a). (The direct de-indexation of the Manitoba income supplement program, especially if other provinces follow suit, will accelerate the trend towards less disposable income in later life.) Dismaying evidence of how this might work is provided in a simulation done by the National Council of Welfare in 1990 which shows that from 1984 to 1991, the federal and provincial tax burdens on poor persons will increase 60 per cent, while for high-income persons, they will decrease 6.5 per cent (James, 1990). The implications are that: more retirees will be poor; more persons who contemplate (or long for) retirement may continue working out of financial exigency, perhaps at reduced efficiency because of their preference not to be working; and more people will be pushed back to work, probably in low-paying jobs in the service sector. To the degree there are future labour shortages of young, low-paid workers, this latter possibility becomes more likely (and we have already seen TV advertisements portraying seniors in the 'McMaster's programme' at the McDonald's fast food chain). These results are likely to be felt by women more than men, given their substantially lower lifetime earnings.

The overall implication of the claw-back is to increase the age at retirement. Recent policy changes in the CPP may have this effect as well. At first glance, the implications for retirement of pension splitting seem minimal, given that so few women are able or willing to take advantage. Yet, in not taking advantage, there are retirement implications; women may be forced to work as long as health and policy allow in order to ensure some income security in old age. Also, if one views the lowered age at eligibility for CPP benefits at a reduced rate as a penalty for early retirement, then this recent change in policy can be seen as reinforcing older age at retirement. Also, if contemporary challenges to the SPA succeed and the predictions we made earlier come to pass, this would create a situation in which more older persons, particularly women, would have to work out of financial necessity.

With respect to private pensions, the issue of indexation is crucial. Without full indexation, those fortunate enough to have private pensions will find it increasingly difficult to fulfil their wishes to retire early. The prospect of a non- (or partially) indexed private pension, in conjunction with the claw-back of OAS, may force people to stay in their jobs longer, especially those with benefits based on years of service and best average earnings.

It seems, then, that one implication of a number of pension policy changes and challenges will be to increase the age at retirement. It should be noted that this prediction is at odds with current trends and the expressed wishes of Canadians. It looks as if Canadians will have to choose between early retirement and lower disposable income in retirement. As it stands now, the majority of Canadians undergoes a drop of at least 25 per cent in standard of living upon retirement (McPherson, 1990). Research needs to address how much more of a drop will be incurred as a result of recent changes, and how much reduction would be acceptable to older people. Armed with this knowledge, we would be able to better predict trends in age at retirement, which is an important variable in economic planning given its effect on the size and composition of the labour force.

MANDATORY RETIREMENT

o

Until the 1991 Supreme Court ruling upheld mandatory retirement at age 65, it was a social practice instituted, not by law, but by a combination of social custom and pension incentives and disincentives. The practice, and now the law, of mandatory retirement reveals the intertwining of retirement policy issues and pension politics and policies.

The first private pension plan in Canada—the CNR (1874)—contained a mandatory retirement (at age 65) provision. The plan was put into place, primarily, in an attempt to stabilize workers (i.e. to create 'company men') and, secondarily, to ensure income security in old age (although benefits could be revoked at any time) (McDonald and Wanner, 1990). In recent times, the goal behind mandatory retirement provisions in pension plans has been to rid employers of older workers, presumably to make way for younger, less expensive workers. The point is that government and business have used the same policy (mandatory retirement) to achieve opposite outcomes (retention of workers vs. expulsion of workers), using the same rationale (older workers are useless), depending upon the economic climate (McDonald, 1991). Thus, the politics of mandatory retirement are not really about the usefulness of older workers, although the mandatory retirement 'debate' is often couched in such terms (Guppy, 1989); rather, they are about the maximization of profits.

How many of today's retirees were forced to retire as a result of mandatory retirement provisions at their place of employment? No one seems to really know, although there is a general consensus that the numbers are quite small (Guppy, 1989). Most people retire before, or at, the mandatory age, sometimes encouraged by early retirement incentive schemes. However, persons forced to retire early due to poor health or the inability to obtain/sustain employment cannot be ignored (McPherson, 1990).

The fundamental question of how many people will be forced to retire at age 65, given the Supreme Court ruling, cannot be answered at this time. One complicating factor is that some provinces[2] have human rights legislation prohibiting mandatory retirement. In other words, depending upon where one lives in Canada, one may or may not be subject to mandatory retirement. Another issue is the degree to which mandatory retirement will be 'circumvented'. Those familiar with the university setting (the site of the majority of the challenges to mandatory retirement) will know that 'post-retirement' contracts are the order of the day. These older professors will, for the most part, be continuing to do their same jobs—what changes is the distribution of the sources of their income (less earnings, compensated for by private and public pension benefits).

Up until now, Canadian research on mandatory retirement has been framed in terms of a debate on its pros and cons (Guppy, 1989). Given the Supreme Court ruling, researchers now need to turn their attention to the consequences of the ruling, at both individual and societal levels. Some questions are: how many people will be affected; what are their social and economic characteristics; what are their opinions; what are their 'post-retirement' employment options (and how do they vary by social and economic status)? How will employers react? What are the social implications of a ruling that states that certain types of age discrimination are just?

At the present time, the effects of the mandatory retirement ruling would seem to be minimal, given trends towards earlier retirement. However, the long-term consequences of the pension changes may have important impacts. Persons facing a grim prospect in terms of post-retirement

income—due to the expansion of the claw-back to the less well-off, the low
coverage rates and low levels of full indexation in private pensions, and the
lack of disposable income to purchase RRSPs in the working years, for
example—may find it necessary to work past the age of 65 and, hence, pressure for changes in the Supreme Court ruling. Or, they may find creative
ways to circumvent mandatory retirement, which would likely be more of
an option for persons with relatively high social and economic resources
who wish to maintain a given standard of living. Or, they may re-enter the
labour force at low-paying jobs, and struggle to make ends meet in later life
(as long as health allows). Or, an 'underground economy' of older persons
may flourish.

Another issue for speculation at this time (and research in the future) is
the interrelationships among mandatory retirement, lower than expected
pension income, labour shortages at younger age groups, and immigration
policy. The present federal government position and practice is to increase
immigration levels as a mechanism to 'compensate' for population aging,
even though public opinion is rather strongly opposed to increasing immigration (Northcott, 1990). If, and when, these public sentiments are combined with the social facts of older Canadians facing low incomes and the
desire/necessity to work later than age 65, the stage will be set for major
public policy conflicts.

INCOME INEQUALITIES IN LATER LIFE

o

Myles' (1989) comparative work revealed relatively high levels of income
inequality in later life in Canada. Recent Canadian data indicate the degree
of financial diversity that exists among the older population. In 1988,
among households with a head aged 65 or over, 15.4 per cent had incomes
less than $10,000 whereas 11.7 per cent had incomes of $45,000 or more (Statistics Canada, 1990b). If household income is divided into quintiles, 34.5
per cent of households in the lowest income quintile had an aged (65+)
head, and 7.1 per cent of households in the highest income quintile had an
elderly head (Statistics Canada, 1990a). While these data show that there are
proportionately more elderly people who are poor rather than well-off, they
also clearly indicate that there are rather large inequalities in income within
the elderly Canadian population. Some elderly are very well-off; in recognition of this, increased advertising and marketing has been aimed at the
'gray market', (perhaps inadvertently directing attention away from the
dire financial situation of many elderly persons, particularly women—see
the following section) and, indeed, an International Association of Gerontological Entrepeneurs had been formed to 'explore the relationship between
the business world and the aging community' (McPherson, 1990:416).

Income inequalities in later life are largely a function of income inequalities at younger ages. However, it is not only the case that the 'poor stay poor and the rich stay rich'; income inequalities in later life tend to widen due to the long-term impact of income- and education-related differences in the ability to generate investment income (Myles, 1981). Other factors contributing to income inequality in old age are worker location in the 'dual economy' (McAllister, 1981) and gender (Gee and Kimball, 1987).

The pension changes outlined above may serve to widen income differentials in later life in the future. The trend towards privatization of the pension system, and the anticipated reforms in private pension schemes, will benefit a small fraction of today's workers. If current trends continue, the focus on individual retirement savings plans such as RRSPs will serve to benefit persons in relatively advantaged financial situations at younger ages, thus exacerbating income inequality in later life. The resistance of employers in the private sector to fully index pensions will serve to differentiate even those with private pensions into the more and less advantaged vis-à-vis real pension income.

Within the sphere of public pensions, the overall implication for income inequality is less predictable. Changes such as the de-indexation of the Manitoba 55 Plus plan will widen income differences, as the poor only will be affected. If the SPA challenges are successful, some of the lower-income persons currently eligible could lose benefits, which would serve to widen income disparities. The OAS claw-back could have the opposite effect, at least in the short-run. It does not appear that the CPP will have much effect on altering income inequities. However, reforms in the implementation of credit-splitting upon marital dissolution could assist in improving the pension income situation for women.

Future research needs to focus on the relative roles of pension policy vs. pre-retirement social and economic factors as predictors of income inequality in later life. If pre-retirement factors turn out to be dominant, this would turn attention to the issue of life-long, structurally-based inequalities and how public policy (via income redistribution, for example) can attempt to ameliorate these disparities that only get larger with age. If recent pension policy changes will have the exacerbating trend that is predicted here, then the issue is one of re-examining those changes, and the political and economic factors underlying them.

RETIREMENT IMPLICATIONS FOR WOMEN

o

It is common knowledge that older women fare much less well financially than older men. Canadian data for 1988 indicate that poverty rates for elderly women are about double those for elderly men: among families with a head aged 65 and over, 14.2 per cent of female-headed households are poor compared with 7.3 per cent of male-headed households; among unattached persons aged 65 and over, 43.9 per cent of women and 23.3 per cent of men are poor[3] (Statistics Canada, 1990b). When one remembers that older women outnumber older men, due to longer life expectancy, these percentages translate into proportionately more poor elderly women in absolute terms.

One of the factors contributing to the poor financial situation of older women is their life-long dependence on men; our society is organized on the premise that women will be financially 'cared for' by men (Gee and Kimball, 1987). And, as long as a woman is married, she is reasonably well protected from poverty. However, only 41 per cent of women aged 65 and over are married (compared with 77 per cent of men)—most of the rest are widows due to the combined effects of differential life expectancy and older ages of husbands (National Council of Welfare, 1990b). Thus, women's poverty becomes evident when their 'financial carer' dies (or leaves).

The characteristics of women's employment play a key role in poverty in later life: the degree of gender segregation (and the associated lower pay levels and lesser likelihood of benefits such as pensions in jobs that women are likely to have); the preponderance of part-time work (which is also associated with low salaries and the absence of fringe benefits such as pension plans); and the non-continuous nature of women's work careers, due to family responsibilities and needs, as well as the fact that women are often in less secure jobs. Thus, a set of social factors operates in tandem to create female poverty in old age, particularly among the 'unattached'.

Pensions have never been 'user-friendly' to women, but recent politics/ challenges, despite some moves towards improvements, make pensions generally even less user-friendly for women (Myles, 1989; National Council of Welfare, 1990a). A major issue is indexation of public pensions, since so few women have access to private plans. The claw-back, while making it difficult for both men and women in retirement, will make it much harder for women in the future. Women have lower pensions to start with, so de-indexation, by whatever means, cuts deeper for women. In addition, women live longer in retirement than men, so experience the de-indexation of their pensions for a longer period. If changes are made in eligibility for the SPA as a result of the forthcoming court challenges, women's quality of life in retirement could be seriously affected. The emphasis on RRSPs will have negative implications for women's retirement income, given the lower salaries of women and the general inaccessibility of RRSPs for many women. Reforms in the private pension system will benefit a small portion of women; however, for them, the hold-out on indexation has serious negative ramifications.

The recent pension changes also have implications for the family context of retirement. It has been found that retirement is often a joint decision between a husband and a wife, i.e. they retire at the same time (Campione, 1987). Different pension prospects may mean that joint retirement is less of an option in the future. Women without pension access might be more likely to work after their husbands retire. Clearly this could have implications for the experience of retirement—it could lead to resentment, to an inability to move in retirement, and to domestic stress. Adding further strain may be the continuing presence of dependents in the home, as grown children do not leave the family home, or return. Also, an increasing proportion of people at around the age of 60 will have surviving parents who require care and time (Gee, 1990).

There are several policy implications of the pension changes. From the point of view of married women, the family context of retirement may change; retirement policy challenges of the future include ways to acknowledge the family context of retirement to facilitate people's family lives rather than viewing the 'retiree' in atomistic terms. From the point of view of the numerically dominant unattached women, the recent pension changes suggest a gloomy future—as an already bleak financial situation worsens, more older women will be in need of health care, chronic care, seniors' housing, etc. These are expensive outcomes of current pension policy changes.

The research agenda for the future in terms of retirement implications of pension policy change for women must first address two differing views of the role of pension change (and reform) for women in later life. Wanner and McDonald (1989:12) state that '[t]inkering with pension policy is probably not the most efficient way for solving the retirement problems faced by Canadian women. . .' given that 'the inequities women face in retirement are rooted in the sexual division of labour, both in the labour market and in the household'. Gee and Kimball (1987), while acknowledging the life-long structural roots of women's economic plight in later life, argue that pension policy changes can have an impact, either positive or negative, on elderly women's economic situation. Second, research efforts should be directed to ascertaining the role of varying family, social, economic, and pension policy situations/conditions in determining women's retirement age, retirement experience, and quality of life in retirement. It may well be that different retirement models for men and women are needed (McDonald and Wanner, 1990). Third, research on the differential impact of the pension changes discussed here for men and women would be a fruitful avenue of inquiry.

NOTES
o

1. The "claw-back" refers to the 1989 legislative change that will tax back some of the Old Age Security (OAS) benefits paid to higher-income seniors—Eds.

2. At the present time, these provinces are New Brunswick, Quebec, Manitoba and Alberta. In these provinces, employers, invoking provincial human rights legislation, may retain employees over the age of 65. While this contravenes the

Supreme Court ruling, the practice can/will continue unless successfully challenged by the federal government or some other agency or individual.

3. These figures are based on Statistics Canada low-income cut-offs, and are conservative, ie., provide underestimates of poverty.

R E F E R E N C E S
○

Campione, W.A.
(1987) 'The married woman's retirement decision: A methodological comparison,' *Journal of Gerontology*, 42:381-6.

Gee, E.M.
(1990) 'Demographic Change and Intergenerational Relations in Canadian Families: Findings and Social Policy Implications,' *Canadian Public Policy—Analyse de Politiques*, XVI:2:191-9.

—————— and M.M. Kimball (1987) *Women and Aging* (Toronto: Butterworths).

Guppy, N.
(1989) 'The Magic of 65: Issues and Evidence in the Mandatory Retirement Debate,' *Canadian Journal on Aging*, 8:173-86.

James, G.
(1990) Keynote address presented at the annual meeting of the Western Association of Sociology and Anthropology, Morley, Alberta, February.

Keyfitz, N.
(1989) 'Aging is not the whole pension problem,' *Popnet* (International Institute for Applied Systems Analysis), 16:5-8.

McAllister, C.
(1981) 'An alternative perspective on retirement benefits: A dual economic approach.' Paper presented at the annual meeting of the Gerontological Society of America, Toronto (cited in McPherson, 1990).

McDonald, P.L.
(1991) Personal communication.

—————— and R.A. Wanner
(1982) 'Work past age 65 in Canada: A socioeconomic analysis,' *Aging and Work*, 5:169-80.

—————— and R.A. Wanner
(1984) 'Socioeconomic Determinants of Early Retirement in Canada,' *Canadian Journal on Aging*, 3:3:105-16.

—————— and R.A. Wanner
(1990) *Retirement in Canada* (Toronto: Butterworths).

McPherson, B.D.
(1990) *Aging as a Social Process: An introduction to Individual and Population Aging* (2nd. ed.) (Toronto: Butterworths).

Myles, J.
(1981) 'Income inequality and status maintenance: Concepts, methods and measures,' *Research on Aging*, 3:123-41.

—————— (1989) *Old Age in the Welfare State: The Political Economy of Public Pensions* (rev. ed.) (Lawrence, KS: University of Kansas Press).

National Council of Welfare
(1990a) *Pension Reform* (Ottawa: National Council of Welfare).
_____ (1990b) *Women and Poverty Revisited* (Ottawa: National Council of Welfare).
Northcott, H.C.
(1990) 'Public opinion regarding the economic support of seniors.' Edmonton Area Series Report No. 67, Population Research Laboratory, Department of Sociology, University of Alberta.
Packard, M.D. and V.P. Reno
(1989) 'A look at very early retirees,' *Social Security Bulletin,* 52:16-29.
Pampel, F. and J. Weiss
(1983) 'Economic development, pension policies, and the labor force participation of aged males: A cross-national longitudinal study, *American Journal of Sociology,* 89:350-61.
Population Research Laboratory, University of Alberta
(1989) *All Alberta Survey, 1989.* Data on computer tape.
Statistics Canada
(1990a) *Income Distributions by Size in Canada,* 1989 (Ottawa: Statistics Canada), Catalogue No. 13-207.
_____ (1990b) *A Portrait of Seniors in Canada* (Ottawa: Statistics Canada), Catalogue No. 89-519.
Wanner, R.A. and P.L. McDonald
(1989) 'Public policy and the future of retirement in Canada.' Paper presented at the annual meeting of the Canadian Association on Gerontology, Ottawa, October.

Canadian Workers and

the New Global Economy

E D I T O R S ' I N T R O D U C T I O N

o

The term "new global economy" refers to an interrelated set of economic, technological, and organizational changes that are dramatically altering the production of goods and services in countries around the world. Central to the concept is a recognition that capital has become much more mobile. Many large multinational companies have been moving their factories around the globe in search of cheaper labour, better access to raw materials, larger markets, and political settings with less restrictive labour and environmental legislation. Free trade agreements in Europe and North America have reduced the significance of national borders; Pacific Rim countries are challenging North American and European economic dominance; and the collapse of the eastern European Communist empire promises an even more integrated global economy.

Global trade in goods and services has been greatly facilitated by microelectronic communication systems linking producers and markets in many different countries. Automated technologies are being rapidly adopted in both the "old" and the "new" producer nations. In some industries, the traditional process whereby goods (automobiles, for example) were produced from start to finish in one location is being replaced by a system in which component parts are produced in various countries and then assembled elsewhere. With high-technology production systems replacing more labour-intensive systems, the need for a well-trained and highly skilled labour force has been increasing. Thus, the term "information economy" is also an apt description of the new global economy, capturing international information flows as well as higher skill requirements for workers.

But there is more to these trends. In many locations, factory shutdowns and new automated technologies have led to higher unemployment rates. Frequently, employers have sought to cut costs by revoking traditional employment relationships, subcontracting work, using temporary workers, developing two-tier wage systems, and attempting to circumvent unions, for example (see Parts 6 and 8 for additional discussions of these trends). Thus, two basic questions underly the discussions in the following readings. First, how can Canada remain competitive in this new global economy? Second, what are the costs and benefits for Canadian workers of the industrial and workplace readjustments taking place?

We begin with short comments from the two co-chairs (in 1989) of the Canadian Labour Market and Productivity Centre, an organization set up to help improve Canada's productivity in the global economy. Shirley Carr, president of the Canadian Labour Congress, explains why many unions have been reluctant to get involved in the push for productivity. In her opinion, there is an obvious conflict of interest between workers and employers. Workers (and their unions) are interested in keeping their jobs, and in obtaining higher wages and improved working conditions. Employers seek higher profits, and many have approached the productivity debate with little more than job cuts and wage reductions in mind. Why would unions not be suspicious? Carr promises that organized labour would be more receptive to productivity concerns if specific workers' rights were protected: the right to know about impending technological and organizational changes; the right to be involved in decision-making; the right to job security; and the right to share in the benefits of productivity increases.

Thomas d'Aquino, head of the Business Council on National Issues, takes the "trust us" approach, arguing that all of society will benefit from growth in productivity, and that overly suspicious perceptions of the profit motives of employers are not helpful. He identifies some of the impediments to higher productivity as seen by the business community: an education system that is not producing enough highly skilled workers; an unwillingness to accept new technologies in the workplace; limited research and development by Canadian corporations; small markets (d'Aquino believes that free trade will be helpful); large government deficits; and too much government intervention in the economy. But d'Aquino also echoes Shirley Carr's concerns about limited labour–management consultation. Thus, there may be room for greater consensus regarding productivity initiatives provided that the benefits are shared more equally.

Andrew Sharpe (the head of research at the Canadian Labour Market Productivity Centre) picks up the discussion of education and training. He points out that, while the average level of education has risen over the years, we still do not have enough highly skilled workers for the types of industries that will make Canada more competitive. He is critical of both the formal education system and the training efforts of Canadian firms that spend considerably less on training than do their counterparts in many other countries. In addition, the amount of government funding for training has also declined. Sharpe concludes that "a potential labour market crisis may be emerging," and that we need to do something about the growing education and training gap.

Free trade agreements, intended to reduce trade barriers between Canada and its neighbours, have been advocated by many business leaders and politicians as a means of strengthening Canada's economy. Trade unions, however, have typically opposed free trade, arguing that job loss, wage cuts, and a decline in the standard of living are more likely outcomes. For example, the Canadian Labour Congress (CLC) presents a very negative assessment of the consequences of the Free Trade Agreement (FTA) with the United States, attributing factory shutdowns, rising unemployment, and an increase in foreign ownership to the FTA and the "ethic of competitiveness" underlying it. John Crispo presents the case for free trade, specifically the North American Free Trade Agreement (NAFTA), which accelerated the economic integration of Canada, the United States, and Mexico. Allowing that the FTA did not produce as many jobs as some had promised, but arguing that many of Canada's current economic problems stem from other sources (a rising government deficit, for example), Crispo insists that NAFTA is a "good deal."

Many critics of free trade have worried about the relocation of Canadian factories to Mexico's Maquiladora. This deregulated, export-based manufacturing zone located near the U.S. border offers very low wages (compared to Canada), is largely nonunionized, and has few environmental and health and safety regulations. Consequently, large profits can be made by manufacturers producing for global markets Crispo discounts these fears, arguing that labour costs form only a small part of total production costs. He believes that higher education levels and better technology in Canada will mean that we will keep the high-technology jobs while Mexico will gain more of the labour-intensive jobs. Our main problem will involve helping those Canadians who lost jobs because of industrial restructuring find new jobs.

There are some obvious inconsistencies among the arguments presented in these readings. For example, if government intervention in the labour market is to be reduced, who will take responsibility for retraining dislocated workers and helping them find new jobs? Given the concerns about insufficient education and training, how do we account for the sizable minority of well-educated Canadians who are underemployed, that is, working in jobs in which their skills and abilities are not fully utilized? If education and training are inadequate, why does Crispo argue that our superior education levels will allow us to benefit from NAFTA? Crispo also suggests that Canadian wages will not suffer given that labour costs are only a small part of the overall costs of production. Yet the business community often complains that Canadian wages are too high, and that workers must accept concessions if we are to become globally competitive.

In his broader assessment of post-industrialism and the service economy, John Myles addresses some of these questions. He points to a growing polarization of the Canadian labour market as the gap widens between those with good jobs and those with less rewarding jobs, between high-skilled and lower-skilled workers, and between the employed and the unemployed. He also notes that young workers entering the labour market are most negatively affected by the shift toward nonstandard work and other polarizing employment trends. But Myles also makes a very important point about such social and economic changes—the outcomes are not predetermined. Instead, they depend on political decisions and power relationships among the various groups affected.

In opposition to those who insist that job security for workers hinders productivity, Myles argues that global competitiveness and a high standard of living in Canada can be achieved only if such security is maintained. Furthermore, cutting back on the "welfare state" will be harmful, not beneficial, in his opinion. Myles concludes by highlighting several very basic questions: What kind of society do we want in the future? Is full employment our goal? How much social inequality are we willing to accept?

DISCUSSION QUESTIONS

1. Is Canada capable of being competitive in the global economy? Is a full-employment policy compatible with "the ethic of competitiveness"?

2. Is organized labour a major impediment to "competitiveness," or is it part of the solution to the problem?

3. Many observers of the Canadian labour force worry about insufficient education and training, suggesting that Canada cannot be competitive internationally unless these problems are solved. At the same time, there is evidence of considerable "underemployment" among Canadian workers. Which view is more accurate?

4. Proponents of free trade argue that it will help Canada's economy grow, lead to more and better jobs for Canadians, and even help improve employment prospects for impoverished Mexican workers. Do you agree?

5. Thomas d'Aquino writes that "less government means more growth, more jobs, more economic rewards." John Myles argues that "Canada's economic disadvantage lies in the fact that its welfare state is too small (and often of the wrong sort), not because it is too large." What do you think?

6. What are the implications of changes in the Canadian labour market for young workers?

SUGGESTED READINGS

○

Bell, Daniel. *The Coming of Post-Industrial Society.* New York: Basic Books, 1974.

Byrne, Edmund F. *Work, Inc.: A Philosophical Inquiry.* Philadelphia: Temple University Press, 1990.

Drache, Daniel, and Meric S. Gertler, eds. *The New Era of Global Competition: State Policy and Market Power.* Montreal and Kingston: McGill–Queen's University Press, 1991.

Economic Council of Canada. *Pulling Together: Productivity, Innovation and Trade.* Ottawa: Supply and Services Canada, 1992.

Gold, Mark and David Leyton-Brown, eds. *Trade-Offs on Free Trade: The Canada–U.S. Free Trade Agreement.* Toronto: Carswell, 1988.

Reich, Robert. *The Work of Nations: Preparing Ourselves for 21st-Century Capitalism.* New York: Alfred A. Knopf, 1991.

Productivity: Labour's Viewpoint*

Shirley Carr

Some view a labour leader talking about productivity at all—let alone in any positive way—as a contradiction in terms. The prevailing wisdom in some quarters is that labour unions are inherently hostile to the concept of productivity.

For example, in a Gallup poll carried out in Canada a few years ago, three-quarters of the respondents believed that Canada had a "productivity problem." While management and labour unions were ranked about equal in their "ability to improve productivity," labour was ranked much lower than business for "willingness to improve productivity."

This perception is not difficult to understand, given that labour is often put on the defensive on the matter of productivity.

First, it is put on the defensive in terms of the very way productivity is usually measured, i.e. as a ratio between output and labour input. This approach can be very misleading. It is a strictly numerical one; it says nothing about cause and effect. The performance of this measure can be affected by many factors other than labour, including the quality of management. Unfortunately, much of the public consciousness about a "national productivity problem" is created by the media, which does not have the time, space or inclination to sort out all the factors at play.

The way productivity improvement efforts are introduced can also put labour on the defensive. Whether the issue is the introduction of new technology at a particular plant or the closing of a plant as part of corporate rationalization, initial decisions are often taken "behind closed doors." Worker and union involvement from step one is very much the exception.

*Abridged from Shirley Carr, "Productivity: Labour's Viewpoint," *Perception* 13, no. 1 (Winter 1989): 29–35. Reprinted by permission of the publisher and the author.

The view is often advanced that labour unions are intrinsically the enemy of productivity. The question here is not the attitude of individual workers and labour leaders, it is rather that unions are, by their very nature, a negative force on productivity. In this stereotype, unions seeking ever higher wages and ever more rigid work rules prevent the kind of flexibility needed to compete in this increasingly competitive world.

Such a view is just a bit galling to me as a labour leader in a country where workers have experienced a decade of real wage cuts. It also flies in the face of a great deal of hard evidence to the contrary. In their book *What Unions Do*, Richard Freeman and James Medoff analyzed mountains of economic data which predominantly showed that companies with unionized work forces were more productive than non-union companies.

Finally, labour is put on the defensive by the motives of much of the productivity gung ho-ism prevalent today. Some of this is explicit and obvious, while some is much more subtle. As an example of the explicit, let me quote a short section of an article that appeared recently in *High Technology* magazine.

"Labour opposition could be the biggest barrier to flexible manufacturing. Flexible automation promises to finish the process of job elimination begun with the industrial revolution. Machine tools have already eliminated many jobs in mid-volume manufacturing. Computer-controlled machine tools have reduced humans to little more than watchers. Tool operators route parts, set up tools, load workpieces, inspect finished parts, and observe their tools at work. Flexible systems will eventually eliminate the need for tool operators. For this reason, many companies are proceeding gingerly, trying to enlist labour support for automation and transferring displaced employees or allowing attrition and recession to do their trimming for them."

In addition to my obvious inability to accept this vision as a trade union leader—particularly the idea that the primary motive is to eliminate jobs, combined with the blatant strategy to co-opt labour in its own demise—the vision is ultimately silly in economic terms.

The question begged is, once the "process of job elimination" is finished, who is going to purchase the output? Eventually, even the most avid automator must face up to the issue of consumer demand. As the great American labour leader Walter Reuther put it, "Robots don't join unions, but they don't buy cars either."

In the "subtle" category, labour is deeply suspicious of the motives behind a great deal of the sloganeering of the "productivity movement." This concern covers the gamut, from issues such as "quality of work life" experiments and gain-sharing programs, to the whole "productivity through people" jargon which shows up in media advertising (for example, "people are our number one asset," or "our strength is people").

While the productivity message is sweet, our experience at the local level has often been very sour. Quality of work life, for example, often creates the illusion of worker participation when, in fact, real decision-making power is left completely in the hands of management. It has too often been our experience that quality of work life is used to co-opt workers, to alienate them from their unions and even to discourage workers from joining unions in the first place.

Similarly, the "soft-sell" of gain-sharing seeks to shift workers' identification from wages to profits, and the vision of "the company as family" seeks to make unions look, at worst, like a housebreaker and, at best, like a relative who stayed too long. Indeed, in the jargon of the management gurus who write the best-sellers and then make a second fortune on the speaking circuit, the word "worker" is definitely out, and even "employee" barely makes the grade.

It is not realistic to expect that labour will carry the productivity torch when the result is to eliminate workers' jobs and to turn back the clock on collective bargaining gains and on unionism itself. However, labour is willing to participate in joint labour-management efforts to improve on the basis of certain rights:

- the right to know,
- the right to participate,
- the right to "security with change,"
- and the right to share benefits.

I could add "the right not to be patronized." One particularly patronizing line is an appeal to labour to be flexible—even to the point of wage and benefit concessions—or else we will be uncompetitive and there will be no economic pie to divide up in the collective bargaining process anyway. And doesn't this really put the interest of business and labour in harmony?

Ultimately the interest of capital (to maximize profit) and the interest of labour (to achieve the best wages and working conditions possible) for its membership) are in conflict. I use the word "possible" deliberately. Collective bargaining is the most effective instrument for dividing up the economic pie but, of course, the pie has to be there to divide up.

Workers know the repercussions of uncompetitiveness better than anyone, for they pay the price in unemployment. Layoffs are a form of economic execution and, to use Samuel Johnson's famous phrase, "The prospect of execution in the morning does wonders to concentrate the mind."

Let me lay out seven concrete guidelines for productivity improvement programs in the work place.

- Broaden the definition of productivity to include such criteria as the quality of a product or service. And, particularly in the public sector, involve the consumers as well as the producers of the service. It may turn out that the answer to a productivity problem is not to cut back on services or staff but to alter or even increase services to meet the consumers' real needs or demands.

- Involve employees at all levels in the overall planning and administration of the program. Don't present workers with a *fait accompli* and then complain that they're not cooperating. And don't dress up attempts to sell workers on the change as true participation.
- Introduce productivity improvement programs in the context of the collective bargaining process: that is, make productivity an issue to be discussed at the bargaining table.
- Where disputes arise, there should be a mechanism in place to resolve them by an independent third party.
- The benefits gained from improved productivity must be shared collectively by the workers. Pitting one worker against the other by promising bonuses and "merit pay" is not conducive to cooperation.
- Where new technology is being introduced, or where there are changes in job functions or other aspects of the job, workers must be guaranteed access to the necessary training or retraining programs. There should be no cuts in wages or benefits as a result of the changes.
- Measure productivity in every sector of the operation, not just on the labour side. Look at the performance of management and the efficiency of administration, planning and decision-making.

In addition, I urge employers and governments to look at productivity in a broader sense than just at the firm or plant. In a national sense, do we really gain much if output per worker is increasing at the same time as large numbers of people become and remain unemployed? If we defined productivity not just as output per worker, but output per worker plus the unemployed, we would get a much different picture of productivity and economic progress in national and comparative international terms.

At an even higher level of social progress, are we really better off when national resources are devoted to the opening of one more hamburger or donut franchise at the same time as essential public services, such as care for our young and elderly, are being starved and neglected? Are we in danger of matching our tendency for plastic and convenience foods with a tendency for plastic and convenience values?

The fundamental point is that productivity cannot be considered in isolation. In particular, it cannot be separated from the employment (and unemployment) issue. Labour will willingly participate in ventures that recognize that productivity efforts must give due recognition to the impact on workers, as well as employment in general.

Productivity: Friend or Foe?*

Thomas d'Aquino

Many of us from different parts of the world praise the virtues of productivity and compare our experiences in the application of this science to economic life in our respective countries. We take satisfaction in pointing to the enormous benefits to citizens everywhere that flow from the steady growth in productivity—the creation of wealth and jobs, the delivery of better products and services, the improvements to quality of life in the workplace and to the environment, just to name a few. And yet I wonder why the benefits of productivity growth are still so little understood. Or why the very word "productivity" continues to be viewed with suspicion and alarm by so many. The reason, I suspect, is that we have not been successful in communicating the idea of productivity to our public constituencies.

Achieving broad public understanding and acceptance of the elements which make up productivity is no easy task, and we have a long way to go yet. Convincing people of the imperative of productivity growth is just as difficult. The hard truth is that productivity growth is critical to a country's ability to generate a high and rising standard of living for each of its citizens. In the words of economist Lester Thurow, "No country's citizens can for long enjoy a higher standard of living than they themselves produce, for no one can divide non-existent output." It follows that if we wish to consume more we must produce more.

Critics often associate the push for higher productivity growth with a blind commitment to growth for growth's sake. Some others suggest that the concern about productivity growth reflects an obsession by the captains of industry with the desire simply to generate more profits, often at the expense of workers. These criticisms miss the point. Productivity growth is

※ Abridged from Thomas d'Aquino, "Productivity: Friend or Foe?" *Perception* 13, no. 1 (Winter 1989): 29–35. Reprinted by permission of the publisher and the author.

essential to meet the growing demand for goods and services, many of these in areas of rapidly expanding importance—education, health care, housing, the environment and leisure, for example.

To satisfy these demands will require massive economic resources— resources that will come only from improved productivity levels. Workers, too, stand to benefit, for it is a well-established fact that real incomes rise in the wake of improved productivity.

Turning to Canada, the need to address the issue of productivity growth is more urgent than ever. In the past we experienced prolonged periods of rising productivity levels. According to the Economic Council of Canada, between 1961 and 1973, there was only one year when the rate of growth of total productivity for the national economy was negative. On the other hand, there were 10 years in which it accounted for at least two percentage points of the growth in total real output. Since 1973, however, the tables have turned and Canada has suffered a deterioration in productivity growth. The Canadian experience is not unique. Other industrialized countries have suffered declines in their productivity growth, although Canada has fared worst among the countries which comprise the Group of Seven.

Why has Canada not performed better in relation to other industrial powers? It is difficult to pinpoint and quantify the sources of the problem. Looking back over the past 15 years, however, a number of factors emerge. It has been argued, for example, that the deterioration of productivity growth was closely linked to the great oil shocks of 1973-74 and 1879-80. It has been suggested that poor fiscal and monetary policies have contributed to the problem. Others have argued that Canadian companies have been a factor because of their failure to achieve economies of scale. Sluggishness in the rate of innovation, industrial research and development, and the adoption of new technologies have been held to blame. So have shortcomings in the areas of education, training, human resource management, and labour-management relations. And often a finger has been pointed at inflation, public sector deficits and the heavy hand of government.

It appears that most Canadian companies, particularly those in the manufacturing sector, do not measure up against established benchmarks for minimum efficient size within a North American context. And this has hampered their productivity performance. It is partly in recognition of this fact that the Business Council and many members of Canada's economic community support the dismantling of barriers to trade within Canada, and the expansion of Canadian exports by means of the Canada-United States Free Trade Agreement and a further round of multilateral trade liberalization. Put another way, Canadian enterprises, both small and large, are hungry for a broader market base. With the expanded scope that this would offer, fresh investment, productivity growth and new jobs would certainly follow, and so would the advantages of the economies of scale.

What about the charge that we are sluggish in our rate of innovation, industrial research and development and the adoption of new technologies?

This is a fair criticism. Indeed, a Business Council Task Force on Science and Technology recently concluded that Canada faces a serious technological challenge from the newly industrialized economies on the one hand, and the larger industrial economies on the other, and that vigorous steps are needed to stimulate science-based innovation and industry-driven research and development if Canada is to improve its productivity.

In adopting new technologies, Canada faces many of the same problems that exist in other industrialized countries. Fear that new technologies lead inevitably to job loss is still a widespread phenomenon in Canada. The fact is that new technologies are powerful catalysts for the creation of jobs and that, generally speaking, those countries that have been most aggressive in embracing new technologies have also experienced the highest rates of growth and the lowest rates of unemployment. In Canada, there is a quickening in the pace of new technology entering the workplace, aided considerably in those cases where labour and management have consulted and cooperated closely in its implementation.

If Canadian enterprises and workers are to benefit from the introduction of new technologies, high priority must be given to superior educational and training standards and a dynamic system of labour-management relations. In Canada we spend relatively more than most industrialized countries on general education. But there is growing concern about how these resources are being allocated, about the gap between our post-secondary institutions and the private sector, about the absence of broadly supported national goals in education, and about the failure to link these goals with national economic priorities. There is an urgent need for action on this front.

In the area of training, on the other hand, we spend considerably less, relatively speaking, than many other industrial nations. We carry instead a bloated unemployment insurance scheme that provides income support but little else for Canadians who want jobs, and who are seeking new skills in a rapidly changing labour market. High rates of unemployment and deteriorating productivity growth are signalling to us that our human resource policies are outdated and grossly inadequate. Throwing more money at the problem is not the answer. The answer lies in new priorities, more flexible policies and closer cooperation between management and labour.

Productivity growth relies heavily on leadership—the ability to manage successfully the variety of resources and assets that are the basis of growth. The quality of management education, therefore, must figure prominently in any strategy to improve productivity. In Canada, our business schools are striving for excellence but have not been as successful as they might be in responding to the demands of a technology-based economy. Both our universities and corporations need to do more to prepare managers for the new challenges that are flowing from global economic integration.

If productivity growth relies on effective leadership on the part of business managers, it relies equally on a committed and motivated work force. Here, the relationship between business and labour is vital. In Canada we have had our share of problems. Work stoppages have been only the periodic symptoms of a malaise that runs deep in our economic life—a malaise stemming from a long-standing adversarial relationship between management and labour—a relationship tinged with ideological overtones and even open distrust.

It is critical that this relationship be repaired, for the sake of productivity growth and for broader reasons as well. The simple truth is that we as Canadians will not remain among the leading industrial powers if the forces of capital and labour fail to unite under a single banner. Many ideas have been put forward as to how this can be accomplished, among them improved consultation, mutual respect for union and management prerogatives, enhanced participation, productivity-based bonuses, more effective training, job enrichment programs, gain-sharing and new and more flexible approaches to the organization of work. These ideas are constructive and deserve to win broad acceptance. But hand in hand with new approaches must be a willingness on the part of business and labour to put aside 19th century rhetoric and outmoded ideologies. Instead, we must build upon the incomparable advantages that Canada offers and create the world's most dynamic economy—an economy capable of providing ample rewards for all of our citizens.

The impact on productivity growth of high inflation rates, big public sector deficits and government intervention in the economy can be summed up in a couple of words—unequivocally negative. It was not long ago that we experienced double-digit inflation and its devastating effects, particularly for the unemployed and those on low and fixed incomes. The Governor of the Bank of Canada is waging a courageous policy to contain inflationary pressures, but he needs more help from the country's fiscal authorities. While the federal government has made progress in reducing the size of public sector deficits, they remain high and our level of indebtedness as a nation continues to rise. After more than six years of strong economic growth, there can be no question about it—our fiscal position should be stronger.

As to the impact of hands-on government on productivity growth, "the answer is blowing in the wind." Social democracies and authoritarian regimes alike are discovering the virtues of the marketplace. From Auckland, Canberra, Madrid, Beijing and Moscow, the message is the same—less government means more growth, more jobs, more economic rewards. The message is alive and well in Canada, but far from being universally accepted.

I suppose there can be little doubt by now that I am a disciple of the productivity growth school and that I believe that productivity enhancement is essential to building a more prosperous Canada. But productivity growth is also the key to economic success in the industrialized world as a whole, and to removing the shackles of poverty and misery from hundreds of millions of people in the developing world.

Training the Work Force: A Challenge Facing Canada in the '90s*

Andrew Sharpe

In recent years there has been a growing debate on the importance of education and training for Canada's future prosperity. As a result, attention has been directed to the role Canada's education and training system can play in developing our economic potential in terms of employment and productivity growth.

This article focuses on Canada's training system and, in particular, on what is required to meet the training needs of the work force in the '90s. For example, is training available to all workers who require it? Is the amount of workplace training sufficient to meet industry's growing need for skilled workers?

THE BASIC SKILLS LEVELS OF THE CANADIAN WORK FORCE

A frequent complaint of Canadian employers is that the basic literacy and numeracy skills of the work force are inadequate. Without such skills workers cannot function effectively in the modern workplace. For example, they may not be able to read manuals, perform numerical calculations, operate sophisticated equipment, use information technologies, or do myriad other tasks requiring a basic level of skills. It follows that workers without these basic skills are less able to adapt to the growth and decline of firms and to the introduction of new technology.

⊕ Abridged from Andrew Sharpe, "Training the Work Force: A Challenge Facing Canada in the '90s," *Perspectives on Labour and Income* (Ottawa: Statistics Canada, Winter 1990), 21–31. Reprinted by permission of the publisher and the author.

It is true that the average level of formal educational attainment of the Canadian labour force has risen significantly over the past several decades and can be expected to continue to increase.[1] This trend arises because young people entering the labour force have, on average, higher levels of educational attainment than those currently leaving the labour force. Nevertheless, concern about the basic skills of the Canadian labour force is well justified for at least two reasons.

First, the proportion of the work force requiring more than the bare minimum of basic skills is rising. Unskilled jobs in many industries and occupations have been eliminated by technological change. New employment opportunities are concentrated in occupations requiring more than basic reading and numeracy skills and very often, advanced skills. For example, employment in primary occupations such as forestry and mining, which in the past have generally required little formal education, has fallen in the '80s. On the other hand, over two-thirds of the net increase in employment since 1981 has been in managerial and professional occupations. Needless to say, skills requirements are relatively high in these occupations.

These trends are expected to continue, if not accelerate, in the future. Employment and Immigration Canada estimates that 64% of all jobs created between 1986 and the year 2000 will require more than 12 years of education and training and that nearly one-half of new jobs will require more than 17 years of education and training.[2]

A second reason for concern is the considerable evidence to substantiate employer complaints about the poor basic skills of their employees, despite the rising formal educational attainment of the labour force. The results of Statistics Canada's Survey of Literacy Skills Used in Daily Activities[3] show that 38% of Canadians aged 16 to 69—6.8 million individuals—do not meet most everyday reading demands. Not surprisingly, the problem is more common among those with low levels of schooling. The proportion is also higher for immigrants, residents of Atlantic Canada and Quebec, and the older age groups.[4]

The implications of the inadequate level of basic reading and numeracy skills of the Canadian work force are significant. The Canadian Business Task Force on Literacy has estimated that in 1988 the direct cost of illiteracy to business in Canada was in the neighbourhood of $4 billion and the cost to society at large was about $10 billion.[5] A recent Conference Board of Canada survey[6] found that a lack of basic reading and numeracy skills leads to firms having difficulties in introducing new technologies and in upgrading the skills of workers.

A key challenge of the '90s will be the development of efforts that raise the basic skills level of the work force. Because of slower labour force growth in the future, the Canadian Labour Market and Productivity Centre estimates that about two-thirds of those who will be in the labour force in the year 2005 are already part of the labour force. In 1989 only one-half of the labour force was participating in the labour market 15 years earlier. This means that the problem is becoming increasingly a question of upgrading the basic skills of those currently in the labour force and less a question of ensuring that those leaving the educational system have acquired basic skills.

Job-related literacy programs in particular offer excellent opportunities to remedy the basic skills inadequacies of workers. The most effective literacy programs have been found to be those that teach reading and math skills in their " functional context" , that is, in direct relation to the trainees' jobs.

CANADA'S TRAINING EFFORT

o

Canada' s training effort includes both basic skills training and training for specialized, higher-level skills. In many occupations the rapidly growing demand for skilled workers is outstripping the abilities of the educational system and immigration to supply the needed number of workers. This development has led to the creation of a skills gap. Evidence of this gap can be found in the growing number of occupations that are currently experiencing skilled labour shortages. Such occupations include air traffic controllers, aerospace engineers, software programmers, systems analysts, and electrical engineers. In the past, economic downturns have eased, if not eliminated, labour shortages. Today skilled labour shortages appear to be concentrated in industries less vulnerable to the business cycle or in occupations vital to the health of a company. Consequently, these labour shortages may be more structural than cyclical in nature and will be alleviated only by increasing the supply of skilled workers through training and, possibly, through immigration.

The effectiveness of Canada' s private and public training effort is thus the key determinant of our ability to meet the growing skills gap. In terms of assessing our training performance, a number of trends should be highlighted.

- on a per-employee basis, Canadian firms spend less than half as much on training as American firms;
- only 31% of Canadian firms do any formal training;
- total federal government expenditures on training have fallen as a share of the gross domestic product (GDP) since 1984-85;
- the poorly educated have a below average incidence of training.

The most comprehensive source of information on the state of private sector training in Canada is the Human Resource Training and Development Survey, an establishment-based survey conducted by Statistics Canada on behalf of Employment and Immigration Canada.[7] This survey found that in 1986-87, Canadian firms spent $1.4 billion on training, an amount equivalent to approximately 0.6% of payroll or 0.24% of GDP. On a per-employee basis this represents about $160 and is estimated to be less than half the level of training expenditure by American firms.[8] A more developed private sector training culture in the United States is one possible explanation for this difference.

One particularly noteworthy finding from the Human Resource Training and Development Survey was that only 31% of firms actually provide formal training for their employees. The incidence of training was low for small firms—27% of firms with less than 10 employees provided training, compared with 76% of firms with 100 or more employees and 92% of firms with 1,000 or more employees.

Additional evidence of Canada's weakness in the area of workplace training is provided by the World Economic Forum, which ranks countries by a large number of competitiveness criteria. In 1990, Canada ranked second among the 23 member countries of the Organization for Economic Co-operation and Development (OECD) in terms of human resources due to its relatively young population, rapid labour force growth, high levels of public expenditure on education and high enrolment rate in secondary schooling and higher education. But in terms of the adequacy of vocational training in meeting the needs of a competitive economy Canada did much more poorly—only 16th place.[9] This is down from 11th place in 1989.

In contrast to the private sector, Canada's public sector training expenditure on a proportional basis exceeds that of the United States. OECD data for 1988 show that Canada's labour market training expenditure on adults was equivalent to 0.20% of GDP and was tenth among 23 OECD countries. Expenditures in the United States represented 0.11% of GDP. Despite the higher public expenditure in Canada, total expenditure on training, which includes both public and private sector expenditure, was still proportionately higher in the United States than in Canada (0.77% of GDP versus 0.46% in 1987).[10]

In absolute terms, federal government expenditure on training has been relatively stable since the mid-80s. In the 1984-85 fiscal year, total federal spending on Canadian Jobs Strategy training, which includes income support, industrial support, and direct purchases of courses, was $1,096.7 million. By 1989-90 the total had risen marginally to $1,122.3 million. As a share of GDP this represents a decline from 0.24% to 0.17%. The Labour Force Development Strategy,[11] announced by the federal government in April 1989, has given increased priority to training. The government proposes to use revenues from Unemployment Insurance premiums to finance additional expenditure on training. This policy shift may reverse the downward trend in federal expenditure on training.

Given trends in federal expenditure on training, the number of individuals enrolled in government-sponsored institutional training courses has, not surprisingly, fallen. From the mid-70s to 1985-86, the numbers fell 20% despite a large increase in the 20-54-year-old age group, which accounts for most of the persons who enrol in government-sponsored institutional training courses. Since 1986-87, a continuing downward trend has been observed.

The results of Statistics Canada's 1987 Labour Market Activity Survey (LMAS) provide interesting information on the incidence of training, by personal characteristics. Participants in the survey were asked if, during 1987, they had participated in any skill training, education upgrading or work experience program sponsored by Employment and Immigration Canada and if they had taken any other training that lasted more than 25 hours to learn a new job-related skill or a new job. Several interesting observations emerge from the survey:

- only 5.3% of the population aged 16 to 69 responded that they had received training in 1987;
- not surprisingly, the incidence of training falls rapidly for those 45 and over, and particularly for those 55 and over;
- the incidence of training is lower for the poorly educated.

The picture that emerges from the LMAS on Canada's training effort is not particularly encouraging. Given the increased importance of training in the '90s because of rising skills demands on the work force, the extent of training undertaken may be inadequate. In addition, persons with no postsecondary education have a significantly lower incidence of training than those who have completed at least some postsecondary education.

The importance of upgrading the skills of the work force for the health of the Canadian economy in the '90s is widely recognized. Mention has already been made of the federal government's Labour Force Development Strategy with its emphasis on training. A recent Canadian Labour Market and Productivity Centre survey of business and labour leaders[12] found that both groups believed training and education was the most important factor in improving Canada's international competitiveness.

IMPLICATIONS AND CONCLUSIONS

o

This article has focused on the training needs of Canada's work force in the '90s. The serious deficiencies that have been found in the basic skills levels of many Canadian workers are likely to become a challenge to both the private and public sectors in the years ahead. Canada currently appears to be lagging behind its major competitors in its workplace training effort.

When combined with the rapidly growing skill requirements of the workplace, a potential labour market crisis may be emerging. Those without skills may find themselves increasingly disadvantaged in the job market. Firms unable to recruit qualified personnel may grow at less than their potential and may be forced to initiate or extend their own training efforts.

A large number of reports have recently drawn attention to this situation and its implications for the Canadian economy. These reports have consequently stressed the importance of making our training effort more effective. All of these reports have emphasized the need for Canada to develop a national training culture where the priority placed on education and training is greatly enhanced.

Rapidly changing technologies and economic circumstances now mean that workers must upgrade existing skills and learn new skills throughout their working lives. Employers, unions, governments, and of course employees, all have a role to play to ensure that the increased training needs of the '90s are met.

NOTES

○

1. Labour Force Survey data show that, in 1975, 20.3% of the labour force had eight years or less of schooling. By 1989 this proportion had dropped to 8.9%. At the other end of the spectrum, the share of the labour force with a university degree has risen from 9.2% in 1975 to 14.9% in 1989. See Statistics Canada, *Labour Force Annual Averages* (1983); and Statistics Canada, *The Labour Force* (1990).

2. See Employment and Immigration Canada, *Success in the Works: A Profile of Canada's Emerging Workforce* (1989).

3. See G. Montigny, *Survey of Literacy Skills Used in Daily Activities: Reading Skills* (1990). This survey classified Canadians aged 16 to 69 into four levels of reading, writing and numeracy skills on the basis of their performance on a series of tests conducted in one of Canada's two official languages. Persons classified to levels 1, 2 and 3 are considered to have skills too limited to deal with most everyday reading demands. The Southam Literacy Study found that in 1987, according to its definition of literacy, 24% of the population aged 18 and over—4.5 million individuals—was illiterate. See The Creative Research Group Ltd., *Literacy in Canada: A Research Report prepared for Southam News* (1987).

4. Similar results were found in the numeracy portion of the survey, the results of which were released on July 17, 1990.

5. See Canadian Business Task Force on Literacy, *Measuring the Costs of Illiteracy in Canada* (1988). The estimates, prepared by management consultants Woods Gordon, are based on a review of the available literature and on interviews with business and government organizations in Canada and the United States. The task force cautions that its estimates are "typically only best guesses, the accuracy of which may be questioned" and that the "main value of this report will therefore be as a preliminary agenda for future research" (p. 3).

6. See B. Des Lauriers, *Canadian Business Review* (1989).

7. See Statistics Canada, *Distribution Report: Human Resource Training and Development Survey* (1989).

8. See Employment and Immigration Canada, *Success in the Works: A Profile of Canada's Emerging Workforce* (1989).

9. See IMEDE International Management Development Institute and World Economic Forum, *The World Competitiveness Report, 1990* (1990).
10. The proportion for the United States is taken from A. Carnevale and L. Gainer, *The Learning Enterprise* (1989). The proportion for Canada is calculated from results of the Human Resource Training and Development Survey, 1987.
11. See Employment and Immigration Canada, *Success in the Works: A Policy Paper: A Labour Force Development Strategy for Canada* (1989).
12. See Canadian Labour Market and Productivity Centre (CLMPC), *Business and Labour Leaders Speak Out on Training and Education* (1990).

REFERENCES
o

Canadian Business Task Force on Literacy. *Measuring the Costs of Illiteracy in Canada.* [Canada], February 1988.

Canadian Labour Market and Productivity Centre. *Business and Labour Leaders Speak Out on Training and Education.* Ottawa, January 1990.

Carnevale, A.P. and L.J. Gainer. *The Learning Enterprise.* Washington, D.C.: U.S. Department of Labor; Alexandria, VA: American Society for Training and Development, 1989.

Creative Research Group Ltd. *Literacy in Canada: A Research Report prepared for Southam News, Ottawa, Ontario.* Toronto, 1987.

Des Lauriers, B. "Functional Illiteracy in Canadian Business." *Canadian Business Review,* Vol. 16, No. 4, Ottawa: The Conference Board of Canada, 1989, pp. 36-39.

Employment and Immigration Canada.

——— *Success in the Works: A Policy Paper: A Labour Force Development Strategy for Canada.* Ottawa, April 1989.

——— *Success in the Works: A Profile of Canada's Emerging Workforce.* Ottawa, April 1989.

IMEDE International Management Development Institute and World Economic Forum. *The World Competitiveness Report, 1990.* Lausanne, Switzerland: IMEDE, July 1990.

Montigny, G. *Survey of Literacy Skills Used in Daily Activities: Reading Skills.* Ottawa: Statistics Canada, April 1990.

Statistics Canada. *Labour Force Annual Averages,* Occasional, Catalogue 71-529. Ottawa, April 1983.

——— *Distribution Report: Human Resource Training and Development Survey.* Ottawa, 1989.

——— *The Labour Force,* Monthly, Catalogue 71-001. Ottawa, January 1990.

Two Years Under Free Trade: An Assessment*

Canadian Labour Congress

INTRODUCTION

o

Two years after the Canada-U.S. free trade deal came into effect Canada has slipped into what may become the worst recession since the 1930's. As the Conference Board remarked, this is the first ever made-in Canada recession. What is also likely is that this is a FTA-induced recession. Moreover, it is a recession that will be made worse by the free trade inspired goods and services tax. . . .

JOB LOSS

o

It is important to establish the context in which the Canadian Labour Congress (CLC) estimates free trade driven job loss. To do this it is necessary to start with Trade Minister Kelleher's 1985 report, *How to Secure and Enhance Our Export Markets,* which first set out the government's intention to enter into free trade negotiations. The government estimated the " job dislocation" from a free trade agreement at 7 per cent of the workforce; that is 850,000 jobs. This slip was never repeated. The Tory PR team moved in with their communications strategy to sell free trade. We heard nothing more of the downside.

The Economic Council, in making the case for a free trade agreement in 1986, set out the spectre of the Americans imposing a 20 per cent import

✠ Abridged from Canadian Labour Congress, "Two Years Under Free Trade: An Assessment," Free Trade Briefing Document, no. 7 (January 1991): 1–13. Reprinted by permission of the publisher.

surtax if a free trade agreement were not reached. The consequences of this, it said, would be 520,000 Canadian jobs lost over nine years. Well that is precisely the effect of a 20 per cent rise in the dollar. Two years under these conditions would imply that 116,000 jobs have already been lost.

Also in 1986, the Ontario Treasury Ministry, responding to rumblings of a possible exchange rate pact tied to a trade deal, estimated that every five cent increase in the Canadian dollar would cost 140,000 Canadian jobs. Since the deal was signed, the dollar has gained ten cents.

In order to get another angle on what our biggest corporations have been doing in the area of job creation, since the Business Council on National Issues was free trade's prime mover, we compared total employment of the top 200 Financial Post Corporations in 1990 with 1988. We found a net drop of 215,000 for these corporations as a group.

We also looked at Statistics Canada figures to observe what has happened to restructuring in the manufacturing sector. We looked at the period June 1989 to June 1990. This period was chosen to give the FTA effects time to show up in the statistics (lag effect) and because it preceded the formal onset of recession.

Overall, they show a stunning acceleration in the deindustrialization of Canada. Manufacturing experienced a net drop in employment of 152,000, 7 per cent of total manufacturing jobs. Contrast this with the period 1981-88 when manufacturing employment remained basically stable, dropping less than one per cent.

During the 1981-82 recession large numbers of jobs were lost. However, those were largely recovered as the country emerged from the recession. The job losses in this pre-recession period have been largely structural. They will not come back when the country emerges from the recession. Ontario government figures on layoffs further clarify this phenomenon. In 1982, plant closures accounted for 22% of all layoffs. In 1989, after one year of free trade driven restructuring, over 55% of all layoffs were due to plant closures.

Sectors disadvantaged by the Free Trade Agreement have been particularly hard hit. Textiles lost 22,000 jobs, dropping 30 per cent; clothing lost 23,000 jobs, dropping 18 per cent; automotive lost 19,000 jobs, or 7.3 per cent of its total; food processing lost 22,000 jobs or 7 per cent of its total; paper products lost 20,000 jobs dropping 13 per cent; chemicals lost 8,000 jobs or 7.6 per cent of its total.

Finally, we looked at job creation in the economy as a whole. In the five years prior to the signing of the trade deal, job creation averaged 326,000 a year net. In 1989 it dropped to 152,000. In 1990 (November to November) it had turned negative; 82,000 more jobs were destroyed than were created. Thus, in two years under free trade 582,000 fewer jobs were created by the Canadian economy than would have been expected under average conditions.

Viewed in this context the latest (November, 1990) CLC estimate of free trade driven job loss, 226,000, seems conservative. Our job loss register picks up only the most visible end of job losses; 80 per cent of them are in the goods producing sector. It cannot trace adequately job losses in the much larger but more diffuse services sector.

Moreover, it covers mainly the larger layoffs or closures. The average size is over 200. Most Canadians are working in firms with less than 50 employees. In a sense it is only the tip of the iceberg. In the majority (75 per cent) of job losses a free trade link can be made. We assume very conservatively that there is an additional spinoff job lost for every lost job we identify.

Let's go back now to examining the various dimensions of corporation restructuring.

FOREIGN TAKEOVERS GROW AND BRANCH PLANTS CLOSE

o

The lifting of regulations on U.S. controlled corporations under the FTA has spurred two somewhat paradoxical processes: an increase in takeover of Canadian companies and the shutting down of U.S. branch plant operations.

Statistics Canada found that during 1988-1989, 460 Canadian controlled companies including major high technology companies with combined assets of $24 billion were taken over by foreign owners, mainly American. During the same period only 136 foreign controlled companies with assets of $3 billion were taken over by Canadian controlled companies. The result was that foreign control of the economy jumped a full percentage pint.

More recently Investment Canada reported that in the two years ending in April 1990, there was a record 1,403 foreign corporate takeovers of Canadian based companies. The combined value of these takeovers was $35.5 billion. (More than 90 per cent of foreign corporate activity in Canada is in the form of takeovers not new investment.)

So foreign (mainly U.S.) control is now on the rise again and the Free Trade Agreement prevents governments from regulating it to ensure that it operates in Canada's interest.

The other phenomenon is the accelerated pace of closure of U.S. branch plants and the transfer of production to locations in the United States, particularly to the sunbelt states and the Mexican border export zone. The liberalization of the Canadian market, the rising dollar and the lifting of regulations on corporate behaviour has made it more profitable to supply the Canadian market from outside. . . .

THE MAQUILADORA

o

Key to the restructuring agenda of U.S. multinationals which are deserting Canada in large numbers is the Mexican Maquiladora. Free trade proponents like the Economic Council assumed that the branch plants would restructure by converting themselves into export platforms for the North American market. The resulting efficiency gains would, they said, lead to additional job creation in Canada. What they failed to grasp was that Mexico was a far more attractive export platform, and that in many cases restructuring the Canadian operation meant closing it down, leaving behind only a warehouse and a sales office.

This deregulated export zone near the southern United States border is a corporation's paradise. Average wages, at 60 cents per hour, are about 4 per cent of what they are in Canada. Effective unions are non-existent. Health, safety and environmental standards are not enforced and taxes are extremely low. Most of the multinationals that dominate the Canadian economy are there. Only a handful of Canadian companies have set up shop there so far, but the list is growing.

The Maquiladora is growing incredibly fast; 400 per cent since 1982. It added 75,000 workers last year. It now employs over 500,000 and is projected to reach a million by mid-decade. Meanwhile the Canadian manufacturing sector lost 150,000 employees in the last year. . . .

CANADIAN INDUSTRY UNDER STRESS

o

Restructuring under free trade is hitting small and medium-sized Canadian companies very hard. This is particularly worrisome because practically all of the new job creation comes from these companies. They are reducing or shutting down their operations for several reasons:

- thousands of firms have shut their doors: 9,407 companies declared bankruptcy in the first 10 months of 1990, up 25 per cent from the same period last year and up 41 per cent from 1988. This is just the tip of the iceberg since most firms that close do not declare bankruptcy. Many have not been able to sustain their debt loads with interest rates so high. Only the large corporations are able to find easier credit on U.S. and other external capital markets;

- the 85 cent dollar has forced many exporters out of the U.S. markets. Others have been forced out of business due to the onslaught of U.S. imports;

- many firms may have lost out because big retail chains are closing down their separate Canadian purchasing operations and are consolidating their buying in the United States;

• still other firms who supplied inputs to U.S. subsidiaries and big Canadian companies have seen their markets evaporate as these companies
have shut down and moved south or consolidated operations in other
communities.

CONCLUSION
o

...The Conservatives claimed during the last election that they were best
equipped to "manage change". In fact, the Free Trade Agreement which was
their main basis for this assertion is the antithesis of managed change. It
embodies a vision, leaves the corporate sector largely free to manage change
themselves—to manage production, investment and trade in accordance
with their own priorities. It is a vision which sees the role of government to
get out of the way and leaves Canadian workers and their families to pick
up the pieces. In the process, the integrity of Canada as economic and political entity is being undermined.

The ethic which drives these corporate priorities is the ethic of competitiveness. David Vice, Chairman of the Canadian Manufacturers Association and Vice-President of Northern Telecom, is an articulate spokesman of
this new morality. He said recently: "All Canadian governments must test
all their policies to determine whether or not they reinforce or impede competitiveness. If a policy is anti-competitive, dump it."

The Free Trade Agreement epitomizes this morality.

Forget the Critics—Free Trade Works[*]

John Crispo

Canada is getting into another wrenching debate about free trade. The contention over NAFTA—the North American Free Trade Agreement—promises to be just as emotional and irrational as the debate over the 1989 Free Trade Agreement with the United States.

Admittedly, there was some exaggeration by FTA supporters in 1988. Those who promised unlimited "jobs, jobs, jobs" and a virtual cure-all for our many economic woes were obviously guilty of overstatement.

But their exaggeration pales in comparison with that of the other side. Remember when you were told the FTA would cost you your medicare and your pensions, not to mention your air and your water?

Yet those who spouted this nonsense are still quoted widely by the mainstream media, as though they were the fountains of all reliable information.

But this is only one reason why NAFTA is in as much trouble, if not more, than the first free-trade deal was at this stage.

More important, perhaps, is the fact that the business lobby in favour of the FTA was much more committed and dedicated than it is to NAFTA. This is because business has a much bigger stake in trade with the United States than with Mexico.

Last, but hardly least, is all the propaganda about the results of the FTA so far. Just as the United States blames Japan for much of its own internal mismanagement, most Canadians blame the FTA for Canada's parallel problems.

Given this perception of the FTA, let's start with some facts about its impact. And remember, the agreement offered Canada and Canadians an

[*] John Crispo, "Forget the Critics—Free Trade Works," *The Globe and Mail* (13 August 1992), p. A17. Reprinted by permission of the publisher and the author.

enviable opportunity (readier and more secure access to the richest single market on the face of the earth), but not a panacea that would somehow solve all our problems overnight.

It was up to Canada to exploit this opportunity—which we could not possibly do after we shot ourselves in both feet with higher interest rates and a higher dollar. These tremendous disadvantages stemmed from our failure to deal with our rising government deficits and debts—federal, provincial and municipal—and our increasing reliance on foreign borrowers to finance them. Foreign money insisted on high rates of interest and pushed up the Canadian dollar as it flowed in to rescue us, at least temporarily.

Despite these and other handicaps, the Free Trade Agreement is having the desired effect on Canada's future industrial structure. Corporate rationalization, realignment and restructuring are evident everywhere as Canadian subsidiaries of foreign firms fight for product mandates and domestic firms struggle for market niches. Our enterprises have to prove that they can do as good a job as anyone else, or better, and more and more of them are doing this.

Meanwhile, the FTA countervail-subsidy dispute-settlement mechanism is working well for Canada by providing a binding non-political procedure—something not available to any other country. Without it, we would be losing rather than winning the growing number of cases that arise because of mounting protectionist pressures in the United States—pressures that have nothing to do with the FTA.

The case for North American free trade is, admittedly, not as compelling as the FTA case was, at least in the short run. Canada's trade with Mexico, while having a huge potential, is still infinitesimal compared with our dealings with the United States.

Still, we couldn't afford to stand idly by while Washington negotiated a separate agreement with Mexico. And this is not just because such a pact could dissipate some of the advantages we derive from our own distinct deal with the United States.

Far more significant is what could happen if the United States continued to negotiate separate bilateral agreements with other individual countries in the Western Hemisphere. This would allow Washington to divide and conquer all those involved, by making the United States the only logical place to set up a new facility—since only from there could any enterprise easily serve all the countries tied to America by different agreements.

At the other extreme, NAFTA will undoubtedly lead to a comprehensive Western Hemispheric free-trade regime—something Canada would have to join at some point whether it liked it or not. By being in on the ground floor, Canada will have an influence on its structure, which it would not have as a Johnny-come-lately.

The critics of NAFTA make much of Mexico's low wages. These pose much less of a threat than the critics would have us believe. If low wages are such an important factor, why do 80 per cent of Canada's imports come from such high-wage countries as the United States, Japan, Germany and Britain? Moreover, 80 per cent of Mexico's imports to Canada already come in duty-free and this still has not led to a flood of cheap, low-wage goods.

The explanation is simple. Except in a limited range of labour-intensive industries, wages are a relatively minor cost in most forms of production. In today's manufacturing, labour amounts to between 10 and 15 per cent of the total costs of production.

Far more important are such factors as the local infrastructure, access to raw materials, a skilled labour pool, modern technology and top-flight management. While Mexico may have lower wages, it has a long way to go to catch up to Canada in most of these categories.

In time, however, Mexico will indeed attract more of our labour-intensive industries. But this is exactly as it should be, as long as Canada replaces its losses in such industries with more high-tech, high value-added jobs, which are the only ones that can draw the high wages to which we have grown accustomed.

It will not matter if we lose some low-paying clothing and furniture jobs, as long as we gain employment in such high-wage key industries as tele-communications and urban transit; we are more than capable of doing well in these in a more open Mexican market.

The only problem we will have then is to help those thrown out of work in Canada because of freer trade switch to comparable if not more lucrative new openings that result from that same trade. This we have failed to do in the past.

All this aside, there are legitimate concerns to raise about NAFTA. One can argue that the treaty does virtually nothing to improve the elementary rights of workers in Mexico to join unions of their own choosing, and to bargain collectively.

One can also object to the relatively weak environmental standards that have been written into the treaty to compel Mexican industry to operate more cleanly. Mexico simply refused to yield much, if any, of its sovereignty in these areas.

Also important, from my point of view, are the protectionist measures written into the treaty. Especially in clothing and autos, the North American content rules go too far. They threaten to create a frightening Fortress North America mentality, which is totally contrary to the spirit of the free-trade principle. However, the treaty is consistent with the General Agreement on Tariffs and Trade, a point to be stressed.

These criticisms aside, NAFTA does create a strong North American free-trade regime in which, over time, the vast majority of goods and services will flow unimpeded among the three countries. To preside over this regime, it introduces a more permanent countervail-subsidy dispute-settlement mechanism that some observers believe is embodied in the FTA.

The treaty also maintains the protection of our cultural industries and our social services that was built into the FTA. And Canada maintains the same right to review foreign investments as under the FTA.

While NAFTA's strengths clearly outweigh its weaknesses, the opponents will have a field day attacking the weak points. Aside from recalling their past misleading propaganda campaigns, one should bear in mind two very disturbing themes that run throughout their thinking.

On one hand, they said they were against the FTA largely because it was a special bilateral deal with the Americans. On the other hand, when we try to widen this to embrace Mexico as well, they remain opposed. Deep down, they are really against any kind of freer trade, even under GATT, despite what they say to the contrary.

Even worse are the liberal and left-wing critics of the FTA and NAFTA, who profess at the same time to care so much about the downtrodden and poor in the Third World. No amount of foreign aid or anything else has helped these disadvantaged people as much as freer access to the markets of the developed countries.

That is why NAFTA is so important to Mexico. It will allow Mexico to raise its people's standard of living in the only real way it can, by trading freely with two of the wealthiest countries in the world.

When I weigh everything, I have to come out forcefully in favour of NAFTA not just because of its importance to Mexico and ultimately to most other developing countries in the Western Hemisphere, but because it is crucial for Canada to be part of this burgeoning free trade. The alternative is to become an economic backwater.

It will be tragic if the paranoia and parochialism of the critics drown out the calls for freer trade. There is no future for an isolated and sheltered Canada. It is essential to participate in NAFTA and what is to follow. Not even our agreement with the United States will save us if we stand aside as the rest of the hemisphere heads toward a freer trading relationship.

Post-Industrialism and the Service Economy*

John Myles

Throughout this century, Canada has led the way in the shift to a service economy where 70 per cent of the Canadian labour force is now employed. The implications of this transition with respect to the future of work and wages has been a topic of considerable attention and debate. Most recently, it has been associated with the thesis of the "declining middle"—the claim that the shift of employment to services is creating a more polarized wage and skill structure than in the recent past. The empirics of Canada's service economy with respect to wages and job skills are now fairly well understood. There is indeed evidence of growing dualization in the Canadian labour market, but this is not a result of the shift to services as such. Rather it is an economy-wide trend that represents one of several "branching points" in the transition to a post-industrial economy.

The transition to post-industrialism is a product of the enormous growth in productivity that has characterized most industrialized capitalist economies in this century. Productivity growth brings the opportunity to either increase the amount of goods and services available or to produce the current amount of output with less labour. Changes in the mix of employment (the service economy), changes in employment levels and in patterns of paid work time are outcomes of this process. But the precise nature and mix of these outcomes are highly indeterminate. Not all things are possible but there is already ample evidence for a variety of alternative national strategies for resolving these issues. The reason for this variation is politics: politics in the sense of strategic choices that are made (or not made) *and* pol-

* Abridged from Daniel Drache and Meric S. Gertler, eds., *The New Era of Global Competition: State Policy and Market Power* (Montreal and Kingston: McGill–Queen's University Press, 1991), chapter 16, " Post-Industrialism and the Service Economy." Reprinted by permission of the publisher and the author.

itics in the sense of institutionalized power relations—between classes, between men and women—inherited from the past and embedded in our social, political, and economic institutions that condition the everyday common sense of élites and publics concerning what is both possible and desirable.

My objective here is to highlight the alternatives to the North American variant of the transition. From a distributive point of view, some of these alternatives are clearly more desirable than others. The risk, however, is that democratic socialists, labour, and the social movements will focus largely on the distributive implications of these alternatives. This would be a mistake. A necessary condition for any alternative economic strategy is that it promises an equal or better solution to the production problem as well—in other words, that it identifies a virtuous circle between employment, wages, inflation, and productivity to take us through the transition. Fortunately there is good reason to think that dualism and flexible labour markets are a less than optimal solution to the productivity problem in a post-industrial economy. . . .

THE SERVICE ECONOMY AND THE DECLINING MIDDLE

o

What of actual trends in job skills and wages? Has the shift to service employment and knowledge-intensive goods production resulted in a more polarized wage and skill structure as [is] often claimed?[1] The answer is yes and no. The results of our research at Statistics Canada in 1988 indicate that the Canadian wage structure has become more polarized over time (more low and high paying jobs and fewer jobs in the "middle").[2] Changes in the industrial and occupational composition of jobs had something to do with this but not much. At most 20 to 25 per cent of the total change in wage structure is explained by changes in industrial and occupational composition. In the 1980s the main source of change has been a shift in the age-wage profile: a very sharp decrease in the relative wages paid to young (age sixteen to twenty-four) workers and a small rise in the relative wages paid to "middle-aged" (thirty-five to fifty) workers. The downward drift in relative youth wages characterizes all industries and occupations. The reason we have tended to identify wage restructuring as a "McJobs" phenomenon is because of the concentration of young workers in consumer services.

This trend is disturbing because it occurred over a period when the labour supply of young workers was declining, when their educational qualifications were rising, and in a period of economic recovery. In sum, the relative wages of young people should have been rising, not declining, over this period. What accounts for this change? One, optimistic, scenario is that the change is temporary. The current generation of young people are entering the labour market in the backwash of the baby boom generation ahead of them. As the baby boomers age and stop clogging up the labour market, youth wages will begin to rise again. The more pessimistic scenario is that a more general wage restructuring is under way that is showing up first among entry-level jobs, a change that Canadian (and American) labour is unable to resist. Two-tier wage contracts, increased use of part-time labour, and contracting out of production to new and smaller work sites are more likely to have their impact on new labour market entrants than on older, established workers with seniority and union rights to protect them. One indication of this is a decline in the percentage of young people in unionized jobs in all industries. The decline is not attributable solely to the fact that young workers are finding employment in sectors where union levels are traditionally low (such as retail sales). Between 1981 and 1986, the share of unionized jobs held by young workers fell from 52 to 30 per cent in resource and resource-based industries, from 35 to 28 per cent in other manufacturing, from 46 to 40 per cent in construction, and from 49 to 40 per cent in social services.[3]

Trends in skill levels are more ambiguous, due in part to measurement problems. But again, the trends in recent years do not appear to be industry-specific.[4] The 1950s and 1960s brought substantial skill upgrading, largely because of the rapid growth in public administration in the 1950s and the welfare state industries in the 1960s. In the 1970s, changing industry mix accounted for little change in the skill composition of the labour force (that is, most change took place within industrial sectors). In the 1980s, measurable skill change has been modest. There is some evidence of a polarized labour market for skills, but not of the sort described by Braverman, with the dividing line between professionals and managers, on the one hand, and the "mass" blue and white collar occupations on the other. Rather, the polarization is within these "mass" occupations, between high and low skill clerical workers, high and low skill blue collar workers, high and low skill sales workers and the like.

REFLECTIONS AND OBSERVATIONS

o

"Manufacturing Matters"

The shift to a service economy does not mean that our economic well-being no longer depends on our ability to produce goods. Declining *employment* shares in manufacturing does not necessarily mean that manufacturing accounts for a smaller share of the total *wealth* produced in Canada. Between 1981 and 1988, the share of all jobs accounted for by manufacturing fell from 19.3 to 17.2 per cent but the manufacturing share of total output remained virtually constant at about 20 per cent.[5] The reason that employment shares in manufacturing have declined while manufacturing has maintained a constant share of total output is higher productivity gains in goods production than in services. If there is a reason for concern among Canadian workers, it is that Canadian productivity gains were not larger. Over the decade, Canada has lagged behind most advanced capitalist countries in this respect. For labour, the issue is not productivity gains per se but rather how the benefits of rising productivity—more wealth or less labour time—are distributed.

Manufacturing also matters for employment growth and the quality of employment in the service sector. Both distributive and business services depend directly on the goods sector for their economic health. Some of the growth in these sectors simply represents the contracting out of services once performed "in-house" by manufacturing enterprises. Canadian competitiveness in the international market for business services depends directly on areas of production, such as telecommunications and energy, where Canada has historically had a competitive advantage. And this advantage is often a direct result of government intervention. The success of Lavalin, for example, is a direct result of its experience with Hydro-Québec in the construction of the James Bay project.

The transformation of post-industrialism, then, does not mean that goods production matters less, any more than the shift from an agricultural to an industrial economy meant a decline in the importance of food production. The transition to industrialism did not mean that food production declined or was shipped offshore. On the contrary, the ability to produce vast quantities of food with very little labour was a precondition of industrialization, and a significant number of our manufacturing firms continue to depend on agriculture both as a source of inputs and as a market for their products. In the same way, post-industrialism does not mean that we can afford to abandon manufacturing to offshore producers and put everyone to work selling services to one another. As Akio Morita, president of Sony, warns, an economy which has lost its manufacturing base has no engine to drive it. As with services, the critical issue for the future is not *whether* to manufacture but *what* and *how*.

"So Does the Welfare State" [6]

Historically, the relative mix of "bad jobs" and "good jobs" in the service sector is reflected in the size of the personal service sector (bad jobs) on the one hand, and public services (good jobs) on the other. This mix in turn depends on the way national expenditure is divided between personal consumption and government spending. Big welfare states tend to "crowd out" low-wage consumer services. If people pay high taxes for comparatively luxurious social services, there is less discretionary income for other things. Esping-Andersen estimates that employment in food and accommodation service is over 7 per cent in the United States but less than 2 per cent in Sweden.[7] A large, high-wage public sector simply makes it difficult for low-wage personal service industries to compete. As a result, in a post-industrial labour market the welfare state can contribute as much or more to economic well-being through its role as employer as through its role as income redistributor. The issue for the future is not whether we will have a service economy but what kind of service economy. But to date, Canada's rather modest welfare state has resulted in a service economy that is more American in its contours than Scandinavian.

The role of the welfare state is important for more than distributive reasons, however: it does more than create jobs that pay high wages. Competitive advantage also depends on the quality of other services in obvious and not-so-obvious ways. An obvious example is the quality (or the lack thereof) of our educational institutions. Less obvious, perhaps, is Canada's competitive advantage vis-à-vis the American labour market because of our ability (through national health insurance) to contain health care costs. The great irony of the free trade agreement is that, if anything, it has led American business leaders such as Lee Iacocca to call for harmonization of American health care with Canada's more efficient, national health insurance system. Universality takes advantage of a basic law of all insurance programs—namely, that the effective cost is inversely related to the size of the insured group.

Finally, a growing body of economic opinion indicates that to compete at the high end of the market for goods and services requires more economic security, not less. At least since the Myrdals, it has been part of social democratic lore that the welfare-efficiency trade-off would be a positive sum precisely because of the labour flexibility and responsiveness to innovation more equality and security would bring. Insecure workers threatened by job loss or a shift from high- to low-paid work will naturally (and correctly) resist innovation and further development of the productive forces. In contrast, workers confronted with an egalitarian wage distribution, active labour market policies, and security of employment will welcome and promote structural change. A growing body of neo-institutionalist economic analysis suggests the Myradals were correct.[8] In this respect Canada's competitive disadvantage lies in the fact that its welfare state is too small (and often of the wrong sort), not because it is too large.

The Service Economy is Not the Enemy

Historically, the service economy has been the source of as many "good jobs" as "bad jobs". This is not to say the "McJobs" economy is nothing to worry about. The personal service industries do provide bad jobs and, in relative terms, these jobs have got worse in the 1980s. The point is rather that the dualization of the labour market into a primary and secondary sector is symptomatic of most sectors of the economy, including the public sector. The disproportionate growth of the low end of the service sector is a symptom, not the cause, of the problem.

Pfeffer and Baron describe this trend in terms of the growing use of "contingent labour." For example, IBM, like Sweden, runs on a full-employment, high-wage labour strategy *inside* the firm. The resulting labour costs are high, so that IBM only wants to provide the "rights" of corporate "citizenship" to their most skilled and valued workers. As a result, IBM attempts not only to contract out the less-skilled aspects of production, such as warehousing and distribution, but also actively assists in the establishment of small firms to do this work. Similar stories and examples can be found in both social services and government.[9]

In effect, the problem is not the service economy per se but the changing "rules" of the labour market in general. Bluestone and Harrison's recent description of the United States' situation could apply to Canada as well.

> Among the "rule changes" we have in mind. . . are erosion of the real minimum wage, the uneven diffusion of wage freeze and concession demands among firms, the growth of two-tiered wage systems, the transformation by employers of full time into part time jobs, and the continued outsourcing of production from work sites whose wage schedules are characterized by relatively high means and low variances (thanks in part to the presence of unions) to suppliers with wage distributions having on average lower means and higher variances.[10]

Policy matters in all of this to extent that labour market, industrial relations, and social policies all either stimulate or accommodate this situation. In other words, they make it profitable for employers to invest or to shift production into the low end of the wage and skill distribution, a point to which I return in the conclusion.

The Youth Labour Market

The growth of low-wage employment is not idiosyncratic to the service sector but is taking place across the whole of the economy, including manufacturing. The main reason we have come to identify the expansion of low-wage employment as a McJobs phenomenon is simply because so many young people are employed there. Transformations in the labour market (including both the shift to services and the dualization of the labour market) tend to show up primarily among new labour market entrants such as women and young people. Expanding industries (as in services) tend to recruit from new labour market entrants and employ more young people and women. Stable or declining sectors have few new recruits and, hence, tend to have a disproportionate number of older, predominantly male, workers. Older, established workers are also more likely to be protected against wage cuts by seniority and other contractual provisions. With female labour force participation rates peaking in the 1980s, the primary victims of dualization have been younger workers who experienced a 15 to 20 per cent wage drop relative to older workers in all sectors of the economy.

The results are manifest in a number of ways: rising enrolments in post-secondary institutions as competition for goods increases: return to the family home and rising welfare rates as the supply of good jobs declines. For young people this means later career starts, delayed family formation, and generally postponed adulthood. For the economy it means we are not fully involving the next generation of workers, either socially, politically, or economically, in finding our way through the current transition.

If wage rates are indicative of other aspects of job quality such as the skill content of work (as human capital theory would suggest), then trends in youth wages are indicative not only of short-term social problems for youth but also of long-term problems for the economy as a whole. The early years in the labour market are typically when job skills and work attitudes are acquired. If, as the wage data suggest, we are excluding our youth from the more complex jobs requiring capacity for self-direction and creativity, they are less likely to become the innovative and responsible employees that we are told the next generation of production systems will require.

It is not clear that any of our social institutions are paying much attention to this development, including political parties, labour unions, or the social movements. The "sixties generation" that is now middle-aged and at the head of these institutions seems to have written the next generation off as "conservative" and disinterested even as their own material conditions have improved. The first political party to make the "youth issue" its own is likely to reap windfall gains; those national economies that prove capable of mobilizing the energies of their youth are likely to enjoy unanticipated dividends in the new global marketplace.

CONCLUSION: POST-INDUSTRIALISM'S   FUTURES

o

The question raised by the post-industrial transition is not whether we will or should have a service economy but what kind of service economy. Actually existing patterns in post-industrial labour markets suggest three emergent scenarios.

1. The first might be called a " high-wage-low-employment" strategy. The exemplar is West Germany. Productivity gains are not translated into a shift of employment into services but into less employment. This does not mean rising unemployment but simply fewer people in the labour market. Here the welfare state is used to implement a labour market "exit" strategy. The pension system, disability and unemployment insurance schemes are used to absorb surplus labour. The main result of such a strategy is to create a cleavage not between high- and low-wage workers but between those inside and those outside the labour market.

Age, sex, immigrant, and family status are the typical divisions along which such boundaries have been constructed in the past.

2. The second alternative is a "high-wage-high-employment" strategy. The exemplar in this case is Sweden. Here the welfare state's main role is that of employer and manager of labour market transitions as employees shift from declining to expanding industries. Work-time reductions do not take the form of reinforcing old or creating new divisions between those who are and are not employed but by reducing working time across the whole of the labour market in the form of paid work absences (sick leave, maternity leave, retraining, vacations). With high levels of employment, this strategy depends critically on a capacity to restrain inflation-generating wage growth, especially at the top of the labour market. This means not just containing wage increases but actually bringing down the relative earnings of the "new middle class" of managerial, professional and technical workers.

3. The third strategy is the "dualization–high-employment" strategy. Canada and the United States are the exemplars here. Both have been successful in creating a large number of new jobs but mainly at the bottom of the labour market. Here, the emergent role of the welfare state appears to be that of "wage subsidiser," providing various kinds of income subsidies to the working poor to keep those at the low end of the labour market alive. Hence the popularity of various guaranteed income proposals not only among social policy experts but also in business circles.

The logic of each system is somewhat different and resolves similar problems in different ways. The way each system solves the employment-inflation trade-off seems especially important. The dualization strategy allows for strong growth in total employment levels without inflation-generating wage pressure by encouraging employment growth at the bottom of the labour market. Many conservatives see this as desirable; many liberals and social democrats see it as inevitable. This seems to be the dominant rationale for the current popularity of a variety of guaranteed income schemes to supplement the incomes of the working poor.[11] We might call this a strategy of "accommodating dualism."

The alternative to accommodation is to institutionalize labour market and social policies to skew investment into the high end of the wage and skill distribution and discourage investment and employment at the bottom. The labour market exit strategy achieves this at the cost of lowering total employment levels. In West Germany inflation-generating wage pressure can be avoided not only for historical and institutional reasons (a political economy organized around the principle of inflation avoidance) but also because a growing share of the population—pensioners—are effectively subject to the "wage controls" of the welfare state.

The Swedish combination of high wages and high employment works to the extent that wage and salary growth at the top of the labour market can be contained. Employers continue to invest to the extent that wages and salaries at the top of the Swedish labour market are lower than they otherwise would be . One might think of this as a strategy where the economy "competes" with the top of its labour market—including the new middle class—rather that its bottom. At the same time, elimination of the opportunity to use low-wage labour compels employers to increase productivity both through technological change and by utilizing a labour force with a higher skill mix.

Either variant of the high-wage strategy requires a strong commitment to continuous productivity growth. High wages are both cause and consequence of rising productivity. Low wages provide no incentive for employers to increase productivity or push their labour mix up the skill gradient, since increases in output can be had more cheaply by hiring more labour. Dualization may enhance productivity for individual firms but not for the economy as a whole. IBM simply exports its problems when it contracts out low-productivity jobs.

A strong commitment to continuous productivity growth (" revolutionizing the forces of production") also requires a strong commitment to the welfare state. A dynamic economy is one that by definition produces change, and change inevitably produces winners and losers among firms, industries, and regions. To make economic change acceptable, the welfare state is required in order to redistribute the costs and benefits of change. Otherwise, workers (and local politicians and often employers) will quite correctly resist change. By providing pathways out of the labour market, the German labour market exit strategy deals with this in one way. By providing employment inside the welfare state and managing labour market transitions within an active labour market, the Swedish model provides another.

In contrast, the dualization strategy—where the welfare state is used to subsidize the victims of low-wage employment—is likely to work against large gains in productivity. With a ready supply of low-wage labour, employers have little incentive to "revolutionize the forces of production" by eliminating low-skill, low-productivity jobs. This is not to say that dualization cannot succeed as an economic strategy in the current transition, but rather that it is a sub-optimal strategy. It brings with it labour market flexibility and the capacity to adapt and change, but it is a flexibility of a particular sort. The capacity to change and innovate may mean that skilled workers equipped with the appropriate technologies are able to apply these skills and technologies on a continuous basis to improve product quality, to change products to accommodate changing markets, and to adopt—even to create—new technologies. But flexibility may also mean the ability to lay off workers, lower wages, and contract out to non-unionized firms. The first—dynamic flexibility—is defined by Cohen and Zysman as the ability to increase productivity steadily through improvements in production processes and innovation. The second—static flexibility—they define as the ability of firms to adjust operations at any moment to shifting conditions in the market.[12] Whereas the former requires a high-skill, high-wage, workforce with security of employment, the latter requires a low-wage, unskilled labour force. The flexibility it offers is characterized as static because of a tendency to adopt new technologies at a slower rate (low labour costs reduce incentives to innovate) and because innovation occurs in a series of successive plateaus rather than on a continuous basis. This fact more than any other provides the political leverage for those who would prefer an alternative future for Canada's post-industrial labour market.

NOTES
○

1. Bob Kuttner, "The Declining Middle," *Atlantic Monthly* (July 1983): 60-72.

2. John Myles, Garnett Picot, and Ted Wannell, "Wages and Jobs in the Eighties: Changing Youth Wages and the Declining Middle," Research Paper 17 (Ottawa: Statistics Canada 1988), 52.

3. Ibid., 96.

4. John Myles, "The Expanding Middle: Some Canadian Evidence on the Deskilling Debate," *Canadian Review of Sociology and Anthropology* 25 (1988): 335-64.

5. Canadian Labour Market and Productivity Centre, "Restructuring in Canadian Manufacturing in the 1980s," *Labour Research Notes* 7 (May 1989): 1-12.

6. The couplet "Manufacturing Matters—And So Does the Welfare State" is shamelessly stolen from Leon Muszynksi's superb paper with the same title, given at a conference to consider the de-industrialization of Toronto, September 1988.

7. Gosta Esping-Anderson, *Post-Industrial Employment Trajectories: Germany, Sweden and the United States* (Florence: European University, Department of Politics 1987).

8. For example, Rune Aberg, "Market-dependent Income Distribution: Efficiency and Legitimacy" in I. Goldthorpe, ed., *Order and Conflict in Contemporary Capitalism* (Oxford: Clarendon Press 1984) 209-30; and Stephen Cohen and John Zysman, *Manufacturing Matters: The Myth of the Post-Industrial Economy* (New York: Basic Books 1987).

9. Jeffrey Pfeffer and James Baron, "Taking the Workers Back Out: Recent Trends in the Structuring of Employment" in Barry Straw and L.L. Cummings, eds., *Research in Organizational Behaviour* (Greenwich, CN: JAI Press 1988). One can also find examples of firms using contingent labour at the high end of the labour market (e.g., professors) to avoid long-term commitments to employees and so maintain a flexible labour market.

10. Barry Bluestone and Bennett Harrison, "Increasing Inequality and the Proliferation of Low-wage Employment in the U.S.: A Review of the Debate and Some New Evidence," mimeo 1989.

11. In view of prevailing forms of family organization, emergent labour market trends, and the growing importance of competing in international markets, it is unrealistic, many argue, to expect the labour market to provide everyone with the high and rising real wage levels we came to expect in the past. Under these conditions, the state cannot afford to "waste" scarce transfer dollars on the middle classes (i.e., on social insurance and public services). A fundamental requirement of the welfare state of the 1990s and beyond, according to the Canadian Council on Social Development, a major anti-poverty lobby, is "to find acceptable ways of accommodating this form of economic development." See Canadian Council on Social Development, *Proposals for Discussion: Phase One—Income Security Reform* (Ottawa 1987), 5. The welfare state must be adjusted to the new reality of a service economy, single-parent families, and a flexible low-wage, labour market through better targeting of benefits on the poor. Instead of a universal system of income security for a nation of high-wage workers, the welfare state of the future will have to provide subsistence to a growing number of low-wage workers. There is nothing wrong with a guaranteed income of course, if it is introduced under conditions where it is largely unnecessary, that is, where there is full and high levels of employment, high minimum wages, and strong unions to defend wage levels. Under these conditions the working poor are an anomaly rather than an institutionalized feature of the economy. Otherwise, a guaranteed income becomes an industrial strategy to encourage investment into the low end of the wage distribution: wage supplements for the working poor are also wage subsidies to low-wage employers.

12. Cohen and Zysman, *Manufacturing Matters*, 131.

Labour Markets and

Inequality

o

A central question in the sociology of work is "Who gets the good jobs?" or, in other words, "What are the sources of inequality in the labour market?" For most people, the defining features of a good job would include high pay, pensions and other benefits, good working conditions, chances for promotion, job security, and the opportunity to use and develop one's skills. Obviously, individual effort plays some part in determining who gets these better jobs. More importantly, access to many of the more rewarding jobs in our society is contingent on higher educational attainment. In fact, "human capital theory" explains labour market inequalities primarily with reference to differences in educational credentials. From this perspective, individuals who invest more time and effort in education acquire more human capital that, in turn, allows them to compete more successfully for better jobs.

However, it is apparent that some people are more advantaged from birth, benefitting from the wealth and opportunities provided by their families. In addition, it is evident that some groups are much more disadvantaged in the labour market because of such factors as discrimination, lack of access to higher education, physical disability, or living in economically impoverished regions of the country. Labour market segmentation theory takes these realities into account in proposing an alternative explanation of employment inequalities. A segmentation model of the labour market proposes that good jobs and less rewarding jobs are found in distinctly different sectors of the labour market, that specific groups are, for a variety of reasons, overrepresented in the secondary (or marginal) labour market, and that large barriers restrict their movement into the primary labour market, even if they are qualified for the better jobs.

The articles in this section provide illustrative material useful in assessing these competing theories. We have chosen five readings that focus on specific disadvantaged groups in the Canadian labour market and the barriers they face in trying to obtain good jobs, or any jobs for that matter. Two of the readings discuss historical patterns of discrimination against specific racial groups, while the other three describe contemporary labour market inequalities. Since 1986, the federal government has attempted to assist four disadvantaged groups—women, people with disabilities, visible minorities, and aboriginal Canadians—by requiring that government departments, crown corporations, and government suppliers initiate programs intended to eliminate employment barriers. Since Part 5 of this reader is devoted to women's employment issues, the readings in this section discuss the employment experiences of members of the other three groups.

Agnes Calliste describes how, for a period of almost eighty years, black railway employees in Canada were restricted to jobs as sleeping car porters while only white employees competed for the better jobs. The origins of this racially split labour market can be traced to the railway companies' desire for cheap labour, as well as to overt racism on the part of employers, the federal immigration department, and the unions representing white railway employees. It was not until 1964 that the contractual arrangements discriminating against blacks were finally removed. Even then, concerns were raised about black porters trying "to take away the white man's jobs."

Such blatant racism and discrimination would not be tolerated in Canada today. But has racial discrimination in the labour market disappeared? The answer is "no," according to Jeffrey Reitz. Noting that there is considerably less racial conflict in Canada, compared to Britain, Reitz goes on to ask whether there is also less racial discrimination, but concludes that racial discrimination is equally common in Canada.

So why do we experience less racial conflict? Among other reasons, Reitz notes that many members of Canada's visible minority communities are first-generation immigrants. Individuals born in Canada, but still experiencing discrimination, might be less willing to accept it. In addition, our selective immigration policies have led to a better-educated group of immigrants who, compared to visible minority members in Britain or the United States, may experience somewhat less discrimination. Equally important, our multi-ethnic political and cultural system is somewhat more capable of responding to the concerns of visible minorities. But because the ethnic and racial composition of Canadian society is changing rapidly, we should not necessarily expect a continued low level of racial conflict. As Reitz observes, the issue of race will have to be given much more serious consideration.

Canadians with disabilities are another severely disadvantaged group in the labour market. In Canada today there are about 1.8 million working-age people with disabilities. It is estimated that about 80 percent are either unemployed or underemployed. Some cannot participate in the paid labour force, but many can with minimal assistance. Shona McKay describes some of the barriers to full and satisfying employment experienced by Canadians with disabilities. Buildings and equipment designed without the needs of the disabled in mind are part of the problem, as is the limited work experience of some disabled labour force participants. But the larger problem is attitudinal; many people have great difficulty believing that someone with a disability could do a job just as well as an able-bodied person. Changing these attitudes is a major challenge for employers, organized labour, organizations representing those with disabilities, and the government. Fortunately, as McKay documents, some progressive employers are making efforts to fully integrate people with disabilities into their work force.

Throughout this century, native Canadians have been among the most disadvantaged labour force participants. The placement of reservations in isolated, economically less developed regions created difficulties for aboriginal groups from the start. A government bureaucracy unwilling to allow native groups anything more than limited control over their own economic affairs compounded the problem. Inadequate education systems added to the dilemma, while discriminatory attitudes and behaviour reinforced labour market inequalities.

Resource development mega-projects in Canada's north have frequently been presented as a solution to problems of unemployment and underemployment among native groups. However, James Waldram's account of the Churchill–Nelson River Hydroelectric Project in northern Manitoba demonstrates just how limited the benefits of such projects have typically been. In this case, native labour force participants managed to obtain some of the unskilled construction jobs, but once this phase of the project was complete employment opportunities for local residents largely disappeared. Relatively few had received any training that might be useful in obtaining permanent employment. Ironically, once the project was complete and operating, traditional native employment options (fishing and trapping) were also reduced, since large-scale flooding of the region had damaged the environment.

Like Reitz, who insists that political leaders will have to make more efforts to counter racial inequalities in the labour market, and McKay, who calls for more efforts to reduce employment barriers faced by Canadians with disabilities, Waldram is critical of token efforts to reduce the employment disadvantages of aboriginal Canadians. He concludes that, with sufficient planning and effort by government and corporations, northern mega-projects might provide more employment options for native Canadians than has been the case in the past.

DISCUSSION QUESTIONS

o

1. Equality of access to higher education is an important social goal given that educational attainment and career success are highly correlated. Is equality of access to higher education a reality in Canada today?

2. "Poverty is not a structural problem; instead, it largely reflects the educational and motivational inadequacies of those who are poor." Discuss.

3. Do ethnically or racially split labour markets still exist in Canada today? How do such inequalities arise and how are they maintained?

4. Should governments be more proactive (via training programs, tax incentives, legislation requiring hiring quotas, penalties for noncompliance, and so on) in reducing the labour market barriers faced by disadvantaged groups?

5. Demographers project a labour shortage in Canada in a few decades, given low birth rates and an aging population. The federal government has begun to address this future problem by raising immigration quotas. What are the social implications of this solution? What additional sources of labour might be targeted?

6. Regional disparities in employment opportunities have existed in Canada for many decades. How did they emerge? Should anything be done about it? Why or why not?

SUGGESTED READINGS

o

Abella, Rosalie S. *Equality in Employment: A Royal Commission Report.* Ottawa: Supply and Services Canada, 1984.

Bienvenue, Rita M., and Jay E. Goldstein, eds. *Ethnicity and Ethnic Relations in Canada.* Toronto: Butterworths, 1985.

Economic Council of Canada. *New Faces in the Crowd: Economic and Social Impacts of Immigration.* Ottawa: Supply and Services Canada, 1991.

Rioux, Marcia H. "Labelled Disabled and Wanting to Work." In Research Studies of the Commission on Equality in Employment (Abella Commission). Ottawa: Supply and Services Canada, 1985.

Stabler, Jack C., and Eric C. Howe. "Native Participation in Northern Development: The Impending Crisis in the NWT." *Canadian Public Policy* 16 (1990): 262–83.

Sleeping Car Porters in Canada: An Ethnically Submerged Split Labour Market[*]

Agnes Calliste

INTRODUCTION

o

The history of black workers in Canada, particularly sleeping car porters, has been largely ignored in labour history.[1] Moreover, research on the Brotherhood of Sleeping Car Porters and its international president, A. Philip Randolph, has focused on the United States.[2] This paper examines the history of sleeping car porters in Canada, and argues that the submerged split labour market[3] in which whites monopolized the higher paid positions (for example, sleeping car conductor and dining car steward) and restricted blacks to portering was a result of market conditions (i.e., the need for cheap labour) and institutional racism.

Split labour market theory was formulated by Edna Bonacich to explain economic sources of ethnic antagonism. A split labour market exists when the cost of labour substantially differs along ethnic lines for the same work, or would differ if they did the same work. In labour markets split along ethnic lines, conflict develops among business (employers), higher-paid dominant labour, and lower-paid ethnic minority labour. Employers aim at having as cheap and docile a labour force as possible to compete effectively with other businesses. Higher-paid dominant labour feels very threatened by the introduction of cheaper labour into the market, fearing either displacement or reduction of wages. Such competition leads to forms of ethnic antagonism: exclusion (keeping lower-paid minority workers out of the territory) and caste (dividing "white work" from "black work"). Both forms

[*] Abridged from Agnes Calliste, "Sleeping Car Porters in Canada: An Ethnically Submerged Split Labour Market," Canadian Ethnic Studies 19, no. 1 (1987): 1–20. Reprinted by permission of the publisher and the author.

represent successful attempts on the part of the higher-paid group to exclude the cheaper group from competing for the same jobs.

B L A C K S   O N   T H E   R A I L R O A D S
o

Black Pullman porters had become a firmly entrenched North American tradition since the Pullman Palace Car Company was incorporated in 1867 as a manufacturer and operator of railroad sleeping cars. When new rail connections with Canada were completed in the 1880s and Pullman service from the United States to Canada began, the black porters came with the trains. Except for the Grand Trunk Railway (GTR) which employed black cooks and waiters in its dining cars, the Canadian Railway companies continued the tradition of hiring blacks almost exclusively as porters until the mid 1950s. The word porter had become synonymous with black. Prior to World War II, portering was an occupation entirely reserved for blacks. Thus, the majority of black men found in the cities were railway porters.[4] For example, in 1941 almost 50 percent of the employed black males in Montreal were railway porters.[5] The early black communities in Montreal and Winnipeg grew largely from the demand for segregated labour on the railways as American blacks were recruited by the Canadian railway companies, particularly the Canadian Pacific Railway (CPR). A number of blacks from Nova Scotia, North Battleford and Amber Valley also migrated to cities such as Montreal, Toronto and Winnipeg to work on the transcontinental trains which, by the 1920s, were crossing the nation regularly in five nights and four days.[6]

Three reasons have been suggested for Pullman's selection of blacks as porters on his sleeping cars. First, they were cheaper, both in terms of wage rates and degree of unionization. Blacks, particularly from the South, were more vulnerable to exploitation as cheap labour because they tended to be desperately poor. Given a tradition of paternalism, they were also less likely than whites to form unions, to make demands for improved conditions (including wages) and to engage in costly strikes. Second, the assumed social distance that existed between whites and blacks meant that the presence of black porters on sleeping cars was considered as impersonal and did not serve as a complicating factor in the intimacies which travel by sleeping cars necessitated. Porters also constantly witnessed the indiscretions that occurred on long trips. The company realized that since white passengers would encounter black porters in no other social context, they were content in their travels—and Pullman desired above all else the contentment of his clientele. Third, Pullman officials were aware that blacks had been traditionally assigned service roles, and that it was a sign of status among whites to be waited on by them.[7] Passengers on the sleeping car could forget the small worries that often trouble people traveling great distances. Porters stowed the passengers' baggage and thereafter ministered to all their needs and wants, including even the shining of their shoes. In order to guarantee the porter's efficiency and because of obvious economies, Pullman took care that the porter's welfare should be inextricably tied up with the type of service he gave passengers. The porter was paid a low monthly wage and had to depend upon passengers to augment his income through tips.

The Canadian Railway companies hired blacks almost exclusively as porters for similar reasons.[8] The process of forming an ethnically submerged split labour market continued in the 1920s when the Canadian railway companies reclassified work categories in order to limit blacks, except for those already otherwise employed, to being porters only. The restriction of blacks to portering on the Canadian National Railways (CNR) began in 1926 when the company took over the Grand Trunk Railway (GTR) and started replacing black employees in the dining car service on former GTR cars with white help. Consequently, a Board of Arbitration heard a complaint made by the black employees that their displacement was contrary to agreement, a violation of status and seniority rights, and created uneasiness as to their security in the minds of other black employees in similar service—an uneasiness which might, in the minds of these employees, be attributed to ethnic prejudice. The CNR claimed that its actions were due to the difficulty of obtaining competent black help. Evidently, the CNR retained the black cooks but the waiters were laid off. A compromise arrangement was agreed to, allowing the displaced black waiters to take employment as porters with full seniority. Black employees who were displaced from waiters' positions on the dining cars were continued on the payroll until they could be assigned to porters' positions.[9]. . .

It is questionable whether the CNR had difficulty in obtaining competent black help. The railway companies had benefitted so greatly from the racist labour practices at that time that prior to the early 1950s many of the best educated and most capable black men in Canada worked as porters. The story of Emerson Mahon makes the point. In 1950 he was a teacher in Grenada, West Indies, and later taught elementary school at Gypsumville, Manitoba. Later he obtained a B.Sc. in Zoology from the University of Manitoba as well as a high school teacher's certificate. Finding it difficult to get a teaching job after graduation, he worked as a CPR porter until retirement. Mahon was not unique. Stanley Clyke graduated from Acadia University with a B.Sc. degree, was king of the campus and was studying medicine; Clay Lewis graduated from Morehouse College with a major in Business Administration. These men worked as railway porters. The CPR "commendations" file also showed that many of its porters were highly educated; all were thoroughly intelligent and resourceful.[10] The harsh irony is that such men accepted jobs as porters largely because the railway companies offered the best opportunities available for black men. . . .

Some researchers[11] have argued that because black labour was cheaper, white workers and their unions erected defensive barriers (for example, exclusion) against the threat of being undermined. While craft unions tended to create protective barriers from competition,[12] one would have expected industrial unions to welcome blacks as members. However, in the early 1900s, the pervasive racism and lack of class consciousness counteracted this logical incentive so that blacks were either excluded or denied equal participation in most industrial unions (for example, the [Canadian Brotherhood of Railway Employees] CBRE).

The literature on occupational ethnic segregation (caste) also emphasizes the role of ethnic typing of work in occupational segregation.[13] Employers, dominant workers and a substantial number of Canadians, including government, shared the same stereotyped conception of what jobs were appropriate or inappropriate for blacks. As W.D. Scott, Superintendent of Immigration stated in 1918:

> Coloured labour is not generally speaking in demand in Canada and it is not only regarded as the lowest grade, but it is the last to be taken on and the first to be discharged in most enterprises.[14]

Portering was normatively defined as an appropriate occupation for blacks. Indeed, it was a menial job with low wages, with little or no job security and very limited opportunities for advancement.[15] In 1920 CPR porters' monthly salary ranged from $75.00 to a maximum of $85.00 after three years. A buffet sleeping car porter's monthly wage was $92.50 with no increments. Out of his meagre salary, a CPR porter had to buy his meals, uniform, a shoe shine kit and even the polish for the passengers' shoes.[16] It was necessary to depend upon tips from passengers to supplement this inadequate pay.

On the other hand, the occupations of sleeping car conductor and dining car steward with greater responsibility and better pay and which required the exercise of formal authority over non-black workers or non-black clientele were normatively defined as inappropriate for blacks.[17] Although a porter in charge did the jobs of both a porter and a sleeping car conductor, both the CPR and the Order of Railway Conductors, for example, argued that black sleeping car porters were not suited for the position of sleeping car conductor.[18] Moreover, porters-in-charge received considerably less pay than did the white conductor for performing one job. In 1951 a sleeping car conductor's monthly wage during his first year of service on the CNR was $286.57; a sleeping car porter in charge made $213.57 and a sleeping car porter $188.57.[19]. . .

The importation of temporary migrant workers from the United States, particularly from the South, was also used to create and maintain a double split labour market between black Canadian and imported black American labour on the one hand, and between black and white Canadian labour on the other. American blacks were brought to Canada as porters by Pullman Company and the Canadian railroads after 1886. In Montreal, for example, American blacks formed the largest portion (approximately 50 per cent) of the black population in 1928.[20] Later the CNR was pressured to hire its porters from within Canada[21] because its porters were unionized in 1918. The CPR, however, recruited porters predominantly from the United States, particularly from the South, both as seasonal workers for the summer tourist season and also as regular workers on six months contracts which could be renewed. Each spring, an agent for the CPR visited black colleges in the South and approximately 300 porters were hired for the summer tourist season. The majority of these men were returned to the United States when their service was no longer required.[22] But more important, the CPR recruited porters as regular workers on six months contracts. In 1949 of the 585 porters on the CNR, 340 were Canadian born and 96 were U.S. born. About fifty per cent of the CPR's 600-700 porters were American born, particularly from the South.[23]

Recruitment of porters from the United States was partly a product of labour shortage, such as during the wars. In 1917-1918, for example, 392 porters were recruited from the United States to work in the Western District. At the end of the war in 1919 only 78 men were recruited.[24] It is also evident that employers wanted cheap and docile labour. The CPR used imported black Americans to displace black Canadian and West Indian porters who attempted to organize themselves.[25] In spring 1924, for example, it was reported that the Welfare Committee of porters met with the CPR.

> While they were seeking an adjustment of impending grievances, a statement acknowledging the present working conditions to be entirely satisfactory was presented to the porters of the Western Region with the option of signing same or quitting service. When this 'Al Capone' policy was put over by Mr. Mathews, Simpson and lieutenants, with the approval of Mr. Cooper, then, without an agreement or compromise of any sort, the committee men were bluntly told to get back to their jobs at once, that Southern immigrants were on the ground to take their place (and it was no bluff as several tourist car loads were then in the yards at Winnipeg being fed and lodged). A number of men were deliberately put out of the service at that time with no pretext of cause. R.J. Hines of the Winnipeg Committee, and D. Sykes of the Montreal Committee were among those who were forced to sacrifice seniority rights, and to seek employment with the Canadian National Railroad where they have continued their valuable service to the travelling public.[26]

The CPR reserved the right to dispense with the service of a porter at any time without being required to give any reason for doing so. On entering the service each porter was required to sign the following clause:

> In consideration of the Canadian Pacific Railway Company, hereinafter called 'the Company' taking me into its services as sleeping car porter, I hereby agree to work as such for the Company on any of its different runs so long as my services may be required, it being understood that my engagement may be terminated by the Company without notice, and without assigning any reason therefor, at any time except during the course of any particular run, and moreover, that it is subject to the terms hereinafter stated.[27]

The company claimed that this clause was necessary because sleeping car porters' work was of a domestic nature and involved close personal relations between the porters and sleeping car travellers. Other employees were not required to sign such a contract. This unfavourable contract further weakened porters' "market position."[28]

Although the CPR's recruitment of American porters slowed down during the depression, and some black Canadians were hired, the importation of foreign labour continued in spite of high unemployment[29] on the grounds that "there were not available sufficient black men of experience and character in Canada to meet its labour force needs."[30] Although the records do not indicate the characteristics which the CPR desired of its porters, it is questionable whether the company could not find sufficient experienced men in Canada. The CNR porters' staff in 1931 comprised about "75% of ex-CPR service trained and experienced porters."[31] Moreover, in summer 1931 the CNR had informed the CPR of its surplus porters (about 60 of them). The CPR responded to local pressure to exclude imported American workers by hiring a few black Canadians. In summer 1931 ten or twelve men were hired in Winnipeg, the Western region, to replace recently imported men who were returned to the United States.[32] This, however, was regarded as a mere gesture. Similarly, CPR's local advertisements for porters were regarded by the CBRE as excuses for importing American men. As McGuire, Chairman of the Brotherhood, wrote to the Honourable W.A. Gordon, Acting Minister of Immigration in July 1932:

> For a number of years past it has been the practice of the Canadian Railways to insert advertisements in certain important daily newspapers in their Parlor and Sleeping Car services. Canadian citizens who applied for such positions were invariably advised that the Railway had succeeded in obtaining all the help of this class they required. Following the insertion of these advertisements the Railways would then make representations to the Department of Immigration, claiming that they were unable to obtain in Canada the class of labour required and asking to be granted permission to bring large numbers of United States negroes into this country, for their summer train services particularly . . . . Even as late as this year, the Canadian Pacific Railway brought more than one hundred United States negroes into Canada for their summer train service, while plenty of experienced colored porters were available in this country, and are at present unemployed. Information we have received indicates that a number of Canadian colored citizens who are taxpayers in Montreal, Toronto and Winnipeg are drawing unemployment relief, while United States citizens have obtained this class of work on the Canadian Railways. [33] . . .

In keeping with the style of powerful, anti-union corporations, the CPR dismissed and/or intimidated porters who attempted to organize themselves. In 1919, for example, when the Order of Sleeping Car Porters began unionizing the porters on the CPR, the company responded by discharging thirty-six porters without giving cause. Seven of the dismissed men demanded a formal hearing under the 1907 Industrial Disputes Investigation Act. In early 1920 a three-man board took evidence. The porters insisted that they had been fired because of their union activities. The CPR officials claimed that the company was exercising its rights according to the contract and refused to give any reason. Moreover, the CPR refused to recognize the bargaining rights of the porters' grievance committee, chaired by one of the dismissed workers. The final decision was two to one against those dismissed.[34] The company, eager to stifle the porters' efforts to organize, recognized the Porters Mutual Benefit Association and requested that the association send to management a grievance committee (i.e., the Welfare Committee of Porters) [35] to discuss matters of mutual interest to employer and employee. In other words, the company ignored the Order of Sleeping Car Porters and preferred to negotiate with the porters through a company-initiated welfare committee which it could control. . . .

UNIONIZATION OF CPR PORTERS

o

Although the Order of Sleeping Car Porters was organized in Canada in 1918 and the Brotherhood of Sleeping Car Porters (BSCP) was organized in New York in 1925, it was not until 1942 that porters with the CPR were unionized and an agreement was worked out in 1945.[36] As in the United States, the fight for collective bargaining rights was most difficult. The company was opposed to outside representation and tried to intimidate the organizers. Some of the porters, particularly the older ones, were reluctant to organize and/or join the union for fear that they might be fired. Previous attempts at organizing had been crushed and the ringleaders fired. Since many of the porters were temporary migrant workers, they were likely to be intimidated and to lack interest in unions since they need not endure undesirable working conditions forever. Moreover, although the porter's grievances were many and serious,[37] the feeling persisted that his job was a good one and some porters were fearful of disturbing one of the largest employers of blacks. Some families had been working with the company for two and even three generations.[38]

A new phase of activism began, however, as a result of World War II and changes in labour legislation protecting workers' right to organize.[39] Membership in the BSCP grew rapidly in Canada, moving on the CPR alone from 153 in 1942 to 620 the following year.[40] With union recognition came higher pay with overtime, shorter working hours, an agreed grievance procedure and a greater measure of self-respect.[41] A regular porter with a good run (i.e., good tips) could adequately support his family,[42] if he did not have to support two homes, one in the United States and one in Canada.

Prior to World War II migrant porters' wives and families were not allowed to visit them. The Canadian Immigration Department discouraged such visits. The excuse given was that since porters were not permanently located in one place, their wives would be better off in the United States. The Department's real reason was to discourage any increase in the black population in Canada. As the District Superintendent of Immigration in Winnipeg wrote:

> For obvious reasons I do not think we would want to add to our coloured population and I do not believe that the arrangement with the Canadian Pacific Railway for the admission of these coloured porters contemplated the entry of their families. We have been discouraging their admission as visitors or otherwise, by every means possible here on this assumption.[43]

Given the demand for porters during the war, the CPR in an effort to retain some of its reliable workers in Winnipeg, made representation to Immigration on their behalf to allow their wives to visit them from the United States. As Mr. Simpson, Superintendent of Sleeping and Dining Cars, advised Immigration, "unless entry was granted he was afraid he would lose some of his porters as they intimated their intention to return to the United States and their families."[44] There was a change in immigration practices to accommodate labour force needs. In August 1943 it was decided that each case be dealt with on its merits and that where Mr. Simpson was satisfied that the porter in question would cease his employment and return to the United States, favourable consideration be given for a maximum of 30 days.[45]

Denial of temporary entry to two porters' wives to visit their husbands in Toronto in 1947 led the Toronto Division of the BSCP to propose to A.J. Joliffe, Commissioner of Immigration, that after a porter had worked regularly for two and one-half to three years for the CPR, he should be classified as a permanent employee with the company. In 1946, seventy-three of the migrant porters had been with the CPR for 2-5 years. The Brotherhood argued that in addition to the hardship of being separated, it was a financial burden on the husbands "to keep up two homes, one in Canada and one in the United States."[46] Moreover, it was in Canada's interest to have satisfied workers. "A man can give better service to the travelling public, when he is satisfied and with his family and not liable to get himself into trouble."[47]

The postwar period was marked by a new sense of militancy in the Brotherhood of Sleeping Car Porters. One effect of this militancy was an attempt to break the CPR's control over its temporary porters. The Brotherhood realised that a migrant or transient porter was a poor union man. Moreover, while the Immigration Branch thought that a migrant worker took his problem with him when he was exported, the Brotherhood realised that transient porters could not contribute to the development of the black community.

The Superintendent of the Eastern District advised the Commissioner of Immigration against granting immigrant status to temporary porters. He states:

While it may raise certain difficulties for the C.P.R. in securing and holding Sleeping Car porters from the United States, I am inclined to be of the opinion that no encouragement should be given for these persons to settle in Canada.[48]

Realising, however, that it would be difficult to refuse these porters immigrant status, the Immigration Branch decided to grant immigrant status, if admissible, to porters who had been in Canada for at least two years.[49] In any case, migrant porters' labour was becoming expensive partly because of unionization and partly because of increasing opportunities for blacks in the United States. Thus, it was more profitable for the CPR "to keep good employees rather than recruit inexperienced men whose qualifications were not known."[50]

Moreover, partly due to the demand for porters during World War II, the railway companies began hiring whites as porters, particularly in the Western provinces. At the same time, the CNR refused to hire blacks as dining car kitchen staff on former GTR cars.[51] However, the enactment of the Canada Fair Employment Practices Act in 1953 which prohibited ethnic and religious discrimination in employment and membership in trade unions,[52] gave porters' unions the leverage they needed to combat discrimination in railway employment. . . .

THE FINAL STRUGGLE

o

In September 1961 an enquiry was launched by the national committee on human rights of the Canadian Labour Congress (CLC). The report found discrimination, but blamed the railway. The porters contended that the fault lay with the union contract. According to Sid Blum, associate secretary of the CLC Human Rights Committee, the CNR, as well as other Canadian and North American railways had "in the past" practised a policy of racial discrimination against blacks and in particular in the promotion of black employees to supervisory positions.[53] He reported that

> The collective agreement does restrict the promotion opportunities of sleeping car porters (originally a 'Negro field of employment') and these restrictions appear to have been influenced by the racial discriminatory employment policies of the company in the years up to the passage of the Canada Fair Employment Practices Act.[54]

The committee's recommendation that Groups I and II be amalgamated was rejected by both groups. Williams labelled the CLC report as a "a whitewash and a carbon copy" to suit the trade union hierarchy.[55] It is difficult to accept Blum's argument that the national officers of the CBRT [formerly CBRE] did not practise racial discrimination against black sleeping car porters given their restriction to promotion in the collective agreement. While the collective agreement did not mention race or ethnicity, prior to World

War II "blacks" and "sleeping car porters" were synonymous. Although H.A. Chappell, national president of CBRT, in 1953 had informed CNR management that he was personally concerned about the lack of promotion for qualified blacks on the CNR,[56] the CBRT did not follow up on Chappell's suggestions after his death.[57] Moreover, the evidence suggests that prior to the porters' struggle for fair employment practices in the 1950s, the CBRT did not try to remove the discriminatory seniority groupings from the collective agreement.[58] There is also the suggestion that blacks were accepted in the union in 1919 on the condition that porters and dining car locals maintain their separate identity. This segregation was intended to protect the white employees from competition from blacks.[59] Moreover, the company claimed that the problem lay with the union contract.[60] This is consistent with split labour market theory which interprets a submerged split labour market as a victory for higher paid workers. The evidence suggests, however, that the caste system on the CNR was a result of a collaboration between the higher paid group and employers. While the union might not have directly influenced the CNR's discriminatory hiring policies, it sanctioned the discriminatory promotion policies (for example, through the collective agreement as discussed above).

Local 130 laid a formal complaint of racial discrimination against its national union under the Fair Employment Practices Act. Local 130 had "a top labour lawyer" and used massive national media publicity to its advantage. In order to avoid embarrassment, in 1963 the Joint Protective Board of the Sleeping, Dining and Parlour Car section of the CBRT approved a merger of the two groups and a combining of seniority lists. Opponents of the merger, however, won the right to a referendum on the question.[61]

The result of the referendum, which was held in January 1964, was an approval of the merger. Out of 843 eligible voters, 536 abstained from casting their ballots. Of the 307 who voted, 196 voted in favour of the proposition, which was negatively worded, i.e., "not in favour" of the merger, and 111 voted against. Under the CBRT constitution, however, all abstentions were recorded as votes against the proposition and the final count was: 196 for and 647 against (i.e., approximately 77 per cent in favour of the merger).

All four Group II locals had completely boycotted the referendum due to a belief that the numerical superiority of Group I made the defeat of the proposal to merge a foregone conclusion. The five Group I locals, however, unsuccessfully sought an injunction to block the amalgamation on the grounds that the referendum was "misleading", and consequently, the amalgamation on the grounds and subsequent loss of positional rights were forced on them by the union.[62] Their petitions and attempts to win the support of passengers against porters trying "to take away the white man's jobs" also failed. Amalgamation led to further ethnic antagonism.[63]

Although the CNR agreed to the amalgamation of the seniority lists, management wanted to maintain promotional classification seniority structure within the sleeping and dining car department. The CBRT, however, objected on the grounds of racial discrimination.[64]

The amalgamation of the two groups opened the way for porters' being promoted to sleeping car conductor, and inspector, as well as for being eligible for employment in the dining car. It also meant that the porter instructor was no longer in a discriminatory category with less pay, but became an inspector or supervisor. Indeed, many porters displaced dining car employees. Williams, for example, a first rate employee with 34 years of service was promoted to conductor and later to supervisor.[65] Both the CNR and CPR porters' victory effected a significant reduction of tremendous discrimination in employment in Canada.[66]

NOTES

o

This article would have been impossible without the assistance from various people, in particular Daphne, Marriett and Matthew Hamilton, David Millar, and Barbara Roberts. Funding for the research in its initial stages was provided by Employment and Immigration Canada.

1. See for example, W.E. Greening, *It Was Never Easy 1908-1958: A History of the Canadian Brotherhood of Railway, Transport and General Workers* (Ottawa, 1961).

2. B.R. Brazeal, *The Brotherhood of Sleeping Car Porters: Its Origins and Development* (New York: Harper and Brothers, 1946); J. Anderson, *A. Philip Randolph: A Biographical Portrait* (New York: Harcourt Brace Jovanovich, Inc., 1972).

3. E. Bonacich, "A Theory of Ethnic Antagonism: The Split Labor Market," *American Sociological Review* 37 (1972):547-59; "Abolition, the Extension of Slavery, and the Position of Free Blacks: A Study of Split Labor Markets in the United States, 1830-1863," *American Journal of Sociology* 81 (3) (1975):601-628; "Advanced Capitalism and Black/White Relations in the United States: A Split Labor Market Interpretation," *American Sociological Review* 41 (1976):34-51.

4. I. Greaves, *The Negro in Canada* (Orillia: Packet-Times Press, 1930):53.

5. H.H. Potter, "The Occupational Adjustment of Montreal Negroes, 1948-48" (M.A. thesis, McGill University, 1949):29. See also W.E. Israel, "The Montreal Negro Community" (M.A. thesis, McGill University, 1928). In 1928 it was estimated that approximately 90 per cent of the black men in Montreal were in the railroad service. Israel, *op. cit.*, p. 71.

6. W.E. Israel, *op. cit.*; Interviews, May 28, 1982; June 14, 1982; May 20, 1983.

7. Though the company's position was that it hired blacks out of concern for their welfare, the fact is that Pullman hired very few of them in its repair and erection shops; in addition, management explicitly excluded blacks from service as conductors. B.R. Brazeal, *op. cit.*; W.H. Harris, *Keeping the Faith: A. Philip Randolph, Milton P. Webster, and the Brotherhood of Sleeping Car Porters, 1925-37* (Urbana: University of Illinois Press, 1977).

8. Public Archives of Canada (hereinafter PAC), Records of Immigration Branch, RG76, Vol. 576, File 816222, C.E. Brower to P. Heenan, the Minister of Labour, April 5, 1930; Brower to R.B. Bennett, Prime Minister, June 12, 1931; Interview, July 30, 1983.

9. PAC, Canadian Brotherhood of Railway Transport and General Workers Papers, MG28, 1215 Vol. 81, File—"The Race Issue," J.E. McGuire to A.R. Mosher, November 6, 1942; *The Labour Gazette*, 27 (January 1927):17-18

10. "The Ambassador of Sleep," *CPR Staff Bulletin* (n.d.); *Winnipeg Tribune* (n.d.); Interviews, July 7, 1982; May 5, 1983; May 19, 1983; July 28, 1983; May 27, 1986. See R. Winks, *The Blacks in Canada* (Montreal: McGill University Press, 1971):425 for a discussion of A. Blanchette and S. Grizzle who worked as CPR porters at one time. I am grateful to Mr. Dave Jones, Assistant Archivist, of CP Rail for sending me clippings on CPR porters. See also S. Young, "Super Porter," *Canadian National Magazine* (January 1949):12, 24.

11. E. Bonacich, "Advanced Capitalism and Black/White Relations"; H. Northrup, *Organized Labour and the Negro* (New York: Harper and Brothers, 1944).

12. Craft unions tend to create barriers to protect their members from competition with all non-members (not just from blacks). Such barriers have historically also been utilized to prevent blacks from gaining access to such occupations. W. Harris, *The Harder We Run: Black Workers since the Civil War* (New York: Oxford University Press, 1982); R. Winks, *Blacks in Canada*; Interviews, June 14, 1982; September 6, 1983.

13. R. Kaufman, "The Impact of Industrial and Occupational Structure on Black-White Employment Allocation," *American Sociological Review* 51 (June 1986):310-323; R. Marshall, "The Economics of Racial Discrimination: A Survey," *Journal of Economic Literature* 12 (September 1974):849-871.

14. PAC, RG76, Vol. 566, File 810666, W.D. Scott to W.W. Cory, April 25, 1918.

15. Prior to the implementation of the Canada Fair Employment Practices Act the only supervisory positions.

16. A CPR porter's meals cost about $16.00 a month more than a CNR porter's meals on the eastern lines. Initially, a CNR porter had to buy a shoe shine kit but the shoe polish and the porter's uniform were supplied free by the company. Later the kit was also provided free by the company. *The Labour Gazette*, 20; H. Potter, *op. cit.*; Interviews, December 21, 1982; May 23, 1986.

17. Occupations which have been normatively defined as appropriate for blacks are those which have low status, low earnings, poor working conditions, menial task performance or heavy physical demands, and high level of routinization. Occupations which have been normatively defined as inappropriate for blacks are those which require interaction with other workers or clientele as a supervisor or equal, those which involve the exercise of formal authority over (white) clientele, or the exercise of informal authority due to technical expertise and/or specialization and low routinization. See for example, R. Kaufman, "Racial Discrimination and Labour Market Segmentation" (Ph.D. thesis, University of Wisconsin-Madison, 1981):174.

18. S. Blum, "Education, Equality and Brotherhood" (Montreal: Canadian Labour Reports, 1958).

19. Trains with less than three sleeping cars were operated by porters in charge. Sleeping car conductors were only assigned to trains with three or more sleeping

cars. "Collective Agreement between the CNR and the CBRT for Employees in Sleeping, Dining and Parlor Car Service" (June 1951):37-38. I am grateful to Messrs. James Durant and Coulter States for giving me access to their files.

20. W.E. Israel, *op. cit.*, p. 80.

21. There is the suggestion that the CNR might have recruited some porters from the United States. W.E. Israel, *op. cit.*; PAC, RG76, Vol. 576, File 816222, Part 2, C.E. Brower to the Minister of Labour, April 5, 1930; C.E. Brower to R.B. Bennett, June 12, 1931; Interview, May 21, 1982. Avery also notes that strike breakers were frequently imported in Canada in spite of the Alien Labour Act of 1897. D. Avery, *"Dangerous Foreigners": European Immigrant Workers and Labour Radicalism in Canada, 1896-1932* (Toronto: McClelland and Stewart, 1979).

22. PAC, RG76, Vol. 576, File 816222, CPR to T. Gelley, April 20, 1920.

23. M. Porter, "Three Thousand Nights on Wheels," *Maclean's Magazine* (March 15, 1949):17; "The Ambassador of Sleep," p. 2.

24. PAC, RG76, Vol. 576, File 816222, Part 2, T. Gelley, Commissioner of Immigration, Western District to the Secretary, Department of Immigration and Colonization, April 22, 1920.

25. Interview, August 27, 1986. Winks points out that quite often West Indians were the source of great activism among porters. Thus, in the 1920s the CPR retained North American blacks while discharging West Indians. R. Winks, *op. cit.*, pp. 325, 425; See also PAC, RG76, Vol. 576, File 816222, C.E. Brower to P. Heenan, Minister of Labour, April 5, 1930; C.E. Brower to R.B. Bennett, June 12, 1931; Canadian Brotherhood of Railway Employees to the Acting Minister of Immigration, July 19, 1932.

26. PAC, RG76, Vol 576, File 816222, Part 6, C.E. Brower to G. Robertson, Minister of Labour, August 7, 1931.

27. *The Labour Gazette,* 20 (March 1920), p. 241. See pp. 245-6 for the other terms of the porter's contract.

28. E. Bonacich, "Advanced Capitalism and Black/White Relations."

29. PAC, RG76, Vol. 576, File 816222, Part 6, C.E. Brower to P. Heenan, Minister of Labour, April 5, 1930; C.E. Brower to R.B. Bennett, June 12, 1931; J.E. McGuire to the Acting Minister of Immigration, July 19, 1932.

30. RG76, Vol. 577, File 816222, Part 6, C.E. Brower to P. Heenan, Minister of Labour, April 5, 1930.

31. PAC, RG76, Vol. 576, File 816222, Part 6, C.E. Brower to G. Robertson, Minister of Labour, August 7, 1931; *The Montreal Daily Star,* May 19, 1928.

32. *Ibid.*

33. PAC, RG76. Vol. 576, File 816222, Part 6, J.E. McGuire to W.A. Gordon, Acting Minister of Immigration, July 19, 1932.

34. *The Labour Gazette,* 20. The porters' efforts were not entirely a failure for they caused the idea of organization to take root in the porters' minds. At the same time the Board of Arbitration realised that the porters had serious grievances and recommended an increase in wages to bring them on par with the CNR porters.

35. The Welfare Committee of Porters consisted of 15 members, three from each of the five districts of Quebec, Ontario, Manitoba, Alberta and British Columbia. PAC, RG76, Vol. 577, File 816222, C.E. Brower to G. Robertson, August 7, 1931; Correspondence of the Porters Welfare Committee, 1940-1942. I am grateful to

Mrs. Vinton Russell-Padmore for giving me access to her files on the Welfare Committee of Porters, the Porters Mutual Benefit Association and the BSCP.

36. "Agreement between the Canadian Pacific Railway and the Sleeping Car Porters in its employ represented by the BSCP" (June 1, 1945); Interviews, February 17, 1983; July 30, 1983; August 11, 1986.

37. Correspondence of the Welfare Committee of Porters, 1939-42; Correspondence between C.E. Russell and A.P. Randolph, May 4, 1939 to October 5, 1939; Interviews, May 28, 1982; July 7, 1982; February 17, 1983; August 25-29, 1986; September 2-3, 1986.

38. Interviews, February 17, 1983; July 30, 1983; August 11, 1986; August 25, 1986; August 28, 1986; "The Ambassador of Sleep."

39. See E. Lorensten and E. Woolner, "Fifty years of Labour Legislation in Canada," *The Labour Gazette* 50 (September 1951):1412-29, 1432-59.

40. B.R. Brazeal, *op. cit.*, p. 223. A.P. Randolph, international president of the BSCP, realizing that the Brotherhood would be more powerful if it represented all porters in North America, attempted to get the CNR porters to join his union. Although the CNR porters were dissatisfied with their representation on the CBRE, they preferred to maintain their membership with the CBRE partly because they had better working conditions than the CPR porters and partly because the BSCP was an international union. A.P. Randolph to C.E. Russell, May 10, 1939; PAC, MG28, Vol. 83; H. Rhodes to A.R. Mosher, July 10, 1945; A.R. Mosher to CNR Porters, July 17, 1945; J.A. Robinson to A.R. Mosher, August 1, 1945.

41. D.G. Hill, "Negroes in Toronto: A Sociological Study of a Minority Group" (Ph.D.: dissertation, University of Toronto, 1960): 107p. 107; Interviews, February 17, 1983; August 11, 1986; August 25-29, 1986; September 2-3, 1986.

42. C. Best, *That Lonesome Road* (New Glasgow: Clarion Publishing Company, 1977):249.

43. PAC, RG76, Vol 577, File 816222, District Superintendent of Immigration, Winnipeg, to the Acting Commissioner of Immigration, August 4, 1943.

44. *Ibid.*

45. PAC, RG76, Vol. 577, File 816222, C.E. Smith to A.L. Joliffe, August 7, 1943; Acting Director of Immigration to C.E. Smith, August 10, 1943.

46. PAC, RG76, Vol. 577, File 816222, J.F. Cromwell to A.L. Joliffe, February 26, 1947.

47. *Ibid.*

48. PAC, RG76, Vol. 577, File 816222, J. McFarlane to the Commissioner of Immigration, May 14, 1947.

49. PAC, RG76, Vol. 577, File 816222, note to and from C.E. Smith, May 1947.

50. PAC, RG76, Vol. 577, File 816222, J. McFarlane to the Commissioner of Immigration, May 5, 1947.

51. PAC, MG28, I215, Vol. 81, S.H. Eighteen to J.E. McGuire, November 1, 1943.

52. *Prefix to Statutes, 1952-53* (Ottawa: Queen's Printer, 1953):27-29.

53. PAC, MG28, V75, Vol. 34, S. Blum, "Inquiry into Charges of Racial Discrimination Against the Canadian Brotherhood of Railway, Transport and General Workers by Mr. Lee Williams, Chairman, Local 130, Canadian Brotherhood of Railway, Transport and General Workers," (1961):2.

54. *Ibid.*, p. 3.

55. *Winnipeg Free Press*, September 25, 1961. Williams thought that Blum and the Jewish Labour Committee could not be impartial probably because of a per-

ceived conflict of interest. The JLC was partly funded by the CBRT. Thus Williams tended to rely on federal politicians (such as J.G. Diefenbaker and L. Pearson) for support rather than on the JLC and the Manitoba Labour Committee for Human Rights, PAC, MG28, V75, Vol. 75, File 45-10, D. Orlikow to S. Blum, August 15, 1961; Interviews, June 14, 1982; September 6, 1983.

56. Chappell suggested to the CNR management that blacks be promoted to supervisory positions (e.g. platform inspectors) which were not covered by the collective agreement. PAC, MG28, I173, Vol. 34, H.A. Chappell to H.B. Parr, December 30, 1954.

57. PAC, MG28, I173, Vol. 8, File "Jewish Labour Committee of Canada 1961," A. Borovoy to S. Blum, May 14, 1961.

58. See for example, PAC, MG28, I215, Vols. 14 and 81.

59. Interview, August 27, 1986.

60. Several porters recalled that when Local 130 decided to take the CNR to court, they were informed by the company that the discrimination in hiring practices was purely a union matter. Interviews, August 25-29, 1986.

61. PAC, MG28, I215, Vol. 14; *The Labour Gazette*, 64 (April 1964):262; *Winnipeg Tribune*, October 16, 1963; November 22, 1963.

62. PAC, MG28, I215, Vol. 14, M.W. Wright to H. Walsh, May 25, 1964; *The Labour Gazette*, 64; *Winnipeg Tribune*, June 4, 1964.

63. Apparently, ethnic antagonism after amalgamation varied by region (for example, ex-porters in Nova Scotia reported more antagonism than those in Quebec); Interviews, May 23-June 26, 1986; August 25-29, 1986.

64. *Winnipeg Free Press*, January 16, 1964.

65. Interviews, June 14, 1982; September 6, 1983.

66. Few porters left the railroads before the 1950s. Of those who did, many of them described the difficulty in transcending the barriers to other areas of employment such as bus driver and civil servant. Interviews, May 5, 1983; July 12, 1983; See also D. Hill, "Negroes in Toronto," *op. cit.*

Less Racial Discrimination in Canada, or Simply Less Racial Conflict?: Implications of Comparisons with Britain[*]

Jeffrey G. Reitz

The view of Canada as comparatively tolerant of racial minorities underlies much of government policy on racial discrimination, but is unfortunately not supported by available evidence. The comparative evidence suggests instead a rather different view—that what may be most distinctive about Canada, in the field of minority relations, is a low potential for racial conflict and tension, not a lesser underlying degree of discrimination. This revised view, if correct, would have important policy implications. It would imply, first, that racial discrimination should have higher priority as an issue in Canada. Other implications go deeper. If lack of conflict explains a failure to address racial discrimination more determinedly, then to achieve change, it may be necessary to reexamine the entire process for establishing priorities in this area....

COMPARATIVE EVIDENCE ON RACIAL DISCRIMINATION: BRITAIN VS. CANADA

o

Credible comparative evidence on racial discrimination in Canada compared to Britain or the United States is sparse, but the evidence that exists runs counter to the usual assumption of less discrimination in Canada. Our interest here is specifically in discriminatory behaviour, that is to say, the denial of access to jobs and other significant resources in society, solely on the basis of race. Such direct discrimination is a clear public policy concern.[1]

✠ Abridged from Jeffrey G. Reitz, "Less Racial Discrimination in Canada, or Simply Less Racial Conflict?: Implications of Comparisons with Britain," *Canadian Public Policy* 14, no. 4 (1988): 424–41. Reprinted by permission of the publisher and the author.

Racial discrimination should be distinguished from attitudes to racial minorities, whether publicly or privately expressed or acknowledged. Comparisons of attitude surveys on race issues have been attempted (cf. Richmond, 1976b; Henry, 1978), but results are ambiguous not only because of non-comparable response categories, but because verbal statements of attitudes may differ between countries, even when the underlying degree of discriminatory behaviour does not.[2] Behavioral data are needed here, not attitudinal data.

The most important behavioral information concerns employment. Generally, in Britain racial minorities are less well off then they are in Canada.... West Indian men in Britain are substantially less well-educated than whites, have lower occupational status, earn somewhat less when employed full time, and have almost double the white unemployment rates. In Canada, West Indian men have comparatively high levels of education in relation to other groups. While their incomes are lower than the incomes of whites, their unemployment rates are only marginally higher than white unemployment rates. Thus West Indian men in Canada experience less economic disadvantage compared to West Indian men in Britain. In Britain, Asians, mainly Indians and Pakistanis, are relatively better situated than are West Indians, but so are Asians in Canada, including many Chinese and Indo-Chinese as well as Indo-Pakistanis.

The higher status for Canadian racial minorities does not necessarily reflect less discrimination. Higher status is expected because occupationally-selective Canadian immigration policies have brought more highly educated and employable immigrants to Canada, and because the buoyant Canadian economy provides opportunities for minorities, insulating them from the 'last hired, first fired' syndrome.

Actual racial discrimination in employment in Britain and Canada can be compared in behavioral data gathered from experimental field trials. In Toronto, such discrimination field trials were conducted by the Social Planning Council of Metropolitan Toronto (SPC) jointly with the Urban Alliance on Race Relations (Henry and Ginzberg, 1985). Results received wide publicity as evidence that discrimination does exist in Canada. Because these studies were modelled closely on similar British studies in London and Birmingham (McIntosh and Smith, 1974), results can be directly compared. The comparison suggests little if any differences between Britain and Canada.

The field trials, including telephone applications by actors with varying accents, and walk-in applications by black and white actors presenting comparable qualifications, produced remarkably similar results in the two countries. In both British and Canadian studies, whites more often received positive responses to telephone applications than did non-whites. In Toronto, whites received positive responses in 86.9 per cent of applications, whereas non-whites received positive responses in only 60.1 per cent of applications, a difference of 26.8 per cent.[3] In London and Birmingham, the corresponding percentages were 89.3 per cent for whites and 73.9 per cent for non-whites, a difference of 15.4 per cent. These data do not support the hypothesis of less discrimination in Canada; if anything they suggest the reverse. In actual in-person job offers, whites in both countries had about a three-to-one advantage over non-whites. Again, the data do not support the hypothesis of less discrimination in Canada.

In other words, the behavioral data show that the measured extent of direct racial discrimination in employment in Toronto is not less than its extent in the British cities of London and Birmingham. There were some differences in research procedures owing to labour market differences in the two countries. The samples admittedly are small. However, the fact remains that these studies, each of which received wide-spread domestic notice and recognition, do not support the hypothesis of less discrimination in Canada. The findings run counter to a key assumption of Canadian race relations policy.

A follow-up SPC employer survey showed how little Toronto employers are aware of discrimination or other race-related problems within their organizations (Billingsley and Muszynski, 1985). Employers oppose government intervention in hiring decisions. These results, too, correspond closely to British findings (Carby and Thakur, 1977), and suggest that in both countries, major voluntary changes in employer behaviour will not occur soon.

Some comparative evidence relevant to racial discrimination in housing is also available. According to demographic analyses, residential concentration of racial minorities in Britain in the first years following their settlement was not significantly greater than current patterns in Canadian cities. Studies in Britain by Collision (1967:281) and Peach (1982:36) found that indexes of residential racial dissimilarity (the proportion of racial groups who would have to move to bring about a similar distribution across all groups) were between 0.3 and 0.6 in the 1960s. For Canadian cities, Balakrishnan and Kralt (1987:143-54) found index values between 0.4 and 0.6 in 1981. Residential concentrations evidently were comparable at comparable stages in the development of racial minority communities in the two countries.

SOCIAL FACTORS MODERATING RACIAL CONFLICT IN CANADA COMPARED TO BRITAIN

o

Unlike the patterns of discrimination which can be denied and may remain hidden, the extent of overt racial conflict in Canada is quite plainly less than in Britain. In the British inner cities of London, Birmingham, Liverpool, and Bristol, hostility and violence have become the norm in relations between young, unemployed blacks and the police. Canada is clearly a contrasting scene. Despite a degree of racial tension in community-police relations in

Canada, and undercurrents of unreported racial conflict in neighborhoods and schools, chronic violence is not nearly as visible a part of race relations. Furthermore, in Canada there is far less controversy about the status of minorities. Canada's Zundels and Keegstras occupy the political fringe. Open expression of hostility to minorities is comparatively rare....

An aspect of the low level of racial conflict in Canada is the level of awareness of discrimination among racial minorities themselves (cf. Breton, 1983:431-3). In the Toronto SPC studies cited earlier, there was compelling evidence of lack of awareness of discrimination, although it was serendipitous and went unreported by the researchers.[4] During debriefing sessions, black actors participating in the study showed genuine shock at the extent of the difference between their own experiences and those of white actors applying for the same jobs. In everyday life, blacks have no access to this kind of information, because whites effectively conceal the relevance of race. When an experience such as this experimental study brings the reality of discrimination home to its victims, the impact can be devastating.[5]

What conditions may be operating to moderate racial conflict in Canada, independent of levels of racial discrimination? As a general distinguishing feature of Canadian social institutions, more has been said about lack of conflict than about lack of inequality. Canadian historians tell us that 'evolution, not revolution, and conciliation, not confrontation have always been... the Canadian way' (cf. Matthews, 1987:384; McNaught, 1970). Sociologists such as Lipset (1970:55-62; 1985) and others emphasize that Canada's counter-revolutionary heritage, and its aversion to conflict as a means of change, are part of the 'founding ethos' of the society. The following discussion will identify four specific factors, some of which may derive from the broader predispositions, which seem to account for lack of racial conflict in Canada compared to Britain. These are: 1/ the generational composition of racial minorities; 2/ the economic status and position of racial minorities in relation to overall economic trends; 3/ the structure of immigration institutions; and 4/ multi-ethnic political structures and culture.

Generational Composition of Racial Minorities

Generational change, the emergence of a native-born generation within immigrant groups, has been crucial to the development of race politics in Britain. British-born blacks have a distinctive social experience, different from the immigrant experience. They often lack the clear economic niche of the immigrant generation, they have no return-migration option, their expectation for equality is greatly increased, and they have an increased identification with minority communities within the country. Increased racial conflict has resulted. Rex and Tomlinson (1979:212), in their study of racial minorities in Birmingham, were 'very struck by the gap between the attitudes expressed by the parents on the one hand (which ... were relatively conservative and complacent), and those expressed by young people ... on the other ... Our data showed increasing militancy amongst this group.'

In Canada, most racial minority group members are recent immigrants, and a major generational transition lies in the near future. Because of the demographic impact of recent immigration, even racial minority communities which have existed in Canada for generations are today composed predominantly of immigrants. Whereas in Britain, 43 per cent of racial minority group members are British-born, in Canada only 23 per cent are Canadian-born. In Britain, there is already a significant adult black British population. In Canada, of the adult members of racial minority groups, only a few are native-born Canadians. For example, in 1981, only 8.4 per cent of black adults over 25 in Toronto were Canadian-born. This is changing rapidly. ...

Racial tensions in Canada, now rather muted, will almost certainly increase with the coming of age of a Canadian-born generation. At the same time, however, the generational transition will not necessarily have the same outcome in Canada as in Britain. Racial tensions in Britain were greater than in Canada even when immigrants predominated in minority communities. There are other factors which may serve to moderate racial conflict in Canada, both in the short term, and over the longer term.

Socio-economic Position of Racial Minorities

As was mentioned above, racial minorities in Canada have higher entrance status than racial minorities in Britain, for reasons unrelated to the extent of discrimination. It is likely that the greater economic integration of racial minorities in Canada will produce lower potentials for conflict, whatever the comparative degree of discrimination, because higher status increases the sense of having a stake in society.

In the short term, any British-Canadian differences in levels of conflict resulting from higher entrance status in Canada probably will be small. In the first years following immigration, immigrants to both countries have jobs more or less as expected. West Indian, East Indian and Pakistani immigrants to Britain in the 1950s and 1960s settled in traditional industrial areas of London and the Midlands (Peach, 1966; 1967; 1968), so initially, unemployment rates were extremely low. Likewise in Canada, the racial minority population has settled mainly in the affluent cities of Toronto and Vancouver, and to a lesser extent in Montreal, cities of southern Ontario and the West.

Few have settled in high unemployment areas such as the Maritimes, or Quebec outside Montreal. Concentration of minorities in affluent regions helps to insulate them from the impact of recessions in both countries, despite racial discrimination. As time passes, however, racial minority groups cannot remain immune to impacts of economic trends. In a buoyant economy, expansion creates opportunities for minorities; in an economic downturn, privileged groups close ranks, carefully guarding their own interests against those of newcomers....

The Immigration and Citizenship Issue[6]

Historical British-Canadian differences in immigration and citizenship policy appear to have affected the levels of racial conflict in the two societies, again for reasons having little to do with predispositions toward racial tolerance. In Britain, controversy over immigration control and the creation of British citizenship clearly aggravated domestic race relations. Canada's immigration and citizenship policies, comparatively speaking, have enjoyed a political consensus. It is well worth considering how differences in levels of racial conflict over immigration and citizenship policy may have been affected by the different historical background of immigration in each society, as much as by pre-existing racial predispositions.

The British immigration policy in place after World War II was, for Commonwealth members, essentially an open door. During imperial rule, the concept of 'British subject' was invented to provide a common citizenship status throughout the imperial domain, and it was maintained to promote continued relations within that domain. The policy, which provided for free movement within the UK, colonies, and independent Commonwealth, was defended as a cornerstone of non-racist international relations.

A changing world economic order in the post-war period resulted in unexpected numbers of black immigrants moving to Britain, and the open-door policy came under severe attack domestically. Because immigrants were being accepted as a Commonwealth obligation, with no controls over numbers or qualifications, they came to be perceived as a welfare problem with an open-ended price tag. Once staunchly supported by Conservative defenders of the Commonwealth, the open-door policy was quickly abandoned by both parties. A series of highly controversial immigration and citizenship acts were passed, instituting skill-based selection criteria and a kind of retroactive citizenship status governing residence rights in Britain. Racial motivations behind these policies were very clear, because the principle of free movement, previously the sine qua non of racial equity, was overridden. These events negatively affected the entire atmosphere of race relations in Britain.

Canada's immigration policy reflects its world-system location, which was very different from that of Britain. Canada, as a new nation with vast, sparsely-populated lands, formulated a nation-building immigration policy directed at national social and economic goals (Hawkins, 1972; Parai, 1975). Toward such ends, Canada admitted immigrants selectively, based on social and economic needs, or 'absorptive capacity'. In the 1960s, in moves to end racial discrimination in immigration policy, geographic selection criteria were abolished, and economic and occupational selection criteria were formalized in a point system. While skill-graded selection criteria may have reduced the number of racial minority Third World immigrants, this was never considered a racially-motivated policy because the legitimacy of selection criteria was well-established (cf. Kalbach and McVey, 1979).

The elimination of geographical selection rules produced, in the late 1960s and early 1970s, a shift in ethnic composition of immigration to those of predominantly non-European origins, and an increase in total immigration.[7] An immigration 'Green Paper'(Canada, 1974) was debated, and a new *Immigration Act* in 1976 empowered Parliament to set annual immigration targets. Total immigration declined to about 100,000 per year. Hong Kong and other Southeast Asian countries became more significant as source countries. In Canada there is popular confidence that immigration serves economic expansion, and this perception dampens controversy. Race has been an issue in these changes, but never the major issue, as it was in Britain....

Canada's broad but selective program of immigration, compared to Britain's open immigration specifically for the Commonwealth, may have had other effects in reducing racial conflict. For one, Canada's selection policy undoubtedly has affected the higher socio-economic status of racial minorities in Canada. The potential effects of this in reducing racial conflict were outlined earlier. Canada's broader policy, which encourages immigration from all sources, not only the Commonwealth, probably also has increased the diversity of cultural origins among the racial minorities in Canada compared to Britain.[8] Ethnic boundaries among racial minorities impede group formation, including the formation of potential conflict groups. Rather than forming political alliances, diverse immigrant groups tend to remain distant from each other. As Ramcharan (1982:49) points out,

> While the common and visible differences of skin colour, which separate the immigrant from the host society, should be sufficient rationale for a united organization and leadership, different cultural traits, class, and national orientations apparently are stronger than the grounds of association.

This factor could operate to reduce racial conflict in Canada compared to Britain, though its force would attenuate as homeland attachments fade over time and through generations.

M u l t i c u l t u r a l i s m ,   B i l i n g u a l i s m ,   a n d   R a c e

Canada's ethnic and linguistic diversity is the feature most often cited as a source of greater racial tolerance, reducing the potential for racial discrimination. It may, however, be much more important as a force deflecting minority group responses to inequality, thus moderating racial conflict.

Bilingualism and multiculturalism, though relatively recently-established policies in Canada, are imbedded within a broader and long-standing Canadian cultural tradition emphasizing the preservation of established values. There is a contrast with the 'melting pot' ideology which insists on change. The Canadian approach reflects a general 'live and let live'philosophy, and in this sense promotes tolerance. However, tolerance for cultural retention does not automatically translate into economic equality for cultural groups. John Porter's (1965) analysis of 'the vertical mosaic' serves as a reminder that the Canadian ethnic mosaic never implied deliverance from inequality. When Pierre Trudeau outlined the ideology of multiculturalism in 1972, equality was one ultimate objective, but no specifics were guaranteed. As Jean Burnet (1975:39) observed in considering multiculturalism and race relations, 'the commonplace that multiculturalism will ease the lot of the visible minorities does not ... seem to be self-evident.'

Multicultural advisory structures in government are far more developed in Canada than in Britain, but such structures are concerned with cultural status, and not with economic status. Racial minorities are represented among other ethnic groups, but attention focuses on cultural retention, an issue of concern to higher-status European minorities, as opposed to equity. Survey data show that equity issues are relatively more important to disadvantaged ethnic groups including racial minorities (cf. Reitz, 1980:381).

Advisory structures specifically devoted to race issues are emerging mostly at the municipal level. These structures appear to have been responsible for more significant accomplishments in Britain than in Canada, at least in terms of promoting employment equity within municipal government itself (cf. Ouseley, 1981; 1984). They have had little independent clout, however, and have been ineffective in producing broader changes. Katznelson (1973) showed that race advisory groups, in Britain and the US, co-opt minority leaders, and marginalize racial politics. When politicians appoint minority group members to race advisory bodies, both have a vested interest in a perception of close links to the respective minority community. Such links, if they exist at all, attenuate as race advisors become creatures of government, isolated from the very people whose interests they formally represent. In the long run, co-optation reduces conflict, not inequality....

The bilingual structure of Canadian society represents a potentially important, and largely unrecognized, factor which impedes the formation of a common political consciousness among racial minorities. Immigrants to Canada include both Anglophones and Francophones, and the process of integration into Canadian society becomes more complex. In Montreal, West Indians, like the white majority, are composed of Francophones (the Haitians) and Anglophones (most other West Indian Montrealers). Each West Indian linguistic community is oriented to a different majority group, leading to a perception that each confronts unique difficulties (Dejean, 1978; Labelle, Larose, and Piché 1983a; 1983b; Neill, 1985; Bernèche and Martin, 1984). Efforts to mobilize racial groups are impeded by the linguistic boundary. (Even research communities are split: Anglophone researchers study Anglophone West Indians, Francophone researchers study Francophone

West Indians!) Thus, race relations in Montreal pose distinct issues not arising elsewhere in Canada. As time passes, the effect of this factor could
increase (unlike the effect of ethnic diversity within linguistic groups), as
each linguistic minority integrates within its respective linguistic majority.

THE NEED TO ASSIGN HIGHER PRIORITY TO THE ISSUE OF RACIAL DISCRIMINATION IN CANADA

o

...Racial conflict is likely to increase in the future with the generational transition. There are many unknowns, however, including economic trends in
specific industries affecting the distribution of opportunities for minority
group members. For the future this analysis suggests that levels of racial
conflict in Canada may remain as high as in Britain....

[Change] will require political leadership which is willing to initiate
action in response to a significant social problem, without regard to the
status of that problem as a political issue, and without regard to opposing
pressures and resistance. Does such leadership exist in Canada, when it
comes to the issue of race? The answer to this question is perhaps the truest
test of whether Canada has special qualities in a multi-racial world.

NOTES

o

1. Indirect discrimination, such as 'institutional discrimination,' exists when the
   use of criteria not explicitly racial but nevertheless unrelated to functional needs
   has the effect of denying to racial minority group members needed access to
   resources such as jobs. Cross-national comparison of indirect discrimination is
   beyond the scope of the present discussion.

2. Expressed attitudes on racial issues change rapidly as a result of specific circumstances. Richmond (1976a; 1976b) reported survey data showing greater hostility
   to blacks as neighbours in Britain compared to Canada, but his Canadian figures
   predated the arrival of significant racial minorities in Canada. Furthermore, the
   hostility toward blacks as neighbours in Britain, which rose during the immigration controversy in that country, declined significantly after the immigration
   issue faded. In Canada, on the other hand, hostility toward non-whites as neighbours appears to have increased (based on a comparison of data reported by
   Richmond with more recent survey data for Toronto; cf. Reitz, 1988:123).

3. The procedure called for non-whites to make the approach first, to ensure that
   negative reactions are not a result of employers regarding the job as already committed to the white applicant.

4. Personal communication to the author.

5. Richmond (1976a) compared discrimination as perceived by racial minorities, and found little difference between Britain and Canada in this regard.

6. The following section draws from Reitz (1988).

7. Some indicative official Canadian immigration figures appear in table at end of the paper.

8. In both Britain and Canada, the proportion of the population which is of West Indian origin is approximately 1%. However, the other non-European origin groups in Canada distributed differently and are more diverse than those in Britain. There are relatively few persons of Indian and Pakistani origins in Canada compared to Britain, and relatively more persons of various Asian origins in Canada.

REFERENCES
O

Balakrishnan, T.R. and John Kralt
(1987) 'Segregation of visible minorities in the Metropolitan areas of Montreal, Toronto and Vancouver. ' Pp. 138-57 in L. Driedger (ed.), *Ethnic Canada: Identities and Inequalities* (Toronto: Copp Clark Pitman).

Bernèche, F. and J.-C. Martin
(1984) 'Immigration, emploi et logement: la situation de la population haïtienne dans certaines zones de la région metropolitaine de Montréal.' *Anthropologie et Sociétés*, 8:2:5-29.

Billingsley, B. and L. Muszynski
(1985) *No Discrimination Here? Toronto Employers and the Multi-racial Workforce* (Toronto: Social Planning Council of Metropolitan Toronto and The Urban Alliance on Race Relations).

Breton, Raymond
(1983) 'West Indian, Chinese and European ethnic groups in Toronto: perceptions of problems and resources. ' Pp. 425-43 in J.L. Elliott (ed.), *Two Nations, Many Cultures* (2nd ed.) (Scarborough, Ontario: Prentice-Hall Canada).

Burnet, Jean
(1975) 'Multiculturalism, immigration, and racism: a comment on the Canadian Immigration and Population Study, '*Canadian Ethnic Studies*, 7:1:35-39.

Canada. Department of Manpower and Immigration
(1974) *Immigration Policy Perspectives,* Canadian Immigration and Population Study, volume 1 (Ottawa: Information Canada).

Carby, Keith and Manab Thakur
(1977) *No Problems Here? Management and the Multi-racial Workforce* (London: Institute of Personnel Management, in co-operation with the Commission on Racial Equality).

Collison, P.
(1967) 'Immigrants and residence,' *Sociology*, 1:277-92.

Dejean, P.
(1978) Les Haïtiens au Québec (Montreal: University of Quebec at Montreal Press).

Hawkins, Freda
(1972) *Canada and Immigration: Public Policy and Public Concern* (Montreal: McGill-Queen's University Press).

Henry, Frances
(1978) 'The dynamics of racism in Toronto,' Toronto, York University, Department of Anthropology, mimeo.

_____ (1986 'Race relations research in Canada today: a "state of the art" review,' Canadian Human Rights Commission Colloquium on Racial Discrimination, September 25.

_____ and Effie Ginzberg (1985) *Who Gets the Work? A Test of Racial Discrimination in Employment* (Toronto: The Urban Alliance on Race Relations and the Social Planning Council of Metropolitan Toronto).

Kalbach, Warren E. and Wayne W. McVey
(1979) *The Demographic Bases of Canadian Society* (Toronto: McGraw-Hill Ryerson).

Katznelson, Ira
(1973) *Black Men, White Cities* (London: Oxford University Press).

Labelle, M., S. Larose and V. Piché (1983a) 'Emigration et immigration: les Haïtiens au Quebec,' *Sociologie et sociétés*, 15:2:73-88.

_____ (1983b) 'Politique d'immigration et immigration en provenance de la Caraibe anglophone au Canada et au Québec, 1900-1979' *Canadian Ethnic Studies*, 15:21-24.

Lipset, S.M.
(1970) *Revolution and Counter-revolution: Change and Persistence in Social Structures,* revised and updated edition (New York: Anchor Doubleday).

_____ (1985) 'Canada and the United States: the cultural dimension.' Pp. 109-60 in Charles F. Doran and John H. Sigler (eds.), *Canada and the United States: Enduring Friendship, Persistent Stress* (Englewood Cliffs, NJ: Prentice-Hall, Inc.).

Matthews, Thomas
(1987) 'The myth of the peaceable kingdom: Upper Canadian society during the early Victorian period,' *Queen's Quarterly*, 94:2:383-401.

McIntosh, Neil and David J. Smith
(1974) *The Extent of Racial Discrimination,* Vol. XL Broadsheet No. 547 (London: PEP, The Social Science Institute).

McNaught, Kenneth
(1970) 'Violence in Canadian history.' In John S. Moir (ed.), *Character and Circumstance: Essays in Honour of Donald Grant Creighton* (Toronto: Macmillan).

Neil, G.
(1985) 'Insertion sur le marché du travail québécois et trajectoire socio-professionnelle: le cas des Haïtiennes et des Haïtiens au Québec.' Montréal, Centre de recherches caraibes, Université de Montréal.

Ouseley, Herman
(1981) *The System: A Study of Positive Action in the London Borough of Lambeth* (London: Runnymede Trust and the South London Equal Rights Consultancy).

_____ (1984) 'Local authority race initiatives.' Pp. 133-59 in Martin Boddy and Colin Fudge (eds.), *Local Socialism? Labour Councils and New Left Alternatives* (London: Macmillan).

Parai, Louis
(1975) 'Canada's immigration policy, 1962-1974,' *International Migration Review*, 9:4:449-77.

Peach, Ceri

(1966) 'Factors affecting the distribution of West Indians in Britain,' *Transactions of the Institute of British Geographers*, 38:151-63.

_____ (1967) 'West Indians as a replacement population in England and Wales,' *Social and Economic Studies*, 16:3:289-94.

_____ (1968) West Indian Migration to Britain (London: Oxford University Press, for the Institute of Law Relations).

_____ (1982) 'The growth and distribution of the black population in Britain, 1945-1980.' Pp. 23-42 in D.A. Coleman (ed.), *Demography of Immigrants and Minority Groups in the United Kingdom* (London: Academic Press).

Porter, J.

(1965) *The Vertical Mosaic: An Analysis of Social Class and Power in Canada* (Toronto: University of Toronto Press).

Ramcharan, Subhas

(1982) *Racism: Non-whites in Canada* (Toronto: Butterworths).

Reitz, Jeffrey G.

(1980) 'Immigrants, their descendants, and the cohesion of Canada.' Pp. 329-417 in Raymond Breton, Jeffrey G. Reitz and Victor Valentine, *Cultural Boundaries and the Cohesion of Canada* (Montreal: Institute for Research on Public Policy).

_____ (1988) 'The institutional structure of immigration as a determinant of coming, interracial competition: a comparison of Britain and Canada,' *International Migration Review*, 22:1:117-46.

_____ , Liviana Calzavara and Donna Dasko

(1981) 'Ethnic inequality and segregation in jobs,' Toronto, Centre for Urban and Community Studies, University of Toronto, Research Paper No. 123.

Rex, John and Sally Tomlinson

(1979) *Colonial Immigrants in a British City* (London: Routledge and Kegan Paul).

Richmond, Anthony H. (1976a) 'Black and Asian immigrants in Britain and Canada: some comparisons,' *New Community*, 4:4:501-16.

_____ (1976b) 'Urban ethnic conflict in Britain and Canada: a comparative perspective.' Pp. 164-204 in S.E. Clarke and J.L. Obler (eds.), *Urban Ethnic Conflict: A Comparative Perspective* (Chapel Hill, NC: University of North Carolina, Institute for Research in Social Science).

Willing And Able*

Shona McKay

"Volk with a V. V as in victory," Lary Volk is telling a telephone caller from his downtown Winnipeg office. His choice of words is appropriate. A 34-year-old computer programmer who has been legally blind since the age of 9, Volk was hired last year by the Royal Bank. It was an event that ended a tumultuous and at times despairing 11-year journey during which the Fort Frances, Ont., native conducted an intensive search for full-time work. "The pattern was recurring," says Volk, who graduated from a computer training course for visually impaired students in 1979. "I would get temporary employment with one or another provincial government ministry, be told that I was doing a great job, and then get laid off. Sometimes I qualified for unemployment benefits and sometimes I'd be forced to apply for welfare. All the while, I papered Canada and the United States with job applications and résumés." Occasionally, Volk was granted an interview. But in spite of the fact that he told prospective employers he would supply his own Braille printer and computer voice synthesizer—a piece of equipment that translates what's written on the screen into the spoken word—he never made it onto anyone's short list. "People were uncomfortable with, even frightened by, my disability," he says. "In most cases, they focused on the things they didn't think I could do. I'd repeatedly get asked inane questions like 'How do you climb the stairs?' or 'Can you use a telephone?' Many times I wanted to scream in rage."

Volk's life changed when he received a call from the Royal Bank in the spring of 1990. "It was a unique experience," he says. "The people here asked me about my abilities, not my limitations. What's more, they not only

✶ Shona McKay, "Willing and Able," *Report on Business Magazine*, October 1991, 58-63. Reprinted by permission of the publisher and the author.

knew about what equipment I would need to do my job, they had already purchased it. It was all quite astonishing."

Happy endings like the one in Volk's tale don't happen very often. There are about 1.8 million disabled people of working age in Canada and some 80% are either unemployed or underemployed. In 1986, a Secretary of State report estimated that 63% of adults with disabilities were living on incomes of less than $10,000 per year. Diane Richler is executive vice-president of The Canadian Association for Community Living (CACL), a national organization of more than 40,000 members representing individuals with developmental impairments. She says: "People with disabilities have traditionally been excluded from the job market. Like our society, business has been more content to give these people a handout rather than meaningful work."

Carol McGregor, a former nurse who lost her sight seven years ago at the age of 41, knows this personally and professionally. "I fully expected to fit right back into the mainstream workforce in spite of my blindness," she says. "But that didn't happen. It was a shock to realize that people didn't see me as a person any longer. The attitude of employers was that I should stay home and be taken care of for the rest of my life." Angry and frustrated, McGregor decided that if she couldn't join business, she'd beat it. Now she's co-ordinator for the Toronto-based Disabled People for Employment Equity, a lobby group that filed complaints with the Canadian Human Rights Commission against nine major Canadian corporations including the CBC, Canada Post and Bell Canada in 1988 for violating human rights in their hiring practices. "Business people have to know that we are here, that we have rights and that they never have done and still are not doing enough to employ people with disabilities," she says.

Across the country, however, a significant number of companies are finally beginning to reach out to people with disabilities and to offer that most desired of commodities—jobs. "As short a time as four years ago, we'd see businesses asking for very basic information," says Rob McInnes, executive director of the Winnipeg-based Canadian Council on Rehabilitation and Work (CCRW), a national organization with the aim of creating more jobs for the disabled. "But now awareness is much higher. Corporations are coming to us asking for more specific tools. They are looking for ways of targeting people with disabilities and including them in their workplace." Judy Waymire, managing director of The Canadian Hearing Society Foundation (CHSF), agrees. "The walls," she says, "are beginning to come down."

Many of the reasons for the shift are pragmatic ones. Recent federal and provincial government legislation requires employers to improve employment equity participation. Since 1986, for example, Ottawa's Employment Equity Act and Federal Contractors Program have required all federally regulated companies, Crown corporations and suppliers to implement hiring and promotion programs that target people with disabilities as well as women, native Canadians and visible minorities. In Ontario, the New Democratic Party government has announced its intention to bring in stiff new employment-equity legislation this fall. Many observers anticipate the new rules will include not only legally binding goals and timetables but also penalties for offenders, which would set a precedent in Canada. Says Lynda White, manager of employment equity for the Montreal-based Royal Bank, an institution that has increased the number of employees with impairments from 1.7% in 1987 to 3.9% last year: "It's fair to say that the government guidelines are encouraging us all to take stock and get our houses in order."

The single most important factor in prompting business to look toward disabled people, however, is demographics. Canadian business will face a labour shortage in the very near future. It's well documented that the traditional source of employees—white, able-bodied males—will make up only 20% of new entrants to the workforce as early as the year 2006. "People with disabilities represent an untapped and valuable resource," says White. "That's a fact that any company that's going to continue to be successful in the future can't afford to ignore."

The Business community is also faced with growing militancy from within the disabled community. The Independent Living movement (IL), an organization founded by disabled Vietnam War veterans during the early 1970s in California, now has scores of offices around the world. Twelve of the IL chapters are in Canada. And more employers are beginning to appreciate the societal costs of their prejudices. A recent CACL report entitled *The Economic Costs of Segregating People with a Mental Handicap* concluded that if the tax dollars now paid out to the approximately 375,000 intellectually impaired individuals of working age in Canada in the form of social welfare benefits were saved and added to the money these same people could put into the economy if they were given fair employment, the economic gain would be $4.6 billion. "You wouldn't believe the number of calls I got from businesses when the report became public last spring," says Richler. "Overwhelmingly, people were asking 'What can I do to change things?'"

The process of hiring and successfully integrating employees with disabilities, though, requires more effort than simply deciding to give someone in a wheelchair a job. Managers and workers need to be sensitized and systems and cultures reviewed, a time-consuming process. But thoroughness has rewards beyond achieving fairness. An employer who takes the time to learn will find that some problems are more imagined than real. Take the issue of workplace accessibility and accommodation. "The majority of uninitiated employers see this as a big obstacle," says Joe Coughlin, a 37-year-old with cerebral palsy who is co-host of *The Disability Network*, a weekly current affairs program airing nationally on CBC that deals with issues of disability. "They imagine spending hundreds of thousands of dollars redesigning buildings and knocking down doors. But that's not what the facts reveal." According to a 1987 study in the United States, in 69% of cases employers spend less than $500 to accommodate an employee's disability. In 88% of the cases the cost is less than $1,000. And thanks to this year's federal budget, Canadian employers are now able to write off accommodation costs.

For employers contemplating equipment like optical scanning devices for people with visual impairments—which can cost as much as $100,000—Dave Fisher, manager of asset sales and loan syndication at the Toronto-Dominion Bank's head office, has this advice. "I'm forever telling employers not to view accommodation as an expense but an investment." Among other initiatives, his employer has installed a swing door on the washroom near his office to help the 42-year-old safely manoeuvre the crutches he has used since contracting polio as a child. "Maybe a company spends money to make a washroom wheelchair-accessible for one person," says Fisher. "But remember, if that same company were to hire 10 people with wheelchairs over the next ten years, the cost will not only be amortized but also negligible."

Not all problems associated with the integration of disabled workers are so easily resolved. Many employers, for example, find it difficult to recruit suitable employee candidates. "We have found the truth to be a little bit behind our original expectations," says Jim Lawson, the TD's assistant general manager of employee relations. "To begin with, there are not that many agencies or organizations that can supply business with a ready pool of trained people." Adds Harriet Stairs, a vice-president of human resources at the Bank of Montreal: "This is a segment of society that usually has less workplace experience and education. [More than 50% of people with disabilities have not completed high school compared to 28.5% of able-bodied Canadians in the labour force.] Given the situation, employers have to go an extra mile to both employ and advance workers with disabilities."

That's exactly what BOM has begun to do. This fall, in co-operation with The Canadian Hearing Society, the federal government and a local community college, the bank will launch a program designed to prepare individuals with hearing impairments for the white-collar career stream. "Each student will not only be given the opportunity to work at the bank while studying but will also be guaranteed employment after he or she has successfully completed the program," says Stairs. "It's an initiative we feel will have lasting benefits for everybody involved."

Employers face more problems arising from what can be a clash of diverse cultures. The CHSF's Waymire points out that any employer contemplating hiring a person with a hearing impairment should realize that someone who is deaf is often the product of a unique upbringing. "For example," she says, "deaf people are usually much more immediately intimate with each other than hearing people. I suspect that a hearing employer or co-worker may judge them as too forward. But they are acting in a way that is very normal to them."

Peter Reynolds, executive producer of *The Disability Network*, who has worked alongside people with mental and physical impairments for several years in both television and radio, also notes that employers must be prepared for some ragged beginnings. "The fact that we have shut away and shut out so many people with disabilities in the past means that not everybody has an easy time making the transition," he says. "In many instances, I've found that people are fearful, intimidated and tentative. As an employer, you have to accept this and work with it."

But the single biggest impediment to the integration of people with disabilities into the workaday world has less to do with the quirks of new recruits than it does with attitudes and values of the old guard. Jamie Hunter can attest to that. A 29-year-old who has minimal control over his limbs as a result of a diving accident at the age of 18, Hunter has been employed as a systems analyst at Esso Petroleum, a division of Imperial Oil Canada Ltd., since January, 1989. He recalls his two-year-long search for work after graduating from York University in Toronto in 1987 with degrees in political science and geography. "With the exception of Esso and a couple of other enlightened companies, the interviews were nightmares," he says. "The interviewers were always extremely nervous. They actually squirmed in their chairs. No one looked me in the eye. I recall one fellow, from the personnel department of a major corporation, who was so uncomfortable he couldn't even bring himself to take me to his office. So we sat in the lobby and he read me back my résumé. 'You're Jamie Hunter? You graduated from York University? You worked for a summer at Ontario Hydro?' Then he said thanks and left. That was it. The interview was over and I never heard from him again."

The TD Bank's Fisher has developed a thick skin. Although he had no trouble obtaining a job during the mid-'70s boom after graduating from the University of Windsor's MBA program, he has since spent years skirmishing with prejudices and ignorance. "You'd be amazed at the number of people I meet in the business world who speak to me in a loud voice," he says. "They assume that because I walk with braces that I'm also hard of hearing or a bit dim." Of course, a hierarchy exists even among prejudices. Once he and a female co-worker met with a senior executive of a leading energy sector company. "The guy came into the lobby, saw the two of us and beckoned me aside," says Fisher. "Out of earshot of my colleague he said, 'Look, I don't mind dealing with you on the crutches but there's no way I'm dealing with a woman.'" Fisher and his colleague left.

The only way to grapple with such attitudes is to first acknowledge that they exist and then attempt to change them. Many corporations, such as the CBC, Bell Canada, Petro-Canada and the Royal Bank, have begun to provide diversity-awareness courses for all employees whether they work in the corner suite or the mailroom. Other companies have decided that the only way to achieve integration is to reward those managers who practice outreach and punish those who don't. Says the TD's Jim Lawson: "We felt that the only way to meet our expectations was to institutionalize the ways and means. That's why we've made employment equity part of the job-performance criteria of each and every senior manager. If one of our VPs doesn't show proof that he's hiring and promoting people from diverse groups, he'll get hit where it counts—in the pocketbook."

Without question, there is a payoff for those employers who do choose to make the effort. "The bottom line is that the company benefits when you start to reach out," says White. "Not only are you putting yourself in a good position to deal with the future, but it's been my experience that the majority of people with disabilities are highly motivated, hard-working employees."

Bob Duncan, manager of Data Entry Services at Markham, Ont.-based American Express Canada Inc., agrees. Three years ago, Duncan hired Jeff Rakoff, then a community college computer programming student. Rakoff has cerebral palsy, a condition that has left him with severely hampered speech and motor control. A one-finger typist, Rakoff, with the help of little more than a software package that allows him to move into upper case by pressing one key, is responsible for compiling and analyzing the department's monthly data reports. "Making Jeff a part of our team has required a little bit of imagination and creativity," he says. "But what's wrong with that when the result is that we have obtained a valuable employee? At our company, we expect x amount of effort from our people. But Jeff gives us an x plus."

Companies have also discovered that it feels good to play a role in transforming human lives for the better. Consider the change in Jeff Rakoff. "When I was growing up, the message was always, 'You won't have a life,'" says the 29-year-old, whose sense of humour—not to mention his participatory interest in sky-diving and white-water rafting—has made him popular with his fellow workers. "It was assumed that I wouldn't get the job, travel or be accepted. But they were wrong. Now, I'm so normal, I'm just like everyone else."

Larry Volk agrees. "For the first time in my life, I don't have to worry about what I'll be doing next week or next month," he says. "I have the time and energy and peace of mind to pay attention to my hobbies and sing in the church choir. I just can't tell you what it means to know that people are beginning to understand that just because I look different or do my job differently, underneath, I'm just the same—and just as good—as the able-bodied guy sitting at the next desk."

Native Employment and Hydroelectric Development in Northern Manitoba[*]

James B. Waldram

INTRODUCTION

o

Hyrdroelectric development in the Canadian north represents one extreme of the spectrum of development projects in which Native people can find employment. Unlike many more stable development projects, such as mining, forestry, and petroleum, where Native people often relocate and are trained in various industrial skills that allow for occupational development,[1] hydro employment characteristically offers short-term benefits with virtually no opportunity for employment when the labour-intensive construction phase is completed. The accelerated pace which utilities adopt in the construction of hydro facilities has rarely allowed for the unskilled or semi-skilled Native labour force to be properly trained to provide them with the option of seeking skilled wage employment within or beyond their communities. Transient professional labour is brought in to fill the vast majority of skilled positions, leaving the Native people to fill jobs which are typically low paying and of short duration. Further, hydro projects, more than many other types of mega-projects in the north, often damage the local environment and the resource base which represents the foundation for Native domestic and commercial economic activity. When the hydro construction has been completed, the Native work force is left to return to this impaired resource base, while the transient professional construction work force moves on to the next project. Hydro development in northern Manitoba provides an excellent example of the dynamics of such a situation: Native people are enticed to become active participants in their own under-

[*] Abridged from James B. Waldram, "Native Employment and Hydroelectric Development in Northern Manitoba," *Journal of Canadian Studies* 22, no. 3 (Fall 1987): 62–76. Reprinted by permission of the publisher and the author.

development by seeking employment on projects that do harm to, rather than benefit, their economic future. . . .

HYDRO EMPLOYMENT POLICY IN NORTHERN MANITOBA

o

The Churchill-Nelson River Hydroelectric Project in northern Manitoba, operational in 1976, involved the diversion of up to 80 percent of the water from the Churchill River south into the Nelson River which, when combined with the regulation of Lake Winnipeg, served to increase the flow on the Nelson River where the generating stations were to be constructed. Six Native communities and three non-Native communities were at least partially affected by the project, through either flooding or reduction in water levels. Residents of these communities found some employment during the construction phase, which lasted from about 1969 to 1976. The community of Pike Lake,[2] the subject of this case study, had two major construction camps established on opposite ends of the lake adjacent to the community, where some residents were able to find periodic employment.

It is evident that, at least publicly, the Manitoba government and Manitoba Hydro believed that the Churchill-Nelson River Hydroelectric Project would be beneficial to the northern Native people. The promise of employment was only a part of an overall package of "benefits" to accrue from the project. For instance, the Assistant General Manager of Manitoba Hydro told the Pike Lake people that "We also believe that developments in the north undertaken by Manitoba Hydro have created new job opportunities and resulted in improved social services for the people of the north."[3] The Manitoba Minister of Finance expanded on this assessment when he stated: "Hydro's Nelson power program would help open up Manitoba's northland and would provide employment opportunities, better educational opportunities, better communications and a general improvement on their standard of living."[4]

Despite this optimism, however, Manitoba Hydro was also cognizant of the likely environmental problems that would be created by the hydro project, and, while not denying these, nevertheless hoped that the benefits offered would reduce opposition to the plan. The promise of employment was a central benefit in this plan of appeasement, even though, in reality, few northern Native people were likely to be qualified for the majority of opportunities that would develop.

At Pike Lake, the promise of employment entailed two components: employment on the hydro construction and related developments, with some training, and a program of training and relocation to other northern industrial communities. The latter was, essentially, a "bail-out" program designed to move people out of the project area, and was clearly contradictory to the publicized benefits to be brought into the community to enhance the quality of life. Only two families undertook the relocation program to a nearby mining community.

Manitoba Hydro's policy was to hire local labour as much as possible in the construction of the project, including peripheral work such as relocation of the community, shoreline clearing, etc., and most able-bodied men in Pike Lake were involved at some time. Further, the people were told by the Assistant General Manager of Manitoba Hydro that training programs, implemented in conjunction with other government departments, would greatly benefit the community, especially the young, and theoretically more mobile, residents. In actual fact, very few local men received specific technical training through their employment activities.

While the Manitoba government seemed anxious to spread the news of impending employment and the concomitant increase in the standard of living, they also acknowledged that employment would be short-term. For instance, Premier Edward Schreyer told the residents of Pike Lake the following:

> In addition, the diversion project has resulted in some job opportunities for [Pike Lake] residents on clearing and construction work. When the construction is finished there would still be a few job opportunities connected with on-going clearing programs and floating debris control. It will be Manitoba Hydro's policy to employ local residents on such work whenever possible.[5]

The inherent contradiction in the policy statements of Manitoba Hydro and the Manitoba government were rarely, if ever, recognized: while acknowledging that the hydro project would probably damage the local economy, and that local people would be hired on the construction, no mention was given to the consequences when the hydro jobs terminated and the people were returned to their old economic activities, now damaged by the flooding of the lake behind the dam.

Much of the hydro construction work was contracted to private companies whose employment policies were more profit-oriented than the policies of Manitoba Hydro or the Manitoba government. Required to compete on construction bids, the crucial factor for these private firms was the extent to which relatively less-skilled local Native labour could profitably replace more expensive, but skilled, professional labour from the south. In general, the contractors were able to stipulate their own employment policies, including experience and certification clauses, independent of the government's statements. A newspaper article of the day described this situation:

> The workers there [Pike Lake] are just hired by construction companies so they really aren't Hydro people. There are a lot of Portuguese, some of whom can't even speak English. This causes a problem in the community. They've brought in people for all the higher-paying and skilled jobs. They've found it easier to import people from Winnipeg than to try training some of the Natives, which might have been a little more tedious in the beginning, but which would have given a better future to the people up there.[6]

It is also evident that no employment quotas for Natives or other minorities were developed. Hence, while the government stated that theoretically Pike Lake labour would be used on the construction, in practice conditions were placed on the use of this labour by contractors. While some training programs were implemented, ostensibly to upgrade Pike Lake labour, most of the labour appears to have been concentrated in the low skill, low pay, and short-term positions.

NATIVE EMPLOYMENT DATA

o

There exists no complete body of data on the involvement of Native northerners during the construction phase of the hydro project. Manitoba Hydro does not have such information since they did not monitor employment by individual contractors. Nevertheless, there are sufficient data to allow some analysis and discussion of the patterns of employment on the hydro project.

Rothney and Watson indicate that, in 1974, a total of 860 individuals were employed on the Churchill River Diversion aspect of the project, in the Pike Lake area, and that 200, or 23 percent, were "northern residents" (including non-Native as well as Native workers). On the Lake Winnipeg Regulation aspect of the project, these authors indicate that there were 360 "northerners" in a work force of 1,385, representing 26 percent of the total labour.[7] The Federation of Saskatchewan Indians presents data indicating that Manitoba Hydro and private contractors employed 3,307 workers at 5 major hydro construction sites in September of 1975. Of these, only 399, or 12 percent, were northern Native people.[8]

In the summer of 1975, Pike Lake labour activity in hydro construction was at its peak, yet relative to the overall labour force in the community, only a minority were actually employed. Elias presents data that demonstrate only 45 Pike Lake residents of a total labour force of 194 (or 23 percent) were employed in hydro construction at this time. For the four other northern Native communities directly affected by the hydro construction, the data is similar: of a total labour force of 2,039 in these four communities, only 212 individuals (10 percent) were employed in hydro construction.[9]

When hydro construction jobs began to develop in the north, many people believed that the wages would be high, that they would learn new skills, and that a new era of lucrative wage employment would ensue. Such was not the case, however, as one former Pike Lake construction employee explained to the author: "Very few men got good jobs on the hydro project. Some moved homes, or cleared brush. But not the high paying jobs we were told about."

Evidently, this new era hinged on the implementation and success of training programs, since it was acknowledged that hydro construction work would be short-term. To this end, a number of training programs were implemented, ostensibly to upgrade the skills of the Pike Lake labour force to allow them to take full advantage of contemporary and future job opportunities. While in a few cases private contractors were involved with training programs, for the most past these were offered by various government departments, in particular the Manitoba Department of Northern Affairs, the Manitoba Northern Manpower Corps, and the Canada Department of Indian Affairs. For this reason, most of the training programs could be tied only to those aspects of the overall construction sponsored by each department. These essentially excluded actual work on the hydro project, and focused on community-based projects such as housing construction and the development of the new townsite. It is significant to note that, for most of these training programs, difficulty in securing a full complement of trainees was encountered. While the reason is not entirely clear, it is possible that these community-oriented employment and training programs could not compete with the private contractors and Manitoba Hydro for Pike Lake labour, or, more accurately, the perception on the part of community residents that such employment would be forthcoming.

The Federation of Saskatchewan Indians, in their investigation of Native employment in hydro construction in northern Manitoba, concluded that, contrary to government policy, the Native people did not have their skill base upgraded as a result of employment and training programs. According to them, of the 399 Native people employed on the project in 1975, 99 percent were in jobs that required less than 30 days of specialized training. Further, less than 1 percent of the Native workers earned more than the Manitoba mean income from this employment.[10]

At the time of construction, both Manitoba Hydro and the Manitoba government were aware that their employment and training programs were not as successful as they had hoped. A 1974 report of the Churchill and Nelson Rivers Study Board stated that "while many jobs are available, there is little evidence of local people acquiring transferable construction skills."[11] The available data for Pike Lake support this observation.

In 1981 and 1982, the author conducted interviews with Pike Lake residents to determine the extent of hydro construction employment and the nature of the skills acquired. In 1972, the total labour force was approximately 129 (consisting of all males between the ages of 16 and 65 who were not in school). Of these, the author interviewed 52 men (40 percent) who had worked on hydro construction.

For the 52 individuals who reported some hydro construction employment, a total of 56 "jobs" were defined. Most indicated only one type of job, while a few indicated multiple employment. Of these jobs, 33 (59 percent) involved the clearing of shorelines and landing sites, or brush cutting; 16 (29 percent) involved general labour activity in construction; and 7 (12 percent) involved surveying. Only 3 men reported receiving any special training for their jobs which involved surveying, photo map reading, carpentry, and blasting.

Overall, employment was very short-term, averaging 10.7 weeks per employee, and ranging from 1 to 40 weeks. However, much of the employment was contracted to local residents on a fee-for-service basis. This was primarily the case for shoreline clearing, landing site construction, and brush cutting. In these projects, an individual simply worked at his own pace and was paid a set fee upon completion (remuneration was usually based on a per acre basis). With these activities, the existing bush skills of the local men were utilized, and no special training was required. A landing site, usually about one-half acre in size, paid $500 upon completion. Other employment activity delivered wages in the area of $3 to $5 per hour, which would represent the lower end of the hydro construction pay scale according to the data presented by the Federation of Saskatchewan Indians.[12]

These data suggest that the local men of Pike Lake provided a temporary pool of labour for the low paying, unskilled, and intermittent labour activities that would have been unattractive in scope and remuneration to most southern professional labourers. Few formal skills were provided. While some men actually became quite proficient in a number of areas through on-the-job experience, particularly carpentry, very few received any kind of certification to allow for job mobility should it be desired. Following the construction period (employment declined dramatically in 1976), most men were left to return to the pre-project activities of hunting, fishing and trapping in an environment that had been altered and impaired by the very project upon which they had worked. Recent hydro-related employment has involved only short-term summer work for 2 to 6 individuals. Ironically, this work has involved clearing the lake adjacent to the community of floating debris and searching for the recently dispersed fish populations in a specially-equipped boat, both of which were necessitated by the flooding of the lake. . . .

CONCLUSION

o

The Churchill-Nelson River Hydroelectric Project provided a number of employment opportunities in construction and related projects for the Native people of northern Manitoba, including the people of Pike Lake. The benefits of this employment were, at best, limited.

There is little evidence that the Pike Lake labourers received significant skills enhancement as a result of the project, and no permanent economic activities were established in the community. Thus, in terms of "benefits," the actual income earned appears to be the major factor of concern. Since no official data exist on the earnings of Native workers, we cannot state definitely that hydro and related work were more lucrative in the short-term than the existing commercial and domestic sector activities. This would probably be the case, however, if we assumed a limited perspective and were able to compare the actual wages earned for the exact period worked with the opportunity costs of the same labour time in the commercial and domestic activities. However, as the letter cited earlier by the Pike Lake resident demonstrates, with a wider perspective the wage labour activity appears less beneficial in comparison to these on-going other activities. In contrast to the non-Native workers, it is apparent that the Native labourers generally worked for short, intermittent periods in the lower paying activities.

The local costs of this labour activity are also difficult to quantify. Certainly there was the loss of alternate income (and income-in-kind) derivable from the domestic and commercial activities, as in the case of individuals lingering about the community in anticipation of hydro jobs instead of working in the other sectors of the economy. There was also a capital depreciation in equipment normally used for these activities, the loss of the Co-operative as a community-owned economic enterprise, and perhaps even a minor disintegration of skills, especially among the young people who were particularly attracted to the hydro employment.

It is difficult to avoid the assertion that Native labour in the construction project was little more than tokenism, politically expedient at the time and in no way essential to the overall project. Granted, some jobs were provided, but most were in the unskilled category, frequently involving activities such as bush and shoreline clearing. Since it was essential for Manitoba Hydro and the Manitoba government to provide *some* employment for the northern Native people as a form of appeasement, we may speculate that some of these jobs were created simply to provide this employment. The ghettoization of northern Native people into preconceived "culturally appropriate" bush-related employment activities, at the expense of formal training programs and more lucrative employment, seems to be an all-too-common practice. In this sense, the Pike Lake labourers were utilized, but were not "proletarianized," by the construction of the hydro project.[13]

Despite the unfortunate experiences of the Pike Lake people, we should not assume that all mega-project employment activities of northern Native people must have negative consequences (an assumption which could lead to policies that avoid hiring Native people). But in order for mega-project employment to have a positive impact on Native communities, it must improve the level of certifiable skills of the Native employees, and result in the development of productive economic activities in the communities to utilize these new skills once the project has been completed. Both are necessary; where they fail to materialize, the "totally intrusive" nature of this wage employment will quite probably have negative consequences. Further, considerable lead time would be required to ensure both of these conditions, in which adequate training and economic development programs could be established in advance of the construction schedule. It is evident that none of these conditions were met in Pike Lake.[14]

For the residents of Pike Lake, the hydro project did not result in new economic activities in the community following the construction period; rather it impaired existing opportunities. Since few residents received certified training during the construction period, employment on the hydro project has meant very little for the residents in recent years. Employment mobility, if desired, was not enhanced, and none of the former hydro employees interviewed presently holds a full-time job in the community. In fact, after the construction period ended, the people of Pike Lake went back to being fishermen and trappers. Unfortunately, these activities were seriously undermined by the damage to the environment caused by the hydro project. The Pike Lake labourers had been enticed into participation in their own underdevelopment.

NOTES
o

1. See, for instance: Jameson Bond, *A Report on the Pilot Project at Elliot Lake,* Ontario (Ottawa: Department of Indian Affairs and Northern Development, 1967); D. Stevenson, *Problems of Eskimo Relocation for Industrial Employment* (Ottawa: Department of Indian Affairs and Northern Development, 1968); John S. Matthiasson and W.S. Chow, "Relocated Eskimo Miners," *Centre for Settlement Studies* (Winnipeg), 5 (1970), pp. 27-52; Charles Hobart, "Wage Employment and Cultural Retention in the Case of the Canadian Inuit," *International Journal of Comparative Sociology,* 23, No. 1-2 (1982), pp. 47-61; Charles Hobart, "Inuit Employment at the Nanisivik Mine on Baffin Island," *Inuit Studies,* 6, No. 1 (1982), pp. 53-74; and Gail Grant, *The Concrete Reserve: Corporate Programs for Indians in the Urban Work Place* (Montreal: Institute for Research on Public Policy, 1983).

2. Pike Lake is a pseudonym. Direct references to the community have been omitted where necessary to ensure anonymity.

3. Minutes, "Pike Lake" Public Hearing, 1969.

4. *Winnipeg Free Press,* 3 May 1969.

5. Letter, Premier Edward Schreyer to the Residents of "Pike Lake," 31 January 1975.

6. Laurence Wall, "Northern Clergy Tell of the Human Effects of a Development That Ignores The People," *The Manitoban,* Special Supplement, November 1974, p. 10.

7. Russel Rothney and Steve Watson, *A Brief Economic History of Northern Manitoba* (Winnipeg: Macro Data and Historical Review Work Group, Northern Planning Exercise, Manitoba Department of Northern Affairs, and Resources and Economic Subcommittee of Cabinet, 1975), p. 108.

8. Federation of Saskatchewan Indians, p. 361.

9. Peter Douglas Elias, *Certain Employment Patterns in the Northern Manitoba Industrial Sectors of Hydro Construction, Forestry, Mining and Provincial Government Administration* (Winnipeg: Manitoba Planning Secretariat, 1975), pp. 125-26.

10. Federation of Saskatchewan Indians, pp. 361-62.

11. J. D. Collinson, *Social and Economic Impact Study of the Churchill-Nelson Rivers Hydro Development* (Winnipeg: Department of Mines, Resources and Environmental Management, 1974), pp. 333-34.

12. Federation of Saskatchewan Indians, p. 357.
13. See Ellen Antler and James Faris, "Adaptation to Changes in Technology and Government Policy: A Newfoundland Example (Cat Harbour)," in *North Atlantic Maritime Cultures*, ed. Raoul Anderson (The Hague: Mouton, 1979), pp. 129-54. Antler and Faris have defined "proletarianization" to mean "making dependent and mobile labourers available to industrial capitalism" (p. 130). It is my contention that the people of Pike Lake were made neither "dependent" nor "mobile" by the project, and hence have not become "available" to industrial capitalism. The fact that the labourers returned to their pre-project domestic and commercial economy argues persuasively that they were not made "dependent" by the project, and the lack of trade certification ensured that they would not yet become very "mobile." Lacking such mobility, they have not become "available" to industrial capitalism as it exists outside their community. Similarly, since the hydro project failed to result in the development of any new economic activities in the community itself, their labour power remains relatively unutilized.
14. Manitoba Hydro and the Manitoba government have since acknowledged the failure of their hydro projects to satisfy the needs of northern Native people. In the spring of 1985, they announced a new Native employment program for the construction of the Limestone generating facility on the Nelson River. This program seeks to improve the prospects of Native northerners through training and preferred hiring programs. For an analysis of this program, see James B. Waldram, "Manitoba's Hydro Employment Program for Native Northerners," *Native Studies Review* 1, No. 2 (1985), pp. 47-56.

PART 5

Women's Employment

EDITORS' INTRODUCTION

○

We endorse a "gendered" analysis of work, which places the different work experiences, roles, and rewards of women and men at the centre of the analytic spotlight. Indeed, we have attempted to capture the gendered dimensions of work in many of the sections of this reader. For example, the historical Part 1 on industrialization juxtaposed male craftwork, women's domestic work, and the administrative revolution that sparked a shift from a male to a female clerical work force. Similarly, Part 2 on contemporary work trends highlighted gender inequalities in service sector employment, the implications of part-time employment for women, and how women are disadvantaged by aspects of pension policy.

Yet we also believe that because gender is a major basis for stratification within work, a separate section on women's employment is warranted. Our purpose is to draw the reader's attention to some of the unique problems and experiences of women in employment. The articles in this section touch upon some of the numerous barriers and problems women confront in workplaces and labour markets. Despite the significant economic progress some groups of women have made in the past several decades, these five essays remind us that women's subordination is tightly woven into the social fabric.

Part 5 begins with a discussion of sexual harassment. Public awareness of this pervasive problem that women encounter in the workplace was heightened by the publicity surrounding Professor Anita Hill's allegations that she was sexually harassed by U.S. Supreme Court nominee Clarence Thomas (now a Judge). As Cynthia Wishart observes, sexual harassment is one form of workplace harassment that can have devastating effects for women. Despite the prohibition of sexual harassment by human rights codes, it is still widespread. Clearly, stronger legislation is required, but also needed to eradicate the problem are effective workplace policies making sexual harassment unacceptable behaviour.

Alexandra Dagg and Judy Fudge address a question that most of us take for granted: who makes the clothes we wear? They reveal how the global restructuring of the clothing industry has resulted in a few giant retailers controlling global networks of suppliers. Retailers and garment makers have reorganized into "pyramids of production." To cut labour costs, they subcontract much of the actual manufacturing work to small jobbers who, in turn, farm out cutting, assembling, and sewing to workers in their homes.

Homeworkers are mainly immigrant women. With limited employment options and lacking adequate child care, these women provide the garment industry with a flexible pool of low-wage but often highly skilled workers. Dagg and Fudge raise a number of fundamental issues about the implications of this chain of exploitation. Do the competitive pressures faced by Canadian industry justify reverting to a pre-industrial form of employment that pays workers less than minimum wage, offers no benefits, and provides no protection under employment standards or workers' compensation legislation? Does the government have a responsibility to regulate this form of employment so that immigrant women (or any other vulnerable group) have the same rights and protections as do other workers? Optimistically, the reading suggests that improvements in this invisible employment sector may result from the organized efforts of the Homeworkers' Campaign, a coalition of labour and community groups.

Thelma McCormack's article takes us from the bottom of the occupational hierarchy to close to the top. The engineering profession has long been a male bastion. The tragic events at Montreal's École Polytechnique in December 1989, when Marc Lépine massacred fourteen female engineering students, prompted public discussions about how these barriers could be removed. The federal government and the Canadian Council of Professional Engineers jointly established the "Canadian Committee on Women in Engineering." The report of the Committee, issued in April 1992, sets out an agenda for change in the school system, engineering faculties, and the profession. As a background, Thelma McCormack's article provides an incisive feminist analysis of the factors underlying the low representation of women in engineering.

A key point made by McCormack is that women are deterred from entering science and math-based careers because of the powerful effects of gender socialization and the masculinization of the scientific world. Lacking encouragement, most young women choose other pursuits. Reinforcing their choice is the sexist male "culture" of engineering faculties, which creates an inhospitable environment for women. For those relatively few (but growing) numbers of women graduating from engineering, the profession accentuates gender differences. The larger issues, McCormack argues, revolve around society's conception of science and technology, disciplines that have been traditionally viewed through men's eyes. McCormack challenges us to consider what the "feminization" of science and technology would entail, and how this transformation could be brought about.

A glaring example of gender inequality is the "wage gap." Today women employed full-time year-round earn about 68 cents for every dollar a similarly employed male earns. Much of this gap is due to the gender segregation of jobs: women are clustered in low-status clerical, sales, and service jobs; men predominate in a wide range of higher-status technical, managerial, and professional jobs. Jane Gaskell's article examines pay equity, the major public policy initiative designed to close the wage gap.

Gaskell cuts to the heart of the male–female wage differential. She argues that pay equity challenges the very assumptions we make about "skill," which, in turn, underpin the judgments about what jobs are worth. But as feminist scholars have shown, what is passed off as an objective basis for assessing the skills required in a job often has more to do with cultural norms that accord greater status to tasks traditionally performed by men. Pay equity policy attempts to replace these socially constructed, and therefore male-biased, notions of skill with a more objective job evaluation system.

What counts as skill has consistently been difficult for sociologists and other researchers to define. Yet what seems clear is that any definition of skill is historically and culturally bound, reflecting existing values and power relations in a society. Furthermore, Gaskell questions whether the length of time spent in school is a good indicator of the skill and complexity of one's work. What accounts for education – job mismatch, whereby some individuals (often women) end up in jobs that do not make use of their education? How does access to on-the-job training affect skill and, in turn, job rewards? Gaskell's case study of clerical work amplifies these points, showing how the actual skills of workers are devalued or not recognized by employers. The crux of the matter, then, is whether or not pay equity programs will bring a re-evaluation of the skills of clerical and other female-dominated jobs.

DISCUSSION QUESTIONS

1. What would constitute an effective workplace sexual harassment policy?

2. What are some of the main ideological and institutional barriers to achieving gender equality in the labour market and the workplace?

3. What unique problems do immigrant women face in the Canadian labour market? Will pay equity help them as much as other groups of women workers?

4. Do employers and the state have any kind of social responsibility to provide women and men with equal opportunities for decent jobs?

5. What are some of the social changes in attitudes, behaviour, and institutions that would contribute to reducing the "double day" many employed women experience?

6. How would men benefit from a workplace that is more accommodating to the needs of women, and in which women are treated equally and fairly?

SUGGESTED READINGS

○

Aggarwal, Arjun, P. *Sexual Harassment: A Guide for Understanding and Prevention.* Markham: Butterworths, 1992.

Cueno, Carl. *Pay Equity: The Feminist – Labour Challenge.* Don Mills, Ont.: Oxford University Press, 1990.

Fudge, Judy, and Patricia McDermott, eds. *Just Wages: A Feminist Assessment of Pay Equity.* Toronto: University of Toronto Press.

Gannage, Charlene. *Double Day, Double Bind: Women Garment Workers.* Toronto: Women's Press, 1986.

Hochschild, Arlie. *The Second Shift: Working Parents and the Revolution at Home.* New York: Viking Penguin, 1989.

Johnson, Laura C., and Robert E. Johnson. *The Seam Allowance: Industrial Home Sewing in Canada.* Toronto: Women's Press, 1982.

McIlwee, Judith S., and J. Gregg Robinson. *Women in Engineering: Gender, Power and Workplace Culture.* Albany, N.Y.: State University of New York Press, 1992.

Workplace Harassment[*]

Cynthia Wishart

Harassment is a complex issue involving men and women, their perceptions and behaviour, and the social norms of the society they live in. Harassment is not confined to any one level, class or profession. Executives as well as factory workers can be subjected to workplace harassment, and even in parliamentary chambers and within the churches, women are not immune.

Two types of harassment are emerging as workplace hazards—sexual and personal.

Sexual harassment is any sexual advance that threatens a worker's job or well-being. It is usually an expression of power made by someone in authority.

Most victims of sexual harassment are women, primarily because most people in authoritative positions in our society are men. The harasser uses his ability to impose work-related penalties to extort sexual favours.

Sexual harassment means being treated as a sex object rather than a worker. It means being judged on physical attributes rather than skills and qualifications, when seeking a job, promotion or salary increase.

Sexual harassment may be defined as any repeated and unwarranted sexual comments, looks, suggestions or physical contacts that create an uncomfortable working environment for an employee.

Sexual harassment can be expressed in a number of ways:
- verbal abuse;

- unwelcome remarks, jokes, innuendoes or taunting about a person's body, attire, age, marital status, etc.;

[*] Abridged from Cynthia Wishart, "Workplace Harassment," *The Facts* (Canadian Union of Public Employees) 9, no. 5 (September/October 1987): 25 – 29. Reprinted by permission of the publisher and the author.

- displaying of pornographic, offensive or derogatory pictures;
- practical jokes which cause awkwardness or embarrassment;
- unwelcome invitations or requests—whether indirect, explicit or intimidating;
- leering or other gestures;
- demands for sexual favours;
- unnecessary physical contact such as touching, patting, pinching, hugging, punching; and
- physical assault.

There are two types of sexual harassment:

1. **Sexual coercion** results in some direct consequence to the worker's employment status or some gain or loss of tangible job benefits.

The classic case would be a supervisor, using his power over salary, promotion, and employment itself, attempting to coerce a subordinate to grant sexual favours. If the worker accedes to the supervisor's request, tangible job benefits follow; if the worker refuses job benefits are denied.

2. **Sexual annoyance** is sexually related conduct that is hostile, intimidating, or offensive to the employee but has no direct link to any tangible job benefit or harm.

This annoying conduct creates a bothersome work environment and effectively makes the worker's willingness to endure that environment a term or condition of employment. Women in non-traditional jobs are often subjected to this type of harassment. Sexual taunts, lewd or provocative comments and gestures, and sexually offensive physical contact fall into this category.

Harassment can also be non-sexual, but nonetheless objectionable.

Personal harassment is any behaviour by any person in the workplace that is directed at, and is offensive to, an employee or endangers an employee, undermines the performance of that job or threatens the economic livelihood of the employee.

Personal harassment occurs when an individual uses his/her authority or position with its implicit power to undermine, sabotage or otherwise interfere with or influence the career of another employee.

Personal harassment may also be defined as repeated, intentional, offensive comments and/or actions deliberately designed to demean and belittle an individual and/or cause personal humiliation.

This definition includes such blatant misuse of power as intimidation, threats, blackmail and coercion, and applies to the distribution of work assignments or training opportunities, promotional opportunities, performance evaluations, or the provision of references.

Also included is favouritism of one employee to the disadvantage of another.

This type of harassment can affect black or immigrant workers, persons with physical or mental disabilities, and homosexuals, as well as other workers. Recently, CUPE's Airline Division and Pacific Western Airlines (now Canadian Airline International) amended their harassment policy to add: "Sexual harassment, for the purpose of this policy, shall include conduct of the nature described above that is directed towards an employee's sexual orientation."

There are two major effects of harassment; one on the victim's working life, and the other on the victim's health.

Tension, anger, fear and frustration are often manifested in physical disorders such as headaches, ulcers, nausea, insomnia and hypertension. In severe cases, medical treatment and even hospitalization occur.

Psychological effects are also common and the victim may feel listless, powerless and emotionally depressed. Decreased ambition a dread of going to work, and loss of self-confidence and self-esteem may also occur. In severe cases attempted suicide is not uncommon.

Arbitrators have awarded financially in complainants' favour to seek psychological counselling as a result of harassment. For example, in *Diesting vs Dollar Pizza (1978) Ltd.*, the complainant had suffered emotional injury as a result of the sexual harassment she had been subjected to during her employment. The degree of emotional suffering was to such an extent that the complainant sought professional help from a psychologist. The psychologist testified that:

> "...The complainant was experiencing anxiety and stress which was particularly related to the incident that occurred with the complainant and the respondents in March of 1980. She was satisfied that this anxiety and stress began with those incidents and there was nothing in the complainant's personality profile that would suggest that she was particularly susceptible to an injury of this type..."

The Board's decision included an award of $500 to the complainant in order to take psychological counselling.

Every province in Canada has human rights legislation. On July 1, 1983, the Canadian Human Rights Act was amended to include protection from sexual harassment. This definition is the most inclusive to date. Although it covers only federal employees, it is expected to act as a guide for legislation throughout the country.

It could be argued in the courts—and is—that sexual harassment is not sexual discrimination because it is not gender-based. That is, both men and women could suffer sexual harassment from a man—or from a woman.

The counter-argument, however, is that it is precisely *because* of the victim's sex that he or she is being sexually harassed. Regardless of whether the victim is heterosexual or homosexual, the harasser has chosen the victim solely because of his or her sex.

Sexual harassment is therefore sex-based, and as such is sex discrimination.

Human Rights Boards across the country have policies prohibiting sexual harassment.The board's interpretations, however, are not binding on the courts. It is left to the courts to decide, and the courts can and do overturn board rulings.

Laws don't prevent sexual harassment, so other channels must be used for redress: existing sex discrimination laws, workers' compensation legislation, occupational health and safety statutes and criminal and tort law (in cases of physical assault or slander).

To solve sexual harassment through legal action—

- is expensive and time consuming;

- can be taken only after the fact; and

- is often emotionally traumatic, because of the tendency to "blame the victim."

One thing is clear: legislation covering sexual harassment must be improved to protect women in the workplace.

The recent Supreme Court of Canada ruling on the Bonnie Robichaud case will have far-reaching effects on employers. The court's decision in July of 1987 ended an eight-year fight for justice and reinforced the four-year-old federal human rights legislation. The Supreme Court ruled unanimously in favour of Robichaud, saying "only an employer can provide the most important remedy—a healthy work environment."

This ruling means that businesses governed by federal and provincial human rights legislation must now create systems to deal with discrimination of all types, including racial and religious.

The spillover effects of this decision are far-reaching, and all employers would be wise to put in place clear workplace policies on harassment.

Unions are taking the lead in recognizing and preventing harassment. Public sector unions in particular are encouraged in this direction by their large female membership.

They are committed to a broad range of women's programs, designed to recognize and protect women's contribution to the workforce:

- affirmative action,

- equal pay for work of equal value,

- maternity leave,

- paid day care, and

- harassment policies.

The crucial role of women within the Canadian labour movement is now a fact. At the highest level of union leadership, women are taking their hard-earned place.

Women's issues are embraced as union issues. Ridding the workplace of harassment takes on a new urgency—

- in leadership statements,
- at the bargaining table,
- in policy and procedures manuals,
- in workshops and training courses,
- in union publications, and
- on the worksite.

Sexual harassment may encourage unionism in the workplace. Employers, especially those whose work force contains a substantial proportion of women, should be mindful that the persistence of sexual harassment in the workplace increases the likelihood of successful union-organizing campaigns.

According to one union organizer "sexual harassment is the single thing in the workplace which radicalizes women more than pay.". . .

Sewing Pains: Homeworkers in the Garment Trade[*]

Alexandra Dagg and Judy Fudge

Who makes the clothes that you buy? Looking at the label won't tell you much, other than the country of origin. Clothing from Taiwan and Hong Kong has long been sold by Canadian retailers, and increasingly garments from countries such as Qatar and Bangladesh are on the market. Clothing from these countries is cheap, mainly because Third World women work long and arduous hours in sewing sweatshops for barely subsistence wages, and in hazardous conditions. But buying clothing made in Canada does not necessarily mean that the women who make the clothes receive a living wage, or work in decent conditions, either. International competition is having a profound impact on the structure of the Canadian clothing industry, and the working conditions of garment workers in this country.

For the last 20 years, the garment industry has been undergoing massive restructuring on a global scale. The popular perception is that the Canadian industry is doomed as a source of jobs and wealth, because of increased competition from low-wage countries. While there are real pressures on the Canadian garment industry, they are much the same as those felt by the manufacturing industry generally.

In 1980, about 73 per cent of all manufactured goods bought in Canada were made in Canada, including clothing. By 1991, we made only 56 per cent of what we bought in manufactured goods.

In the United States, firms have responded to the restructuring of the garment industry in two ways. "Outward processing" is accelerating in light of the North American free trade agreement. This is a production system in which garments are cut and bundled in the U.S., and then sent to low-wage countries to be assembled and sewn. Other manufacturers are

[*] Alexandra Dagg and Judy Fudge, "Sewing Pains: Homeworkers in the Garment Trade," *Our Times* (June 1992): 22–25. Reprinted by permission of the publisher and the authors.

responding to the cut-throat competition by setting up domestic subcontracting structures. Since outward processing is not permitted in Canada (although there's pressure to change this with the North American free trade deal), domestic subcontracting proliferates.

The Canadian garment industry is increasingly dominated by large retailers who call the shots for the manufacturers. While American retail chains such as The Gap, Talbots and Nordstrom are moving into the Canadian market, large Canadian retailers have embraced the free trade deal in order to dump Canadian manufacturers, and to enter into integrated supply arrangements with American producers.

A powerful example of this trend is the Hudson's Bay Company, the most "Canadian" department store. Founded in 1670, it operates 486 stores throughout Canada. The Bay is North America's seventh largest department store, with sales of $5 billion in 1990. The Bay controls a large piece of the mid-level retail market and, through its ownership of Zellers, it has a large presence at the lower end as well. The Bay recently announced that it plans to increase its purchases from the U.S. from the current 15 per cent level to 40 per cent within the next three years.

A close examination of the Bay's relationship to its suppliers reveals the increasing Americanization of the goods it sells. It also provides a stark example of the pyramid structure of the garment industry.

At one point, many of the Bay's suppliers manufactured the clothing which bore their labels, selling the apparel in relatively large quantities to the Bay. However, under pressure from the Bay, these relationships are being refashioned. Take, for instance, the Bay's supply arrangement with Jones of New York, an American supplier of women's clothing.

Instead of keeping an inventory of Jones of New York apparel, the Bay has introduced an electronic data interchange system which enables it to drastically reduce its inventory. As individual items are sold, the Bay electronically transmits its orders to Jones of New York, which then fills the specific demands of the giant retailer. Moreover, increasingly retailers are accepting goods on a consignment basis. Consequently, the risks are shifted from the Bay to Jones of New York, which has responded by reducing its overheads.

Instead of manufacturing the clothes bearing its label, Jones operates as a jobber, designing the garments and buying textiles for them. It then subcontracts cutting and assembly operations to contractors. Contracting shops employ as few as two and up to 30 workers. The larger contractors often subcontract work out to still smaller contractors, and to women working in their own homes—or "homeworkers."

The Hudson's Bay is just one example of a general restructuring trend. This hierarchical chain, or pyramid, of production is developing in the garment industry as a consequence of employers' strategies to try to lower direct labour costs, in competition with low-wage imports. Large retailers dominate at the top, while the work at the bottom is performed by women working in their homes. In some cases, manufacturers run "inside shops," where they directly employ workers who cut and assemble garments. But the trend is toward pure jobbing, and the creation of what has been called the "hollow" corporation, where no actual production is done on the premises of the manufacturer.

So what's wrong with this strategy? Isn't it simply a way for garment manufacturers to survive global competition while, at the same time, permitting women with young children to combine child care with opportunity to earn a bit of money on the side? The answer is no. The popular illusion is that homeworking is a cottage industry similar to pre-industrial household production, where workers produced goods or services in the household for sale on the market, using supplies which they provided, under conditions which they controlled. But nothing could be further from the truth.

Last spring, researchers with the International Ladies Garment Workers Union interviewed 30 homeworkers in the Metropolitan Toronto area. The homeworkers were all Chinese-speaking, so the interviews were conducted in Chinese.

The homeworkers interviewed work on average 46 hours per week, with some reporting up to 82 hours a week. All of them have to provide their own equipment; usually sewing machines that cost between $2,500 and $3,000. Two thirds report that their schedule has to fit the employer's demands, which often means working for more than one employer. Almost all the homeworkers say that their wage rate is set by the employer, and that they simply have to accept it, or find work elsewhere. Several say they are told what they will be paid only after the work is completed. Most of the homeworkers are paid less than the minimum wage.

The average wage is $4.50 an hour, although some are being paid as little as $2.50 and $1 an hour. Almost all of them do not receive vacation pay, or overtime. Their employers do not make unemployment insurance or Canada Pension Plan contributions on their behalf. In addition, almost half of the homeworkers say they have trouble getting employers to pay them for completed work. Many of these women are being helped by their children, which means child labour is growing, too.

The single most important reason that women work as homeworkers in the garment industry is the lack of child care. With very few exceptions, the last job outside the home for the homeworkers interviewed was in a garment factory, and their reason for leaving the job was pregnancy. Almost all of these women say that, if they could afford child care, they would prefer to work outside the home.

The ILGWU estimates that there are 2,000 homeworkers in Toronto in the garment industry alone. Unfortunately, there is simply no way of obtaining reliable statistics on the extent of homeworking in the garment industry across Canada. In many cases, homeworking is virtually a clandestine activity, since small contractors employ homeworkers in order to avoid both unions and minimum employment standards legislation.

Homework is not chosen freely by women. It is rooted in their economic vulnerability in industrial societies such as ours, which do not provide the social services to support their full and equal participation in the workforce. The most fundamental of these services is affordable, quality child care. The other major factor confining these workers to homework is the lack of their ability to speak English, and other job skills which would allow them to work at jobs which paid enough to enable them to afford child care.

Government policies have contributed to the exploitation of women working in the garment industry. Child care services and training are government responsibilities. In failing to provide these services, governments help create a pool of labour which is highly vulnerable economically, and available for exploitation by unscrupulous employers.

Moreover, governments have failed to provide homeworkers with the same legal entitlements as other workers, and have failed to ensure that homeworkers receive the benefit of employment standards which they are entitled to by law.

Homeworkers in Ontario are denied the protection of significant sections of the province's Employment Standards Act, under the regulations to the Act. They are excluded from maximum hours of work, overtime pay and statutory holidays.The argument that homeworkers have the independence to determine their own pace of work simply does not stand up to serious scrutiny. These exceptions should immediately be repealed. Homeworkers should stop being treated as second-class citizens.

The pyramid subcontracting structure of the garment industry contributes to driving homework underground. Small contractors faced with cutthroat competition pay homeworkers less than minimum wage. However, merely imposing liability on a small contractor won't solve the problem. A contractor may simply go out of business, with another springing up in its place. Any enforcement mechanism for minimum labour standards for homeworkers must address the pyramid subcontracting structure in the garment industry.

The related employer provision currently in the Ontario Employment Standards Act is designed to prevent employers from manipulating their corporate form, and the organization of their operations, "if the intent or effect of the arrangement is to defeat, either directly or indirectly, the true intent of this Act, which is to provide minimum standards for workers."

This provision basically empowers the Employment Standards Branch, which enforces the legislation (or the referee who is appointed to resolve disputes) to look beyond the corporate or organizational form. Since the provision imposes joint liability on related employers for any contravention of the Act, it is possible to hold retailers, jobbers and manufacturers liable, who are all part of a subcontracting chain.

The problem is that the already over-burdened Employment Standards Branch has not taken an aggressive approach to determining when employers are related. This creates an incentive for each level of the garment industry pyramid to shift the burden of complying with minimum employment standards legislation on to the subcontractors. In turn, subcontractors may seek to avoid minimum standards altogether by having the work they have contracted to perform done by homeworkers.

The simplest and most effective means of ensuring compliance with minimum standards legislation is to impose joint liability for minimum labour standards on the businesses at the top of the pyramid. Manufacturers and jobbers control the labour process, and they are economically stable. They also set the terms which the contractors must comply with. To ensure that they will not be liable for any breaches of minimum standards, the manufacturers and jobbers could easily demand that their contractors meet minimum statutory obligations. In this way, wages and working conditions will not be subject to a constant downward pressure.

Several organizations have formed a coalition [the Homeworkers' Campaign] to push for changes to Ontario's Employment Standards Act which would provide homeworkers with equal and enforceable minimum labour standards. The organizations include the ILGWU, the Workers' Information and Action Centre of Toronto, the Ontario Coalition for Better Child Care, the Chinese Workers' Association, and the Parkdale Community Legal Services clinic in Toronto.

The coalition plans to mount a concerted campaign involving labour unions, visible minority and women's groups, and organizations for social justice for the working poor, to press the Ontario New Democratic government to make the necessary changes to the employment standards legislation.

As the current process of economic restructuring continues and deepens, it is essential that coalitions mobilise to prevent the exploitation of the spreading forms of precarious employment, of which homework is the most extreme example. But legislative reforms of the employment standards legislation are just the first step in this campaign. Other reforms are also necessary to ensure the enforcement of revitalized legislation, and to reduce the economic vulnerability of homeworkers. These reforms include more effective enforcement of the Employment Standards Act, the channelling of government resources to the building of a quality system of affordable child care on a priority basis, the increase in government resources going to the training of workers who need basic upgrading (particularly in English language skills) and to bridging programs which allow homeworkers to exercise their choice to work outside the home. As well, unionization and broader-based bargaining structures are necessary to end the exploitation of homeworkers....

Post Mortem—Lépine: Women in Engineering[✠]

Thelma McCormack

In 1965, shortly after *Sputnik,* a conference was convened at the Massachusetts Institute of Technology on "Women and the Scientific Professions." Bruno Bettelheim was the keynote speaker and Erik Erikson delivered the closing address. Two men—two psychiatrists; neither of them had the remotest idea what it meant to be a woman in a group of professional disciplines created by men and dominated by them. To their credit they were encouraging and supportive. Both thought more participation of women in science and engineering would balance the predispositions of men. Women, Bettelheim said, embrace their work; men conquer theirs.[1]

All of this came back in the days following the tragedy of the École Polytechnique de Montréal when Marc Lépine killed fourteen engineering students. Most of the discussion in the media concerned Lépine's motivation. Was he deranged? A deviant? Was he a misogynist acting out the violence most men feel toward women? Or was he a political actor, a terrorist in an on-going struggle by women to change the power structure? Each of these explanations is to some degree true; however, it is the last one, the political scenario, that is the least understood and of most concern to feminists.

Lépine's message to the feminist movement was straight-forward: high-tech is high risk. Ironically, this comes at a time when feminists are sharply divided on the issues of science and technology. Eco-feminists denounce science and technology as inherently destructive to nature, a way of thinking which leads us to dominate nature rather than live in harmony with it. Other feminists are critical of the abstract logic of science and technology that creates an insensitivity to human concerns. Some feminists are less concerned with the logic or value system of science and technology than they

[✠] Thelma McCormack, "Post Mortem—Lépine: Women in Engineering," *Atlantis* 16, no. 2 (Spring 1991): 85–90. Reprinted by permission of the publisher and the author.

are with the historical abuses, in particular, the close connection between technology and the military establishment. Still others consider science and technology as a false ideology which promotes the search for a quick technological fix to profound moral issues and social conflicts. Most of the research on women and technology has focused on the negative impact on employment, that is, problems of workplace automation, deskilling, unemployment and further labour force segmentation.[2]

Leaving aside some of the philosophical questions about science and technology, and leaving aside as well the studies of technological effects on employment, there is a more proximate and political question: What is the relationship between women and engineering in the context of the movement? Was our feminist revolution being fought for equal opportunity in Silicon Valley? Was the women's struggle nothing more than the right to conduct military experiments in space? Should the feminist movement become the conscience of technology rather than join men in the mainstream who idealize and endow it with a metaphysical status?

Lépine's terrorism was intended to deter women from going into engineering. The socialization process has been delivering the same message—the gender differences in toys and hobbies as well as the absence of role models. Girls see their mothers glue handles into cups, shove rags into leaky plumbing and change bulbs, but seldom see them repair the car, install new wiring or rebuild radios. Daughters are more often praised for their people skills and verbal competence han their curiosity about motors. In addition, the educational system streams girls away from science and math, not always intentionally, but the teachers of science are male, the textbooks are written by men, and the histories of science and technology give almost no attention to the achievements of women or show great interest in those fields of science where women have excelled.

When the Soviet rocket *Sputnik* was launched in 1957, there was a major policy change. Embarrassed by the achievements of Soviet scientists, the Western industrial nations poured money into educating young people for careers in science and engineering. Girls benefitted from the attention, but boys more so; the latter were the primary beneficiaries of the new equipment, enriched courses, better teachers, more tutoring, science clubs, field trips, computer camps and science fairs. Thus the floor was raised but the gender gap widened. As a result, women arrived at universities better prepared than they were in the past but with less confidence in themselves or less confident than their male cohorts to do science or engineering. Then, as now, women had few role models. Engineering faculties are primarily men, including those who work in the new areas such as information technology.[3] A few universities have made special efforts to assist women (and minorities) to overcome their insecurity in math and upgrade their skills. However, none have adopted affirmative action policies. At the same time, feminists, among others, have begun to question the prerequisites needed for engineering—specifically, mathematics. Is advanced calculus really relevant to the discipline or is it, as Latin used to be, a measure of character?[4] There is also some controversy among educators whether, in view of the differences between men and women—differences that are either innate or the result of socialization—engineering should be taught differently to women.[5]

Meanwhile, the situation remains the same. Insufficient math is still the reason most often given by women for avoiding engineering and science, and by men for excluding them. Yet, the same women are capable of performing high-level statistical analyses in psychology and sociology, where women are in the majority. There is nothing in probability theory that overwhelms them nor are they any less able in deductive reasoning. (Recently, two young Hungarian women, sisters, astonished the male chess world by becoming grandmasters—one at the age of 13, the other at 15.) In these contexts, women lack neither logic nor the ability to do some fast number crunching. Had we looked more closely at their bridge-playing mothers, we would have realized sooner how much talents for mathematics and logic were being wasted because they were undeveloped. The problem, then, is not an inaptitude for math or linear thinking, but a gendered system and organization of education that anticipates a gendered system of work and economic production.

Women who enrol in engineering courses find themselves in a minority.[6] Four out of 150, two out of 60 are typical, and that number will dwindle by the time they graduate. They feel isolated and are excluded from the day-to-day camaraderie of the men who commute together, study together, relax together and have probably come out of a secondary school where their math and science classes consisted predominantly of boys and were taught by men. Mature male students are less likely to have family obligations than mature female students. Women students in engineering, like university women generally, are inevitably asked by someone—a student, a teaching assistant, a faculty member—if they are only there to find a husband. The campus culture is preparation for the work culture. Hence male alumni do not find the puerile behaviour, vulgarity and coarseness of student behaviour unusual or offensive. Hacker, who audited engineering classes at MIT and later enroled in engineering courses, found that men created a chilly atmosphere for women: locker-room humour, sexist language used in connection with the naming of machines and mechanical processes as well as in informal conversations among students and faculty, and what she calls the erotic pleasure men find in the achievement of some new, extremely narrow technological problem.[7] Like the army, engineering faculties appealed to "tough guys" and screened out any lingering traces of effete sensibility. If the behaviour has become more discussed in recent years, it is, in part, because women on campus (not necessarily women in engineering, who tend to retreat) have become less tolerant—in part because, in a neoconservative environment, it is bad public relations to have engineering students profaning womanhood, but mostly because engineering deans want to attract a small number of women. Alarmed by declining grade-point averages of incoming male students and concerned about the increasing number of foreign students, admissions officers have decided to bring in an elite group of women. The operative word here is "elite," for the men who deplore the manners of their students and publicly reprimand or discipline them have yet to demonstrate any serious intention of democratizing a profession that, in addition to being sexist, is racist and anti-Semitic as well.

Since their earliest days in the 19th century, Canadian engineers have mainly been from Scotland and England.[8] They created the rules, the licensing and the organizations. They became the deans of engineering schools, presidents of large engineering firms and vice-presidents of industrial organizations. That legacy has meant that, when admissions officers today are seeking women applicants, what they want is someone who is brainy, WASP and will be "one of the boys." Yet progress is slow. In Ontario between 1975 and 1985, undergraduate enrolment of women in engineering and applied sciences went from 5.9% to 12.3%, while overall enrolment of women went from 42.6% to 49%. Women are still in a minority and, without some system of quotas or affirmative nation, the gap will not close.[9] The story is slightly better on salary differentials, although one U.S. study found that women engineers with Ph.D.s and 25 years of experience were earning 62 cents on the dollar. Furthermore, the unemployment rate in all branches of engineering was significantly higher for women.[10] The data on Sweden suggest that there may be generational differences. Among younger women, the salary differences and differential rates of unemployment are better. I suspect the same may be true elsewhere. . . .

It would help to change the male culture of engineering faculties if a critical mass of their faculties were women. Academia may be the hope of women, for ambitious men with four-year engineering degrees head toward private industry. There, the starting salaries are among the highest for any group with comparable education and the pay-offs in terms of consumerism, the fastest. Typically, women with four-year degrees in engineering are in the public or semi-public (e.g., utilities) sector, where starting salaries and professional ceilings are lower.[11] Women are often marginalized or underemployed, doing a technician's work.

No wonder they drop out.[12] Educators and employers who worry about the poor retention rate among women engineers usually attribute it to the desire of women to raise families. However, since employers do very little in the way of flextime, daycare or maternity leave to insure that women with children will not drop out, it becomes a self-fulfilling prophecy.

When push comes to pull, the structure of employment, with its incentives and disincentives, overrides the influence of socialization. Women are drawn to engineering when the opportunities are there. Equal opportunity policies may be more important than sexism. This is illustrated by a study comparing high-tech and aerospace industries, which found that women's salaries and promotional opportunities were better in aerospace than in hightech.[13] Why, especially when, according to the women themselves, the aerospace industries were more blatantly sexist than high-tech? In the aerospace industries, there is more harassment, derogatory language and patronizing behaviour from men who were older, more traditional, and often from the military. The difference was that aerospace industries, which depend on government contracts, were required by Title VII of the 1964 Civil Rights Act to observe affirmative action policies. The Equal Employment Opportunity office was there to monitor contract compliance. Therefore, despite the informal work environment, women had better chances of moving up. While they were not welcomed, they were entitled.

By contrast, in the computer industries, more is left to managerial prerogative. There is another factor, however, which also works against women, and that is the system of financing through venture capital or "junk bonds." Women do not attract risk capital, and seldom accumulate much of their own. For the same reason—the inability of women to attract capital or credit—women are less able to start their own enterprises. Hence, a woman with a combined MBA and engineering degree may have all the same entrepreneurial qualifications as a man but still be disadvantaged.[14]

At the low end of the scale, women are overrepresented in the microelectronic industries, where they produce the chip, assemble the hardware, and risk their health through shift work, exposure to chemical solvents and low-level radiation, for wages below or just at the minimum levels.[15] It has been estimated that between 75 and 90 percent of assembly workers in the electronics industry around the world are women, most of them in Southeast Asia where they are new entrants to the labour force, young, unmarried and highly mobile. There is no job security, no unionization, and women who marry and take on family responsibilities can be fired. Work on the assembly line in these industries is as monotonous and alienating as elsewhere. Far from embracing their jobs, as Bettelheim suggests, women endure them.

If the few women in engineering were distributed randomly across the various industries and specializations—electrical, mechanical, civil, aeronautical, and so on—the aggregate income discrepancies would not be so great. Instead, what appears to be happening is a trend toward resegregation. Having moved out of the traditional occupational ghettoes, women are finding themselves in new ones.[16] Is there an "iron law" of job-gender segregation? In Sweden, which scores high on almost all measures of gender equality (for example, 30% of members of parliament are women; paid maternity leave is available to either fathers or mothers up to eighteen months), job segregation along traditional lines persists. According to the 1985 census, women were 8% of all engineers, and in both the largest and the smallest specializations (mechanical and metallurgical), they were only 3%. Although Sweden has a strongly segregated labour force, the case of engineering is extreme.

How much job satisfaction is there in the work? Do women have the same job satisfactions as men? If Bettelheim was right that women bring a different style to the workplace, if eco-feminists are right that women are not naturally comfortable with techno-logic, there should be a significant difference between men and women on measures of job satisfaction. The evidence so far suggests that there is not, but it is possible for men and women to differ on reasons for dissatisfaction. They may agree on what makes a job interesting or challenging or good, yet disagree on what makes it bad. While women resented sexual harassment on the job—everything from pin-up calendars to provocative remarks—they often interpreted these gestures as a lack of professionalism rather than the intrusive presence of patriarchy.[17]

However, the discontents of engineering seldom produce the radicalization Thorstein Veblen envisaged when, in the early 1920s, he wrote *Engineers and the Price System*. If capitalism was to be overthrown, Veblen said, it would be by a soviet of engineers who, better than anyone else, understood how wasteful, stupid and irrational was the traditional mind-set of capitalist owners and stockholders. Engineers held the levers of power, he said, and they could manage the companies more efficiently and profitably.

How far could a soviet of feminist engineers go? Women engineers are about as likely to overthrow patriarchy as male engineers were to overthrow capitalism, but they do not necessarily buy into it uncritically. In her 1990 Massey Lectures, Ursula Franklin described what she calls a "redemptive technology," a technology that is holistic rather than assembly-line; participatory rather than compliant; a technology that minimizes harm and counts environmental costs; a technology that is accountable to people.[18] A soviet of feminist engineers could make science and technology more accessible to women by intervening in the school system and questioning the criteria university gatekeepers use. Feminist engineers could establish a networking relationship with women who work with tools in the crafts but do not want an engineering degree, women who have had to struggle against male-dominated craft unions and male-dominated work sites. Women engineers could be more responsive to women who use a medium technology in offices, shops, small businesses, households, schools, neighbourhoods and hospitals, women whose fears of automation need to be dealt with rationality and through careful transitional planning. A soviet of feminist engineers could incorporate its users into new coalitions and lobby groups. They could blow the whistle on unsafe technology and, perhaps most important of all, develop their own agenda for technological development. These are among a few of the alternatives to the individualism and careerism of a profession integrated with a capitalist economy. More generally, what these examples suggest is that the problems of women in science and engineering lie not in their *method or objectives* but in their *organization*.

This feminization of science and technology stands in opposition to the dystopic view that science and technology oppress women, and that women should remain outside as a form of protest. The women at École Polytechnique wanted to be inside; they were risk-takers who made their own choices in a game where the deck was stacked against them. It is precisely because they were making choices that they represented a threat to men who just want to be left alone to reproduce a labour force in their own image. This will not be the first or last time in history that men fear change or the process more than its outcome.

Lépine may or may not have been a paranoid schizophrenic; he may or may not have hated all women, but he sensed that the system of male privilege was endangered. "Feminists," he told his victims, "are ruining my life." He was not a very politically astute man but he was, as terrorists are, more political than the people who try to understand them socially or psychologically. Meanwhile, this is the occasion for feminists to clarify their thinking about the participation of a younger generation of women in science and technology. Boycott it? Excel in it? Or redeem it?

NOTES

○

1. Mattfield, Jacquelyn A. and Carol G. Van Aken (eds.) (1985) *Women and the Scientific Professions*. Cambridge, MA: MIT Press.

2. Cockburn, Cynthia (1985) *Machinery of Dominance*. Boston: Northeastern University Press. See also Greve, RoseMarie (1987) "Women and Information Technology: A European Overview," in Davidson, M.J. and C.L. Cooper (eds.) *Women and Information Technology*. New York: John Wiley & Sons.

3. Davidson, Marilyn J. and Cary L. Cooper (eds.) (1987) *Women and Information Technology*. New York: John Wiley & Sons.

4. Hacker, Sally (1983) "Mathematization and Engineering: Limits on Women and the Field," in Joan Rothschild (ed.) *Machina Ex Dea*. New York: Pergamon, pp. 38 - 58.

5. Chivers, Geoff (1987) "Information Technology—Girls and Education: A Cross-Cultural Review," in M.J. Davidson and C.L. Cooper (eds.) *Women and Information Technology*. New York: John Wiley & Sons.

6. Carter, Ruth and Gill Kirkup (1990) *Women in Engineering*. London: Macmillan.

7. Hacker, Sally (1989) *Pleasure, Power and Technology*. Winchester, MA: Unwin Hyman.

8. Millard, Rodney J. (1988) *The Master Spirit of the Age: Canadian Engineers and the Politics of Professionalism, 1887-1922*. Toronto: University of Toronto Press.

9. Dagg, Anne Innis and Patricia J. Thompson (1988) "Science and Engineering," in *MisEducation: Women and Canadian Universities*. Toronto: Ontario Institute for Studies in Education, pp. 15 - 23. See also Council of Ontario Universities, Report from the Committee on the Status of Women (1988) *Attracting and Retaining Women Students for Science and Engineering*.

10. Vetter, Betty M. (1981) "Women Scientists and Engineers: Trends in Participation," *Science*, 214(3), 1313-1321.

11. Humphrey, Sheila M. (1982) *Women and Minorities in Science.* Boulder, CO: Westview Press.

12. CAUT Bulletin ACPU. "Women Scientists and Engineers." October 1989, p. 6.

13. Robinson, J. Gregg and Judith S. McIlwee (1989) "Women in Engineering: A Promise Unfulfilled?" *Social Problems*, 36(1), 455-472.

14. Rogers, Evers M. and Judith K. Larsen (1984) *Silicon Valley Fever.* New York: Basic.

15. North-South Institute (1985) *Women in Industry: North-South Connections.* Ottawa: North-South Institute, pp. 11-17.

16. Perrucci, Carolyn Cummings (1970) "Minority Status and the Pursuit of Professional Careers: Women in Science and Engineering," *Social Forces*, 49, 245-259.

17. Carter, Ruth and Gill Kirkup (1990) *Women in Engineering.* London: Macmillan.

18. Franklin, Ursula (1990) *The Real World of Technology.* Toronto: CBC Enterprises.

What Counts as Skill?
Reflections on Pay Equity[*]

Jane Gaskell

Much of the ideological power of pay equity lies in its promise of a process that substitutes objectivity for politics, technical expertise for power relations. A pay equity committee judges the worth of a job by assigning points on an agreed-upon scale. Numbers seem objective and neutral. The scale is based on criteria that are shared within the committee and can be communicated to the sceptical. Where collective bargaining, the market, and employer's decisions have demonstrably disadvantaged women, a technical process that insists on 'unbiased' assessments of the characteristics of jobs, and, therefore, of their worth, seems enormously promising.

But is the promise real or illusory? Can employers, or management consultants, or even teams of workers and managers, come up with assessments that are not biased? Can assessments of jobs be done objectively, without a political point of view implicit in the analysis? The simple answer is no. Any rating scale, any determination of job value is based in judgments that can be politically contested. The job-evaluation process involved in pay equity looks like a technical process, but it is a political one.

This kind of argument is not a new one for feminist analysis. Revealing the hidden ideological underpinnings of 'objective assessments' has been grist for the feminist academic mill. Feminist scholarship has continually pointed to the ways in which what have been described as taken-for-granted, neutral, and objective judgments are actually partial, if not completely wrong and misguided. Feminist analysis has shown that what has been taken as objectivity and political neutrality has too often been simply what powerful males think and say. 'Subjectivity' and 'politicization' enter

[*] Abridged from Judy Fudge and Patricia McDermott, eds., *Just Wages: A Feminist Assessment of Pay Equity* (Toronto: University of Toronto Press, 1991), chapter 7, "What Counts as Skill? Reflections on Pay Equity." Reprinted by permission of the publisher and the author.

in when someone with less power raises questions. This general lesson applies to the determination of pay equity.

Pay equity committees are asked to evaluate jobs on the basis of four criteria—skill, effort, responsibility, and working conditions. My academic work has been directed at one of these issues, the historical and social processes that have shaped our evaluations of skill. My argument, in short, is that there is no one correct, objective version of how much skill is involved in doing a job. In making statements about and evaluations of skill, we stand in our historical time and place, in our culture. We stand in traditions of thought that have been thoroughly dominated by men. And we come face to face with basic questions of value, of power, of women's place in the world. When people overlook women's skills, devalue them, give them low ratings, it is not a technical glitch, but a reflection of the status and power women have not had in the world. . . .

W H A T   C O U N T S   A S   A   S K I L L ?

o

In the sociological literature, Braverman (1974) has been an important stimulus to rethinking what counts as skilled or unskilled work. He points out that, according to census categories, work today is considerably more skilled than work a century ago. The census mirrors the assumption that life today is more complicated, as technology is more complicated, and that people have obtained more education in response to the requirements of the more complex jobs they do. 'The idea that the changing conditions of industrial and office work require an increasingly "better trained", "better educated" and thus "upgraded" working population is an almost universally accepted proposition in popular and academic discourse,' he wrote in 1974 (p. 424).

Braverman notes that working with machines was what originally set skilled factory workers apart from unskilled labourers in the U.S. census. As an extension of this line of thinking, the census classified drivers of motorized vehicles as skilled and drivers of horse-drawn vehicles as unskilled. But Braverman comments,

> in the circumstances of an earlier day, when a largely rural population learned the arts of managing horses as part of the process of growing up, while few as yet knew how to operate motorized vehicles, it might have made sense to characterize the former as part of the common heritage and thus no skill at all, while driving, as a learned ability, would have been thought of as a 'skill'. Today, it would be more proper to regard those who are able to drive vehicles as unskilled in that respect at least, while those who can care for, harness and manage a team of horses are certainly the possessors of a marked and uncommon ability. There is certainly little reason to suppose that the ability to drive a motor vehicle is more demanding,

requires longer training or habituation time, and thus represents a higher or intrinsically more rewarding skill. (p. 430)

Census categories reflect common ideological assumptions and patterns of informal learning abroad in the land—assumptions that, as technology gets more complex, jobs get more complex; that, as education levels increase, the jobs workers do become more skilled; that everyone can drive a car. What we take to be a noteworthy skill is fundamentally shaped by what is taken for granted in the society, what the social context is, where and how we learn to do something.

Having pointed out that the government classification system does not accurately describe skill levels, Braverman reverts to his own definition of skill, although he has difficulty describing it in one phrase. He sees skills as 'traditionally bound up with craft mastery,' and, as he indicates above, tied to training time and the 'commonness' of skills. He assumes this definition is shared with his readers and validated by common sense. He is uneasy with 'relativistic or contemporary notions' (p. 430) of skill that degrade the concept by having it refer to those 'able to perform repetitive tasks with manual dexterity.' His political concern for craft workers (he was a copper-smith, pipe-fitter, and sheetmetal worker, among other things) shapes the way he begins to think about skill himself. He points to craft skills, not to the interpersonal and social skills involved in being a waitress or a recep-tionist. His experience shapes his perceptions—understandably. None of us can avoid it.

Braverman's analysis of the shifting definition of skill suggests the importance of inquiry into the social processes involved in producing the shifting skill labels. He did not explore gender issues, but others have. Mar-garet Mead wrote, 'One aspect of this social evaluation of different types of labour is the differentiated prestige of men's activities and women's activi-ties. Whatever men do—even if it is dressing dolls for religious ceremonies —is more prestigious than what women do and is treated as a higher achievement.' Being treated as a 'higher' achievement can easily translate in a more scientific world, into being considered a 'higher' skill. Mental labour is more prestigious than manual labour. Science is more prestigious than caring for children. Giving directions is more prestigious than working out what they mean and following them closely. It is not clear that one is more difficult than another. These are cultural values. Things associated with dominant values and with power are counted as higher skills....

Providing an account of a worker's abilities is not a neutral descriptive process. The terms of the account are highly conditioned by the social con-text in which it takes place and by the social purposes to which it will be put. Labelling and valuing particular abilities involves an ongoing historical struggle between workers and employers, and among different groups of workers.

And women have not fared well in these struggles. Barrett (1980) argues: 'Women have frequently failed to establish recognition of the skills required by their work, and have consequently been in a weak bargaining position in a divided and internally competitive work force... we need to know precisely how and why some groups of workers succeed in establishing definitions of their work as skilled.' (p. 166).

This more thorough-going recognition of the social and political content of skill categories is one feminists must embrace. To revalue women's skills involves seeing the ways that our knowledge and abilities have been taken for granted. It involves fighting for the revaluing of women's work, because it is important and necessary work.

E D U C A T I O N   A S   S K I L L

o

Views of skill are based not only in abstract constructions of what we value and what we take for granted. They are based quite concretely in the length of educational preparation required for a job. More educated workers are more skilled. Workers who have spent longer in training programs are more skilled. Questions of value are given a material form in educational requirements and training programs....

Even those who point to the ideological content of skill ratings tend to rely on time spent in training as a legitimate way to differentiate between skilled and unskilled work. Time is a useful measure for administrators, labour negotiators, or social scientists trying to come up with ratings, as it can be turned into a number and used to compare things that are actually quite unlike. Time becomes a mode of exchange of value, like money, and it creates the same problem of losing sight of what it actually represents and how it is produced. Thus, time in training is turned into skill ratings, reifying skill into a undimensional 'thing.'

Taking training time as a sign of skill assumes that the length of training depends on the difficulty, complexity, and breadth of understanding necessary for performing the work. There is a long tradition in the sociology of education that treats skill in just this way, as something accumulated through years of formal education and justifying a claim to a higher-paying job.

But Braverman for one points out that increased educational levels cannot be used as a measure of skill upgrading in the work-force. 'A complete picture of the functions and functioning of education in the United States and other capitalist countries would require a thorough historical study of the manner in which the present standards came into being, and how they were related, at each step of their formation, to the social forces of the society at large. But even a sketch of the recent period suffices to show that many causes, most of them bearing no direct relationship to the educational requirements of the job structure, have been at work' (p. 437).

Changes in labour legislation, in the unemployment rate, in state investment in educational institutions, and in employers' use of education as a screening device are among some of the important factors that have increased the educational levels of workers. None of these means that the skill levels of jobs have changed.

How are we to determine the amount of training 'necessary' to an 'adequate' performance of a job? Some people learn faster than others. Some employers are more demanding. Some people will already know a lot of what they need, because they have picked training up informally. The length and form that training will take are decided through political and economic struggle. Collins (1979) comments: 'The "system" does not "need" or "demand" a certain kind of performance; it "needs" what it gets, because "it" is nothing more than a slip shod way of talking about the way things happen to be at the time. How hard people work, and with what dexterity and cleverness, depends on how much other people can require them to do, and on how much they can dominate other people' (p. 54).

Lots of different kinds of training will do to prepare people for their jobs. No single version is 'necessary.' What training programs do is control the supply of labour and certify its skill. Turner has argued that workers are considered skilled or unskilled 'according to whether or not entry to their occupations is deliberately restricted and not in the first place according to the nature of the occupation itself' (1962, 184). Barrett (1980) echoes this observation: 'Training and recruitment may be highly controlled and skill rendered inaccessible for the purposes of retaining the differentials and privilege of the labour aristocracy' (p. 168).

Collins (1979) documents how some groups have successfully struggled to restrict entry through educational requirements, while others have not. Doctors and engineers were able to insist on university preparation for their work; nurses, child-care workers, and carpenters were not. Tool-and-die workers were able to maintain their apprenticeships on the job; clerical workers were not. Women's occupations—child care and clerical work, for example—are much more likely to be open to people with a wide range of educational and vocational backgrounds, and therefore to be treated as unskilled occupations. Women have not had the political might to keep wages in their occupations up by restricting entry to a narrow band of suitably credentialled workers.

There is evidence that many of the skills learned at school or in formal training programs have little direct importance on the job (Berg 1970; Hall and Carlton 1977). Educational attainment may act as a 'signal' or a 'screen,' without imparting any necessary skills (Spence 1973). The time training takes can vary for the same job, depending on which country a worker is in, or which employer she works for. Requirements for training change when the actual skills involved in the work do not. The training of teachers is an example. It has increased over the years as the demand for teachers eased and as the general educational levels of the population went up. Changes in the skills 'required' for a classroom have been produced by social changes extending well beyond the 'needs' of children.

The provision of on-the-job training is also negotiated. Women have been less able to get formal training after they are hired, as they are assumed to be short-term workers. If employers believe that women really belong in and will therefore return to the home, investment in their training is considered wasteful. As a result, women must often pick up skills in more informal ways, on the job or in the family. Opportunities for mobility through education are not built into their jobs.The difference between advancement and training opportunities for secretaries (women) and for general-purpose clerks (men or women) is the most obvious example.

In other words, the correspondence between schooling requirements and work demands need not be very strong, and certainly does not need to be based on 'skill.' While there undoubtedly are instances where training does develop necessary skills, this must not be assumed to be the case.The form that specific skill training and vocational education will take has been one of the major areas of struggle, within the public-school system as well as in the workplace and in state-run training programs.

And it is clear that training for women's work is organized in ways that are different from training for men's work. Women have been less able to insist on licensing and regulation of training, and have been less able to get on-the-job training (Wolf and Rosenfeld 1978). Rather than being an indication of skill differences in men's and women's jobs, these differences reflect the fact that the jobs have been filled predominantly by one sex or the other.

AN   EXAMPLE: THE   SKILLS   IN   CLERICAL   JOBS
o

I will briefly illustrate some of these issues with reference to clerical work. Clerical work is an interesting example because, today, it is an overwhelmingly female occupation. It accounts for the employment of about a third of the female labour force. Secretary, typist, and receptionist are some of the jobs most fully identified with women. Yet the skills involved in these jobs are unclear, unrecognized, and learned haphazardly. Entry into the occupation is unregulated and unstandardized. Paying for existing educational levels, skills, and training would clearly help many women who work in clerical jobs achieve higher pay. But to recognize the worth of clerical jobs would entail more than this. It would entail recognizing the complexity and importance of the tasks that are done....

Today, clerical work remains an area where skills are not recognized, where women experience the disjuncture between what they do and what others see. Pringle (1988) notes that secretaries are defined more by who they are (women), and by their relation to a boss (helpmate and subordinate), than by what they do. There are few agreed-upon job definitions, few clearly defined skills, few agreed-upon training requirements, and few ladders out of the job into more responsible positions, even though unions have increasingly addressed these issues. The extreme variability in jobs broadly labelled 'clerical' also contributes to the struggle around the meaning of the work, a struggle that is contested by workers, educators, and employers.

Comments like these from clerical workers express their sense of being undervalued in a variety of ways:

> I don't think a lot of people realize that a lot of work done in offices isn't done by the boss ... most of it is done by the staff and everyone doesn't look at it that way.

> A man [manager] was hired at one time who had no experience, and he got twice as much wages as I did. You know I had to train him. And it really got under my skin.[1]

The skills, the knowledge, the language abilities that are necessary in clerical jobs provide the motivation for these women to engage in further education. But their frustration is that their skills are not visible to others, and are not rewarded by high wages or respect in the office. They may need better language skills than the boss because they must fix his grammar, and they may have more knowledge of how the office runs, so they show the boss what to do, but theirs remains a job that is not perceived as skilled.

The training for clerical work remains unregulated. Some employers will prefer and hire clerical workers with university degrees, while others prefer and hire women with less than high-school diplomas. Some educators will argue that a single typing course is enough, if combined with general academic skills, while others stress the necessity of elaborate programs of training in accounting, dicta-typing, shorthand, computer technology, and office practice offered at a community college. BAs in secretarial science are offered at a couple of universities in Canada, indicating that one might construct the training requirements as quite elaborate. But, for the most part, clerical training is short, even while the skills involved in the job are many.

In order to prepare women for a job that can be quite complex within the terms of a short training program, instructors must admit into training women who already know most of what they need to know. Clerical training gets women to quickly recognize, label, polish, and feel confident in skills they already possess. Neither the resources nor the time are available for teaching what needs to be known.

In a twenty-six-week government-sponsored clerical-training program I studied, students who had already worked as clerical workers were chosen as students. The instructors instituted a screening interview, and made grade 12 completion a requirement for students. Applicants were chosen if they were emotionally secure, well dressed, used the English language correctly, and already had basic clerical skills, most importantly typing. Some had university degrees. The instructors were worried about this phenomenon, pointing out that the women most in need of training were not getting it, but the structure of the situation made such selection procedures necessary.

The curriculum centred on life skills and work experience. The technical skills were at a very introductory level—more advanced skills were seen to be necessary for the work, but would have to be learned on the job. The students spent time on typewriters upgrading their typing speed. They also learned Multi-Mate, a software program for personal computers that gave them an idea of what word processing was all about. There were no accounting courses taught, no spread-sheet or data-base-management programs, no other word-processing packages. There was no dicta-typing; no shorthand; no basic grammar, spelling, or arithmetic.

In other words, successful clerical training, at least in short-term programs, depends on students having already informally learned the skills that the training is meant to impart. Training can be short because it depends on everywoman's skills. More advanced technical training is not provided, a phenomenon that reconfirms the notion that clerical workers lack skills and allows the government to continue to underfund women's training.

What was taught in the program also speaks to the construction of clerical skills. 'Life skills,' including dress codes, were taught because they would have an immediate pay-off in an interview, because they mattered to employers. What is taken for granted as femininity must be taught. It is not natural. It is a 'skill.'

In the class on dress, clear rules were adduced. 'Buy fake pearls that are knotted in between the pearls and don't have too high a gloss; buy beige. It's boring as hell, but it goes with everything.' But at the same time, the contextual discussion was fairly sophisticated. 'Whatever I'll tell you today, someone else will tell you something else tomorrow' (and, later, as the students make clear the variety of their actual work situations), 'It all comes down to, you'll have to figure out what your interviewer will be like.' In other words, figure out the social relations of the office and conform in ways that recognize your social position.

The objective of the class was described as 'to identify a professional look ... Women don't know how to dress. Men do ... There are things your mother never told you, the best things to wear to get ahead in business.' The discussion was interspersed with scientific findings: '75% of women from Harvard thought their appearance was important in getting a position.' Through looking at pictures of men and women, students were encouraged to examine critically the meaning of various styles of clothing, what clothes say. 'The jacket puts the woman at the top. Jacket is a mantel of authority. Men know it. They put it on when they see a client. A sweater is textured. It says touch me, it seems more friendly.' As the class goes on, each look is critiqued for how powerful it makes the woman appear. 'I think it's a very successful look. It says money. Off white or cream. Only the rich can afford to have them dry cleaned. Pearls are quite successful'; 'Fake it till you make it. Dress like where you want to go, but never more than the boss.'

There is a gender code that must be learned. Sexuality must be controlled, but cannot be denied. The discussion of dressing like or for men included the following comment: Student: 'We don't want to look like them, but they are the ones that hire you. You need to understand them.' The problems with dressing like a woman were that 'there's nothing that will put you down in authority more quickly than a little pink sweater. You look like a housewife.' Long hair is too 'counter culture,' and yellow is 'not a power colour.'

The description of this class provokes laughter from many of the educators to whom I have described it. These skills are not skills that are valued and respected and put in most curriculum outlines. But these are skills the women wanted, felt they needed at work, and would be hired because of. The instructors, who had a good deal of experience with placing students, agreed that the ability to dress appropriately was an absolutely critical skill, a skill women are expected to have and punished for not having. How should these skills be valued? The answer depends on who is asked.

Another point in the training program where the social construction of skill becomes explicit is in constructing a résumé. The instructors pointed out that the résumés is a way of communicating to employers what you can do. It 'is the packaging for you—you're writing a real box package—making it appealing. The purpose is to sell yourself.' The instructors advised women to highlight skills on their résumés, to thereby construct themselves as skilled workers. The résumé was a place where they could decide what counted as a skill, and where they could communicate their competence using a frame of reference that suited them. The instructors showed students how to 'trick,' as they put it, employers into seeing them as skilled. As the instructor explained, 'We try to show that everything that they've been doing in their life, the things they are dismissing as just housewifely chores, are all really skills that they've learned and that they can help make a contribution in the business world.'

In class, the instructor explained, 'We do skill right up front, not education but skills—that's a functional résumé ... we'll forget about chronological résumés here. In traditional application forms they want you to list your work, starting from the most recent. It makes me freeze.' Student: 'That's what Canada Employment wants you to do.' Instructor: 'Well, we're going to trick them— assemble it so that the gaps don't show ... Because you have so many skills—look at all the ones you've got. I'm impressed ... Look at page 15, we're going to use some of these words. They've been designed by experts—action words that people can hang on to ... Most words are "ing" words. A résumé is not in past tense.'

Instructor: 'With skills, what you list you don't have to be paid for it ... in a functional résumé your skills are what you've been paid for or not. You did the work, you had the skill. In the last group one woman ran her husband's trucking business for twenty-five years while her husband was out on the road. Never got a penny. But she had to do invoices, phoning, contracting. Doesn't matter if you've been paid or unpaid—doesn't connect with traditional paid employment.'

The skills that the instructors particularly encouraged the women to recognize, value, and write down were social skills.

Student: 'What are interpersonal skills?' Instructor: 'Counselling, interviewing, dealing with people all day. A lot of secretarial work is interpersonal—handling complaints, conferences, handling people is distinct from technical ... Dealing with people is one of the hardest things to do. Those who go to management school—it's all people skills. The reason why women are doing well in the workplace is that they have good people skills. Don't forget the interpersonal—like handling complaints.' Student (indicating here that she is getting the idea of 'packaging' her skills): 'Handling is not a good word.' Instructor: 'What else could we use? Dealing?—mediating is a good word.

'Interpersonal skills—there are thousands of women who can type and use word processors but if they are being difficult or get in cliques—'

What is the value of these skills and abilities? There is no simple answer to these questions, but it is important to see them as questions. Too often knowledge of dress and social graces are taken for granted as personality characteristics. Their association with women makes them lose value. Sitting in these classrooms makes one aware of how the skills are learned and how they are taken seriously by women returning to the labour market. They should be recognized as we struggle over our assessments of skill. They will be recognized only if the women who do the work are able to insist on their importance, their scarcity, and their value.

C O N C L U S I O N

o

The process of defining and valuing the skills necessary for a job is a complex one that is based in someone's point of view. It has rarely taken the point of view of women workers. The devaluation of women and their work has shaped the assessment of women's skills, and affected the kind of training women receive for their work. Training programs symbolize skill and restrict job entry. Women workers have not been able to insist on long and regulated training programs. They have not been able to insist that on-the-job training be provided.

Any processes that hope to produce pay equity must make the politics of skill attribution explicit, and abandon the idea that skill is an objective criterion to which we can appeal to get away from politics, power, and struggle. Can pay equity legislation be used to raise consciousness about women's skills and training at work? Can it be used to show women that their skills are important and real, and that they can legitimately make demands based on them?

The answer probably depends on how pay equity is implemented, how it is discussed by unions and employers and lawyers and all of us. The requirement of pay equity committees means that the question of what skills are required at work must be confronted and discussed. The terms in which this discussion takes place are critical. If the discussion simply leads everyone to discuss where on a taken-for-granted scale of value their own job fits, the politics of pay equity will consolidate in the workplace a version of skill that was arrived at with little input from women. If the scales themselves are discussed and re-evaluated, there is an opportunity for a fundamental revaluing of women's work.

There seems to be preliminary evidence that both processes occur. Women do sometimes discover that they have skills they had never thought about, and they force employers to recognize it too. But sometimes, the process can confirm for women their place at the bottom, and legitimate ways of valuing that obscure women's skills. Pay equity has no single necessary outcome. It can have one effect in one workplace, and another next door. What will happen will depend on how we all engage the process, and over time perhaps we will see its ideological impact on all of us.

NOTE

○

1. These comments are taken from transcripts of interviews with women in clerical-training programs in Vancouver. The research was funded by the Social Sciences and Humanities Research Council of Canada.

REFERENCES

○

Barrett, Michele. 1980. *Women's Oppression Today.* London.

Berg, I. 1970. *Education and Jobs: The Great Training Robbery.* New York.

Braverman, Harry. 1974. *Labor and Monopoly Capitalism.* New York.

Collins, Randall. 1979. *The Credential Society.* New York.

Hall, O. and R. Carlton. 1977. Basic Skills at School and Work (Occasional Paper No. 1, Ontario Economic Council). Toronto.

Pringle, Rosemary. 1988. *Secretaries Talk.* Sydney.

Spence, M. 1973. 'Job Marketing Signalling.' *Quarterly Journal of Economics* 87: 355 -74.

Wolf, Wendy and Rachel Rosenfeld. 1978. 'Sex structure of occupations and mobility.' *Social Forces* 56/3: 823-44.

Organizing and
Managing Work in the
New Economy

EDITORS' INTRODUCTION
o

The articles in this section offer contemporary examples of the challenges employers—and workers—face in the wake of massive economic change nationally and globally. There is no single survival strategy. Nor is there a consensus regarding how to meet what are often competing objectives: improved quality of working life for employees and, for managers, greater productivity and flexibility. New technology, for its part, cannot be viewed as a simple solution to the complex problems of adjusting management styles and organizational forms to accommodate new economic and social realities. What does emerge from the following articles, however, is that some of the most successful and innovative organizations have adopted a course of change that emphasizes human resource development.

The 1988 federal Auditor General's report provides a fascinating glimpse into what makes organizations perform well. The research began by asking senior government managers to identify federal government departments, agencies, or crown corporations that were highly effective. A consensus emerged about eight such organizations. This was a diverse group in terms of types of clients, size, and the kind of work performed. These eight well-performing organizations shared twelve attributes. Foremost was an emphasis on people. Good performance thus appears to have resulted from organizational structures and management styles that enabled people to use their talents and abilities, encouraged them to take responsibility and be innovative, and did not shackle them with bureaucracy. Managerial styles were participative; work was flexible and creative; clients were a major focus. High performance was developed and maintained largely through a commitment to continuous improvement. Values, or "organizational culture," played a major role in reforming these work organizations. What the report does not address, though, is how the employees of these eight organizations perceived their jobs. Were they as motivated and satisfied as the Auditor General would lead us to expect? Or was performance defined largely in terms of management's goals?

These are important questions, especially in the face of public sector cutbacks and privatization. The private sector, wracked by the recession and struggling against the competitive pressures of the new global economy, has also undergone massive restructuring.

Many North American-based corporations have been slow to adapt to the new economic environment. The threat of Japanese competition has been a major catalyst for change, especially for the auto manufacturers. Conventional wisdom holds that superior management largely accounts for the success of Japanese corporations. Will these techniques work in Canada? Answers to this question are provided in Ann Walmsley's look inside Japanese transplants in Canada. Especially fascinating is her analysis of management practices, production methods, and working conditions in Canada's three new Japanese auto plants—Toyota, Honda, and CAMI.

Walmsley leaves little doubt that some features of Japanese management are not acceptable to Canadian workers, or managers for that matter. For example, production workers object to frequent mandatory overtime, while managers complain about conditions in huge open-plan offices. Regimentation also grates on employees, as does the policy of expecting production teams to cover for absent members. But there are compensations. Jobs are less boring and learning opportunities greater. Teams build camaraderie among workers, and consensus decision-making boosts morale. Job security and pay are good. The general trend seems to be for Japanese firms to adapt their practices to the Canadian situation. Eventually, perhaps, this will produce a new hybrid management approach that will be adopted more widely in Canadian industry.

A contrasting perspective on contemporary management is provided in the articles by Jerry Zeidenberg and David Olive. The workers in the Japanese transplants may be the lucky ones, if the practices described by Zeidenberg and Olive are at all widespread. In a twist on Japanese just-in-time inventory systems, Zeidenberg describes the advantages of a "just-in-time work force" for small business. Surviving in the recession means keeping labour costs down, especially in the labour-intensive service sector. A solution, Zeidenberg argues, is creating a flexible work force by using part-time and temporary workers as dictated by the changing volume of business. From Zeidenberg's examples, it is evident that this practice will create a two-tiered employment system: full-time and relatively well-paid core staff, and the "flexible" work force of temps and part-timers who receive low wages and no benefits.

Yet David Olive's portrayal of the get-tough mentality in some large corporations suggests that many full-time workers also may feel insecure about their jobs. Olive detects a shift away from the people-orientation, championed in the previously cited report of the Auditor General, to a survival-of-the-fittest style of management that pressures staff to work harder and faster. Essentially, this management style places blame for corporate woes on employees, rather than taking stock of failed executive strategies, resistance to change, or outmoded structures and procedures.

Technological innovation is a prime ingredient of organizational change in Canada. But it is naive to think that computers and automated technology alone can lead to improvements in productivity or the quality of working life. New technologies are only part of a larger change process that also includes human and organizational factors. Ignoring the latter will limit the positive effects of technology. A model of workplace innovation that addresses the concerns of management, workers, and unions is the sociotechnical systems (STS) approach. STS moves beyond traditional top-down management and adversarial industrial relations, forming a new partnership based on employee participation and teamwork. Quality of working life is a paramount goal, and technology is introduced accordingly.

Despite the fact that most technological change has not been accompanied by this kind of organizational reform, there are some Canadian examples of successful sociotechnical designs that optimize the advantages of new technologies for both workers and managers. One of the most famous of these STS workplaces is the Shell Chemical plant in Sarnia, Ontario. A joint initiative by Shell Canada and the Energy and Chemical Workers Union, the plant represents a significant departure from old-style management, bureaucratic organization, and industrial relations. The development of the team-based organizational design at the plant is detailed by Louis Davis and Charles Sullivan. The plant is the ultimate high-tech operation, yet it is also very people-oriented given the direct involvement of its worker teams in decision-making and its emphasis on continuous learning. Perhaps the most notable feature of the Shell sociotechnical model is the cooperation between union and management. Many Canadian unions remain sceptical of management's motives in such "participative" schemes—with good reason. As other articles in this section point out, management's agenda of slashing labour costs and boosting worker productivity will seriously erode the quality of working life. Reconciling the apparently conflicting principles of human resource development and improved quality of working life, on the one hand, and the drive for competitiveness and productivity, on the other, may be one of the keys to our economic prosperity.

DISCUSSION QUESTIONS

1. Are the principles of well-performing organizations that the Auditor General found in public sector organizations equally applicable to the private sector?

2. Should a decent job be a basic right for all Canadians?

3. What factors account for the variations in management styles and organizational structures described in the various articles?

4. How important is "leadership" in bringing about organizational change? What are some of the other main ingredients of successful change?

5. What are some of the implications of the employment practices described in the articles for social stratification and inequality in Canadian society?

SUGGESTED READINGS
o

Betcherman, Gordon, Keith Newton, and Joanne Godin, eds. *Two Steps Forward: Human Resource Management in a High-Tech World.* Ottawa: Economic Council of Canada, 1990.

Kanter, Rosabeth Moss. *When Giants Learn to Dance: Mastering the Challenges of Strategy, Management, and Careers in the 1990s.* New York: Simon and Schuster, 1989.

Milkman, Ruth. *Japan's California Factories: Labor Relations and Economic Globalization.* Los Angeles: Institute of Industrial Relations, University of California, Los Angeles, 1991.

Peters, Tom. *Thriving on Chaos: Handbook for a Management Revolution.* New York: Alfred A. Knopf, 1987.

Rankin, Tom. *New Forms of Work Organization: The Challenge For North American Unions.* Toronto: University of Toronto Press, 1990.

Zuboff, Shoshana. *In the Age of the Smart Machine: The Future of Work and Power.* New York: Basic Books, 1988.

Zussman, David, and Jak Jabes. *The Vertical Solitude: Managing in the Public Sector.* Halifax: Institute for Research on Public Policy, 1989.

Well-Performing Organizations[*]

Auditor General of Canada

AIM OF THE STUDY

A general consensus indicates that some government organizations continue to perform better than others in delivering their programs productively. They do so not necessarily with respect to any one specific criterion— least cost, for example—but in terms of overall performance, including quality and level of service, timeliness, responsiveness, cost-effectiveness and satisfaction of employees.

This realization, and the observation that some of these organizations seemed to be using innovative approaches to achieve their level of performance, led us to undertake the present study. Our aim was to discover why some organizations perform well and then to document and report our findings. The expectation was that similar approaches might lead to similar successes in other organizations that are not performing as well. It should be noted that this study was not approached as an audit in a verification mode. It represents an attempt to discover and understand; the evidence we present is qualitative rather than quantitative.

THE STUDY DESIGN

As the first step in our study design, we sought to identify, by peer consensus, some six to eight organizations that were considered to perform well.

[*] Abridged from Auditor General of Canada, "Attributes of Well-Performing Organizations: A Study by the Office of the Auditor General of Canada (Ottawa: Minister of Supply and Services, 1989), chapter 4, "Well-Performing Organizations." Reprinted by permission of the Minister of Supply and Services Canada.

We knew that no organization would be perfect, and we didn't look for perfection. To reach a consensus, we interviewed senior officials in various departments and in central agencies.

Next, we interviewed senior officials of the suggested organizations, obtaining their agreement to participate. During these initial discussions, we also agreed on a focus, or "theme of good performance", on which we would concentrate when examining their organizations. This was important to us, because it would focus our analysis and help us scope out aspects of the organizations to which this particular study didn't relate.

The next step was to identify and analyze the attribute that produced good performance in the organizations. Was it leadership? Was it autonomy? Was it technology? What attribute or combination of attributes was the basis for success?

We interviewed people who represented each of the selected areas within the organizations—senior and middle management as well as staff at lower levels. We also interviewed sources outside the organizations, such as suppliers, clients, observers and "owners". By observers we meant overseeing agencies such as, for example, the Office of the Comptroller General. By owners, we meant individuals responsible for overall policy and accountability for the organization. Depending on the organization, this could be a Deputy Minister, a Minister or other Member of Parliament, or a member of a Board of Governors. In addition to conducting interviews, we reviewed various records that were available in the organizations, including surveys of clients and of employees.

Once we had identified and verified the distinguishing attributes of each well-performing organization, we would determine if some of these attributes existed across all or most of the organizations. If they did, and if it were then possible to document them in a way that would make them useful to other organizations, our aim would be achieved. . . .

COMMON ATTRIBUTES OF THE PARTICIPATING ORGANIZATIONS
o

Our study included interviews and observations at various levels of each participating organization and we spoke with people both at headquarters and in the field. It also included discussions with knowledgeable outside people. We talked with suppliers, clients, boards of governors, Deputy Ministers and Ministers. As we collected data, we reviewed and analyzed them to identify those attributes that seemed to be common to all or most of the participating organizations. During feedback sessions with people in the organizations, we discussed the set of attributes we were developing, and confirmed and refined them. . . .

Following, in summary form, is a set of twelve attributes that we found to be common to the organizations we examined. They are grouped in four categories: Emphasis on People, Participative Leadership, Innovative Work Styles, and Strong Client Orientation. Some of the attributes overlap, yet they are distinct enough to warrant individual reference.

EMPHASIS ON PEOPLE

o

The most striking attribute of the well-performing organizations is the emphasis they place on their people. People are challenged, encouraged and developed. They are given power to act and to use their judgment. There is a "caring" attitude in these organizations, based on the belief that, in the long run, high performance is a product of people who care rather than of systems that constrain. Typically, people in these organizations do not preoccupy themselves with the risk of failure, but instead are confident that they can tackle virtually any challenge.

The empowering organization. Well-performing organizations become and remain that way by developing and empowering their people. People are challenged, stretched and encouraged to grow by being given authority, responsibility and autonomy. They are given the power to act, to make decisions and to represent the organization based on their own best judgment. One of our interviewees put it this way: "People work not only with their hands, but also with their minds and their hearts".

The "caring" organization. The values, attitudes and policies of the organization are based on an overall sense of caring: for its own people; for its clients; for the organization as a whole and for the organization's owners. These values are based on the belief that, in the long run, high organizational performance is a product of people who care rather than of systems that control.

The "successful" organization. The organization tries to ensure "success experiences". It sets easily attainable goals at first. In time, the goals are set higher, but always within reach. Initial success creates an appetite for further success, and eventually failure becomes inconceivable: success has been made part of the culture. Typically, people in these organizations are not blind to the risk of failure. However, they are not preoccupied with it and are confident that they can tackle virtually any challenge.

PARTICIPATIVE LEADERSHIP

o

Leadership in the well-performing organizations is not authoritarian or coercive, but participative. The leaders envision an ideal organization, define purpose and goals, then articulate these and foster commitment in their people. They see the organization as always becoming more and more like the ideal. The well-performing organizations communicate easily internally and with others. Staff feel comfortable consulting their peers as well as those above and below them. Although formal levels exist for administrative purposes, there are no boundaries that inhibit collaboration in achieving organizational goals.

The organization with participative leadership. Instead of directing through authoritarianism or coercion, this participative leadership guides by being creative, by detecting patterns, by articulating purpose and mission, and by fostering commitment to the goals of the organization.

The "becoming" organization. Here, the leaders envision an "ideal type" of what the organization could and should be. Once this ideal is defined, they continually strive to reach it. They see the organization as always "becoming" more and more like the ideal.

The communicating organization. One of the prime functions of the leaders in this type of organization is seen as communicating, rather than as commanding. The leaders inspire and foster communication: they hear, they notice, they encourage, they articulate policy and purpose, they counsel and they reward. Staff at all levels feel comfortable consulting their peers as well as others above and below them. Although formal levels exist for administrative purposes, there are no boundaries that inhibit consultation and collaboration in achieving organizational goals.

INNOVATIVE WORK STYLES

o

Staff in the well-performing organization reflect on their performance, on the environment and on opportunities. They learn from experience. They are innovative, flexible and creative. They maintain strong monitoring, feedback and control systems, but only as useful tools. In effect, the well-performing organization seeks to be self-reliant and to control itself rather than relying on control from outside.

The learning organization. Staff are involved in continual scrutiny of the organization, of its environment, and of its performance in relation to the ideal. They seek to learn from the effects of their actions. They use evaluations, standards and assessments, but always for a productive and defined purpose, never simply because of convention.

The problem-solving organization. The organization thrives on identifying opportunities and solving problems. It is innovative and flexible, and it seeks to solve problems creatively.

The intelligent organization. Members of the organization review, consult and collaborate with each other as a matter of course. They understand the organization's purpose and mission. They know what needs to be done and what needs to be measured. They build monitoring, feedback and control systems that are useful tools. The organization controls itself rather than depending on control from an outside authority.

STRONG CLIENT ORIENTATION

○

People in these organizations focus strongly on the needs and preferences of their clients. They derive satisfaction from serving the client rather than the bureaucracy. There is an alignment of values and purpose between the well-performing organizations and their political and central agency masters with a view to strong performance and high achievement.

The organization that is supported by its owners. Goals are congruent between political, central agency and departmental levels, all of which actively support and reinforce the overall mission. There is an alignment of values, of purpose and of resources toward high organizational achievement and performance.

The organization with strong client orientation. Instead of focussing on a hierarchy and on the authority that rules the hierarchy, people in the well-performing organizations focus on client needs and preferences. People in the organization derive their satisfaction from serving the client, rather than from serving the bureaucracy. Interaction is strong within the organization, but it is perhaps even stronger between the organization and its clients.

The "concretizing" organization. Organization members are able to talk in concrete terms about intangible things such as mission and values. They are also able to talk about abstract results in such a way that these become visible and easily discussable. For example, achieving zero mortgage defaults over a long period of time would normally be reflected only in routine paperwork. The well-performing organization finds ways to make such achievements visible by recognizing them through, for example, plaques and awards. As a result, people can better identify with achievement and are motivated to extend their reach.

THE PROCESS BY WHICH THE ORGANIZATIONS ACQUIRED THESE ATTRIBUTES

○

Our aim in this study was to discover why some organizations perform well and then to report our findings, so that others might profit from them. In the early stages of this study, we believed that documenting the common attributes would be sufficient to serve as a guide for other organizations. However, further reflection and discussion suggested that a specific set of attributes is not necessarily ideal for all situations. Different organizations, and even the same organization at different times, may need different attributes for good performance.

Accordingly, we tried to go beyond the attributes and search for the underlying process that allowed the well-performing organizations to develop and maintain their optimum set of attributes. We reasoned that such a process would be both more generic and more informative than simply a list of the attributes themselves. If we could point to such a process, people in other organizations might use it for developing a suitable set of attributes for themselves and thereby improve their performance.

Perhaps the most significant finding from this phase of the study was that people need to have a certain mindset to initiate such a process. This mindset seems to be a function of strongly held beliefs, of values such as dedication and the innate need to improve the organization in which they work. It became apparent during our discussions that people were not conscious of having used a specified pattern or prescription for success. What they recognized was their need to improve the performance of their organizations.

One of the deputy ministers told us about posing a challenge to his various branches, after he was appointed, to improve on what they were doing. The response in most cases was that they would try to do better, but that additional resources would be required. One branch, which participated in this study, provided an exception to that general response. Its leaders consulted with their people and found new and better ways, with the same resources, to provide products and services to their clients.

In another case, a newly-arrived Deputy Minister visited all his branch heads individually and asked them what problems they were having and what help he might be able to provide. The branch heads outlined their various problems, with one exception. That branch, again one in this study, assured the Deputy Minister that they did not have any problems; they were doing just fine. Across the country, wherever the Deputy Minister visited regions and asked representatives of this branch about their problems and difficulties, he received the same answer. Initially, he was skeptical and assumed that the branch head had instructed his people not to tell the DM about any problems. However, as it turned out, it was part of the branch culture to genuinely feel that no problems existed that they couldn't solve on their own.

In some cases, we found that the process of developing positive attributes was prompted by a crisis or a threat, by a strong demand from an outside influential group, or by an obvious opportunity. Such an opportunity was sometimes created by a newly arriving leader who posed strong challenges while creating an environment of trust and participation.

The process, once initiated, tends to drive itself. People at various levels discuss, explore, reflect and scrutinize themselves and their activities. They bring together ideas which sometimes result in disagreements. However, because of the mutual trust and respect among people at different levels, these ideas and difficulties become starting points for innovations that result in new ways of working and of achieving. This process gradually becomes ingrained in the culture of the organization, and, ultimately, people tend not to be conscious that this is something special or remarkable.

For example, it was not until after three in-depth conversations that one Assistant Deputy Minister was persuaded his branch was doing something worth highlighting. He was not conscious that they were doing anything special that wouldn't also be done in similar branches elsewhere in the public service.

CONCLUSIONS

o

When we began this study, several people were surprised that there should be well-performing organizations in the public service. One of our interviewees, however, put it another way: "Good performance is expected. It shouldn't be a surprise, then, that there is good performance in these organizations. The interesting part is that good performance has been successfully suppressed in most others".

We realize that we have not been able to find definite answers for all questions that arose during this study. Finding these would require a much more extensive examination than was possible with the resources we had available. One unfinished task, for example, is a detailed study of the underlying process of developing attributes of success, which we have described only briefly. Another question that requires further investigation is whether there is a difference in approach between *changing* the performance of an organization from average to excellent and the challenge of *maintaining* it at that level. We are not at all certain, for example, that the same forces that cause a turnaround are also instrumental in maintaining a high level of performance. A third question yet to be answered is what prompts some managers to initiate a process of reform and improvement. Why would they behave differently from other bureaucrats? Are leaders born like that? Can they be developed? Can such a mindset or such a set of values be acquired from textbooks or courses, or are these values developed by observation and imitation of role models?

These questions deserve further discussion and further investigation. When we first presented the outline of this study to some of the senior people in the public service, we benefited from insightful advice. Some of the advice dealt with the question of how far to go with this study. Should we attempt to make it comprehensive and complete within our one-year time frame? Should we publish the findings as definitive results and develop authoritative recommendations? The advice said otherwise. Do what you can, it was suggested to us, and publish the best answers you can find. But do not imply that they are final answers. Publish the chapter with the aim of generating thoughtful and wide-ranging discussion at all levels of the public service.

We have followed that advice. We present this chapter not as a definitive answer to some of the most difficult questions of public service management, but as a starting point for reflection and discussion. The challenge will be to answer more completely the question we posed at the beginning of this study: why do some organizations perform significantly better than others, and what can be done to encourage and assist others to do likewise?

Trading Places*

Ann Walmsley

At the Honda car plant in Alliston, Ont., the theme music from *Miami Vice* summons workers to Japanese *taiso* exercises before the afternoon shift. But only about half of the plant's 1,500 employees put their hearts into the three-minute routine of bends and stretches. In the shipping area, several people perfunctorily sway, others lean against a wall or chat. Jack Bouwers, 23, who inspects car interiors, does knee bends but draws the line at arm-flapping. "Not necessary," he says dismissively. Even the concessions to Canadian taste—*Miami Vice*, instead of the Japanese piano music that Honda used to play, and less strenuous movements than in Japan—have failed to inspire plant-wide enthusiasm for *taiso*. The same problem is evident at the Toyota plant in Cambridge, Ont., where exercises scheduled during unpaid time were one of the several Japanese practices that drove Sino Briski, 30, to quit his job in the primer department. "We were told that every minute was important during our shift," says Briski. "But that idea worked against Toyota when it came to exercises, because people started to sense the value of their personal time. We said, the hell with them. These are my five minutes."

Such grumbling is rarely heard above the general praise for Japanese management techniques in North America. "There's a fascination in Canada for Japanese manufacturers," says Charles McMillan, a professor of international business at York University in Toronto. "The evidence is overwhelming that they are more productive and successful than we are. In Wales, Tennessee, Wisconsin or Ontario, Japanese managers are taking the same plants, the same workers, making some fundamental changes and getting productivity equal to what they get in Japan."

✠ Ann Walmsley, "Trading Places," *Report on Business Magazine*, March 1992, 17–27. Reprinted by permission of the publisher and the author.

But little known to most outsiders, Japanese managers are finding that the methods that worked at home sometimes backfire in Canadian plants, with their ethnically diverse and more spontaneous North American workforces. In Japan, ideas of teamwork, constant improvement and bottom-up management grew out of deeply ingrained cultural values that stress harmony and conformity at the expense of individual expression. Nothing could be more foreign to the fiercely independent North American workers, nor to the middle manager groomed in a corporate star system geared to personal recognition.

Certainly the Japanese have had phenomenal success in transplanting production know-how to Canada and the United States. You need only look at the television picture tube plant owned by Mitsubishi Electronics Industries Canada Inc. in Midland, Ont., which revamped a tired RCA Inc. production line and is now exporting to television assembly plants in Japan; or witness the Alliston-produced Honda Civics, whose stellar performance (4.6 litres of gas per 100 kilometres) sets a daunting bench mark for managers at the Big Three domestic auto makers. But attempts to implement Japanese-style management don't always work. So Japanese manufacturers ranging from Toyota to Matsushita Electric Industrial Co. Ltd. are now being challenged to develop hybrid systems of Japanese and North American management.

The impact of these experiments to reinvent the Japanese miracle will be felt in every Japanese-owned-and-managed facility in Canada. And there are plenty of them. In the past two decades, Japanese direct investment in Canada has grown from a smattering of sales operations to giant "greenfields" projects—all-new, non-unionized plants with young workforces, usually located at the perimeters of small towns. Most notable among these facilities, of course, are the auto plants: Honda of Canada Manufacturing Inc., which opened in 1986, Toyota Motor Manufacturing Canada Inc. in 1988 and CAMI Automotive Inc., a General Motors-Suzuki joint venture in Ingersoll, Ont., in 1989. Following the auto makers, about 25 Japanese auto-parts suppliers, and companies that build and service assembly lines have appeared in the past five years. In Western Canada, the Japanese have invested heavily in forestry and coal production. In Central Canada, their big investments concentrate on cars and consumer electronics. According to a count by the Japanese External Trade Organization, Japanese-owned-and-managed plants in Canada now number more than 530, of which 164 reported revenues of roughly $26.2 billion in 1990. That figure almost triples if you include the many Japanese-North American joint ventures, which are usually run by Japanese managers.

A good example of a Japanese turnaround in Ontario is Mitsubishi's Midland plant, which employs 600 people on the southeast shore of Georgian Bay. When Mitsubishi bought the plant from RCA in 1983, it inherited the production line, the employees and a fractious union. As part of "Mitsubishi-ization," the new owners imported automated Japanese production equipment, bumped up production from five to seven days a week and cracked down on absenteeism and untidiness by sponsoring competitions with a Toshiba Corp. plant in New York state. Already the plant has halved absenteeism to 6%, which helped it to break into the quality-conscious television assembly market in Japan—a steppingstone to shipping to clients around the world. Until now, the plant's customers have been limited to Canada, Southeast Asia and the soft U.S. market.

While Mitsubishi's progress is inspiring, all eyes are on the three pristine Japanese auto plants in Canada—Toyota, Honda and CAMI—to see which Japanese methods work here and which don't. The complexity of auto assembly brings every element of Japanese theory into play. And all three plants are new operations from the ground up. U.S. auto analysts at DRI McGraw-Hill predicted in 1989 that every three cars made by these Japanese transplants in North America would displace one import and two vehicles made by American companies. The ability of Japanese transplants to claim such a sizable chunk of North American production—17%—is implicated as a factor in GM's recent decision to close 21 plants in North America and cut its workforce by 74,000 people, according to Dennis Des-Rosiers, a Toronto auto analyst.

At the Japanese plants in Canada, many workers (known as production associates or team members) and managers embrace the Japanese approach wholeheartedly, fascinated by its novelty and efficiency and seduced by the guarantee of a job for life. Others, however, bristle at the notion of wearing a company uniform instead of a power suit, or working overtime several times a week without advance warning. The culture clash also reaches beyond the plant walls, as the Japanese struggle to find Canadian parts suppliers with whom they can set up long-term relationships. "Japanese manufacturers in North America have made some mistakes and are really struggling," says David Cole, director of the University of Michigan's Office for the Study of Automotive Transportation. "We are still in the early stages of merging the two cultures."

Some Japanese managers even contend that Canadians are more receptive than Americans to Japanese-style management. That's the view of Shinichi Kawai, the 52-year-old president of Honda's Alliston plant. "We feel that Americans are more self-interested and less willing to do things the Japanese way," says Kawai, lighting a Marlboro Light and speaking through a translator in the map-lined Alliston boardroom. "Americans always try to proceed straight ahead to the target. Canadian associates are more like Japanese. Canadians always think about factors surrounding a goal. They have a feeling for balance." Kawai is speaking from experience. Before coming to Canada, he spent three years leading the expansion at Honda's huge Marysville, Ohio, car plant.

As if to illustrate his theory, some of Canada's Japanese plants are soundly out performing their sister factories in both Japan and the United States. Last fall, Toyota's three-year-old Cambridge plant won the coveted

J.D. Power and Associates award for highest quality in North America, based on surveys of more than 33,000 new-car owners. Canadian-made Toyota Corollas averaged only 65 problems per 100 cars in the first 90 days of ownership, compared to 78 per 100 at the Corolla plant in Toyota City, Japan. Toyota's Camry plant in Georgetown, Ky., rated 79 problems per 100. The production system at Cambridge is identical to those in other Toyota plants. But what the workforce lacks in experience it makes up for in youthful enthusiasm. And Toyota's president at the Cambridge plant, the tall, silver-haired Tom Kawamura, has been putting on the pressure for top performance. Kawamura, 54, is frustrated by the small size of the plant, which limits management's clout in negotiating contracts with suppliers. He is pushing his bosses in Japan to expand significantly beyond its 70,000-car-per-year production. "I went to Japan in September to explain how nice we are doing and how big potential we have," he says, sitting at his metal desk and signing Christmas cards to hundreds of the plant's suppliers and visitors. Kawamura's work cap displays the plant's logo—a mountain peak flanked by a C (Canada) and a J (Japan), symbolizing that combining the best of Canadian and Japanese management techniques could produce a new generation of superplants.

What will these superplants be like? Honda, which pioneered Japanese car manufacturing in North America, styles itself as the most North American operation. Although it is top-heavy with Japanese managers, Honda farms out plant and production design to local engineers. Toyota on the other hand, is more conservatively Japanese, preferring to export its production line almost intact. CAMI is the youngest of all the Japanese auto ventures in Canada. Despite the fact that it is the only unionized shop and operates as a joint venture with GM, it adheres strictly to Japanese methods, partially because it is just two years old and still in the honeymoon phase of operating in Canada. As in many Japanese factories, the plant floor is so immaculate that it could be mistaken for a pharmaceutical laboratory. Even outside the plant, the only noticeable fumes are from cow manure in the surrounding fields. And unlike Honda or Toyota, CAMI bedecks the plant with signs bearing Japanese terms and slogans. Its long, narrow layout is a *nagare* design, visitors are informed, meaning "flowing like a river." Although it takes ages to walk from one end of the plant to the other, the needlelike shape allows delivery ports all along the assembly line so that suppliers can ship goods several times a day to a dock directly adjacent to the appropriate spot on the line—the ultimate in just-in-time delivery.

At CAMI, the local farm kids who work on the line have not rebelled against the widespread use of Japanese terms. Because of their inexperience with factory line life, they tend to accept the cultural indoctrination as simply workplace jargon. They are immersed in it from the minute they sign on. In the training and human resources area, each room bears a Japanese name. Newly hired hourly workers train for the Tracker, Sidekick and Metro production lines in the *Yubisasha Kosho* room ("look and point both ways when you come to an intersection in the plant"). Next door in the *Yaruki* room ("can-do attitude"), production associates charged with improving participation in the suggestion system are having a brainstorming session. They call themselves *teian* ("suggestion") advisers.

One innovation that has proved highly successful is adopting the Japanese term teian. Its psychological value lies in its clean break from the worn-out notion of the suggestion box. "The last place I worked, the suggestion box had dust in it," says one adviser. "CAMI's *teian* is different. Here you add up a few points for making suggestions and, after a few years, you might earn a car." With those kinds of incentives, CAMI's *teian* advisers say they can't envisage a time when a process is so perfect that there would be an end to suggestions for its improvement. "Not when it is Canadian people," they say. "Money talks."

Recognizing that fact, the CAMI plant has borrowed ideas from Honda, Suzuki and North America companies to implement a much more extensive suggestion program and more generous incentive plan than Suzuki's in Japan. Employees accumulate points for each suggestion they make and redeem them to purchase goods from the Consumers Distributing catalogue—55 points for every $10 worth of goods. Year-end awards are worth up to $1,000 each and, in 1991, 17% of the plant's employees qualified for an award. The result: CAMI workers are coming up with an average of 4.9 suggestions per person per month, compared with only three at Suzuki's plant near Hamamatsu, Japan. And at CAMI about 90% of suggestions are implemented by hourly-rate team leaders, avoiding the frustration of delays of waiting for management approval. "That's because the focus of the suggestion system is on small improvements that you can make yourself," says John Lounsbury, a CAMI manager who oversees the plant's product changes. "Our president Mr. [Masayuki] Ikuma, always tells us we are not looking for home runs, we are looking for base hits."

At CAMI, as at the other Japanese auto plants in Canada, most elements of the manufacturing system have transferred flawlessly to North America —apart from having to raise the height of the line because Canadian workers are generally taller than Japanese. CAMI's *kanban* system, originally conceived by Toyota for just-in-time delivery, has enabled the plant to keep inventory low and receive one to four shipments of the same part each day. Every box of parts comes with a *kanban* card, inserted by the plant's inventory department. Team leaders file the cards in colour co-ordinated slots on a nearby *kanban* board where inventory workers on bicycles collect them. The number of cards filed indicates if a part is running low and should be reordered from the supplier.

One of the most popular Japanese innovations among Canadian associates is the *andon* board communication system. Workers who encounter a problem on the job can pull a red cord and stop the line without fear of discipline, or pull a yellow cord to request assistance. Pulling cords illuminates a portion of a giant *andon* light board hanging near the area and causes it to play a tune. Each *andon* board plays a unique piece of music ranging from a nursery rhyme to a piano sonata. This helps a team leader quickly recognize who needs help and where to go. "Most people really want to do a good job," says Lounsbury. "This gives them the opportunity to do that."

But there is grumbling on the line about *kaizen*—the Japanese term for "continuous improvement." Under *kaizen*, workers are encouraged to come up with ways to improve their job—to speed it up, save walking time, reduce waste, or improve safety. It also entails finding ways to cope with fewer workers when colleagues are sick or injured, instead of relying on replacements. "The Suzuki philosophy is that people will be creative if they have to be," explains Lounsbury. But some workers see it differently. "Under *kaizen*, our problem is we have people away with repetitive strain injury and we don't get a replacement for them," says a woman who installs wipers and windows. "I am three people short and I find that hard. But they say you are only allowed so many people on the line, even if those people can't work."

Another complaint heard by Tom Grygorcewicz in the bargaining unit is that the company is undermining the Japanese philosophy of teamwork by plucking people from one team and moving them to another. Production associates learn all the jobs performed by their team of roughly 10 people and must be flexible at rotating from one job to another. But jumping from team to team has stretched their patience. The issue has been so prickly that at one point union members orchestrated an unofficial work slowdown. "They preach about the togetherness of the team and say people should party together after work," says Grygorcewicz. "But as soon as the team starts to get close-knit, they move some people out."

The marriage between Japanese and Canadian managers is also shaky at times at CAMI. The Canadians are unaccustomed to the Japanese inclination to criticize rather than praise. "I guess, for them, praise is false flattery, insincere and shallow," says Lounsbury. One of the most jarring instances of differing expectations occurred before the plant opened, when Lounsbury gathered together the first group of hourly workers and praised them for doing a fine job painting the plant floor. "After the people dispersed, my Japanese adviser told me that this was a very inappropriate thing to do," says Lounsbury. "He said that one day two people were talking when they should have been painting and that there was half a can of paint left over. His mentality was to think only of things that had not been done right. There have been a lot of strained relationships because of differences in culture."

Canadian CAMI managers also have grown to view the Japanese open-office concept as something of a myth. At CAMI, as at most Japanese plants, senior executives reject the comforts of a private office in favour of sitting at plain metal desks in a vast common office. Both management and line workers wear the same unflattering uniform of blue pants and a white shirt. The message is that the barriers are down and everyone is part of the same team. But the reality is something else, according to the Canadians. "In Japan, they have a very regimented hierarchy," observes Richard Conrad, CAMI's vice-president of production. "You do not approach your boss and disagree with him. If you are a manager, you talk with people on your own level, but you do not speak to peons. They are completely flabbergasted that I would deal with production associates on the line. But in North America we are trying to eliminate such hierarchies and deal with the person you need to deal with."

At Toyota's and Honda's Canadian plants, there have been other problems in adjusting to North America. The most notorious case occurred in 1987, when Honda asked an employee to remove his Remembrance Day poppy because the pin could have scratched a car. The company goes to great lengths to avoid scratches—even buttons on the all-white company-issued uniform are concealed beneath flaps. In the ensuing disagreement, the Honda worker left the line. In Alliston, the poppy issue upset some residents, who linked the incident with remnants of wartime bitterness. Today, Honda observes two minutes of silence every November 11.

Toyota and Honda may represent CAMI's future. They have found compromises that both the Japanese and the Canadians can live with. That has meant, for example, dropping the Japanese custom of coercing colleagues to extend the workday and socialize over drinks in the interests of promoting company spirit. North Americans not only guard their time off more jealously, but they have to consider the tough Canadian laws on drinking and driving. Unlike their Japanese counterparts, they do not have the convenience of commuting home by train. Other compromises include forgoing the Japanese practice of paying workers salaries to erase the difference between them and management. "We toyed with the idea of paying salaries," says Bill Easdale, Toyota's senior vice-president of administration. "But they all asked what they would be paid per hour." Yet if you ask the presidents of Honda and Toyota what frustrates them most about the transition to a North American environment, the answer is not their workers, but their suppliers. In Japan, automakers establish intimate long-term relationships with suppliers based on quality and trust. They inspect not only a windshield wiper itself, but the conditions in which the wiper is made. They can also expect parts makers to go beyond the prototype stage and gear up for full production without a purchase order. But parts producers in Canada have had difficulty convincing Canadian bankers to lend money without a purchase order. Parts makers are also having difficulty adjusting to the Japanese expectation that the price of a part will go down each year, not up. "And when you are asked to quote on a part that you know you need to sell for $1.10," says Neil DeKoker, president of the Automotive Parts Manufacturers' Association, "you walk in to quote and the Japanese have a target price written on the blackboard of, say, 52 cents—less than your materials costs." Not surprisingly, Japanese-owned parts makers have proliferated in Canada. One Japanese-owned seat manufacturer, Bellemar Parts

Industries Canada Inc., occupies a corner of Honda's 182-hectare Alliston property.

On the flip side, the rigorous requirements of the Japanese have begun to rejuvenate Canada's auto-parts industry. Parts suppliers are attending seminars in *kaizen*, sending teams of workers to Japan to train and adopting the Five Ss of plant organization. Mitchell Plastics Ltd. in Kitchener has landed a contract with Toyota to make five or six parts for the 1993 Corolla, thanks to its involvement in a series of programs on Japanese plant cleanup. "I was heavily involved myself," says Murray Ariss, president and part-owner of the company. "In the past we had half-full material bins that workers would sometimes throw garbage into. Now we paint old material bins blue and yellow and use them for waste." The company's automotive business has increased so much that Ariss is building a new $1.3-million facility to produce such parts as dashboard components, air louvres and map pockets.

Overall, the Japanese companies' adaptation to North America is marked by innumerable success stories. The manufacturers' legendary employee screening process, which ranges from three to seven hours, has worked as they had hoped. Employee turnover at the Honda plant is now down to about 0.5% a month, compared with a high of 5% to 6% in its first year. Following the example of the Japanese plants in the United States, all three manufacturers chose to locate in small towns and hire in the surrounding farm communities where they found young, hard-working people with no union background and a commitment to community values. And unlike the U.S. sister plants, the Canadian plants have not been accused of anti-civil rights and anti-union activities for operating that way. While the Canadian Auto Workers union is monitoring what is happening at Toyota and Honda, and there is muted talk from time to time, production associates say that people are too happy with their pay and work conditions to contemplate organizing. At Toyota, workers have even begun to imitate their Japanese trainers and hold *karaoke* parties and play paddle tennis on the floor during lunch breaks.

Moreover, increasing numbers of employees at the plants are gung-ho about coming up with money-saving improvements through, as they say, *kaizening* their job. In the middle of the Honda plant, a bulletin board displays several teams' solutions for improving their work process. "Rags to Riches" is one solution originated by the paint shop. The shop was discarding wiping rags after one use and had problems with them sticking on shoes and marking the floor. The team researched the idea of sending them out to be washed and reused 10 times. The annual savings for Honda: $600,000. As more improvements are implemented, particularly engineering changes, the employees are gradually Canadianizing Honda's manufacturing process.

For Toyota and Honda, the next major challenge is to decide to what extent they will allow their Canadian managers to take control. Even though Honda is the oldest Japanese transplant in Canadian auto industry, three of the top four positions are still held by Japanese and there are 60 Japanese on staff. Honda is also unwilling to allow the Canadian plant to conduct its own model changeover without significant assistance from Japan, even though the plant had successfully switched from producing Accords to Civics in 1988. Last fall, Honda Japan dispatched 100 temporary trainers to Alliston to oversee the model changeover. But the plant's management explains this as only partly due to the Canadians' lack of experience. The Japanese trainers provided additional manpower so that there would be no interruption in production during the model change, unlike most North American plants, which shut down during changeovers.

For now, the Japanese have no plans to change the system of rotating Japanese presidents and senior executives every five years or less and installing new envoys. The presidents themselves remain largely mystery men in the Canadian business community. They point out that they are rarely in Canada long enough to gain confidence in English. Tom Kawamura at Toyota and Shinichi Kawai at Honda have succeeded the presidents who oversaw the plant start-ups. Both are now concentrating on reinforcing certain elements of their imported management styles, while at the same time saying politely that the style must be a blend of Canadian and Japanese.

Kawai, an avid ice fisherman and golfer, sees his mandate as pushing managers to circulate more and do visual inspections, known in Japan as the 3 Gs: *genba, genbutsu, genjitsu* (translation: "actual thing at the actual place in an actual situation"). He distrusts written reports and says you will only get the truth through watching and talking. He wears white safety shoes with his uniform at all times to facilitate a quick jog to the line.

Kawai's predecessor, Hiroshi Hayano, was also famous for hands-on management. Instead of asking for a written report on the first car off the line in 1986, Hayano insisted on driving it himself. He climbed into the Accord, sped down the test track behind the plant at about 80 kilometres an hour, locked into a four-wheel skid and landed off the track. Climbing out, he told his concerned staff: "It pulls a little to the right." Taking the hands-on approach one step further he asked who was responsible for installing the brakes. When a nervous employee stepped forward, Hayano handed him the keys and said: "Here, you drive it back."

Certainly there is much that Japanese executives and Japanese transplants can teach Canadian business. And Canadians are realizing that they have no option but to learn. Japan is expanding its industrial empire internationally at a remarkable pace. But it is unlikely that the much-vaunted Japanese style of management will survive in quite the same form.

The Just-in-Time Workforce*

Jerry Zeidenberg

Kathy Sayers started her Vancouver technical-writing company in the chill of the 1981 recession. Nearly 10 years later, she still gets the shivers. "The last recession scared the pants off me," she says. "I still haven't quite gotten over it." Sayers remembers the downturn as her nightmare years—rife with strained phone calls from bankers and creditors trying to squeeze money out of her fledgling firm.

But the experience taught her a valuable lesson: stay lean and flexible. Sayers' firm, International Wordsmith Ltd., had employed too many writers—technical specialists found it difficult to write about financial matters, and financial experts struggled with computer terminology. The company, which produces policy manuals and instruction guides for industry and government, was overextending itself trying to cover its clients' needs—all in the depths of a recession.

Faced also with hot-and-cold running contracts, Sayers and partner Sheila Jones seized hold of temporary workers as the solution to their accordion-like labor requirements. By turning to temps, they could hire a financial specialist—or any other expert—just when they needed one. That kept productivity up and costs down. At any given time, says Sayers, International Wordsmith now employs 10 to 20 part-time technical writers in addition to its six full-time staff. She expects sales this year to hit $750,000, up 25% from $600,000 in 1989. To increase the local supply of skilled labor, she and Jones have even helped set up a continuing education program in technical writing at Simon Fraser University in nearby Burnaby.

While the temp strategy still keeps the company flexible year in, year out, Sayers says it's also part of a plan to deal with the next recession. After

* Jerry Zeidenberg, "The Just-in-Time Workforce," *Small Business*, May 1990, 31–34. Reprinted by permission of the publisher and the author.

seven straight boom years, she says the economy is ripe for a fall. "That's why they call them business cycles," she says. "A recession is unavoidable."

When the downturn hits, International Wordsmith will be ready and able to retrench quickly and wait out the storm. It won't have a big payroll to cut, nor high overhead costs. "It takes a load off your mind and lets you sleep easier," says Sayers, when your company has a plan to deal with a change in the economic weather. When the economy perks up—with its usual fits and starts—the partners will quickly hire more temporary employees for stints lasting just weeks or months.

Like Sayers, business owners across Canada are learning to manage their labor requirements more flexibly—to cope with minor dips in the economy, as well as the dive that many entrepreneurs expect later this year. "Labor is one of the biggest cost components of any business," notes Alex Mersereau, research director for the Society of Management Accountants of Canada in Hamilton. Management experts estimate that labor accounts for 10% of costs in a manufacturing concern and 50% or more in a service business.

To slash their labor costs, companies of all sizes are starting to draw on the services of workers as they need them, instead of carrying them on the payroll all year round. "Flexibility is a major competitive advantage," says Mersereau. The trend goes beyond bringing in technical, financial and management experts to tackle special projects; many companies now hire blue-collar labor and even sales people on a pay-as-you-go basis. The structure of the relationships between employers and their flexible workforce varies: part-time arrangements, time and materials contracts, and project assignments to professionals, home-workers and service companies.

Mersereau calls this "just-in-time employment," tipping his hat to Japan's just-in-time inventory management, a technique that reduces warehousing costs considerably by ordering and receiving parts only as needed. Just-in-time employment means you pay for workers only when you really need them. "Companies have tried this in the past," notes Mersereau, but as management seeks ever-increasing productivity, the trend is taking off.

According to the Economic Council of Canada, jobs lasting less than six months, self-employment in work such as one-truck moving companies, and positions in temporary-help agencies accounted for about 50% of the jobs created between 1980 and 1988. Those jobs now make up 30% of total employment, and the Economic Council says more of these part-time, project-oriented positions are emerging.

Over the next 10 years, says Don Eastcott, managing director of the Canadian Organization of Small Business in Edmonton, temps and contract employees will become the norm. Independent businesses will operate with a lean core of employees who regularly draw on a wide range of outside "buffer" companies and lone-wolf workers. "You'll call on computer programmers, marketing specialists, accountants, as you need them," says Eastcott. "You couldn't afford to keep these people on staff." Skilled freelancers offer another benefit, too: they breathe an air of professionalism into even the tiniest companies. Bankers will love it, says Eastcott: "When a small company shows them it has top management people to draw on, they feel better about giving out money."

Manufacturers can turn to just-in-time workers as readily as service firms. Gary Pursley, general manager of Toronto auto parts maker Springco Industries Ltd., will rely increasingly upon temporary factory workers over the next six to 12 months while his biggest customers, the automakers, spin their wheels through the current automotive slump. Springco, which makes springs for car seats, still received some impressive orders from the Big Three. But Pursley doesn't wager on how long that will last. "You would have to be insane to employ more people right now," he says. "There are some big orders today, but the auto plants may shut down a few months from now."

Detroit's automakers have already laid off thousands of employees in Canada and the U.S. in recent months due to falling demand. Springco was forced to cut a dozen employees from its payroll last fall, and now operates with 71 full-timers. To cope with unexpected orders, it hires temporary workers on a week-to-week basis from agencies such as Manpower Temporary Services. At any given time, says Pursley, Springco may have five or six temporary blue-collar workers on hand, saving the company the costs of hiring and firing permanent employees with every sputter, cough and wheeze in the auto business. Another saving: lower workers' compensation payments. "If you take on a new employee, your risk of an accident is highest during the first three months," says Pursley. "When we use temps, Manpower takes the risk, we don't."

There is a cost, however. Whenever the company brings a temp on board, it invariably suffers a brief productivity drop. "We have our own ways of doing things, and our own equipment," says Pursley. "There's always a learning curve for new employees, but they're usually on-stream after two or three days." Temps generally require less training than new employees, says Pursley, because they're already accustomed to working in factories. Nonetheless, some industrial companies are wary of blue-collar temps. Pursley considers that penny-wise but pound foolish. "They're reluctant to call for temporary help, because temps cost you $3 to $4 an hour on top of the $6 to $7 you normally pay a worker," he says. But companies that ignore temps fail to account for the costs of training new full-timers, as well as the cost of benefits paid to permanent staff members. Says Pursley: "Benefits add 20% to your hourly wages."

For some workers, staying at home is the benefit they value most. Home-based programmers, accountants, graphic artists and designers, for example, frequently serve several client companies from afar. But work sometimes travels from factories to homes as well. The garment industry employs this technique with astonishing success. While Canada has been flooded with cheap clothing from offshore countries, domestic firms are cutting costs by farming out jobs to pieceworkers in their own homes.

Both sides of the arrangement seem to win. The part-timers, usually women, work at their own pace at home with their children. Manufacturers enjoy lower overhead. They require less factory space, and don't have to pay benefits to part-time workers. The result: hundreds of clothing manufacturers have thrived, largely in Quebec and Ontario, despite the onslaught of imports. And, in the event of a recession, garment makers can quickly pare down their operations without incurring lay-offs or letting factory equipment stand idle.

"It's an ace up my sleeve," says Sol Mandel, president of Trail-Mate Products Ltd., a Toronto-based manufacturer of jackets and bags. Mandel employs about 40 people in his Toronto shop, and farms out jobs to 20 home-workers at between 10¢ and 30¢ an item. "If there's a recession, I'll just reduce the amount of work I send to the home-workers. My factory workers are the last people I'd lay off."

Not everyone, however, is happy with the rise of home-workers. Gerald Roy, director of the Montreal-based International Ladies Garment Workers Union, burns at the mention of the topic. "It's devastated our union," he says. As the number of home-workers in Quebec alone surged to 30,000 this year from 20,000 just five years ago, ILGWU membership fell to just 7,000 from 15,000. While new employees often join a union automatically when they start work at a factory, home-workers are under no such obligation. What's more, it's difficult for organizers to recruit home-workers, who are scattered across a city or town.

Roy claims garment companies are creating sweatshops in workers' homes with children dragooned by parents into forced labor. "Women get their kids to help mommy turn the piece, to help mommy move the bundles," he says. "She's got free labor, and she thinks it's O.K." Roy says his union is lobbying government to check conditions in home-workers' dwellings. For their part, garment makers like Mandel say they simply provide the work to qualified people who want to work at home.

A flexible workforce helps keep labor costs under control—whether it's part-time computer programmers updating your CAD/CAM-capability, or home-based laborers taking on special design projects. But if sales are your problem, firms are emerging that can add value to what you already spend, assembling "dedicated" sales teams for your products. You can even hire a polished sales force to put your product on the road during a peak selling season or to launch a special promotion. Unlike traditional sales reps, who may flog nine or 10 different lines—bath soap, gumballs and your product—the newer breed will represent just you alone.

The four-year-old Sales & Merchandising Group of Mississauga, Ont., doubled its revenues to about $10 million in 1989 by training and managing platoons of dedicated merchandising mercenaries. These sales-reps-for-hire pay regular visits to retail outlets, restaurants, gas stations—virtually any place where your product is sold—to see that the product is well stocked and visible. They also help store managers build displays and set up promotions, and prompt them to order more product when stocks are low. "Our clients can concentrate on their main job— manufacturing and marketing to the head offices of their customers," says Tony LaSorda, S&MG's chief executive officer. "We make sure that what they negotiate with their customers is executed at the store level."

Some firms use S&MG's hired sales guns throughout the year. Through diligent visits to drugstores and mass merchandisers like Woolco, the company's 24 reps last year increased sales by 20% for Mississauga-based Foster-Grant Canada Ltd., an eight-person firm that distributes the sunglasses made by its U.S. parent.

Before turning to S&MG, Foster-Grant sold its glasses through regular manufacturers' reps—the kind with suitcases full of different products. "In some cases, they wouldn't call on our stores in months," says general manager Rick McChesney. "If they had a drive on shampoo, they would sell shampoo, and they would get around to selling our sunglasses eventually." By contrast, McChesney says S&MG reps service his account rigorously. "They only wear a Foster-Grant hat when they go into a store, and they even use our business cards."

With the new just-in-time workforce, entrepreneurs don't have to be merchandising experts, production wizards or computer gurus—even in a recession when hiring such professionals is out of the question. All of this expertise can be purchased on a pay-as-you-play basis. What an entrepreneur must possess is the flair and flexibility to draw on these resources as they're needed. As we learned in 1981, companies that stay lean and flexible stand the best chance of staying healthy throughout the next downturn—and beyond.

The New Hardline[*]

David Olive

The concept of the benevolent business enterprise has always been something to be skeptical about. A *New Yorker* drawing of several years' vintage captures the cynicism. It depicts a boardroom gathering at which one of the directors shocks his colleagues by musing, "You know what I think, folks? Improving technology isn't important. Increased profits aren't important. What's important is to be warm, decent human beings."

No need to guess where satirists of corporate life come up with their material. They simply watch business in action, and try to top the exercises in unwitting self-parody that go on in that world. An example is the current retreat by business from its experiment with putting the pride, self-worth and personal fulfilment of employees at the top of the corporate value system.

A recent full-page ad in *The Wall Street Journal* touting the services of a corporate insurance provider reminds us that social Darwinism is respectable again. The ad's headline reads, "He who hesitates is lunch." Stanley Bing, *Esquire's* popular expert on executive life, begins his July column with the cheery salutation, "Wake up, maggot. Smell the coffee." Stop finding yourself, pal: It's time to get back to work—if you still have a job, that is.

Only yesterday, employees were held to be the most valued assets of a corporation. Then the recession began to do its work. Today the job market is awash with *curricula vitae*, and people don't seem so valuable any more. Where are they now, the workers who were invited to conceive and embrace a company vision? Many are gone, swept up in the dehumanizing process of "body-count reductions."

[*] David Olive, "The New Hardline," *Report on Business Magazine*, October 1991, 15–16. Reprinted by permission of the publisher and the author.

Thinking seriously about the important role of the individual in the corporation, as we began to do in the late 1980s, was a useful and overdue exercise. But after that short-lived burst of introspection, coming hard on the heels of the materialistic excesses of the past decade, business leaders appear to be driven again. Driven to fight off the demons of recession, inefficiency and global competition and to swing the pendulum back to career-obsessed workaholism. Business is hell, so let's get on with it.

Witness Toronto venture capitalist Gordon Sharwood, who is alarmed that the public has yet to embrace Brian Mulroney's austerity agenda. He chides soft-hearted Canadians for being "strongly resistant to competitive pressures" and "much more interested in a *caring* society" (his italics).

Witness also Donald Fullerton, CEO of the Canadian Imperial Bank of Commerce, who has taken management to task in an internal memo for not being tough enough in employee evaluations, fretting that the bank's 49,000 workers are being managed in a "country-club" fashion. Fullerton wrote, "There is no way that CIBC can survive, let alone prosper, if we allow even one of our personnel to be unchallenged in our pursuit of providing value to our customers."

Fullerton would know about the country-club life, being a member of two exclusive recreational retreats and the posh Toronto Club, besides. In the trenches, meanwhile, Commerce employees are being exhorted to work faster, harder, smarter to repair the damage wreaked by a few highly placed individuals who approved a whack of bad loans. Who knows, maybe the spear-carriers can find a way to make up for the board's mistakes out of the paper-clip budget, and by smiling harder at customers.

The most high-profile disclosure of a CEO's displeasure with apparent sloth in the workplace has been John Akers's outburst in the spring, when the IBM chief executive said, "The fact that we're losing [market] share makes me goddamn mad.... Everyone is too comfortable at a time when the business is in crisis."

If the intended message was that Akers can lead IBM back to prosperity by browbeating his galley slaves, the ploy has backfired. Not a few IBMers are convinced that their helmsman is more to blame than they for the company's faltering fortunes. IBM's operating income peaked long ago, at $11.2 billion in 1984. Akers's tenure at the top, which dates from that same year, has been marked by a steady erosion of market share and profitability.

They're also painfully aware of IBM's recent departure from its vaunted no-layoffs policy—the firm is looking to cut 14,000 names from the payroll. And this after Akers's pay and bonus has soared 185% in 1990, to more than $2.2 million.

The threat of job cuts and the selective application of the "pay-for-performance" principle are not terrifically effective morale builders in the lower ranks, of course. Worse than that, Akers fails to recognize that it's the "little people," not him, who will determine IBM's ability to turn itself around.

To wit: If IBM is to recover lost market share, its 30,000 systems-software writers will have to speed up new-product development. The company will have to form key strategic alliances with other firms in order to reap the benefits of shared technology. IBM will have to break with its habit of waiting for rivals to create a new market before entering that market with its own copycat products. It will have to improve quality, which lags behind that of Japanese rivals; and shed a reputation of highhanded arrogance toward customers and suppliers.

Not everyone has decided to treat employees as disposable commodities. Canada's Northern Telecom Ltd., facing the same global competitive threat as IBM, has not escaped the pain of workforce reduction. But Nortel is sending a different signal than IBM. In July, Nortel unveiled a college-recruiting campaign unique in North America in which successful candidates will be given a three-year employment guarantee. At a time of economic uncertainty, Nortel has reasserted its conviction that it can only succeed if it has the industry's most talented and committed engineers, marketers and finance experts on its team. The *quid pro quo* is that these people will be treated with respect—as much out of necessity as an instinct for altruism.

Nortel is hardly a touchy-feely organization. It bears the same militaristic hallmarks as IBM. But even the military recognizes that a chief goal in any strategy is to minimize losses, and that no campaign can work without a system of security and rewards for individuals. Success is not a function of the supreme commander alone—a truism that gives rise to Nortel's example of what can be termed "pragmatic sensitivity."

Today's rampant *in*sensitivity has been encouraged, I suspect, by the decisive actions of certain players in the Persian Gulf crisis, who may have triggered this wave of Pattonesque get-tough messages now heard in corporate corridors. But captains of industry who favour the military model are wise to adopt it whole. This means resisting the urge to find fault with the troops. It also means CEOs must accept a measure of blame when things go wrong.

At the risk of keeping alive an overused term, the concept of empowerment has much to recommend it. Quality will not improve, breakthrough products will not issue from the lab, and creative alliances with partners will not bear fruit unless the people who do the real work are persuaded, gently but with conviction, that their own best interests lie in that direction.

It's no wonder talented people defect from insensitive, impersonal organizations, often to create the nimble competitors that typically bedevil huge corporations. The exodus starts with episodes like these, when CEOs isolated from their comrades in the ranks shout angry words into the void and flatter themselves that this is leadership.

A Labour-Management Contract and Quality of Working Life*

Louis E. Davis and Charles S. Sullivan

INTRODUCTION

o

In the North American tradition of evolving theory from practice, this paper reports what may become a significant innovation in union-management relations. This pragmatically evolved development may be crucial to the evolution of new forms of union-management collaboration. Reported are the extremely rare events of union participation in the design of a new chemical plant organization and the evolution of a new form of union-management contract developed through collective bargaining and responding to the organizational philosophy that guided the design....

BACKGROUND TO THE DESIGN

o

The background to the design starts in the early 1970s when the manufacturing division of Shell Canada, Ltd. began studies of its own way of managing its workers and utilizing their capabilities. Substantial recommendations were made, some of which were implemented and many of which seemed to be waiting for 1975 when the design of the polypropylene-isopropyl alcohol plant was to begin. The sum of the recommendations of the earlier studies pointed to the need to enhance the quality of working life of refinery and chemical plant workers. Such workers, with good pay and

✠ Abridged from Louis E. Davis and Charles S. Sullivan, "A Labour-Management Contract and Quality of Working Life," *Journal of Occupational Behaviour* (1980): 29–41. Also published in Graham S. Lowe and Harvey J. Krahn, eds., *Working Canadians: Readings in the Sociology of Work and Industry* (Toronto: Methuen, 1984), pp. 191–200 [reprinted by Nelson Canada in 1991]. Reprinted by permission of the publisher and the authors.

working conditions, were found to be seeking greater control over the decisions affecting their lives in the workplace and were inhibited from fully utilizing the considerable skills and experience they had acquired. The usual roles of a traditionally operated organization, enlightened though it may be, imposed needless restrictions on workers. Typical of their comments were: "I operate a 5 (or 10) million dollar machine but have to obtain approval from the foreman for an overtime meal when I am asked to stay at work beyond my usual departure time." "I have to wait for the foreman to arrive to sign off on a maintenance request. All he does is add his signature to the form after he asks me if the work is needed." The primary concern of Shell management and a major concern of OCAWIU [Oil, Chemical and Atomic Workers International Union, now the Communications, Energy and Paperworkers Union of Canada] was the physiological and psychological problems associated with shift work.

In the early 1970s the worker issues of remuneration, security, control over workplace decisions, shift work, development of self, participation in governance of one's work life taken together came to be called the quality of working life. By the time the design began the participants were well aware of this concept and that it could be strongly affected by organization and job designs....

UNION-MANAGEMENT JOINT DESIGN PROCESS

o

There was considerable discussion regarding union jurisdiction. Some expected that the refinery union would have jurisdiction over the new plant when completed; others thought the union would not. Some said this did not matter since it was management's prerogative to design and organize work. Others were concerned with the negative consequences of placing a completed design before the union as a *fait accompli*. The consultant to the design team questioned whether excluding the union was contrary to the organization philosophy and to the congruency principle of socio-technical systems design which calls for design methods to be congruent with the features of the organization (Cherns, 1976). All came to see that success of the future operation of this costly, leading edge technology plant was in various ways bound up with participation by the union.

Finally, following considerable examination, the design team recognized that the union would represent the future members of the plant and invited it to join as a partner in developing the design of organization, jobs, rewards, training and controls. Such participation of the union as a basis for successful operation is contrary to conventional wisdom about advanced technology, large corporations, and engineering and management processes.

The union accepted with two stipulations—(1) that it be a full partner in the design process and (2) that it would maintain a high profile. This was quickly accepted. The participation of the union representatives provided the means of capturing and utilizing organizational learning at the shop floor level. Initial concerns were quickly forgotten as the high quality of union contribution unfolded and managers congratulated themselves for their statesmanship.

Later the external consultant had opportunity to interview the Canadian national director of the union. He was asked to indicate why he supported his union's participation in the design process in the face of the history, in North America, of rejection by many unions of quality of working life activities. His reply is very instructive. He said that

> We would be poor union leaders if we did not utilize the opportunity given us by management to participate in providing for satisfaction of quality of working life needs for workers. If you think that only managers have problems with our members as their workers, then you are unaware that we have many similar problems with our members, particularly younger members. We must grasp each opportunity that becomes available to learn how to find the means of responding to quality of working life issues raised by our members if we are to be a strong viable union.

What was the role of the union in the design process? What was their contribution to the design? Would the design have been the same without them? How were they beneficial to future union members who would be joining the new organization? These questions are difficult to answer because of the relationship that evolved. Quickly managers accepted the union leaders as equals and vice versa. Each contributed as an individual whose membership on the design team was highly valued. The team called on its members as experts on the basis of their reputations, knowledge, and experiences. Many proposals were generated through synergistic interaction among team members, whether union or management. Proposals for features of organization and jobs were examined by both union and management for secondary and unintended effects on members at all levels. The union representatives' greatest contributions seemed to be centred on proposals regarding the knowledge and skill modules for advancement, maintenance, working hours, shift teams and their rotation. Additionally the union representatives helped develop the team coordinator role, shop steward role and the Good Work Practices Handbook. The details of the structure of the organization and jobs will be described in a separate publication.

DESIGN PROCESS AND OUTCOMES

o

....The design selected treated the entire plant and its processes as one organizational unit. One team of 18 people plus a team co-ordinator operates the entire process including laboratory, shipping, warehousing, and many aspects of maintenance on each shift. The teams needed for 24 hour, 365-day operation would be supported by some planners, engineers, and managers as well as a team of 14 maintenance craftsmen-instructors and two laboratory specialists on days. The organization design was further influenced by societal issues stemming from strong negative pressures about shift work. The design team sought to minimize shift work and to share equally the positive and negative aspects of working life. The design provides for six shift teams, each consisting of 18 people plus a co-ordinator. Each team rotates and controls, in turn, all the work activities of the plant. Based on the 37.5 hours per week schedule of the plant, 4.5 shifts are required for continuous around-the-clock operation. The design selected calls for 1.5 shift teams, on average, to join on days, with the following groups: 14 maintenance craftsmen-instructors, 2 laboratory specialists, and 2 warehousemen-schedulers. The shift team joins with the maintenance craftsmen to become the maintenance work force while obtaining cross-skill training in maintenance crafts. In this manner, a maintenance response capability becomes available on all shifts for emergency situations, with a concentration of maintenance capability during days. The six shift team arrangement provides the means whereby the members of all shift teams spend 53 per cent, approximately, of their work time on days. Should a future experiment with the 12-hour day work out then 72 per cent of each member's work time would be spent on days as compared with 33 per cent on days in a conventional shift arrangement.

Thus a team of 18 with its team co-ordinator operates the entire plant including its administrative, laboratory, shipping, warehousing and maintenance activities. Not unexpectedly the organization structure is flat, having three levels—the shift teams and their co-ordinators, operations managers, and plant superintendent. The day foremen level present in conventional refineries and chemical plants is omitted since these people are not staff technical advisors. Within the teams the structure is deliberately amorphous, permitting the team to assign tasks to its members as required. Additionally, for organizational continuity, various leadership functions including planning and co-ordination have been assigned to the team members. Team members have received training to perform a variety of social system maintenance functions including problem solving, confrontation, conflict resolution, norm setting, etc. Each team has a [union] shop steward who is one of its members. This is particularly useful since very few rules exist and the labour-management contract language is permissive, leaving to team members the determination of their day to day working lives. A Good Work Practices Handbook was developed, with union input, which serves as an administrative guide governing specific job-related activities such as overtime-meals etc. What is frequently described in labour-management contracts, making them rigid and subject to legal quibbling, concerning work-related activities is now in the Good Work Practices

Handbook. The collective agreement thus remains as the enabling document it was originally intended. The team co-ordinator, who stays with his team as it rotates through the shifts, serves as the intershift team link and the link with management. His major functions are to provide boundary protection for the team acting as a mediator or buffer between his team and demands from the environment; to provide technical expertise and training on the processes; and to serve as the management representative on the shifts when he may be the only such present. In addition to the shop stewards, the union structure has a five-person executive committee including the union officers in the plant.

Members of the team do not have specific job titles or assignments but rather grade levels or competence levels based on the knowledge and skill attained. Advancement depends on qualifying examinations and performance tests covering specific groups of knowledge and skill modules. This arrangement supports open progression and satisfaction of individual differences through the many career paths available to an individual. Each team member must acquire all the process or operations knowledge and skill modules. Some are present in every wage grade level. Beyond this there are choices available for individuals to combine knowledge and skill modules from six specialty areas with operations modules to make up each individual wage grade level. The specialty area skills include maintenance crafts, quality laboratory testing, warehousing and production scheduling. The various combinations provide six career paths along which an individual can choose. The specifics of the path chosen depend on joint organization needs and individual desires. The interests of the plant and of the individual member come together in the provision and support of training which is always available, reinforced by the system of wage payment and reward. The more groups of knowledge and skill modules learned, the higher the wage level and each member may move at his or her pace right to the top level that each individual is capable of achieving; time limits are not imposed for doing so. No one, however, is forced to move and failure to learn and advance cannot impede anyone else's progress. These are norms developed by team members at the start of plant operation.

COLLECTIVE AGREEMENT

o

As the organization design was completed (some specifics were later added) recruiting, selection, and training were designed. At this time, the union representatives took on dual roles—continuing their work on the design team and engaging in the collective bargaining process for a labour-management contract for the new plant. Participating in the bargaining process for management was the manager of the manufacturing centre, the chemical plant superintendent, and the employee relations manger. The union negotiating committee was composed of the local and regional officials who were serving on the design team joined by five of the craftsmen-instructors who had been transferred from the refinery to the chemical plant to form the maintenance team.

After hard bargaining, a first-of-its-kind labour-management contract was developed. As indicated earlier, this contract is unique in that it is the first labour-management agreement developed in consonance with the design of a post-bureaucratic organization giving specific emphasis to achieving high quality of working life for its members. Both union and management representatives at the bargaining table understood the central nature of the new organization with its emphasis on self-control, learning and participation, its flexible work assignments, and its evolutionary structure based on specifying only what is critical to organizational functioning, i.e., minimal critical specification (Cherns, 1976). They understood that the design was in effect a skeleton structure that would be further evolved from subsequent experiences. This learning was the opposite of their prior experiences in living in a bureaucratic organization where all aspects of structure and relationships were completely specified. They agreed that the survival of the organization and enhancement of the quality of working life for its members would come from the detailed structures and practices that would be evolved by those living in the organization, from the participation of members in solving the problems of the organization and from the feedback and utilization of organizational and individual learning.

Both union and management appeared to conclude that protecting and developing the organizational form would best discharge their responsibilities and advance the satisfaction of their own needs and the needs of those they represented. Their shared understandings led to agreement that flexibility and support should be the central features of the labour-management contract. The contract emphasizes and reflects flexibility and is itself and evolutionary document providing enabling conditions consonant with the organization design. It was as if the principle of minimal critical specification had been applied by the negotiators. Both sides made some signal concessions in support of developing the collective agreement. Management did not insist on the customary management rights clause in the contract accepting general rights stated in law. At the same time it accepted mandatory deduction of union dues as necessary for continuity of the union. Not as a concession, the union for its part did not require a seniority clause, except for lay-off, since open progression was one of the central features of the organization. With provision of continual training and objective qualification examinations each worker has an equal opportunity to advance to the highest level the individual's aspiration, capacities and energy will take him or her. Under these conditions, the union saw no need for the usual seniority clause.

An examination of the agreement indicates how flexibility and support were translated into contract language. The agreement unconventionally begins with a unique foreword that sets the tone for what follows. The complete text of the foreword is as follows:

> The purpose of the agreement which follows is to establish an enabling framework within which an organizational system can be developed and sustained that will ensure an efficient and competitive world-scale chemical plant operation and provide meaningful work and job satisfaction for employees. Recognizing that there are risks involved and that there are many factors which can place restraints on the extent to which changes can occur, both management and union support and encourage policies and practices that will reflect their commitment to the following principles and values:
>
>> Employees are responsible and trustworthy, capable of working together effectively and making proper decisions related to their spheres of responsibilities and work arrangements—if given the necessary authority, information and training.
>>
>> Employees should be permitted to contribute and grow to their fullest capability and potential without constraints of artificial barriers, with compensation based on their demonstrated knowledge and skills rather than on tasks being performed at any specific time.
>>
>> To achieve the most effective overall results, it is deemed necessary that a climate exists which will encourage initiative, experimentation, and generation of new ideas, supported by an open and meaningful two-way communication system....

SOCIAL SYSTEM SUPPORT

The first year of the collective agreement was taken up largely by training of new employees, team formation, equipment testing and some plant commissioning. Actual operation of the plant by work teams looks as if it will begin during the second year of the collective agreement. Late in the first year or the agreement, when all workers were on site, the stresses of not having rules or norms and no specific contract language led to some extended developmental meetings between the union executive committee and plant management. One of these meetings evolved a collaborative social system support mechanism to deal with grievances as called for in Section 3 of the collective agreement. Established was a Team Norm Review Board composed of seven employee representatives, one from each team, three management representatives and the union vice president. Consensus is required in reaching recommendations by the Board and in introducing new norms. The Board audits team norms. It cannot discipline. In the event that a team member's problem is not resolved at team level, i.e., face to face with the team co-ordinator and shop steward, the member may appeal to the Team Norm Review Board to adjudicate the issue. To date the Board has been an effective vehicle for problem solving and for developing guides at shop floor level.

Later in the first year a Joint Information Committee was established to aid with the very considerable task of communicating and sharing of information among teams who operate around the clock every day of the year. The Information Committee is composed of one team co-ordinator and one team member from each team making 14 members. This committee should also prove to be an important part of the social system support mechanism by which the organization maintains itself.

The union's view of developments that took place during the first year of the collective agreement is revealed in part of an article written for publication by the National Director of the union. Reimer (1979) states:

> Our program with Shell Canada, Ltd., at the Sarnia Chemical Plant has received much notice. Programs of this nature and others of course require continuing attention. However, one can already observe that in this "open society" operation, where people speak up more frequently, there is less fear in the plant and indeed higher attendance at Union meetings. The nature of the operation tends to keep people more informed and the meetings where decisions are made affecting their welfare have a higher priority. I understand there is very little absenteeism and the quality of training and the versatility in the plant are concrete attainments. The more the worker is trained, the higher is his income and management can put him to better use. Our Collective Agreement has a statement of purpose and is about five short pages in length. We expect that nothing will be written into the Agreement arbitrarily and that if anything is added, it will have stood the test of time. It is interesting to note that in this Agreement, management does not incorporate the traditional Management's Right clause.

The first year under the collective agreement came to an end and negotiations for renewal are completed. Management and union agreed that, with the exception of changes in salaries, the contract finally signed remains the same as the collective agreement described above.

CONCLUSION

The design process and the resulting organization design as well as the collective agreement for this non-bureaucratic chemical plant indicate that there is another path available better suited to the post-industrial era. This path is marked by a co-operative process and by the objective of a high quality of working life for all members of the organization. Once again we see a demonstration of the powerful outcomes of substantive collaboration as compared with confrontation in union-management relations. It may be that only by such collaboration will a high quality of working life be truly provided for the members of the organizations.

The collective agreement informs us that the "contract as an enabling document" is essential to evolutionary design and thus to a post-bureaucratic form of organization. Counter-intuitively we are instructed that high technology increases dependence on workers for economically successful operation. Increased reliance on workers further emphasizes the obligation during design to examine the needs, aspirations and goals of members, i.e., their quality of working life. The joint union-management process more easily satisfies this examination and the development of useful responses. It also demonstrates that shared responsibility for the development of a new organization evolves through union-management collaboration.

We may well close by examining a duality of questions. First, would this innovative collective agreement have been developed without the prior experience of the joint union-management process? Second, would the new form of organization have survived without the collective agreement as an evolutionary and enabling document?

The answers to these questions are inferential. The long period of working together, the trust developed, the shared experiences, the agreement on organizational philosophy, and the early-on exposure to sociotechnical systems concepts and quality of working life concepts had their effects. Undoubtedly union and management had likely developed a substantial set of shared understandings which served as a base for considering their individual and joint needs as well as those specific to this new form of organization. At this period in the life of the new organization, given both the fragility of any new social system and the open evolutionary form of the design, it would appear doubtful that this new form of organization can survive for very long without the collective agreement as an enabling and supporting instrument.

REFERENCES

o

Cherns, Albert
    (1976). "The principles of sociotechnical design." *Human Relations*, 29(8), 783-792.
Reimer, C. Neil
    (1979). "Oil, chemical and atomic workers international union and quality of working life—a union perspective." *Quality of Working Life: The Canadian Scene,* Winter, 5-7.

P A R T

Unions And

Industrial Relations

E D I T O R S ' I N T R O D U C T I O N

o

Unions are the main institutions that act as advocates for ordinary workers in a democratic society. Now representing 36 percent of Canada's nonagricultural paid labour force, unions have had a large impact on pay and benefits, working conditions, and the organization of jobs. Yet many unions have been slow to adapt to a new era characterized by globalization, high technology, recession, new management strategies, a more hostile legislative environment, and a rapidly growing service-based labour force. Some observers, looking to the U.S. where union fortunes have been in steady decline for decades, wonder if Canadian unions also will begin to lose ground. The readings in this section are intended to enliven the debate about the future of Canadian unions.

To begin, Mary Lou Coates poses a fundamental question: does the Canadian labour movement even have a future? In other words, will it successfully adapt to the new political, social, and economic realities of the 1990s? The union leaders she quotes are very optimistic, and the Canadian situation looks rosy when compared with the sharp membership declines that have crippled unions in other industrial countries. But on the negative side, Coates points to shrinking employment in the traditional union bastions of manufacturing and mining, and the fact that recruitment of new members in banking, retail chains, and other service industries has been exceedingly difficult.

Put simply, many unions never recovered from the one-two blow of the 1981–82 recession and the subsequent get-tough stance toward unions by both government and employers. The changing composition of the work force— exemplified in the growing numbers of women and youth, part-timers,

and professionals—has meant that unions' once reliable recruitment strategies, bargaining agendas, and internal procedures are becoming far less
effective. Coates argues that unions are also unsure about how to react to
the new management strategies outlined in Part 6. Corporate reorganization, teamwork, participative management, Japanese-style quality circles—
unions fear that these reforms will erode their traditional collective bargaining strength. To be sure, such techniques are sometimes explicitly used to
keep a firm union-free. Coates leaves us wondering whether Canadian
unions will adjust to the multitude of forces reshaping the industrial relations environment.

Many observers have concluded that the industrial relations environment became more restrictive and hostile during the 1980s. Governments
are the largest employers in the country, so when they plead fiscal restraint
and clamp down on their employees' collective bargaining rights, demand
concessions, legislate the end to legal strikes, or alter "the rules of the game"
with tougher labour legislation, the effects are felt throughout the labour
force. Bryan Palmer's account of public sector restraint in British Columbia
and Quebec is testimony to the rancour such actions generate among state
workers. In an ironic twist, Quebec's Parti Québécois government, which
raised the ire of public sector unions in the early 1980s by unilaterally
extending collective agreements and curbing strike activity, was elected
with union support.

By contrast, the Social Credit government in British Columbia was
unabashedly anti-union. In 1983, it introduced legislation aimed at imposing a neo-conservative agenda, the centrepiece of which was a direct attack
on collective bargaining rights and civil service jobs. The labour movement
and community groups joined forces in Operation Solidarity, a powerful
grass-roots response. The coalition orchestrated massive anti-government
public demonstrations and threatened a province-wide general strike.
However, it was subdued by a deal struck between the premier and Jack
Monro, an old-style labour leader. In Bryan Palmer's view, in the aftermath
of Operation Solidarity and open displays of "class war," the B.C. labour
movement, like its Quebec counterpart, became more conciliatory toward
the government.

Two prominent themes in Palmer's account of public sector industrial
relations are militancy and the role of union leaders. These are pursued in
Charlotte Yates's analysis of Canadian autoworkers' growing militancy
during the 1980s. Canadian members of the United Autoworkers Union
(UAW), drawing on strong rank-and-file traditions and forceful leadership,
parted company with the American UAW in response to the "Big Three"
automakers' restructuring and demands for concessions. While the American UAW essentially acquiesced, the Canadian UAW embarked upon a
two-pronged strategy of plant sit-ins to protest closures and no-concession
bargaining.

By the mid-1980s, this approach had forged a new, more militant organization independent of the American UAW: the Canadian Auto Workers Union. As Yates notes, the tough but reasoned line that the union took to protect Canadian autoworkers' jobs and income security was widely supported by other unions and in the community. Bob White, the union's president, became the leading labour spokesperson in the country (not surprisingly, White was recently elected president of the Canadian Labour Congress, the national labour central). Thus, while other unions were struggling to survive in a recessionary climate, the autoworkers' resistance to these pressures from the auto industry helped to build a stronger union. This strength undoubtedly will be needed as the union faces the challenges of continued restructuring, work organization, new production methods, and free trade.

Internally, a major new influence on how unions operate is the growing proportion of female members. Women are demanding a different style of unionism, one more sensitive to their needs and problems. Linka Briskin examines the role of women in unions, observing that many unions have instituted women's committees and now place sexual harassment, pay equity, child care, and employment equity high on their list of priorities. But in raising these issues, women have had to push for reforms to internal union structures, and to oppose the traditional conception of "business unionism," which focused narrowly on bread-and-butter issues. Part of the difficulty women face is that they are still underrepresented in union leadership positions. Their numbers are growing, in part because of the designation of affirmative-action positions, but the scope of feminist change is limited by entrenched male leaders and union bureaucracy. It is clear from Briskin's discussion that feminist unionists have a leadership approach that is more grass roots, participatory, and empowering than traditionally has been found in unions. The promise this holds out for the future, argues Briskin, is reinvigorated unions with greater member involvement.

DISCUSSION QUESTIONS

1. What are the major factors accounting for the divergent trends in union membership in Canada and the United States?

2. Assessing the current state of unions and the industrial relations system in Canada, are Canadian unions holding their own, declining, or growing in strength?

3. What role does the state play in industrial relations, both as legislator and employer?

4. What reforms are required in unions themselves if they are to be responsive to the needs of the work force of the 1990s; that is, a work force that

is increasingly well-educated, female, and with a growing proportion of visible minorities?

5. Are there indications that women have had a positive impact on union priorities and collective bargaining outcomes? Would it be accurate to portray the Canadian labour movement as male-dominated today?

6. What, in your view, would be the key elements of a survival strategy for Canadian unions? Alternatively, should unions survive into the 21st century, or would Canadian workers and the economy be better off without unions?

SUGGESTED READINGS

○

Anderson, John C., Morley Gunderson, and Allen Ponak, eds. *Union–Management Relations in Canada*. 2nd ed. Don Mills: Addison-Wesley, 1989.

Freeman R.B., and J.L. Medoff. *What Do Unions Do?* New York: Basic Books, 1984.

Heron, Craig. *The Canadian Labour Movement: A Short History*. Toronto: James Lorimer, 1989.

Panitch, Leo, and Donald Swartz. *The Assault on Trade Union Freedoms: From Consent to Coercion Revisited*. 2nd ed. Toronto: Garamond Press, 1988.

Russell, Bob. *Back to Work? Labour, State, and Industrial Relations in Canada*. Scarborough, Ont.: Nelson Canada, 1990.

White, Jerry P. *Hospital Strike: Women, Unions, and Public Sector Conflict*. Toronto: Thompson Educational Publishing, 1990.

White, Julie. *Male and Female: Women and the Canadian Union of Postal Workers*. Toronto: Thompson Educational Publishing, 1990.

Is There a Future for the Canadian Labour Movement?*

Mary Lou Coates

INTRODUCTION
o

At first glance, all seems well with the Canadian labour movement and the prognosis looks good. Four million Canadians belong to labour unions, a record high. Except for a short plateau in the early sixties and a decline in 1982-83, union membership in Canada has increased steadily each year and since the 1981-82 recession, union ranks have increased by one-half million members. During the past decade, membership growth has averaged almost two percent per year. Currently, over one-third (36.3 percent) of the total non-agricultural paid workforce in the country is unionized. Those who have studied the Canadian union movement have commented that:

> ... the Canadian labour movement remains strong, exhibiting a remarkable resiliency in the face of a difficult and unfavourable economic, social and political environment. (Kumar 1991, 1)

> ... the strength and vitality of the Canadian labour movement has been reflected in greater organizing activity and success, widespread rejection of concession bargaining, and prowess in achieving legislative goals. (Chaison and Rose 1990, 596)

Canadian union leaders, as expected, also appear confident about the health of their labour movement:[1]

> ... we continue to grow, and have credibility. I think we have an exciting labour movement. *Shirley Carr, President, Canadian Labour Congress*

✳ Abridged from Mary Lou Coates, "Is There a Future for the Canadian Labour Movement?" Current Issues Series (Kingston: Industrial Relations Centre, Queen's University, 1992), pp. 1–13. Reprinted by permission of the publisher and the author.

... I think we're holding our own. In some places we're moving ahead, in other places we're being forced onto the defensive, but we'll be around for a long time to come. *Jeff Rose, Past President, Canadian Union of Public Employees*

I think the percentage of organized non-agricultural people in Canada will continue to grow in the next 10 years. I think that the Canadian Labour Movement, in total, is healthy. *Cliff Evans, International Vice-President, United Food and Commercial Workers Union*

... I think that generally the labour movement is alive and well and fighting back. I think the future of the labour movement is not at all down, I think it can be up ... the future for the labour movement is one in which the labour movement is going to continue to fight back and we'll continue to grow. *Bob White, National President, Canadian Auto Workers*

DECLINING   UNION   GROWTH?

o

By international standards, unions in Canada have not suffered the steep membership losses that the United Kingdom, France and the United States have experienced during the 1980s (Visser 1991). Compared with the United States, the degree of unionization in Canada is twice as high.

However, there are indications that all is not well. Despite steady increases in union membership, union growth in Canada has certainly not been as robust in recent years as it was in the 1960s and 1970s. Furthermore, membership growth has failed to keep pace with the rise in the non-agricultural paid workforce and, as a result, union density, which hovered around 38 percent in the early 1980s, has declined to 36 percent in recent years. While some would argue that this pattern indicates 'stability' in union penetration, others brand it 'stagnation' or 'decline.'

There is even more cause to ponder the future of union activity in Canada when one moves beyond the aggregate measures to look at what has been happening in the private and public sectors and across industries. Two major concerns include the decline in private sector unionization and the union presence, or lack thereof, in the faster growing segments of the Canadian workforce.

In the traditionally strong sectors of unionization such as mining and manufacturing, union membership growth has fallen over the past ten years. In forestry, union growth has been marginal in the 1980s although healthier than it was in the 1970s while in construction it has slowed compared to the previous decade. In transportation, communications and utilities, union growth has been steady but not robust.

As a proportion of paid employment, union membership in forestry, mining and manufacturing has declined substantially over the past two decades. Over one-half of the paid workforce in construction and in transportation, communication and utilities remain unionized, roughly the same proportions as twenty years ago.

On the other hand, over four-fifths of the overall increase in union membership during the past decade has been in the service industries and public administration, evidence that unions have been expanding into new and growing areas of the economy. Nevertheless, the majority of workers in the service industries, trade and finance, insurance and real estate remain non-unionized. With three-quarters of employees organized in public administration, there is concern that unionization is at or near its saturation level in this sector. By occupation, density is less than average in professional occupations outside of teaching and medicine and health, in clerical and related occupations, sales occupations, service occupations such as food and accommodation and personal services, and wood, rubber, plastic and other product fabricating, assembling and repairing occupations.

WHY THE DECLINE?

o

Numerous reasons have been given to explain the decline or stagnation in unionization in the private sector and the relatively low levels of union representation in growing sectors: structural shifts in the economy, labour legislation and public policy that restricts organizing and collective bargaining, employer hostility to unions, and unfavourable public opinion. The 1981-82 recession appears to have marked a turning point for organized labour during the 1980s. The severe economic downturn had a deleterious impact on employment in the goods-producing industries and blue-collar occupations, traditional strongholds of union strength.

For the first time in recorded history, there was an actual reduction in the number of union members and many unions, faced with losses in their dues-paying memberships, were also forced to rationalize union administrative structures and cut back on staffing and servicing the membership. Union bargaining power was also weakened as many unions came face to face with concession bargaining (including wage cuts and freezes, wage settlements below the rate of inflation, lump-sum payments in lieu of wage increases, reductions in employee benefits and modified work rules) as well as public sector wage restraint legislation and restrictions on the right to strike.

Moreover, on the heels of the recession came massive corporate restructuring, rationalization and consolidation in response to international pressures which meant continued losses in jobs, many permanent, and related employment upheaval, particularly in the unionized sectors of manufacturing and the resource-based industries. Against the background of plant closures and relocation, privatization, deregulation, fallout from the Canada-US Free Trade Agreement, technological change, and contracting-out, the union's ability to bargain improved wages, benefits and working conditions and provide employment and income security has been severely hampered. Several of the larger private sector unions, such as the United Steelworkers,

Carpenters, International Brotherhood of Electrical Workers, Machinists, Woodworkers and several construction unions have therefore been unable to regain the membership lost during the recession.

With unionization rates declining or stagnating in those areas where membership had traditionally been concentrated, unions are also facing the labour market realities of new workforce—a workforce with diverse interests from traditional rank and file members, one that unions have historically found more difficult to organize and where existing union structures, policies and practices have often been inadequate in reflecting some of the concerns of these new groups of workers. For example, women comprise 45 percent of the labour force but only 30 percent of employed women are union members and the proportion of Canadian women members elected to union executive boards remains relatively low. The rate of unionization tends to be relatively low among part-time workers (26.2 percent) who have accounted for over one-quarter of net employment creation in Canada in the 1980s (Economic Council of Canada 1991, 72). About two-thirds of the net employment growth in the 1980s was in managerial and professional occupations and the demand for highly skilled workers, particularly in managerial and administrative occupations, is expected to rise dramatically (Employment and Immigration Canada 1989). Many managerial and professional workers are not legally eligible to unionize at the present time and some of these groups consider themselves to be outside the mainstream of the trade union movement. Almost 90 percent of the net employment creation since the 1950s has taken place in the service sector (Economic Council of Canada 1991, 1), which tends to be characterized by high turnover, either very large employers (eg, banks, department stores) or small-sized firms, and a high proportion of women, part-time workers, professionals and youth—factors which have made union organizing more difficult.

Unions have also contended that labour legislation and labour board policy, while successful in extending collective bargaining to workers in the resource and manufacturing sectors, has not been conducive to organizing either part-time workers or workers in the growing finance and service industries (Partnership 1991, 3). Unions have also had problems making inroads in the private service sector because there tends to be more contact between the worker and the consumer which creates an incentive for employers to adopt human resource strategies that reinforce this identification (Betcherman 1989).

NEW   FORMS   OF   WORK ORGANIZATION

o

This points up another area of concern for the future of the labour movement—increased employer demands for new forms of work organization, that is, alternative approaches to how work is organized and managed. In attempting to become more responsive to changing business conditions and to cope with a fiercely competitive environment, management is placing greater emphasis on flexibility in production methods as well as compensation and working arrangements. Employers have been flattening management structures by eliminating layers of management, pushing for fewer or broader job classifications and multiskilling, looking to more variable compensation schemes (eg, lump-sum or cash bonus payments, two-tier wage systems, pay for knowledge and pay for performance, productivity gain-sharing, incentive pay, employee stock ownership plans and profit-sharing) and making greater use of part-time and temporary employees and contracting-out.

With an erosion in the effectiveness of traditional competitive tools such as technology, product innovation, financial resources and access to raw materials, organizations are beginning to discover that their human resources represent a 'fundamental source of competitive advantage' and a 'significant force in achieving organizational effectiveness' (Benimadhu 1989). Many organizations feel a growing need to become more directly involved with employees, foster greater worker commitment and cooperation and make their human resources more involved in managing change and improving competitiveness. Quality circles, team concepts, quality of worklife, and other initiatives aimed at increasing worker participation and employee involvement are receiving increased attention. A recent survey of over 400 public and private sector organizations found that 'companies appear to be more active in responding to changing worker values and in building a new management style than in any other area' (Towers Perrin 1991, 19). For example, more than 50 percent of the survey group have introduced, or plan to introduce, a quality management or improvement program *involving employees* while almost 50 percent have adopted other types of programs that focus on greater productivity or morale enhancement. In terms of organizational strategy, over 40 percent of the companies had undertaken strategic changes ranging from the design of communication processes to help build employee commitment to business objectives, the reorganization of work tasks or activities to create greater labour efficiencies, programs to encourage innovation and productivity at the operating level, and the development of a more supportive 'culture' to reduce turnover and enhance productivity.

UNIONISM AND THE NEW HRM

The implementation of alternate forms of work organization has important implications for labour unions not only in unionized settings but also in terms of nonunionized workplaces where the desire for and ability to unionize may be thwarted by such schemes. Some of these issues were explored in a recent paper which examined the compatibility of strong unionism with alternate forms of human resource management (Wells 1991). Although some argue that the effectiveness of such human resource management strategies depends on the presence of strong unions, Wells' study of some of the alleged 'successful' experiments (eg, Shell, Eldorado Resources, Xerox, Dominion Stores and Willet Foods) points out that the 'new human resource management' leads to weak unions or the absence of unions.

THE CANADA/US DEBATE

Evidence that private sector unionization has been declining in Canada in recent years has led to a controversial debate on whether the path of Canadian unions is paralleling that of unions in the United States. In the United States, membership levels have steadily declined since 1975 and union density has fallen from a peak of 32.5 percent in 1953 to 16.1 percent in 1990, more than one-half the current Canadian rate. Two contrasting views have emerged in this debate raising some startling and critical issues for the future direction of the Canadian labour movement.

Unionization in Canada—Is It Following the American Route?

The conventional view is that although unionization in the United States has been 'dying on the vine', Canadian unionism has been 'thriving' and that, given the close economic and institutional relationship between Canada and the United States, the United States has been unique with respect to this deunionization. More recently, however, this mainstream view has been challenged by the counterclaim that not only has declining unionization in the United States *not* been unique but the experience of private sector industrial relations in the US indicates that the size and strength of Canadian private unionism will be reduced (Troy 1991b).

Leo Troy, Distinguished Professor of Economics at Rutgers University in New Jersey, has taken strong exception to the comparisons made between the 'robust' and 'vibrant' Canadian labour movement and the 'flabby' American one and any suggestions that American labour relations policy emulate the Canadian model. Troy has long held the opinion that the conventional view of divergent trends in Canadian and US unionization, which relied on aggregate measures of union membership levels and density, misdiagnosed the invulnerability of Canada's private sector union movement because it failed to distinguish private from public sector markets, union movements, and industrial relations systems. Therefore, instead of diverging, trends in private sector density have been similar in Canada and the United States except that the US 'led the way'...

Troy believes that the robustness of Canadian unionism applies to the public not the private sector. Moreover, he argues that public sector unionism owes its strength to favourable government intervention which, unlike unions in the private sector, sheltered public sector unions from market forces and blunted the impact of competitive pressures. However, he feels that the economic costs of unionism in the public sector will encourage more privatization and public management will be under increased pressure to reduce negotiated wage increases in the public sector. Given the role that public policy and legislation has played in giving 'instant unionism' to the public sector, Troy questions whether public sector unions have the 'allegiance' of their members. The growth of public sector unionism 'ran out of steam' during the 1980s and was unable to offset the decline in private an d therefore, overall union density. Over time, the Free Trade Agreement, privatization, technological change, public resistance and the growing weakness of private sector unions will mean that public sector unions will no longer be able to remain immune to the erosion taking place in private sector unions and Troy expects stagnation in Canadian public unionism (Troy 1990a and 1991a). In the private sector, Troy believes that as 'the Canadian labor market get[s] swept into the vortex of the more competitive North American free trade economy, Canadian private sector unionism, already in a state of decline, will become more vulnerable to the "American disease"' (Troy 1991b)....

Pradeep Kumar, Associate Director of the School of Industrial Relations at Queen's University in Kingston, Ontario also acknowledges that public sector unions in Canada have outperformed those in the United States and that private sector unionism has declined in both countries but debates whether the size of the decline is similar (Kumar 1991). In his paper, he carries the debate further to examine the more qualitative measures of the extent and influence of unionism. The difference in union strategies and approaches, he states, is what accounts for the growing divergence between the labour movements in Canada and the United States. In his analysis, Kumar transcends some of the 'gloom and doom' scenarios and offers a more optimistic outlook for the Canadian labour movement by focussing on the strategic role that unions have assumed in organizing, collective bargaining and in their political and social approaches.

According to Kumar, it is the broader 'social' concept of unionism in Canada which accounts for the strength of the labour movement in this country. In particular, he distinguishes between the Canadian unions' emphasis on social and political strategies compared to the American reliance on collective bargaining as a key factor in the divergence. This divergence is manifested in the more active and aggressive organizing efforts by Canadian unions, their opposition to concession bargaining and resistance to contingent compensation and employee involvement/participation programs, the negotiation of social issues (eg, pay and employment equity, child care, human rights, etc), legislative lobbying, coalition-building with various groups outside the labour movement, and the bilateral consultation and consensus-building initiatives with employers at the national and sectoral level (eg, the Canadian Labour Market and Productivity Centre, Canadian Steel Trade and Employment Congress).

CONCLUSION
o

Despite the various strategies and approaches taken by the labour movement, unions are still faced with the grim reality that unionization in the private sector has declined, remains relatively low among the faster growing segments of the Canadian workforce, and is near saturation in the public sector. Furthermore, there is no indication of any 'wave' of new organizing on the horizon. These developments raise serious questions about how the labour movement is preparing for the future and whether a transformation is taking place in Canadian industrial relations.

NOTE
o

1. Based on interviews by Pradeep Kumar and Dennis Ryan with prominent business leaders (Kumar and Ryan 1988).

REFERENCES
o

Benimadhu, Prem.
  1989. *Human Resource Management: Charting a New Course.* Report 41-89. Ottawa: Conference Board of Canada.
Betcherman, Gordon.
  1989. 'Union Membership in a Service Economy,' in Michel Grant, ed., *Industrial Relations Issues for the 1990s. Proceedings of the 26th Conference of the Canadian Industrial Relations Association,*120-31.
Chaison, Gary N. and Joseph B. Rose.
  1990. 'New Directions and Divergent Paths: The North American Labor Movements in Troubled Times.' *Proceedings of the Spring Meeting of the Industrial Relations Research Association.* 591-96. Madison, WI:IRRA.
Economic Council of Canada.
  1991. *Employment in the Service Economy.* Ottawa: Supply and Services Canada.
Employment and Immigration Canada.
  1989. *Success in the Works: A Profile of Canada's Emerging Workforce.* Ottawa: Employment and Immigration Canada.
Kumar, Pradeep and Dennis Ryan.
  1988. *Canadian Union Movement in the 1980s: Perspectives from Union Leaders.* Research and Current Issues Series no. 53. Kingston: Industrial Relations Centre, Queen's University.

Partnership and Participation in the 1990s: Labour Law Reform in Ontario.
1991. Report of the Labour Representatives to the Labour Reform Committee of the Ministry of Labour. April 14.

Towers Perrin and the Hudson Institute of Canada.
1991. *Workforce 2000: Competing in a Seller's Market: Is Canadian Management Prepared?* Toronto: TPFC.

Troy, Leo.
1990a. 'Why Canadian Public Sector Unionism is Strong,' *Government Union Review* 11, No. 3: 1-32.

Troy, Leo.
1990b. 'Is the US Unique in the Decline of Private Sector Unionism?' *Journal of Labor Research* 11: 111-43.

Troy, Leo.
1991a. *Convergence in International Unionism Et Cetera: The Case of Canada and the US.* Queen's Papers in Industrial Relations 1991-3. Kingston: Industrial Relations Centre.

Troy, Leo.
1991b. 'Can Canada's Labor Policies Be A Model for the US?' Paper prepared for the 28th Conference of the Canadian Industrial Relations Research Association, June.

Viser, Jelle.
1991. *Employment Outlook* (July). Paris: Organization for Economic Development and Cooperation.

Wells, Don.
1991. *What Kind of Unionism is Consistent with the New Model of Human Resource Management?* Queen's Papers in Industrial Relations 1991-9. Kingston: Industrial Relations Centre, Queen's University.

A Tale of Two Provinces: The Assault on the Public Sector in Quebec and British Columbia*

Bryan D. Palmer

There appear to be few similarities between Canada's Pacific coastal province, British Columbia, and its distinctive Francophone society, Quebec.

Their economies, cultures, and politics are as different as night and day. And yet, in 1982-83, the provincial states in these divergent regions set their coercive sights directly on the public sector and attempted to ride out the difficulties of hard times on the backs of government employees. In the process, trade union and civil rights were trampled and popular resistance peaked in massive mobilizations. Yet the state, for the most part, emerged from this self-created cauldron of conflict intact and triumphant, however bruised. Some of the players ended up being displaced, but the nature of state power remained basically unchanged.

No provincial government, it could be argued, did more to consolidate a positive working relationship with its own labour force than the early Parti Québécois (PQ). Quebec's working class was the most combative, militant, and radical in Canada throughout the 1970s. From the Common Front days of 1972 on it was an activist contingent quick to strike and willing to place a wide range of social issues on the bargaining table of class relations. Some of this got translated into the national arena as militant Montreal locals of federal unions stood their ground against the tide of repression or thrust leaders like Jean-Claude Parrot into the national limelight.

When the PQ came to power in 1976, it alone among the provincial governments bucked the Trudeau restraint program. Headed by René Lévesque, the PQ was engaged in a higher politics than economic controls, squaring off against the federal Liberals in a sovereignty-association push

* Abridged from Bryan D. Palmer, *Working-Class Experience*, 2nd edition (Toronto: McClelland & Stewart, 1992), chapter 7, pp. 361–69. Reprinted by permission of the publisher and the author.

that was to be tested in a 1980 referendum on Quebec independence. Lévesque and the PQ bought a bit of time and labour support for sovereignty-association in 1979 when they placated a common front of public-sector unionists, but this mortgaging of class relations was torn up as the 1980 call for a "Oui" vote soured and the Quebec economy faltered badly in the early 1980s recession. Cuts in social spending resulted, and the PQ experimented with the privatization and deregulation so championed by the New Right. But it wasn't enough. By 1982 it was apparent that the PQ could no longer pay the price of keeping labour on side. Instead, it desperately needed to shore up its fragile and now gutted economy, structured around the most vulnerable kind of small, consumer-goods manufacturing—textiles, shoes, garments—and to dispel the debilitating view common among Anglophone and American investors that the province was a hotbed of labour radicalism as well as a region of socially progressive government programs with a corresponding tax structure to foot the bills.

With sovereignty-association shelved and the bill for past labour relations largesse now overdue, the PQ moved to counter the economic downturn with the programmatic overkill of the rights of public-sector unionists. It began inauspiciously with the legislating back to work of some Montreal transit workers in January, 1982, but quickly escalated in mid-year. When the Common Front public-sector unions of teachers, CNTU affiliates, and the QFL balked at demands that they forgo salary increases, the Quebec state passed Bill 70. This legislation tabled previously signed contracts and decreed in advance of their impending expiration a 19.5 per cent wage cut for the first three months of 1983. Affecting some 300,000 public-sector workers, Bill 70 effectively banned strikes, extended collective agreements and lowered salaries.

As if this were not enough, Bill 105 was introduced. It extended the coverage to a few previously excluded sectors of workers, secured a further extension of all public-sector collective agreements through to December 1985, and limited wage increases to less than the annual rise in the consumer price index. Job security and working conditions were eroded, as well, with seniority clauses taking a beating and working-class autonomy limited by the centralizing of power and decison-making in the hands of administrative personnel. Some 109 contracts were altered, and public-sector workers' pockets were looted to the tune of over $650 million.

The Common Front unionists quite correctly perceived this as a war waged against them, an aggressive action that commenced with their being stripped of the traditional means of counter-attack, the right to strike. Still, they defied the PQ and its legislative arsenal and walked off the job illegally, some 300,000 in number. This January "general strike" was met with yet another piece of labour legislation, Bill 111, an Act To Ensure the Resumption of Services in the Public Sector, which was passed in February. It provided for fines, imprisonment, and the decertification of bargaining agents, overriding the federal Charter of Rights and Freedoms and the provincial

Charter of Human Rights. Those targeted were refused the right of trial and denied the opportunity to present evidence or secure legal protection. To be absent from work was to be guilty. Most union leaders quickly complied with the state's dictatorial demand that they get their members back to work, although the teachers stayed out for a month. Nevertheless, in the face of what was undoubtedly the harshest legislative assault on unionism since 1919, the strike was broken.

For the rest of the decade this guillotine of state attack hung over the collective neck of the Quebec working class. As the 1982-83 legislation lifted in 1985, the PQ simply added on some new bills, amending the provincial labour code and tightening its regulatory control over monetary decisions in the public sector. More and more public-sector workers were designated "essential" and thereby denied the right to strike. Other trade unionists were split off from their brothers and sisters as the state stipulated that collective bargaining was to take place, not in concerted constituencies of solidarity, but within a host of sectoral "sub-tables." This effectively squashed Quebec's historic Common Front.

To be sure, forces beyond the state contributed to this sorry end, among the most significant the rivalries and acrimony within the labour movement and its hierarchy that were encouraged by the repressive divide-and-conquer tactics of the PQ. Nor would the PQ itself ride out the storm. But when it went down to electoral defeat in the mid-1980s, the regrouped Liberal Party was able to pick up where it had left off. The Bourassa Liberals made no move to restore the 20 per cent cut in public-sector wages that PQ Finance Minister Jacques Parizeau secured over the course of his years in office. They simply upped the legislative ante in 1986 with the passage of Bill 160, which, as we have seen in terms of the struggles of Quebec's nurses, provided for the crushing of any unionists who would defy government orders and engage in illegal strike activity. The Quebec Federation of Labour's Louis Laberge called Bill 160 "vicious, illegal, immoral . . . an atomic bomb to sink a canoe."

Laberge's angry rhetoric was, however, matched by a curious nationalistic defence of Quebec labour's own distinctive society relation to the state. In a 1987 interview he remembered with fondness the positive contribution of the PQ, stressed the tripartite climate in Quebec, and was surprisingly generous in his assessment of the new Liberal provincial government:

> I believe the climate in Quebec is a lot better than it's been before. The climate was bad in 1973 when three of us—myself, the president of the CNTU, and the president of the teachers' group, were jailed. The election of the PQ in 1976 helped improve the climate. We did get good pieces of legislation on health and safety and others under the PQ regime. Even today you cannot find anything comparable to what we've had from the PQ government. We cannot forget that. The PQ lost the last election because of internal disputes. They were so divided amongst themselves that nobody could help them, even we couldn't. With this new government we have been pleasantly sur-

prised. The government started off with deregulation, privatization, for instance, the sale of Quebecair. . . .Since then they have been more careful. . . . Management and labour and government have all been working a little closer together for the past 15 years.

Perhaps Laberge's head was clouded by his heavy involvement in the Solidarity Fund, a Quebec trade union exercise in venture capital that by 1989 boasted 72,000 shareholders, assets of $232 million, and a piece of fifty-six small and medium-sized companies. Tax-exempt by agreement with the government, the Solidarity Fund aims, according to its president, former Campeau Corporation VP Claude Blanchet, to create jobs. Laberge sees it as changing the very "mentality" of workers and managers. But just how saving the Quebec Nordiques hockey team with a $3 million investment transforms anything is a little hard to answer. So are dissident unionists' questions about why the Solidarity Fund investments are overwhelmingly in non-union companies....

Thousands of miles away, on the other side of the country, things were also very different in the 1980s than they had been a decade before. In British Columbia, an NDP government was replaced by Social Credit, and under Premiers Bill Bennett and William Vander Zalm the once ostensibly socialist province was turned on its political head. Throughout the 1980s, B.C. would be the most uncompromising site of the politics of the New Right in Canada.

British Columbia's introduction to the downturn came early, with the Barrett NDP government in power, but the recessionary collapse of the 1980s was stayed for a time as the more developed manufacturing economy of central Canada was hit with a pronounced wave of plant closures. When the regional economy finally came to feel the pinch of hard times, however, the pain was perhaps more forceful. Almost entirely dependent on the resources of its forests, British Columbia's export-oriented economy tumbled in the early 1980s. Unemployment, seemingly under control in 1980-81 at roughly 7 per cent, soared to 16 per cent in 1983, well above the national average. Natural resource revenues fell catastrophically. As the new global division of labour lessened reliance on North American products and resources, British Columbia came to the shocked realization that timber could be secured more cheaply from the once obscure corners of the world than it could from the harvests of its own backyard. For the provincial state the economic collapse spelled disaster: the government took in less because the forest industries were selling less, people were cutting back on their buying, sales taxes were reduced, and, finally, personal incomes were cut by unemployment, meaning income tax revenues were reduced. At the same time, state expenditures on welfare and social services necessarily climbed. By mid-1983, a budget deficit of over $1.6 billion was projected.

Obviously concerned with the state of the regional economy and the new international division of labour, the ruling Social Credit Party—a curious right-wing coalition, a segment of which was a natural environment for the most vitriolic neo-conservatism—looked around the province and saw an economic apocalypse looming. There were those willing to tell them what must be done. Consultations were soon arranged with Michael Walker and his colleagues in the B.C.-based New Right "think tank," the Fraser Institute. Premier Bill Bennett took kindly and quickly to the blunt advice he received from Walker and others.

Between February, 1982, and March, 1984, British Columbians were treated to a series of televised chats with Bennett. They were not unlike those mounted nationally by Trudeau, although Bennett had more trouble reading his lines than did the federal Liberal leader. The views of the British Columbia governing party were unequivocal. There was a need for "restraint"; British Columbians could not "picket their way to prosperity"; the province, like it or not, must adapt to "the new economic reality," where victory could only be won by those tough and able enough to compete in world markets. If the west coast could become a high-tech Silicon Valley of the North, or if B.C. could catch some of the rays of a new economic order's "Pacific Sunrise," basking in the light of the prosperity of the Far East, well, so much the better.

On July 7, 1983, Bennett and the Social Credit Party introduced a provincial budget, accompanied by some twenty-six bills. These bills represented a direct attack on trade union rights, human rights, and the autonomy of communities and groups to control or influence spending in the social arena. As a collective assault on organized workers and all oppressed sectors of society, as well as a concerted attempt to centralize power in the hands of the provincial state, the 1983 legislation was as forceful a political move as any Western New Right government had made. It was applauded by none other than ultra-conservative American economist Milton Friedman, who appreciated that Bennett was attempting to do in one fell swoop what Thatcher, Reagan, and others only dared to do over a number of years and campaigns.

Much has been written about the 1983 Bennett budget. Here it is important to stress how central the assault on public-sector workers was to the project. Five of the twenty-six bills attempted to curb the much-maligned powers of civil servants and their trade union organizations. The Public Service Relations Amendment Act, for instance, removed the right of the British Columbia Government Employees Union to negotiate anything but wages. Wage restraint, however, was quickly addressed by the Compensation Stabilization Amendment Act, which extended previously established controls and limited bargaining to a range of minus 5 per cent to plus 5 per cent. More ominous still was the Public Sector Restraining Act, which in its original wording would have given the government the right to fire employees at the expiration of a collective agreement "without cause." Later that wording was removed, but broad termination conditions remained. In one devastating blow, Bennett and the Socreds sought to liberate capital and the state from the fetters of the post-war settlement, striking out at public-sector unionism as the weak link in the chain of trade union defence mechanisms. . . .

. . . Before presentation of the budget the government reduced school financing, eliminating 1,000 teaching posts. The day after the twenty-six bills were introduced the state indicated the direction in which it intended to proceed: 400 employees received pink slips, and the state expressed its resolute intention of terminating 1,600 civil servants by October 31, 1983, when the BCGEU contract would lapse. Many of these posts were in the Human Resources ministry, and the 400 firings severely disrupted social services, affecting battered wives, abused children, welfare recipients, and the disabled. The devastating forecasts were that full-time equivalent positions for employees of government ministries would be reduced from about 46,800 to just under 40,000 in 1983, and further slashed in 1984-85 to about 35,400. In the parlance of Social Credit and the New Right this was "downsizing."

Done in the name of economy, these job eliminations also had their convenient ideological and political sides. Bennett made much of civil servant "laziness," lack of productivity, and privileged "job tenure." Fraser Institute head Michael Walker noted that public-sector workers provided "an ideological consistency and a lag in adjustment to new ideas and political directions." In the age of the new reality, "when the government of British Columbia is attempting to make the transition to a new vision of the future, it is appropriate that the continuity of ideas provided by the civil service is broken." Materially and ideologically, then, jobs had to go and with them the people who had been doing the work and thinking the wrong political thoughts.

This sledgehammer attack, coupled with the deep cuts in almost all areas of social spending, mobilized a vibrant mass opposition. From mid-July through mid-November, 1983, B.C. was an intensely politicized province. A *Globe and Mail* correspondent wrote, "Class warfare used to be a joke in this province. . . . [Now] no one is laughing." Trade unions in the public and private sectors banded together in a provincial opposition known as Operation Solidarity. Human rights groups and their supporters came together in a massive province-wide organization known as the Solidarity Coalition. Orchestrating all of this was the British Columbia Federation of Labor president, Art Kube.

An impressive culture of resistance broke somewhat out of Kube's tight organizational control and encouraged thousands to attend nightly meetings, read the movement's newspaper, *Solidarity Times*, and involve themselves in politics and daily discussions in ways never before imagined possible. Demonstrations of 50,000-80,000 were held. As the BCGEU prepared to go out on strike at the end of October there was talk of a general strike and a timetable of strike action that threatened massive public-sector walkouts and private-sector union involvement if the state intervened with a heavy hand to order protesters back to work or to jail their leaders. As

Bennett and the Socreds made a mockery of the traditions of the legislature, using their majority to stifle debate and ram bills through the House, it was obvious to many in the province that parliamentary procedures were a charade. The real opposition was in the streets with the Solidarity mobilization, something that Bennett himself—always keen to poke hard at the NDP—enjoyed acknowledging.

In spite of the intensity of working-class protest, little was won by the anti-Socred stand of literally millions of British Columbia workers and their supporters. BCGEU workers stayed off their jobs for a couple of weeks, teachers struck successfully and illegally, militants called for a general strike, but the state stood firm. And in the face of this firmness the leadership of the Operation Solidarity Coalition, always tightly in the hands of a few trade union leaders, folded. When the going got really tough, a broken Kube retreated to the sidelines. In the end, in what was perhaps one of the sorriest denouements in the history of Canadian class struggle, International Woodworkers of America leader Jack Munro flew on the state's own jet to Premier Bennett's Kelowna home. There, only hours before the B.C. Federation of Labor-led Operation Solidarity promised province-wide labour walkouts to defeat the oppressive restraint legislation, Munro and Bennett shook hands. The tap of class struggle was turned off. No workers were told why or for what. In the weeks to come they would learn: the teachers were victimized; the BCGEU settled for zero per cent in the first year of its new contract and sacrificed workers laid off, part-timers, and job conditions; *Solidarity Times* found its trade union financial support withdrawn; and the "social unionism" promoted by many labour leaders was crudely sacrificed as none of the human rights issues of the massive mobilization were addressed in the Munro settlement that many bluntly called a sell-out.

The fallout from this derailment was immense. Within the workers' movement, acrimony and internal dissent were rife. Munro was reviled by those on the left, defended by those on the right. He was voted out of a B.C. Federation of Labor vice-presidency a short time later. Two years later, Art Kube, mastermind of the Solidarity mobilization, retired from the provincial labour scene to take up a CLC posting in Ottawa: he was the federal body's new "expert" on coalitions. His own coalition, however, was in tatters. Bill Bennett had no Ottawa backers, although his own chief adviser, Norman Spector, was able to land a powerful behind-the-scenes post with the Mulroney Conservative government.

However much the players changed, the British Columbia "reality" was not all that new. As the 1980s wore on Vander Zalm replaced Bennett, the usual skirmishes between the BCGEU and the state took place, the building trades were locked out, and the provincial labour code went through a series of revisions, all of which, not surprisingly, undercut trade union rights and powers. In 1987 the Vander Zalm Socreds implemented legislation that increased state involvement in collective bargaining to an unprecedented level in Canada, allowed employers to restructure their productive relations to avoid unions, and curbed what few powers remained for organized labour, cutting back working-class capacity to resist. The mainstream B.C. Federation of Labor unions called for organized workers to boycott the Labour Relations Board, and tripartite experiments such as the Pacific Institute for Industrial Policy, bankrolled by the federal Labour Market and Productivity Centre, took a nosedive in the estimation of the trade union tops. B.C. Fed head Ken Georgetti described the Institute as "in a very, very deep coma." Bombastic Jack Munro, having now worked his way back into the labour hierarchy after his 1983-84 wrist-slapping, seemed to have been rudely awakened from his class-collaborationist dream. Noticing that Vander Zalm and the employers were cracking down hard on labour, Munro publicly attacked the co-operative tenor of the Institute as nothing less than a sham. "We were duped," he yelled. "We were double-crossed."

This seesaw of seeming militancy, derailment, and co-operation with capital and the state has, in fact, been the trajectory of a 1980s workers' movement constrained by both hard times and a vacillating trade union leadership. As in the case of Quebec's Louis Laberge, B.C.'s labour leadership has often talked tough, done little, and retreated into the pipedream of corporatist collaboration. Whereas Ken Georgetti replaced Art Kube in the aftermath of the latter's Solidarity failure, inching toward opposition and militancy in the later 1980s, he, too, like Quebec's Laberge, now epitomized the new pragmatism of the trade union bureaucracy. As one newspaper report from 1990 noted:

> The B.C. Federation of Labor, once the knee-jerk, extra-parliamentary opposition, now does extensive public-opinion polling every three or four months to tailor its message and moderate its policies. Jack Munro, the longtime sometimes irascible head of the woodworkers, currently sits on at least two provincial councils, alongside employers to advise the Vander Zalm government on various land-use options. Mr Georgetti has just been named to the premier's new environmental round table. The Federation and its arch enemy, the Business Council of British Columbia, have just agreed publicly—for probably the first time—on a major new government initiative, the restructuring of the workers' compensation system.

This process underscores the extent to which hard times, and the state's response of cannibalizing the public sector, push labour's leadership into ever more restricted corners of certain defeat. . . .

The Internal Dynamics of Union Power: Explaining Canadian Autoworkers' Militancy in the 1980s[*]

Charlotte Yates

In 1980, Canada, like most other Western industrialized nations, entered a period of economic decline. The North American auto industry was particularly hard hit. Faced with growing international competition from Japan and Europe, and falling consumer demand due to the recession, it was caught in a compound crisis. Parts of the industry became victims of this crisis and were forced to close down plants. Meanwhile the 'Big Three' auto makers (General Motors, Ford, Chrysler) tried to increase their competitiveness by rationalizing and restructuring production and demanding concessions from workers. These company initiatives threatened to weaken, if not displace, the largest auto union, the American based International Union of Automobile Workers of America (UAW). Canadian autoworkers fought against becoming the scapegoats of the recession and through their union, the Canadian region of the UAW, pursued a militant mobilization strategy of plant sit-downs and a no-concessions policy. Both these strategies left the union stronger and more united than ever. . . .

Restructuring the Auto Industry in the 1980s: UAW Responses in Canada and the US

The economic uncertainty of the 1970s became world recession in the 1980s, combined with continued high inflation, double digit unemployment and a severe drop in productivity. The auto industry was particularly hard hit. In the short term, it suffered an immediate drop in profitability owing to

✠ Abridged from Charlotte Yates, "The Internal Dynamics of Union Power: Explaining Canadian Autoworkers' Militancy in the 1980s," *Studies in Political Economy* 31 (Spring 1990): 73–105. Reprinted by permission of the publisher and the author.

declining consumer incomes and the increased penetration of foreign cars into the North American market. More serious, however, was the long-term prospect of the North American auto producers' loss of their position of world dominance in auto production. The root of the problem lay in the North American auto industry's failure to meet the Japanese challenge with a more efficient use of resources and organization of production. North American auto producers therefore began searching for means to restore their competitiveness.

In the short term, auto parts makers responded with plant closures and layoffs. To increase long-run efficiency and competitiveness, corporations mechanized their plants, introducing robots and computer technology. Streamlined production and reduced costs were obtained by using fewer parts in cars, producing standardized car designs which could be sold in any market, shifting production to cheap labour zones in Third World countries and, more recently, entering into joint ventures with foreign corporations. Corporations also downsized their cars in the hope of competing with the Japanese in the small car market.[1]

Rationalization of the production process was accompanied by corporate attempts to reduce labour costs and restructure relations with the UAW. The restructuring process constituted a move to dismantle existing collective bargaining arrangements and replace them with a system characterized by flexibility in the allocation of labour and variability in wage and benefit calculations. Management saw these moves as imperative. Master and pattern bargaining, seniority arrangements and structured wage and benefit increments were viewed as fetters on corporate initiatives to restore competitiveness. Concessions from workers became the means to achieve both these goals.

While auto corporations willingly used threats of plant closure and job loss as a means to force workers to accept concessions, they also attempted ideologically to mobilize workers and the UAW behind corporate strategy. A new management discourse of team work, joint decision-making and 'equality of sacrifice' accompanied corporate demands for concessions, heightened pressure for QWL [Quality of Working Life] programmes and the reorganization of production. The auto corporations were intent upon allying workers and the UAW in corporate struggles to restore their competitiveness.[2]

This reformulation of labour relations, aimed at tying workers' wages and interests to the productivity of a corporation, constituted a threat to the relationship between the union and its members. First, in the not-so-long-run, the union could find itself demanding measures which would ensure the profitability of the company at the expense of wages and the protection of union members. Furthermore, union locals could become tied to the interests of the corporations, resulting in a weakening of the union organization itself. Second, proposed labour-management committees could result in a devolution of the union's role as protector of workers' interests to these newly created committees. Third, in negotiating and 'selling' concessionary agreements to their members with no guarantees of job security, unions could find themselves the object of growing membership discontent, thereby threatening the capacity of the union to pursue a strategy of collective action. Finally, since the late 1940s, the UAW had relied upon institutionalized collective bargaining practices for its organizational strength. By accepting the reformulation of labour relations, the UAW faced the possible erosion of its established organizational position and an accompanying loss of power in the work place and ultimately the political arena. Yet, if the UAW did not accept concessions it was possible that corporations would either shift production to cheap labour zones or face possible bankruptcy. This would both threaten the jobs of autoworkers and lead to a decline in union membership.

In spite of this uncertainty, the Canadian UAW chose to pursue a strategy of militant mobilization of its membership in an attempt to resist concessions and plant closures. In doing so, the union hoped in the short term to protect its organizational integrity and bolster membership support for the union. In the long term, the Canadian UAW anticipated that successful resistance to concessions and plant closures would stall, if not reverse, management's chosen strategy for recovery which threatened to destroy the union.

The Canadian UAW's first major act of resistance to corporations came in response to plant closures. After lobbying failed to gain government action to protect workers thrown out of work due to closures, the UAW Canadian Council formulated a strategy of plant sit-downs. Rank-and-file autoworkers were anxious for action and rushed to offer their plants as the first targets for a sit-down.[3] With the pending closure of a number of small, older plants and the poor severance packages offered by corporations to workers, the Canadian UAW was pushed into action. On August 9, 1980, 200 autoworkers occupied the Houdaille plant in Oshawa. With the help of strike pay, for which White pressured the reluctant international union officers, the workers held fast until August 21 when a settlement was reached. Severance pay was to be increased almost 6 times the amount originally offered by the company and pensions were improved and extended to include workers of 55 years of age.[4] By September, autoworkers at Beach Appliance and the Bendix plant had also staged sit-downs, meeting with similar successes.[5] Soon after, the Ontario government passed severance pay legislation to protect workers faced with plant closures.

The scenes of solidarity and vitality amongst UAW members at the subsequent Canadian Council meeting were reminiscent of the 1930s and 1940s. The importance of this victory went beyond the immediate gains for the workers involved. The union had successfully mobilized the rank and file at a time when most unions were in retreat. A renewed pride in the union reinforced the militancy and solidarity amidst the rank and file and between the leadership and membership, preparing the ground for what would prove to be more difficult days ahead.

The success of the sit-down strikes was all the more important as it coincided with the early demands for concessions. In 1979, the financially-troubled Chrysler corporation first asked for concessions from its workers. Both Canadian and American autoworkers accepted these demands. Nevertheless, by 1980, Chrysler seemingly on the verge of bankruptcy, appealed to the American government for help. Congress offered to bail out the corporation if Chrysler could gain further concessions from its workers and loans from other governments, in particular the Canadian government. While the American members of the UAW International Executive Board (IEB) accepted concessions as the only way to save the corporation (and hence jobs), Bob White, Canadian Director of the UAW, refused to go along with the deal. He rejected the notion that Canadian collective bargaining could be determined by a foreign government.[6] The Canadian autoworkers' hand was strengthened by the Canadian government's position on the Chrysler loan negotiations. Contrary to the American government position and largely as a result of the dependent nature of the Canadian economy, the Canadian government made any loans to Chrysler conditional upon corporate guarantees of increased investment and jobs in Canada.[7]

While White's move represented the first step towards what would become major strategic differences between the Canadian and American sections of the UAW, neither section of the union had yet determined a long-term strategy for dealing with corporate demands. This was illustrated when the Canadian Director, along with the American UAW, agreed to a third round of concessions demanded by Chrysler. White argues that these concessions were imperative as they were based on the very real possibility of bankruptcy and loss of jobs and not the result of a Congressional decision.[8]

The dangers of accepting these and other concessionary deals quickly became apparent to Canadian UAW leaders. Only 2,921 Canadian Chrysler workers voted in favour of the agreement containing concessions while 2,664 rejected it.[9] The union was being divided. This point was clearly brought home when White's administrative assistant went to a membership meeting of a local which had previously accepted concessions and was entering negotiations once again. Whereas these workers had previously been frightened by company threats of closure and had accepted concessions, they now felt the pinch of these give-aways and blamed the union for forcing them down their throats. The most striking feature of this confrontation was that these were not traditionally militant workers.[10]

In the face of growing rank-and-file discontent and the prospect of a flood of concessions from other corporations following Chrysler's lead, White announced that this contract was the last to be reopened. The Canadian Council then voted in favour of a strategy of resistance to concessions.[11] The American UAW appeared bent on a similar strategy of resistance when in July 1981 the IEB voted not to open other contracts for concessions. This strategic convergence proved, however, to be short-lived. When General Motors demanded concessions late in 1981, the IEB agreed. Backed by the 1981 Canadian Council decision to resist concessions, White cast the lone dissenting vote against the GM decision.[12]

White risked the displeasure of the International union administration because he saw the alternative to be serious weakening of his union's credibility among its rank and file and therefore general weakening of the UAW. White argued:

> I predict we will before this is over see large numbers of our members attacking each other and fighting each other for jobs. We will have large numbers of our members attacking not the corporation or the governments, but the leadership of our union, and will eventually see them turn against our union as an institution.[13]

The prediction was borne out within weeks. Forty-six percent of the American GM union leadership voted against the UAW president's proposal to reopen the GM contracts. Nevertheless, the slightly favourable majority was taken as a mandate to reopen the contract and the re-negotiated agreement made $3 billion in concessions. Discontent and splits within the American rank and file were reflected in the ratification vote; only 52% of the GM workers voted for the contract.[14]

The Canadian UAW's no-concessions policy appeared at one level to be a strategy to bargain 'as usual'. Rather than reopening contracts to pave the way for concessionary bargaining, the Canadian UAW entered into collective bargaining with an agenda of demands and the threat of a strike. The Canadian UAW aimed to protect structured wage and benefit increases, seniority arrangements and master and pattern bargaining. It therefore rejected profit-sharing and lump-sum payments in lieu of wages, the drastic reduction of job classifications in existing plants and the two-tier wage system whereby new workers were to be paid on a lower scale than the older workers. While Canadian autoworkers experimented with QWL projects, the scope of these projects was automatically restricted by the union's hard line stance with respect to accompanying changes, such as the reduction of job classifications.[15] For Canadian autoworkers, these programmes were seen as a possible means of improving life on the assembly line, not as a vehicle for joint decision-making of which autoworkers were highly suspicious.

To some, this strategy may appear as one of defensive maneuvering with the goal of preserving a labour relations system unsuited to new technology and production techniques. The objectives sought by the union through this strategy were, however, much more than this. The no-concessions strategy was intended to preserve the Canadian UAW's organizational strength. Once in a position of power, the Canadian UAW would be able to shape the type of restructuring undertaken in the auto industry rather than accepting the chosen corporate strategy which threatened to undermine the position of the UAW.

The no-concessions strategy would bolster the Canadian UAW's organizational strength in a number of different ways. By resisting rather than selling concessions, the Canadian UAW could reduce the likelihood of the membership blaming the union for any concessions exacted by management. In this way the union hoped to preserve membership support. Secondly, by rejecting the various corporate demands for reformulating wage calculations, the Canadian UAW hoped to prevent competition between different locals with the accompanying threat of internal union disintegration. Finally, the protection of master and pattern bargaining became the organizational means through which the Canadian UAW could advance their goals.

For this strategy to work, the Canadian UAW had to mobilize membership support. This was a difficult task. Large numbers of autoworkers were against concessions; others were afraid of the possible loss of jobs should their union fight the corporations. Moreover, by fighting concessions the Canadian UAW was asking its membership to abandon the historic practice of abiding by International union policy. The Canadian UAW therefore had to construct a unity of interest amongst the membership.

The militant syndicalist tradition of the Canadian UAW provided a necessary ideological basis for UAW appeals to workers to reject management solutions to the economic crisis and fight back using militant forms of work place action. Canadian autoworkers' experience in the 1970s had rekindled a trade-union centred world view in which the interests of the trade union were understood as independent of it, if not in opposition to, those of the corporations. While corporate interests lay in maximizing profits, workers' interests lay in protecting their jobs, improving wages and escaping the misery of the assembly line. This interpretive framework made Canadian autoworkers and their leaders suspicious of the new 1980s management discourse of 'team work' and of attempts to equate the interests of workers with those of individual corporations. Finally, experiences in the 1970s had laid the groundwork for appeals to Canadian UAW members for a national course of action. Consequently, the union's syndicalism tradition provided the ideological space for mobilizing membership support for a no-concessions policy. The union's organizational structure further enhanced its capacity to unify membership behind such a course of action. Through its educational forums, the Canadian Council, shop stewards and the communications network of newspapers and fact sheets, the Canadian UAW disseminated information on both the effects of concessions and the union's strategy. To ensure compliance with the no-concessions policy, the union carefully monitored all negotiations, a practice that was facilitated by the centralized collective bargaining system and the Canadian Council. In addition a no-concessions fund based on special membership levies, which increased the level of strike pay and provided resources for the union to mount its anti-concessions campaign, was set up. Consolidation of membership support for this strategy was facilitated by the early victories over plant closures and by the growing success of the union's resistance to concessions.

To further bolster the union's position, the Canadian UAW sought widespread union and community support for its no-concessions policy. This was important, for if the UAW 'went it alone' in its no-concessions stand, the union might become the target of criticism from the public, governments and corporations and be vilified for its unwillingness to sacrifice in the name of economic recovery. In turn, this may have led to pressure being put on the UAW by other Canadian unions to reverse its position and join with the rest of organized labour in its retreat. Therefore, the Canadian UAW mobilized the support of the Canadian Labour Congress, the Ontario Federation of Labour, the International Woodworkers and Dave Patterson, District Six Regional Director of the Steelworkers, for an all-Canadian union policy against concessions. Secondly, the UAW leadership adopted a strategy of openness and availability to the media in order to place its agenda before the public and into national debates on economic restructuring.

In addition to its work place strategy, the Canadian UAW stepped up its efforts to have the federal government adopt a trade policy which dealt more adequately with the question of international competition. Rather than advocating protectionism, the Canadian UAW demanded that the Autopact be extended to cover all automakers so that, in exchange for access to the Canadian markets, non-American auto producers would be forced, like their American counterparts, to invest in Canada and create a certain number of jobs.[16]

The no-concessions strategy paid off for the union. In negotiations with GM and Ford in 1982 and 1984, the Canadian UAW successfully resisted the replacement of regular wage increases and COLA [Cost of Living Adjustment] clauses with profit-sharing and lump-sum payments and maintained master bargaining and seniority. While it lost paid personal holidays and certain other benefits, the basic structure of bargaining was maintained. Perhaps the most important victory came during the 1983 Chrysler negotiations. This strike resulted in a substantial wage increase in the move towards regaining parity between Chrysler and the other automakers. In turn, this proved to Canadian autoworkers the viability of their union's analysis that management's strategy of restructuring through concessions was not the *only* one available. Rather, faced with union resistance, Chrysler had been forced to back away from this strategy. . . . [17]

As a result of these victories, the Canadian UAW and, in particular, Bob White, became the darling of the media and a symbol for all Canadian workers of the efficacy of militancy and the justice of labour's fight to protect its position in the work place. The cost, however, was high. Following internal union struggles over the 1984 GM negotiations, Canadian autoworkers found themselves forced to move towards independence. In 1985 the founding convention of the new National Automobile, Aerospace and Agricultural Implement Workers Union of Canada (CAW) was held and a new chapter in the history of Canadian autoworkers began.[18]

CONCLUSION

o

The Canadian UAW strategy, and now that of the CAW, has increased the power of the union in both the work place and the political arena. Not only is membership support for the union at an all-time high, but CAW has become the union of choice for various groups of unorganized workers as well as those disillusioned with their existing union. For instance, east coast fishers recently voted in favour of abandoning their old union, the International Food and Commercial Workers, and joining the CAW.

The CAW's strategy has had the unintended consequence of catapulting the union into the vanguard of the labour movement. The CAW has become a symbol of militancy and hope for workers. While this has engendered hostility from many international unions who feel threatened by the possible sucession movements, it has also provided the CAW with more widespread support in its drive to have an effective union voice in the economic restructuring of the 1980s. This can be seen at both the corporate and the government level. The Canadian UAW (CAW) has been drawn into various discussions on new auto investments in Canada, policy forums investigating the future of the Canadian auto industry and trade and, at the provincial level, a task force on technology. These involvements combined with the Canadian autoworkers' media image made the CAW a pivotal figure in the national debate on free trade with the US and a counterpoint to conservative visions of the Canadian nation.

All these effects combined have enhanced the power of the CAW. At the same time, the CAW faces new challenges which may undermine its renewed strength. Although the mergers and organizing drives by the CAW have increased its numerical strength, they have also increased the diversity of union membership. In so doing, these organization drives may have created future obstacles to the articulation of a unity of interest amongst Canadian autoworkers and hence the capacity of the union to engage in united collective action. Moreover, the CAW has undergone some major organizational changes since independence. In taking over the functions once performed by the International and in meeting the demands of a larger, more diverse membership, the CAW has rapidly bureaucratized, increasing its staff and possibly the distance between the leadership and membership. Heightened tensions at the CAW office between office-clerical staff and union leaders are a small reflection of the changing internal dynamics of the union. While Bob White's willingness to walk a picket line and distribute leaflets at plant gates tempers this pessimism, the degree to which this can and will continue remains to be seen as the union grows larger. The relative autonomy of the Canadian Council from the union administration has also been reduced as members of the executive now function as part of the Council. This in turn reduces the Council's historically important role as a site for organizing the internal opposition which has made the union what it is.

The CAW continues to face the challenges of restructuring and, now, free trade, which may alter the dynamics of the union. New Japanese auto plants located in Canada pose an organizational challenge to the CAW. While successful in its bid to represent workers in the new CAMI Automotive plant, a joint venture between GM and Suzuki, the future of the union remains uncertain in the new Honda, Toyota and Hyundai plants. Unless it is successful, the CAW will lose its near-monopolistic position in the auto industry and face the prospect of wage competition. Moreover, it remains unclear how the CAW will mesh demands for Japanese-style labour management relations with those existing in the older auto plants. More flexible arrangements in the new plants may place more pressure on older plants for concessions and once again open up the union to membership competition and the disintegration of internal unity. While acceptance of flexibility may be the only means for the CAW to gain a foothold in these new auto plants, it may well sow the seeds of competition among autoworkers and thus prove a weakness in the future.

Finally, the spectre of free trade haunts the CAW. The union's success in protecting structured collective bargaining and decent wages and benefits for its membership may have increased the incentive for automakers to attempt to meet the demands of the Canadian market with vehicles built in the US. The recent announcement of shifts in production from Canada to the US by both GM and Honda have been interpreted by some analysts as proof of this effect of free trade.[19] Such competition with the US for jobs narrows the choices open to the CAW and raises the possibility of increased internal membership rivalry as each local vies for a declining number of jobs. Thus, the loss of the battle against free trade, along with new challenges in the nineties may undo the CAW's victories of the eighties.

NOTES

○

1. For a discussion on restructuring in the American auto industry see Alan Altshuler *et al*, *The Future of the Automobile: The Report of MIT's International Automobile Program* (Cambridge: MIT Press, 1984); on Canada, see Patrick Lavelle and Robert White, *An Automotive Strategy for Canada*, Report of the Federal Task Force on the Canadian Motor Vehicles and Automotive Parts Industries (Ottawa: Minister of Industry and Commerce, 1983); Marc Van Ameringen, "The Restructuring of the Canadian Automobile Industry" in Duncan Cameron and Francois Houle, eds, *Le Canada et la Nouvelle Division Internationale du Travail* (Ottawa: University of Ottawa Press, 1985).

2. For an excellent example of this new corporate discourse see Lee Iacocca with William Novak, *Iacocca: An Autobiography* (N.Y.: Bantam Books, 1984).

3. Minutes of meeting of Canadian UAW Council, 21 and 22 June, 1980.

4. *Globe and Mail*, 9 and 21 August, 1980.

5. Canadian Regional Director's Report to Canadian Council, 14 and 15 September, 1980, pp. 4 and 10.

6. Canadian Regional Director's Report to Canadian Council, 26 and 27 January, 1980.

7. Canadian Regional Director's Report to Canadian Council, 21 and 22 June 1980, p. 16; *Globe and Mail*, 1 May 1980.

8. Canadian Regional Director's Report to Canadian Council, 31 January and 1 February 1981, p. 8.

9. *Globe and Mail*, 30 January 1981.

10. Interview with Robert White, Canadian UAW Regional Director, 31 December, 1985.

11. Minutes to meeting of Canadian Council, 31 January and 1 February 1981, p. 8.

12. Canadian Regional Director's Report to Canadian Council, 12 and 13 September, 1981, 30 and 31 January 1982.

13. Canadian Regional Director's Report to Canadian Council, 30 and 31 January 1982, p. 23.

14. Minutes to meeting of Canadian Council, 30 and 31 January 1982, p. 32; *Globe and Mail*, 16 April 1982.

15. C. Yates, *From Plant to Politics: The Canadian UAW, 1936-1984* (Ph.D. dissertation, Carleton University, Ottawa, Canada, 1988).

16. Lavelle and White, *An Automotive Strategy...*, 1983.

17. Yates, *From Plant to Politics...*, chapter 8.

18. For an insider's view of the split of the Canadian Region from the International UAW, see Sam Gindin, "Breaking Away: The Formation of the Canadian Auto Workers," *Studies in Political Economy* 29 (Summer, 1989), pp. 63-89.

19. *Hamilton Spectator*, 14 October 1989.

Women, Unions and Leadership[*]

Linda Briskin

In the past fifteen years the movement of union women has posed a creative and often successful challenge to the structures, strategies and ideologies of unions in Canada.

The understanding of what is a legitimate union issue has expanded to include abortion, childcare, affirmative action, pay equity, sexual harassment. New structures have emerged, such as women's caucuses and committees, generated by women unionists on the margins of traditional union organization. By highlighting women's concerns as workers and unionists, these committees have mobilized women in larger numbers than ever before. Recognition of the significance of gender has also helped to create space to take account of racism and homophobia. Women organizing within these alternative structures have accepted as fundamental the necessity for rank and file involvement. This has posed a challenge to business unionism and to the service mentality of many unions.

Despite the fact that workplace conditions faced by women have not improved dramatically over the last 15 years, women unionists can point with pride to these shifts in the internal life of unions. As a result of their efforts, unions are increasingly taking up women's issues in negotiation, targeting financial and staff resources for specific educational programs designed to suit women's needs, and making unions more hospitable to women.

These successes have shifted the debate about women and unions: from a focus on the barriers which prevent women from participating in unions, and specifically in leadership positions, to the barriers women in leadership positions face from union hierarchies and bureaucracies traditionally dom-

[*] Linda Briskin, "Women, Unions and Leadership," *Canadian Dimension* (January/February 1990): 38–41. Reprinted by permission of the publisher and the author.

284

inated by men, and further to the emergence of a new feminist-informed union politic.

Obviously it is difficult to generalize. The sectoral and industrial location of the union, the region of the country, the political and economic context, the ratio of women to men in the union all impact on the shape, and degree of success, of women's organizing. This article highlights, then, emerging trends, often initiated by feminist unionists, rather than deeply rooted and widespread practices.

DESIGNATED AFFIRMATIVE ACTION POSITIONS
o

Despite the increasing numbers of women in unions, women continue to be underrepresented in the halls of union power. Overall, from 1980-86 the percentage of women on central executive boards has remained fairly constant: at about 17 per cent. More encouraging is the participation of women in local leadership positions. In 1986 women represented 50 per cent of the membership in the Public Service Alliance of Canada (PSAC) and held 40 per cent of all executive positions (although 70 per cent of those were in the position of secretary).

Unions have attempted to address the under-representation of women in top elected positions through designating affirmative action positions. In 1983 the Ontario Federation of Labour broke new ground by amending its constitution to create five 'affirmative action' positions on its executive board. In 1984 the Canadian Labour Congress followed suit by adopting a constitutional change calling for a minimum of 6 female vice presidents. Subsequently many large labour federations and unions across the country followed suit.

These high profile positions give visibility to women in leadership positions, challenge stereotypes and provide role models. Since many of these women are committed to addressing the specific concerns of women, as workers and unionists, the visibility of these issues has also increased.

Although these positions do represent a significant turning point for the union movement, some cautionary notes are worth sounding. The first relates to the limits of any strategy of numerical representation based on sex alone. There is no guarantee that a woman, by virtue of her sex, will have progressive politics on women's issues. Therefore, increasing the numbers of women in leadership has limited potential when not part of a larger strategy of concretely addressing the needs of women. The representational strategy must be linked directly with the political perspective of feminist unionism.

Gains in numerical representation may also create a false sense of accomplishment and weaken the drive to more pro-active and substantive solutions. There is no doubt that it is easier to appoint/elect a few women vice-presidents than to challenge the deeply-rooted male domination of union structures, strategies and ideologies. The existence of a few high profile women leaders can make it appear, mistakenly, that great strides toward 'women's liberation' have been made.

Some feminist union activists have confronted, with a degree of success, the limits of designated affirmative action positions. Through women's caucuses and committees they have brought politics, and rank and file involvement, to the process of selecting a candidate. They have highlighted the political perspective of the candidate rather than her sex; and by establishing accountability to a constituency of union women, created the base from which to organize for broad workplace and union transformation.

In recounting such a process, a leader of a large public sector union had this to say: "I hold an affirmative action position. We deliberately set out to follow a feminist process and collectively decide who would run. And I was the one who ran and was elected. We defeated the establishment candidate and showed very strongly that this collective process was pretty successful. What's more it was successful because they didn't divide us. In the past they'd been able to divide us against each other because of competition between the women who want to run for these positions. I now offer a challenge to them in the way that they want to proceed, although there are some very common basic union principles that I share with those that I work with."

This strategy is not without its price. Elected through affirmative action, women may face an uphill battle for credibility; systematic exclusion from information networks and from formal and informal decision-making processes; and ghettoization in 'women's issues' narrowly defined. These problems can be compounded if the woman has deep roots in an organized political (feminist) constituency of women, who are simultaneously perceived to be both marginal and threatening.

"I hold an elected position and am in charge of women's issues. I am shut out by other elected officers, some of whom are women and some of whom are men because I am compartmentalized into something called 'women's issues'. ... The most problematic thing is that they don't share their knowledge with me nor do they share information..."

A N E W P O L I T I C O F L E A D E R S H I P

In response to male-dominated and hierarchical union practices, a new politic of leadership is emerging among feminist unionists which emphasizes process and accountability, and which goes well beyond superficial style. Informed by the organizing strategies of the grassroots women's movement, this politic fundamentally redefines leadership practices. It supports decentralization of the power traditionally associated with leadership positions and emphasizes "providing members opportunities to develop their own power and the self-reliance required to effect democratic changes in the union." It is an inclusive rather than exclusive politic; it relies on participation more than on representation. It moves toward greater democracy and openness of union structures and decision-making; it underscores accountability and operates on the basis of a strong and active link between leadership and constituency. And it operates with a consciousness of gender, and of the specific barriers which women face in the household, the workplace and the union.

A move toward such a politic is an essential ingredient for a resilient and visionary union movement. However, the practice of this form of leadership is not without contradiction. Within a women's caucus—a somewhat protected environment—it may be possible to structure decision-making in an inclusive way, and to develop a team-oriented relationship. But attempts to operate with greater accountability in other arenas can be counteracted by various forces. Linda Torney, the president of the Labour Council of Metro Toronto with its 180,000 affiliated members has struggled with the difficulties of maintaining a feminist commitment to process in the face of the daily pressure of large and crisis-ridden union organizations.

"One of my major problems is process: how to deal with things on a consultative basis, arrive at consensus with adequate communication, empower people, develop new leadership; in fact, build a team. That's what I want to do. So far I'm holding on to that as a process but I got to tell you, it's incredibly hard to maintain. It is not that somebody tries to coopt me into doing something else. It's time. All of those things take time. The organization is crisis-ridden. There's at least one a day and it's much easier sometimes to say 'Just do it this way. I don't have time to discuss it.' I have to really resist that. It's too easy to slide into making a decision on your own because of time constraints. And it becomes more difficult to hang on to the process as people begin to trust you. Because they don't watch you as closely. So it's easier to say, 'Well just this one little time I won't make these six phone calls that I need to make to get clearance to do this.' So it's a problem: holding on to the process in a crisis organization."

Attempting to use such strategies can provoke deep ideological resistance. A woman in a senior staff position in a large public sector union describes her attempts to introduce new practices in the union office:

"My role was essentially to coordinate and supervise. I went into a situation which was very traditional and my bosses—the union staff hierarchy—expected me to take a very traditional role. A kick ass role, it you like, and senior reps who couldn't do that were seen to be quite weak people. I didn't see myself particularly as a person who wanted to do that or who was very effective at doing it. When I got appointed most of the reps were men and they were not only men but overwhelmingly had an authoritarian approach to the membership. They were not interested in encouraging the rank and file to participate. They were politically very conservative and they operated mainly through the leaders of the union. They really didn't see theirs as a role to activate the rank and file. I did resolve to try and change the process in the office but attempts at team work were quite overtly rejected. One guy just simply said, 'I work best as an individual. I do not want to work as a team. I will not work as a team.' Downright refused to even deal with the idea that we might cooperate together."

A women's caucus representative on a local executive describes some of the tensions which arise because of the traditional structures of union decision-making and union organization.

"We have an executive and a union that's generally very supportive of feminism but, at the same time, it's very committed to a traditional union structure... My legitimacy is sometimes challenged because I was elected from the women's caucus. I wasn't elected from the traditional representative structure of the union as a whole. In fact, I am more accountable to the women's caucus because this is a strong group and I would always have to take things back to the women's caucus. I would say at the executive that I can't decide immediately. They could decide immediately because between elections, the executive has a fair bit of autonomy."

Not only are union structures resistant to the practice, if not the principle, of accountability, but a commitment to these new forms of leadership cannot erase the inevitable differences in power between union leaders and those they represent. Often unacknowledged is the power that accrues to union leaders by definition—a power that is expressed in greater access to information, union educationals, time, resources, travel, credibility, time off from work, etc.

Women leaders who adopt new leadership practices may assume that such practices, and the common bond of womanhood, can overcome these power differences. As a result, they may face a distance, and even hostility, from their constituency, and sometimes a message that they have sold out. The *recognition* of differences in power—be they based on race, class, gender, sexual orientation or leadership position—provides the foundation to build the solidarity we need to transform the union movement.

But the contradiction for women leaders goes deeper yet. Women in leadership positions are, more often than not, excluded from access to the power that should accrue to them by virtue of their position; they are marginalized and isolated by the structures and ideologies of male domination. They are caught between the reality of their power relative to the rank and file, and the absence of their power relative to male leaders. The solution is not to retreat from the challenge of the new politic of leadership but rather to acknowledge openly the power differentials: both those that separate women in leadership positions from the rank and file, *and* those that separate women in leadership positions from men in similar positions.

This consciousness must be reflected in structural changes, in particular the decentralization of leadership. This might take the form of more financial and staff resources to locals and women's committees, and more rank-and-file authority to shape union policy and strategy.

FEMINIST PROCESS INSIDE THE UNIONS

○

In general process focuses on *how* we organize. Feminist process in the unions has tended to concentrate on three areas: developing decision-making practices that rely on consensus; building skills; and sharing knowledge and responsibility. It includes taking account of the emotional climate in the union, and legitimizing concerns that are often seen to be irrelevant to the effective functioning of the union. Feminist process encourages more responsive, hospitable, democratic, participatory and inclusive practices.

Union women have developed unique feminist forms of sharing knowledge informally and of building skills through formal educational programs. In emphasizing both collective strategies and self-activity, the skills building approach of feminist process has posed a direct challenge to the service mentality of many unions and to the deadening effect of business unionism. Feminist process also encourages the informal sharing of knowledge. Marg Bail from the Alberta Federation of Labour sees this as a challenge to the competitive strategies often adopted by men.

> Women trade unionists have learned the value of 'networking', of sharing concepts with other women in other unions, of borrowing successful strategies to win their arguments rather than 'reinventing the wheel' on every issue... We have also learned of one area where women and men are not equal. Union feminists willingly share with one another their secrets of success—male labour leaders hoard theirs.

Inside the unions, this experimentation with process has taken place mainly within women's committees, at women's conferences and within educational programs—at the margins of union structures—or in newer, less bureaucratized unions. For example, the Canadian Union of Educational Workers (CUEW) has been struggling to put in place a form of collective leadership informed by feminist process at the national level of their union.

Feminist process has its immediate roots in the grassroots women's movement and in that context has been the source, not only of strength, but also of problems. Given these difficulties *and* the degree of enthusiasm for feminist process among some feminist unionists, it is worth examining some of the contradictions inherent in the focus on process.

The unifying thread that underlies most problems with feminist process is the way in which process gets separated from politics. Although the critique from which feminist process arises is highly politicized, the actual practice of feminist process is often depoliticizing and demobilizing. Politically correct process itself becomes the objective rather than a means to achieve political goals.

An overemphasis on process can disrupt the internal life of groups. It can be time-consuming and inward-looking as the group turns its attention to its own workings. In an attempt to develop new forms and reject traditional ones what has often resulted is what Jo Freeman called 'the tyranny of structurelessness' where the rules are not clear, the leadership informal and therefore not accountable, where those who don't agree are silenced through the pressure of consensus decision-making. Internalization and structurelessness can make outreach to new women problematic, marginalize and isolate women inside of women's committees, make it difficult for women to move into more public political arenas and weaken organizing for change.

Finally, an overemphasis on process can make women's groups less accessible to women who are not white, or middle class. The detailed scrutiny and resultant transformation of group process can have the contradictory effect of creating a safe and supportive environment for those inside, and an inadvertent means of excluding those on the outside. Feminist process as an exclusionary practice is exacerbated when groups are class and race homogeneous; and when assumptions about process are made which do not take account of a diversity of cultural and class experiences. For example, what constitutes a safe environment for some women may be experienced as dangerous by others; interpersonal practices which emphasize sharing experiences may be more comfortable in some cultural contexts than in others. Further, the time commitment necessary to make 'process' work can easily exclude women who work full time, face a double (triple) day, are single parents, etc.

Despite the importance of sounding some cautionary notes about feminist process, the daily reality of the workplace and the union may prevent, or at least minimize, some of the problems. In the women's movement, feminist process is often situated in a non-institutional setting where the focus on political goals is more difficult to sustain, and the desire and potential to create a haven from the 'world out there' is stronger. The women's movement is also an extraordinarily heterogeneous political, ideological, and class context which makes consensus, prioritizing of issues, and strategic co-operation more difficult. By contrast, the unions provide an institutional structure, a resource base, and a clear raison d'être. The skills developed through feminist process are directly and immediately applicable to work and union situations. The union reality grounds feminist process and provides a counterweight to the inherent tendency in feminist process toward marginalization.

C O N C L U S I O N

o

Although the numbers of women leaders have not increased as quickly as we might like, feminist-informed leadership practices in the union movement are having an important impact, and have the potential to inspire a creative rethinking of union organization. More inclusive, participatory, and democratic practices can empower and mobilize a rank and file that is often apathetic in the face of the service mentality of business unionism. Feminist consciousness goes beyond other progressive rank and file forms of unionism in its identification of the material and ideological barriers that face women. This convergence of feminism and rank and file unionism is exciting not only for the links it can generate between the community-based women's movement and the movement of union women but also for the possibilities it suggests for a new kind of unionism as we move into the 1990s.

Power and Control

at Work

EDITORS' INTRODUCTION

o

Work essentially involves relations of power, the most fundamental of which is between employer and employee. The power of employers is exercised through managers' control over the content, organization, pace, and rewards of work. Yet regardless of how ingenious managers are in devising ways to regulate workers' activities, the goal of total control will always remain elusive. This is because workers are equally adept at finding ways of resisting, renegotiating, or redefining managerial objectives—such as a fair day's work, output quotas, or detailed procedures for executing specific tasks. However, it would be naive to conclude that the resulting compromises balance out the interests of both employers and employees, given that the former holds the keys to the store, office, or plant, and, therefore, the workers' jobs. A critical perspective on work highlights the complexities of the labour process by focusing on managerial power, struggles for control, and the potential for conflict over outcomes.

The articles in Part 8 take a worker's perspective, and thus indirectly engage in a critical debate with the managerial perspectives presented in Part 6. This debate is neatly framed by James Rinehart in his critique of quality of working life (QWL) schemes, such as participative management, autonomous work teams, and job enrichment. Rinehart notes that QWL addresses the negative impact of Taylorism (scientific management) and Fordism (mass-production assembly-line technology), but falls well short of transferring authority to workers or significantly improving job content. Rather, Rinehart argues that the overriding goal of QWL tends to be changing workers' attitudes so that they are more supportive of management objectives, rather than significantly altering workplace authority relations.

In other words, QWL rests on the assumption that participation and higher job satisfaction will create a more compliant and diligent work force. QWL also is based on a "win–win" model whereby everyone equally benefits, a claim that rings hollow in Rinehart's view because improvements for workers are overestimated.

Recall that QWL and sociotechnical job design can also result from collaboration between union and management, as in the case of the Shell chemical plant described by Davis and Sullivan in Part 6. But Rinehart argues that Shell management embarked on a sociotechnical approach not out of a humanistic concern for the welfare of workers, but because of cost factors in operating expensive continuous-process technology. Lower maintenance costs and reduced risk of shutdowns or accidents were the desired results. Rinehart does admit that the kind of "team concept" used at Shell probably has the greatest potential to reform the workplace. But the fact that Shell carefully screened all employees to weed out those with a "them–us" attitude toward management indicates that the workers themselves are unlikely to push the team logic beyond the limits set by management.

Technology is a driving force in the continued rationalization of work. From a critical perspective, automation extends and refines managerial control over the labour process. Unions are especially concerned about the negative impact of technological change on workers. David Robertson and Jeff Wareham report some of the findings from a Canadian Auto Workers Union's (CAW) case study of Northern Telecom, one of Canada's premier high-tech corporations in the telecommunications field. They underscore the crucial link between, on the one hand, Northern Telecom's changing labour requirements and organizational restructuring, and, on the other, the introduction of new automated systems.

The primary goal of Northern Telecom's automation strategy was cost reduction, which was to be achieved largely through increased productivity with fewer workers. The application of this "more-with-less" manufacturing philosophy is described in detail by Robertson and Wareham. For example, flexible manufacturing systems and "just-in-time" inventory controls significantly reduced the number of production workers required (direct labour), as well as related materials-handling, clerical, administrative, and maintenance jobs (indirect labour). A major result of automation is a change in the composition of the firm's work force toward more information-based jobs in marketing, design, and customer services. It is important to note that occupational changes within this firm parallel the rise of information work in the service economy as a whole, as described in Part 2. Similarly, the new job structures have created a more polarized job hierarchy within Northern Telecom. Robertson and Wareham raise the prospects of reduced union strength, as CAW members at Northern Telecom adjust to blurred job lines, the contracting-out of work, and the transfer of unionized technical work to nonunion engineers.

Joel Novek investigates the impact of corporate restructuring and technological change within a very different context: the meat packing industry. Meat packing was once a core mass-production industry in which unionized workers enjoyed relatively decent wages and benefits. However, recessionary pressures and more competitive markets have brought hard times to the industry, resulting in a deterioration of wages and working conditions and an intensification of the labour process. Novek's bleak message, then, is that workers have borne the brunt of restructuring.

Novek attributes the peripheralization of what was once a core industry to the fact that employers seem to be locked into mass-production techniques. The industry has not been innovative, moving beyond mechanized mass production, in large part because of the nature of the raw material— live animals. Collective bargaining has created elaborate and rigid job classifications that virtually guarantee major conflicts if management departs from the mass-production methods. And market share is determined by a plant's ability to mass-produce large volumes of a standardized product— fresh meat. For these reasons, unlike the high-tech strategy adopted at Northern Telecom, managers in meat packing plants have resorted to faster, more repetitive, and closely regulated work. The most immediate effect on workers is a rise in accident and injury rates. Novek is careful not to use the meat packing scenario to propound generalizations about other industries, although his research certainly lays out one path management could follow when confronted with a difficult economic environment.

A different kind of worker control is the subject of Vivienne Walters and Ted Haines's article. Occupational health and safety legislation in Ontario (and most other jurisdictions in Canada) gives workers the right to participate in creating healthy and safe workplaces. Walters and Haines address Rinehart's concern about the tension between management control and worker participation, and Novek's interest in the effects of working conditions on health. But they do so from the vantage point of legislated participation within the workplace through joint worker/union–management health and safety committees and worker health and safety representatives. The core principle of the Ontario legislation is "internal responsibility," which requires workers' involvement in creating healthy and safe working conditions. Walters and Haines's interviews in six firms sought to determine if, in fact, workers had the resources to put this legislated responsibility into practice.

The findings of this research are cause for concern because they reveal major inadequacies in the system of worker involvement in occupational health and safety. For example, while most workers interviewed had experienced job-related health problems and were aware of a wide range of health risks, few requested information about hazards or had exercised their legal right to refuse to perform unsafe work. The inconsistencies between workers' concerns and their actions partly reflect their reliance on their own supervisors rather than on designated worker health and safety

representatives. As Walters and Haines argue, the health and safety representatives are the weak links in the system. Supervisors—the front line of
management—can hardly be expected to have workers' best interests at
heart. Other important determinants of workers' inaction were a lack of
objective information about hazards, a blaming-the-victim mentality, and a
sense of fatalism. In short, despite the good intentions of Ontario's health
and safety legislation, there are powerful institutional and ideological constraints that undermine true worker participation.

To summarize, while examining diverse topics, the four articles in this
section converge upon several important issues. The first concerns the limits imposed on workplace reforms because of existing organizational structures and power arrangements. The second issue underscores how corporate restructuring strategies frequently have detrimental effects on workers.
Of course, this second issue raises, once again, the dilemma of whether the
alternatives could result in even fewer jobs, or jobs of worse quality. Yet the
third issue—the potential for workers to have an influence on the future
direction of their workplace and industry—offers some hope that more
truly participatory forms of workplace democracy may be a viable option.

D I S C U S S I O N   Q U E S T I O N S

o

1. From Rinehart's perspective, what kinds of reforms would create a more
   humanized and participatory workplace?

2. Are there situations in which industrial restructuring, automation, or
   QWL produce a "win–win" situation, that is, one in which management
   and workers equally benefit?

3. What, if anything, should be done to save declining Canadian industries
   such as clothing and textiles or meat packing?

4. How useful are the concepts of power and conflict for explaining the
   internal dynamics of some unions?

5. Are the changes described by Robertson and Wareham the inevitable
   results of automation? What might alternative models of technological
   change involve?

6. How could Ontario occupational health and safety legislation be
   amended to empower workers to create healthier and safer workplaces?

S U G G E S T E D   R E A D I N G S

o

Armstrong, Pat, and Hugh Armstrong. *Theorizing Women's Work*. Toronto:
Garamond Press, 1990.

Braverman, Harry. *Labor and Monopoly Capital*. New York: Monthly Review Press, 1974.

Dwyer, Tom. *Life and Death at Work: Industrial Accidents as a Case of Socially Produced Error*. New York: Plenum, 1991.

Heron, Craig, and Robert Storey, eds. *On the Job: Confronting the Labour Process in Canada*. Montreal and Kingston: McGill–Queen's University Press, 1986.

Rinehart, James. *The Tyranny of Work: Alienation and the Labour Process*. 2nd ed. Toronto: Harcourt Brace Jovanovich, 1987.

Thompson, Paul. *The Nature of Work: An Introduction to Debates on the Labour Process*. 2nd ed. London: Macmillan, 1988.

Wells, Don. *Soft Sell: 'Quality of Working Life': Programs and the Productivity Race*. Ottawa: Canadian Centre for Policy Alternatives, 1986.

Improving the Quality of Working Life through Job Redesign: Work Humanization or Work Rationalization?*

James Rinehart

Corporate executives, government officials, and trade union leaders increasingly are attracted to possible workplace reform embodied in what is known as work humanization, the new industrial relations or Quality of Working Life (QWL). The appeal of QWL can be found in the reformers' diagnosis of workplace problems and in their claims about the character and consequences of QWL programs. The principles of conventional work arrangements, especially Taylorism, are condemned for being neither humane nor cost effective. Authoritarian work milieux and highly fragmented jobs over which workers exercise little or no control impede work performance by breeding discontent and resistance. Resistance is expressed through carelessness and indifference, absenteeism and turnover, sabotage and strikes. These problems can be rectified by creating a more democratic enterprise, by constructing more complex jobs, and by entrusting to employees some responsibility for and control over the work process. Although initiated by management, QWL programs are seen as mutually advantageous to capital and labour. This mutual benefits thesis is the key to understanding the broad appeal of QWL. With QWL there are no losers—everyone wins. Workers get a democratic workplace and gratifying jobs. In return, employers receive a diligent, cooperative workforce and, as a consequence, greater productivity and profits (Hackman and Lawler, 1971; Herzberg, 1968; Nightingale, 1982; Trist, 1981)[1].

This paper subjects the foregoing portrayal of QWL to two lines of criticism. First, QWL programs are indiscriminately conflated into a resistance-

* Abridged from James Rinehart, "Improving the Quality of Working Life through Job Redesign: Work Humanization or Work Rationalization?" *Canadian Review of Sociology and Anthropology* 23, no. 4 (1986): 507–30. Reprinted by permission of the publisher and the author.

integration explanatory model. In this model, reforms are undertaken by management in order to minimize resistance and maximize cooperation.[2] Anticipated increases in output and profits, then, are contingent upon the programs' inducement of changes in employees' attitudes toward work, management, and the company. . . .

A second critical thrust is directed at the thesis that capital and labour are mutual beneficiaries of workplace reforms. QWL schemes can reduce a company's costs and increase productivity and profits. In contrast to these tangible outcomes, employees' gains are realized largely in the intangible sphere of intrinsic work satisfaction.[3] While improvements in job satisfaction are undeniably important to workers, proponents of QWL 1/tend to exaggerate QWL-induced modifications of hierarchy and job content (and hence overestimate resultant psychological gratifications), and 2/ ignore or play down QWL's impact on workers' material and collective interests. The latter include job security, the wage-effort bargain, and the maintenance of organizations which protect workers from management and promote struggles to achieve better working conditions. These interests of employees are threatened by QWL programs.

T Y P E S   O F   Q W L

o

This paper examines two types of management-initiated QWL programs— participative management and job redesign. Examples of the first approach include consultative supervision, works councils, management-by-objectives, joint committees, quality control circles, and the Scanlon Plan. Integral to these programs are the relaxation of supervisory controls and the involvement of workers and local union leaders in decision making. Implemented by management to raise output and profits, participatory programs can achieve these ends only when the erosion of rigid hierarchical structures and autocratic styles of supervision transform recalcitrant workers into co-operative ones. Where unions are present, participation may be used for cooptative ends—to temper militancy, to open up divisions in the membership, to extract concessions. In either case, the key to attaining management's purposes is altering the attitudes of subordinates. Since participation is adopted to develop a cooperative workforce, this approach can be subsumed under the resistance-integration explanatory framework. This framework does not provide an adequate understanding of job redesign.

Job redesign restructures job content by expanding employees' tasks and responsibilities. This is done by increasing the task cycle and by assigning to workers, either singly or as a group, duties ordinarily performed by supervisors, inspectors, and other categories of indirect labour. These modifications of the division of labour are implemented through programs called job enlargement, job enrichment, and autonomous groups. The psychological well-being of the workforce usually is advanced by managers as a rationale for such programs, and job redesign indeed may improve employees' work attitudes. However, this paper will argue that the profitability of restructured work is not dependent on motivational change. Job redesign facilitates capital accumulation less through altering workers' consciousness and reducing resistance than by *rationalizing* the work process. Rationalization of productive activity normally is equated with progressively degraded work procedures, resulting in a labour process which is highly specialized and standardized and which divests workers of any semblance of control. However, there are economic and organizational conditions under which extreme job fragmentation and low worker discretion are not the most productive/profitable modes of structuring work. In these circumstances, rationalization entails some degree of despecialization, destandardization, and restoration of workers' discretion. These departures from Taylorism and Fordism can cut labour costs and reduce the time required to produce or process an item because they entail outcomes such as work intensification and labour elimination.[4]

To differentiate QWL programs is not to argue that the types do not overlap in important ways. First, management may simultaneously employ both types of programs. Companies intent on redesigning the labour process have implemented participative mechanisms to weaken opposition to new work methods and the abolition of 'restrictive' work practices. Also redesign programs whose success is predicated on workers performing 'responsibly' often use participation to elicit the appropriate behaviours. Second, limited levels of participation frequently are built into redesigned jobs. Third, one possible consequence of both redesign and participation is improved worker motivation. Finally, what unifies both approaches to work reform is management's ultimate interest in capital accumulation. The expectation of increased profits underlies the corporate adoption of all varieties of QWL. These points of concurrence do not alter the contention that participation and job redesign programs often reflect distinct management purposes (proximate) and realize these purposes via distinct mechanisms. . . .

Production Uncertainty and Autonomous Groups

Multi-skilled and self-regulating work teams (autonomous groups) are the central feature of QWL programs instituted in industries like oil refining, chemicals, and coal mining.[5] Common to these industries are uncertainties related to the raw materials or technology of the production process which make the rigid subdivision of work difficult and costly (Heckscher, 1980; Kelly, 1982; Perrow, 1970). An examination of a QWL program recently implemented at the highly automated Shell Canada plant of Sarnia, Ontario reveals the character of autonomous groups and the corporate rationale for their adoption.

The Shell Sarnia plant manufactures polypropylene and isopropyl alcohol and runs around the clock with process operator shift teams. Each operator is encouraged (through wage increments) to develop the capacity to operate all sections of the plant and to handle routine craft functions, such as equipment maintenance and repair. According to a Shell Sarnia design consultant the work system is structured to permit 'any employee to undertake any task required for the efficient operation of the plant ... artificial, traditional departmental or functional demarcation barriers should be eliminated and work allocated on the basis of achieving the most effective overall results' (Halpern, 1984: 68). The company's wage form is tailored to fit this work system. Operators' remuneration is tied not to the job being done but to the level of skill acquisition. Ideally, operators progress through twelve skill stages, a process scheduled to take a minimum of seven years.

QWL proponents single out plants like Shell Sarnia as proof of their commitment to humanizing the workplace. However, Shell Sarnia's flexible work patterns are less an outgrowth of the humanistic concerns of QWL consultants and progressive executives than of their considerations of profitably operating process technology. The noted redesign expert, Louis Davis, who was involved in planning the Shell plant's work system, candidly observed: 'Industrial relations officers in the oil industry are proud of their "advanced and enlightened" practices. And indeed these practices may be accurately described as enlightened. But they were not adopted for the sake of enlightenment. They were adopted because they are a necessary functional response to the demands of process technology' (Davis, 1972:421). And Heckscher (1980: 96) maintains that the conditions of continuous processing 'almost compel the granting of substantial autonomy to groups of workers.'[6] Indeed, flexible role definitions and self-regulating work teams appear in continuous process plants in general, not just in automated facilities whose labour processes have been constructed by QWL experts (cf. Blauner, 1965; Bright, 1958; Cooper, 1972; Gallie, 1978; Mallet, 1969; Mann and Hoffman, 1960; Naville, 1963; Susman, 1972b; Taylor, 1971; Woodward, 1965).

There are several technologically related conditions which make flexible work roles a cost-effective means of running continuous process operations. Work is usually intense during crises, shutdowns, and start-ups and comparatively relaxed when production is stable. Because the contribution of an individual to output is unrelated to physical effort, it is meaningless to apply conventional work measurement methods to the jobs of process operators. Second, always alert to labour intensification, management strives to keep operators busy during normal production periods by requiring them to perform duties like housekeeping and equipment maintenance and repair.[7] QWL advocates like to define this extension of duties as job enrichment, but besides keeping workers busy the practice also reduces or eliminates the wage costs of indirect and craft workers. Shell Sarnia, for example, employs journeyman craft workers only on the day shift. Maintenance and repair problems encountered on the other shifts are handled by process operators. This represents a significant savings in the wage bill, since it takes process operators at least six years to reach the basic wage of a craftsman (cf. Halpern, 1984).

Process operators monitor an entire complex of machinery and work in an environment where important events occur unpredictably. If a component of the machine complex malfunctions or if there is a change in the rate or character of the output, the problem must be quickly detected, information about it rapidly conveyed throughout the plant, and appropriate corrective action taken. Otherwise, substantial costs are likely to be incurred. Since the appropriate responses to unpredictable events cannot be decided in advance, specialization inhibits workers' capacity to deal with such contingencies. A particular difficulty in this regard is the likelihood of highly unbalanced work loads. When emergencies arise, some specialized workers are intensely occupied while others remain idle. At Shell Sarnia, for instance, 'it seemed desirable for every member of each team to be fully capable of operating all sections of the plant ... there was seen to be much value in having the flexibility within the work force for operators from various units to assist one another during upset conditions' (Halpern, 1984:41). One important 'value' of autonomous groups (as compared with a Taylorist work design) in automated industries, then, is labour intensification.[8] Moreover, because delays in reacting to production problems can involve enormous costs, a premium is placed on developing effective communications among workers and in allowing them the discretion to take remedial action (rather than awaiting orders from supervisors). For example, at Shell Sarnia the 'design team opted for organizational forms that would ... improve response time in dealing with disturbances as they arose' (Davis and Sullivan, 1980: 34). The structure of autonomous groups facilitates rapid and effective reactions to emergencies by encouraging workers to cooperate in coordinating their activities (Wrenn, 1982). There is an additional rationale. Autonomous groups are formed because communication and work allocation are less costly by mutual adjustment of operators than by coordination by management personnel (Susman, 1972a; Gallie, 1978). As Fantoli (1979: 72) observed:

> ... there comes a stage (of technological development) at which the mechanistic logic of the Taylorism model reduces efficiency because of the specialization of functions and of unduly remote, high-level control over the factors that can produce a variety of unexpected breakdowns; and at that stage it becomes advantageous to integrate functions at the operative level. Increased efficiency is then sought not in centralization of decision-making but in the redistribution of decision-making powers according to the nature of the variables that have to be monitored.

The wage cost advantage of a flexible over a Taylorist organization of work was illustrated by two proposals for staffing requirements at a new

automated plant in Norway. Design consultants using socio-technical systems (QWL) concepts compared their recommendations for arranging work
with those advanced by conventionally minded industrial engineers. The
engineers suggested specialized, geographically restricted work roles and
work loads calculated on the basis of standard time study methods. The
result was a many-tiered chain of command, three shifts of process operators, a special maintenance crew, a days-only force of general labourers, and
many first-line supervisors. From labourers to plant manager, the plan
called for ninety-four employees. The proposal forwarded by the sociotechnical systems consultants, which centred on autonomous work groups,
required only sixty employees from top to bottom. An important basis of
this whittled-down model was the consultants' awareness that in plants
with similar technology and specialized work roles many workers were idle
for extended periods, while others struggled with temporary work over-
loads (Emery and Thorsud, 1976).[9]

While flexible work designs can be more profitable than Taylorism, the
realization of this advantage for capital depends on the initiative of workers.
QWL experts insist that flexible work roles intrinsically motivate workers to
diligent work performance. But however much workers appreciate flexibility, the intrinsic gratification they enjoy is often demonstrably insufficient to
induce the level of performance desired by management. When autonomous groups have been instituted in existing plants, the resultant increased
productivity of methods improvement and labour intensification was realized in 80 per cent of the cases not via improved intrinsic motivation but
through wage increases (Kelly, 1982). In new facilities (greenfield sites in
QWL jargon) the typical approach to the problem of motivation is to employ
1/ a highly discriminatory, multi-stage screening process for workforce
recruitment, and 2/ supplementary integrative programs of the participa-
tory/human relations varieties. Shell Sarnia relied on highly selective
recruitment procedures, utilizing autonomous groups in conjunction with
participatory mechanisms and the abolition of hourly wages, time clocks,
special parking lots, and cafeterias for office personnel. These practices have
the goal of 'eliminating the traditional "we-they" atmosphere' (Halpern,
1984: 49). . . .

Corporate Costs and Job Enlargement

The typical form work redesign takes in large offices is job enrichment. This
approach despecializes individual jobs by 'loading' them 'horizontally'
(more task variety) and 'vertically' (adding tasks calling for skill and
responsibility) (Herzberg, 1968). 'Enriched' jobs purportedly allow individuals to realize their personal goals and, as a consequence, evoke work
behaviour congruent with the objectives of the enterprise. As we shall see,
job enrichment programs also have a hidden agenda which more directly

addresses the problem of overspecialization. A major job enrichment project launched by AT&T exemplifies the dimensions of this approach.

Between 1965 and 1968 AT&T 'enriched' the jobs of over 4 000 employees in Canada and the United States.[10] The stated objectives of the program—reduced personnel turnover, lowered costs and improved quality and quantity of output—allegedly were attained at most of the locations where work was restructured. Work changes in the complaints division are typical of the redesign strategy employed throughout the company. Clerks who answered customers' complaints by letter originally were required to respond in terms of a standard answer format. All of their work was checked by verifiers, and cleared letters were signed by supervisors. Under the revised procedure, the women were allowed to use a more personalized mode of response, had only 10 per cent of their work checked, and signed their own names to the letters. In addition, the clerks were monitored for the first time by means of a Customer Service Index which measured the speed and accuracy of their responses.

These measures allegedly ensured that workers would be more satisfied with their jobs, and that the consequent boost in motivation would translate into outcomes favourable to the company. But in this case (and most others at AT&T) higher output and reduced labour costs had less to do with enhanced worker motivation than with the fact that the enrichment measures rationalized the work process.[11] The duties of clerks originally were defined so narrowly that a large and expensive cast of verifiers and supervisors was needed to get out the work. By consolidating verification, minor supervisory duties, and clerical tasks fewer employees were required to handle a given volume of work. Consequently, the number of first- and second-line supervisors was reduced and verifiers were eliminated for an annual saving in salaries at this site alone of $76 000 (Ford 1969).[12] As the AT&T redesign expert remarked: 'When you load people with responsibility ... you find you don't need so many checkers, verifiers, work assigners, and "pushers" of various kinds' (Ford, 1969: 66).

In effect, 'enriched' workers were subjected to a speed-up. The heavier work loads were assumed by the clerks, I submit, not because of improved intrinsic motivation but because of the application of more systematic management control devices. The Customer Service Index allowed management to keep an output record on each worker. The use of the CSI was made possible by applying a key element of job enrichment—the job 'module' or the 'natural unit of work.' In the case of complaints clerks, drafting, verifying, and signing letters constituted a 'natural unit of work.' (In other sections of the company modules were created by replacing random work assignment with a system where each clerk was responsible for work emanating from a specific geographic region or company department.) According to the company's design consultant, modular work triggers the 'motivators' of responsibility, achievement, and recognition. Work modules also purportedly promote psychologically gratifying 'feedback' (enabling workers to evaluate their own performance) and facilitate workers' identification with or 'ownership' of the product (Ford, 1969; Hackman, 1977; Walters, 1975). There may be some truth to these claims, but heightened management control offers a more parsimonious interpretation of improved worker performance. By requiring clerks to sign their names to letters they had composed, management was able to scrutinize and hence control individual work performance. As an AT&T manager said:

> Before we did not really know who was competent because verifiers or supervisors checked everything, making sure no one failed and seeing to it that errors were low. Now I know whom to drop. If they cannot do the job, if they cannot take the responsibility for producing a good letter of reply, then we cannot carry them (Ford, 1969: 35).

There is nothing unusual about AT&T's redesign program. The American management consulting firm of Roy W. Walters and Associates has 'enriched' jobs in several hundred enterprises (Heckscher, 1980). This firm's implementing mechanisms and outcomes parallel those observed at AT&T (cf. Dettelback and Kraft, 1971).[13] However, orthodox job enrichment is not the only approach to restructuring office work. For example, in the mid-1970s Air Canada instituted a Work Improvement Program at its Winnipeg and Toronto branches. In a section of the Winnipeg office which handled customer refunds, each clerk originally performed a one-minute task in the claims process. In contrast to the principles of orthodox job enrichment, which modifies *individual* jobs, the claims are now processed by teams of clerks. Each team is required to process all phases of claims coming from a particular geographic region of the country (work modularization). The new system reduced the number of supervisors. Moreover, both in Winnipeg and Toronto (passenger agents) an integral element of the Work Improvement Program, which management billed as an expression of company concern for employees, was the introduction of computers. Computerization led to the automatic monitoring of workers' performance and to deeper labour elimination (Parker, 1984b; Wright and Lareau, 1984).[14] . . .

IMPACT OF REDESIGN ON WORKERS

o

Work redesign programs provide workers with greater task variation and discretion than conventional modes of organizing the labour process. It is mainly these changes that management invokes to support the claim that restructured jobs benefit employees. Two questions should be addressed to this claim: Are job content and workplace authority relations altered significantly by redesign programs? Are workers' interests in any way threatened by job redesign?

Many redesign programs construct jobs which still entail the repetitive performance of a quite limited number of standardized tasks. Consider the kinds of task addition that pass for job *enrichment*: signing your name to a letter you have composed in your own words; checking your own work; sweeping your work area; getting your own paper for typing; cleaning your machine. These cases illustrate the fact that most redesign initiatives add repetitive tasks to an absurdly fragmented job or allow workers to take turns doing repetitive jobs, the result of which is best described by the term 'routine variety' (Tausky and Parke, 1976). Even if we grant that forms of job redesign reduce repetitiveness and alleviate boredom, task variability is not the *sine qua non* of challenging non-alienated work. The critical determinant of an intrinsically gratifying job is the control over work exercised by individuals and groups of workers (Edwards and Scullion, 1982; Rinehart, 1975). The effectiveness of redesign programs on this score cannot be evaluated, then, by counting the number of tasks added to a job or timing the length of the task cycle. It is necessary to ask, what is the scope of activities and issues about which employees in redesigned jobs make decisions, and how great is workers' influence?

While the parameters of discretion vary across redesign programs, management draws carefully defined limits on the scope of workers' power in all of them. The focal points of decisions are workers' immediate jobs, work areas, and co-workers. Widening employees' influence beyond these spheres, especially in North America, is rarely suggested by even the most progressive exponents of job redesign. Just as the scope of employees' decision making is circumscribed, so too is their degree of influence. Employees' decisions are accepted by management only to the extent that they facilitate the achievement of company objectives. Redesign programs give workers more discretion in how they pursue the ends of employers, but they do not extend workers' influence on management and management policy. Moreover, with redesign projects control over work is not a zero-sum game. Job enrichment permits workers to exercise more control over the details of their tasks, but modularization simultaneously enables management to more effectively monitor and control overall work performance. Similarly, restructured assembly operations provide relief from the inexorable movement of the line and allow workers some discretion over work methods, assignments, and pace. However, management still monitors work performance and dictates output quotas established by time and motion study (Coriat, 1980; Delamotte, 1979; Wood and Kelly, 1982). This observation applies even to Volvo's Kalmar plant, which has restructured work more drastically than most mass manufacturing facilities. Here the assembly line has been replaced by moving platforms that transport cars from one work station to another, where work teams assemble sub-sections of the vehicle. Ideally, the teams can decide how fast to work, since each platform is equipped with a button that accelerates or retards the platform's movement. In the mid-1970s the company expected 12.6 cars per hour to be produced. This meant that the platform stopped at a work station for three or four minutes and then moved on, governed by a management-instructed computer (Rinehart, 1978). The chassis of each car to be assembled received a number which was kept throughout the entire assembly process, and the progress of each car was monitored by the computer from start to finish (Dundelach and Mortensen, 1979).[15] The output quota, established by time and motion study, was set at 11 per cent over the output level at which a worker normally becomes 'healthily tired' (Kelly, 1978). This pace virtually precluded workers from speeding up—the reward for which was a maximum of two extra ten-minute breaks. If workers slowed down and failed to meet production standards they were subject to disciplinary action.

Of all the types of work redesign, autonomous groups have the greatest potential for expanding workers' control and for threatening traditional structures of workplace power. Work teams are responsible for assigning, pacing, and scheduling work. In some cases the teams have taken on responsibilities for recruitment and internal discipline. Foremen are replaced by team leaders or coordinators whose function is to facilitate rather than police work. Operators are given economic and technical information rarely available to subordinate workers. As Heckscher (1980: 94) says, because they are based on flexible work roles and the informal regulation of interdependence, autonomous groups 'involve extensive and fundamental challenges to bureaucratic organization.' However, capital's domination of the labour process should alert us to the constraints placed on the potentially liberating force of this redesign approach. . . .

By extolling the psychological gratifications (individual job satisfaction) of their reformist efforts, consultants and managers obscure the impact of job redesign on workers' material and collective interests. Over many years workers have struggled against speed-up and for reduced working hours, better wages, and greater job security. Job redesign programs pose a threat to these interests. Flow-line reorganization is a form of methods improvement used to reduce the time required to produce an article. Hence, work intensification is regularly associated with this type of redesign. The expansion of assemblers' jobs also has led to the elimination of jobs of indirect workers. Where production is permeated with uncertainties, job consolidation and the creation of teams intensifies labour by reducing the size of the plant workforce and balancing individual work loads. By combining office jobs, job enrichment speeds up the clerical labour process and enables management to release more expensive workers. Labour elimination is not simply an occasional outcome of redesign programs. After examining the literature on European and North American redesign programs of all varieties, Kelly (1982) isolated 178 cases where information on this condition was available. Of these cases 121 (68 per cent) involved labour elimination. Data on the extent of job loss was available for 60 cases. Of 2 317 jobs redesigned, 572 (about one out of four) jobs were made redundant. Finally, the heavier work loads established by redesign programs frequently are not compensated by increased earnings, particularly but not exclusively in the non-unionized service sector.

Because redesign programs achieve their ends by rationalizing work, they generally have fewer implications for workers' formal and informal organizations than participatory schemes, which are directed at encouraging identification with management and corporate goals. This is not to say that negative outcomes of redesign in this sphere are entirely absent or inconsequential. The expansion and rotation of jobs can abrogate union rules and customary worker practices regarding job classifications, work assignments, and seniority provisions on promotions, job bidding, and transfers (cf. Halpern, 1984). Traditional areas of union control were waived at the Shell Sarnia plant where a contract was struck which covered 'very little of importance' (Ondrack and Evans, 1980: 263). While it is true that this contract contains no management's rights clause, neither does it specify union limitations on management's customary, de-facto prerogatives. If work redesign weakens or eliminates traditional union controls over key spheres of shop floor activity, the union may come to be viewed by members as ineffectual or irrelevant.

Divisions between workers have appeared when only one segment of a workforce is given the preferential treatment usually associated with involvement in a redesign 'experiment' (Goodman, 1979; Wells, 1983). Management-constructed work teams may strengthen intra-group cohesion and foster inter-group competition at the expense of overall worker solidarity (Boisvert, 1984; Gryzb, 1981; Rinehart, 1984; Wells, 1983; Walton, 1977). When work teams assume duties normally handled by foremen, such as discipline, divisive antagonisms and formal grievances may arise from the pressures applied by workers to their team mates. In this situation unions sometimes must ignore the principle of solidarity and contest decisions made by their own members (Brossard, 1981). Where these effects occur, the capacity of workers and unions to engage in effective collective action—the historical basis of improvements in the quality of work life—is undermined.[16]

C O N C L U S I O N

o

Job redesign is heralded as a means of improving the quality of working life and corporate performance. Redesign programs do represent a retreat from the strict tenets of Taylorism and Fordism. These revisions of the labour process, however, are not introduced primarily to pacify workers but to meet corporate exigencies arising from technological and economic conditions which make maximum job simplification unprofitable. When job redesign programs do contribute to the realization of corporate goals, they do so not mainly through the motivating effects of complex jobs and greater worker discretion but through the introduction of rationalized work arrangements.

The enlargement of jobs under special organizational circumstances can improve ineffective work designs, strengthen managerial control systems, eliminate or reduce the need for labour, and intensify the work process. Because their techniques are used to fine-tune the division of labour to operating exigencies, job redesign consultants can be characterized as modern efficiency experts.

Job redesign benefits accruing to employees are restricted largely to the sphere of job satisfaction. This may be appreciated by employees, but gains in this area are restricted because work reforms introduced by employers and their agents are defined, limited, and evaluated by the criteria of profitability and the reproduction of the social relations of production. Moreover, improvements in job satisfaction must be weighed alongside effects of redesign which endanger worker interests. These effects include uncompensated work intensification, labour elimination, and the weakening of organizations to protect workers from management and to enable them to improve the quality of working life.

NOTES

o

1. Where unions are involved in QWL programs they allegedly can expect to deal with a more understanding management, time spent on grievances declines, and contract negotiations are conducted openly and rationally.

2. This model also is employed by QWL critics. For example, neo-Marxists such as Bosquet (1972), Edwards (1979), and Friedman (1977) maintain that workers' resistance is the source and worker integration the goal of all varieties of QWL.

3. With the onset of the current economic crisis companies also began to promise that QWL programs, especially forms of participative management, would promote job security by making companies more competitive (Rinehart, 1984; Wells, 1983).

4. The distinction between participation and job redesign being advanced here may be clarified by Gordon's (1976) differentiation of qualitative and quantitative efficiency. The former refers to management techniques adopted to maximize employers'/managers' capacity to dominate the labour process and minimize workers' opposition to such domination. The latter embraces techniques geared to yielding the greatest physical output from a given set of physical inputs, or yielding a given output from the fewest possible inputs. Using this terminology participatory schemes can be characterized as a qualitatively efficient technique and job redesign as a quantitatively efficient technique.

5. Autonomous group initiatives have been informed and stimulated by sociotechnical systems theory (see Trist, 1981).

6. These determinist statements obscure the fact that autonomous groups are established in automated facilities not because of technical imperatives but because management has decided that such patterns of work are more profitable than less flexible procedures.

7. At the Esso refinery in Fawley, England twenty-five tasks were added to process operators' jobs, including cleaning the plant's toilets (Flanders, 1964).

8. For excellent accounts of how autonomous group structures facilitate work intensification see Cotgrove et al. (1971) and Kelly (1982).

9. Similarly, the celebrated Topeka, Kansas General Foods plant, originally scheduled to start with 110 production workers, actually opened with only 70. The staffing difference was attributed to the QWL designers' reduced reliance on inspectors, custodians, and repairmen. Their tasks were added to the 'enriched' process operators (Walton, 1972).

10. Job enrichment projects at AT&T are estimated to have reached between 10 000 and 100 000 jobs by the mid-1970s (Wrenn, 1982). Despite this humanizing crusade, telephone operators at many locations still must ask permission to go to the bathroom. The Communication Workers of America complained throughout the 1970s about equipment and supervisory actions 'that turned people into robots and measured their work in classically Tayloristic ways' (Simmons and Mares, 1983; 245; Kuyek, 1979).

11. This conclusion is supported by the negative results of attitude tests administered to 'enriched' clerks and control groups before and after jobs were changed. Absenteeism remained constant in the 'enriched' and control groups, while turnover was unchanged in the latter and 'greatly reduced' for those in redesigned jobs. However, supporting data were not provided (Ford, 1969).

12. In AT&T's Treasury Department a combination of job enrichment and mechanization eliminated both supervisory and non-supervisory jobs for an annual saving in salaries of $275,000. Cutbacks also were reported at many other departments where jobs were restructured. At two comptroller offices work redesign did not cause job loss because the volume of work increased. This increase 'offset the fact that fewer people were needed for existing work' (Ford, 1969: 66).

13. Despite outcomes favourable to the company, job enrichment is not an infallible management tool. There is an estimated 50 per cent failure rate for such projects. The apparent reason—the resistance of supervisors whose jobs may be at stake—is understandable (Heckscher, 1980).

14. Because it is a more certain means of cheapening office labour power, monitoring worker performance, and boosting output, the proliferation of micro-technology does not bode well for the future of job enrichment.

15. This is the equivalent of job enrichment's modular principle. Restructured assembly operations in Europe and North America are accompanied by devices which enable management to trace defects to their source. Management control of work performance on standard assembly lines is much less effective (Coriat, 1980; International Labour Organization (vols. I and II), 1979; Rush, 1971).

16. Acutely aware of these consequences, European trade unions have formulated guidelines for dealing with redesign projects. The unions favour reversals of Taylorism and Fordism, but reforms are acceptable only if management provides guarantees that work loads will not increase, jobs will not be lost, job classifications will be maintained or upgraded, trade union power will remain secure. In other words, only when job redesign projects humanize rather than rationalize work can companies anticipate union support (International Labour

Organization (vol. 1), 1979). To the extent that unions insist on these safeguards, management's enthusiasm for job redesign is likely to wane.

REFERENCES

o

Blauner, Robert
1967 Alienation and Freedom. Chicago: University of Chicago Press
Bosquet, Michael
1972 'The Prison Factory.' New Left Review (May-June): 23–34
Bright, James
1958 Automation and Management. Cambridge: Harvard University Press
Brossard, Michel
1981 'North American Unions and Semi-Autonomous Production Groups.'
Quality of Working Life: The Canadian Scene 4(1): 1–5
Cooper, Robert
1972 'Man, Task and Technology: Three Variables in Search of a Future.' Human
Relations 25(2):131–57
Coriat, Benjamin
1980 'The Restructuring of the Assembly Line: A New Economy of Time and
Control.' Capital and Class 11 (Summer): 34–43
Cotgrove, Stephen, Jack Dunham, and Clive Vamplew
1971 The Nylon Spinners: A Case Study in Productivity Bargaining and Job
Enlargement. London: George Allen and Unwin
Davis, Louis
1972 'The Coming Crisis for Production Management: Technology and Organization.' Pp. 417–47 in L. Davis and J. Taylor (eds.), Design of Jobs. Harmondsworth: Penguin
Davis, Louis and Charles Sullivan
1980 'A Labour-Management Contract and the Quality of Working Life.' Journal
of Occupational Behaviour 1: 29–41
Delamotte, Yves
1979 'France.' Pp. 47–75 in New Forms of Work Organization (vol. I). Geneva:
International Labour Organization
Dettelback, William and Philip Kraft
1971 Organization Change Through Job Enrichment.' Training and Development Journal 25 (8): 2–6
Dundelach, Peter and Nils Mortensen
1979 'Denmark, Norway and Sweden.' Pp. 9–43 in New Forms of Work Organization (vol I). Geneva: International Labour Organization
Edwards, Richard
1979 Contested Terrain: The Transformation of the Workplace in the Twentieth
Century. New York: Basic Books
Edwards, P. K. and Hugh Scullion
1982 The Social Organization of Industrial Conflict: Control and Resistance in
the Workplace. Oxford: Basil Blackwell

Emery, Fred and Einar Thorsrud
    1976 Democracy at Work: The Report of the Norwegian Industrial Democracy
    Program. Leiden: Martinus Nijhoff
Fantoli, Alessandro
    1979 'Italy.' Pp. 65–76 in New Forms of Work Organization (vol. II). Geneva:
    International Labour Organization
Flanders, Allen
    1964 The Fawley Productivity Agreements. London: Faber and Faber
Ford, Robert
    1969 Motivation Through the Work Itself. New York: American Management
    Association
Friedman, Andrew
    1977 Industry and Labour: Class Struggle at Work and Monopoly Capitalism.
    London: Macmillan
Gallie, Duncan
    1978 In Search of the New Working Class: Automation and Social Integration
    Within the Capitalist Enterprise. Cambridge: Cambridge University Press
Goodman, Paul
    1979 Assessing Organizational Change: The Rushton Quality of Work Experi-
    ment. New York: Wiley
Gordon, David
    1976 'Capitalist Efficiency and Socialist Efficiency.' Monthly Review 28 (July-
    August): 19–39
Hackman, Richard J.
    1977 'Work Redesign.' Pp. 96–162 in J. R. Hackman and J. L. Suttle (eds.),
    Improving Life at Work. Santa Monica: Goodyear
Hackman, J. R. and E. E. Lawler
    1971 'Employee Reactions to Job Characteristics.' Journal of Applied Psychology
    55: 265–86
Halpern, Norman
    1984 'Sociotechnical Systems Design: The Shell Sarnia Experience.' Pp. 31–69 in
    J.B. Cunningham and T. H. White (eds.), Quality of Working Life: Contemporary
    Cases. Ottawa: Labour Canada
Heckscher, Charles
    1980 'Worker Participation and Management Control.' Journal of Social Recon-
    struction 1(1): 77–101
Herzberg, Frederick
    1968 'One More Time: How Do You Motivate Employees?' Harvard Business
    Review (September-October): 53–62
Hill, Stephen
    1981 Competition and Control at Work. London: Heinemann
Kelly, John
    1978 'A Reappraisal of Sociotechnical Systems Theory.' Human Relations 31(12):
    1069–99
    1982 Scientific Management, Job Redesign and Work Performance. New York:
    Academic Press
Kuyek, Joan Newman
    1979 'The Phone Book: Working at the Bell.' Kitchener: Between the Lines

Mallet, Serge
1969 La Nouvelle Class Ouvriere. Paris: Editions du Seul
Mann, Floyd and L. Hoffman
1960 Automation and the Worker. New York: Henry Holt
Naville, Pierre
1963 Vers L'Automatisme Social? Paris: Gallimard
Nightingale, Donald
1982 Workplace Democracy: An Inquiry into Employee Participation in Canadian Work Organizations. Toronto: University of Toronto Press
Ondrack, D. and M. Evans
1980 'The Shell Chemical Plant at Sarnia (Canada): An Example of Union-Management Collaboration.' Pp. 257–72 in H.C. Jain (ed.), Worker Participation: Success and Problems. New York: Praeger
Parker, Mike
1984 'Canadian Airline Union Resists QWL Scheme.' Labor Notes (April 26)
Perrow, Charles
1970 Organizational Analysis: A Sociological View. London: Tavistock
Rinehart, James
1975 The Tyranny of Work. Toronto: Academic Press
1978 'Job Enrichment and the Labour Process.' Paper presented to Conference
on New Directions in the Labor Process, State University of New York, Bingham-
ton
1984 'Appropriating Workers' Knowledge: Quality Control Circles at a General
Motors Plant.' Studies in Political Economy: A Socialist Review 14 (Summer): 75–
97
Rush, Harold
1971 Job Design for Motivation. New York. The Conference Board
Simmons, John and William Mares
1983 Working Together. New York: Alfred A. Knopf
Susman, Gerald
1972a 'The Impact of Automation on Work Group Autonomy and Task Specialization.' Pp. 357–73 in L. Davis and J. Taylor (eds.), Design of Jobs. Harmondsworth:
Penguin
1972b 'Process Design, Automation and Worker Alienation.' Industrial Relations
11: 34–45
Tausky, Curt and E. Lauck Parke
1976 'Job Enrichment, Need Theory and Reinforcement Theory.' Pp. 531–65 in
Robert Dubin (ed.), Handbook of Work, Organization, and Society. Chicago:
Rand McNally
Taylor, James
1971 'Some Effects of Technology on Organizational Change.' Human Relations
24(2): 105–23
Trist, Eric
1981 The Evolution of Socio-Technical Systems. Toronto: Ontario Quality of
Working Life Centre
Walters, Roy W.
1975 Job Enrichment for Results: Strategies for Successful Implementation.
Reading: Addison-Wesley

Walton, Richard
    1972 'How to Counter Alienation in the Plant.' Harvard Business Review
    (November-December): 70–81
    1977 'Work Innovations at Topeka: After Six Years.' The Journal of Applied
    Behavioral Science 13(3): 422–33
Wells, Don
    1983 Unionists and Quality of Working Life Programmes. Toronto: Humber Col-
    lege Centre for Labour Studies
Wood, Stephen and John Kelly
    1982 'Taylorism, Responsible Autonomy and Management.' Pp. 74–89 in
    Stephen Wood (ed.), The Degradation of Work: Skill, Deskilling and the Labour
    Process. London: Hutchinson
Woodward, Joan
    1965 Industrial Organization: Theory and Practice. London: Oxford University
    Press
Wrenn, Robert
    1982 'Management and Work Humanization.' The Insurgent Sociologist 11(3):
    23–38
Wright, Susan and Serge Lareau
    1984 'An Analysis of a Work Improvement Program at Air Canada.' Pp. 145–71
    in J. B. Cunningham and T. H. White (eds.), Quality of Working Life: Contempo-
    rary Cases. Ottawa: Labour Canada

Technological Change and Shifting Labour Requirements[*]

David Robertson and Jeff Wareham

Jennifer works on the line in an area adjacent to the robots. For her the relationship between technology and jobs is as clear cut as it is alarming. "It's scary watching the automation next to you," she confides. "You know you're next. They're going to get your job eventually."

At a different plant in a different city another Northern Telecom worker expresses a similar reaction. For Victor the issue is also one of growing job insecurity: "You go home on Friday and come in on Monday and all of a sudden there is this monster sitting there that's going to do everything that I have done, but not go for lunch or take a coffee break or anything else that I do."

For Jennifer and Victor the role of technology in changing labour requirements is obvious. At other times, however, the casual chain is tangled in other factors. But even in those situations when casual relationships are not clear, outcomes can still be described. At Northern Telecom labour requirements are changing. The *demand* for labour is changing, the *distribution* of labour is changing and the *composition* of the labour force is changing. Behind these developments are the converging elements of technological change: changing product designs, changes in machinery and equipment and altered procedures and processes.

What follows is a series of observations which explore the changing requirements for labour in Northern Telecom and the importance of procedural innovations and computer automation in driving those changes. The

[*] Abridged from David Robertson and Jeff Wareham, *Changing Technology and Work: Northern Telecom,* CAW Technology Project (North York and Willowdale, Ont.: CAW/TCA, 1989), chapter 1, "Technological Change and Shifting Labour Requirements." Reprinted by permission of the publisher and the authors.

transitions occur in a context shaped by corporate policy and this is the starting point for the following observations.

T H I N   I S   P R O F I T A B L E
o

Corporations are engaged in an aggressive effort to contain staff numbers, what some in management refer to as creating "thin organizations." And Northern is a charter member. At corporate H.Q. Northern's manufacturing strategy gets expressed as adding value without adding cost. In the offices and plants the diet plan gets interpreted to mean cut cost.

Throughout the Northern organization there is a preoccupation with the "head count", an overriding emphasis on cost improvements or "CIs". As one manager explains:

> ...We have goals and objectives for our people. We have product cost reductions. We have objectives set at corporate level. We have to look at employee levels everywhere. ...

In such a context job reduction, while predictable, is not always a direct effect or even a necessary outcome of technological change. It is often a product of managerial intent. Management's cost-cutting ideology has treated technology as a diuretic and has created a cycle of computer dependency. Without computer based automation the ranks could not be kept 'so thin'. In turn, 'reducing head count' is a powerful justification for adopting new technology. A Northern manager presents the corporate edition of the riddle about the chicken and the egg. In this case, which comes first, 'technology' or job loss?

> ...Very seldom are my projects related to head count... (Our automation efforts) never respond directly to a downsizing pressure. Now what probably does happen is that those who are left have a lot of work to do and suggestions are made, there will be identified improvements in how to make their jobs easier. So when business picks up again there may be a tendency to need less people because of the improvements in productivity. It's just the way the business works....

The corporate rationale for adopting advanced office, design and manufacturing technology is straightforward. In boardroom terms automation is the road to the twin destinations of increased productivity and reduced costs. Northern uses situations of technological change—new product designs, automated equipment and changes in work procedures—to reduce labour content and increase profits.

MORE WORK BUT FEWER JOBS
o

Management is quick to argue that everyone at Northern owes their job to new technology, a claim which does little to reassure anyone outside of management. Instead workers face it as a technology paradox—technology may save the operation but it might cost their jobs.

What can be seen at Northern is job decline. What can be hoped for, at best, is jobless growth—a trend where corporate growth is required just to hold the line on jobs rather than to make employment gains. A manager discusses the trend.

> ...The volume of work can go up dramatically. In the past if you would add x amount of product you would add x amount of people. Not anymore. It (technology) reduces the need for people. We won't be creating the jobs....

Labour is displaced wherever computer based automation replaces conventional processes. When new technology is introduced substantially fewer people are required to produce the same level of output. This is true whether the measure is telephones, design drawings or invoices and whether the application is in plants, administrative offices or technical departments. Northern's impressive productivity gains provide the evidence.

In the Plants

—At London, in 1981, 1725 hourly workers produced 1 million telephone units. In 1987 909 hourly workers produced 1.8 million units. Staff has been cut almost in half but output has almost doubled.

—At Kingston the old extruder lines had a throughput capacity of 3500-4000 feet per minute. The new extruders are capable of 6500-8000 feet per minute. On the old lines there was one operator for every line plus a helper for every two lines. Now there is one operator for every two lines and a robot that serves all the lines.

—At Belleville Sydney St. the introduction of new computer controlled, semi-automatic machines (Royonics) used in circuit pack assembly cut the labour time in half for certain printed circuit boards.

—At London the new automated plastic moulding presses require only one operator for every two machines. The old presses had one operator for every machine.

—At Brampton the FMS line currently produces, on average, 25 circuit packs per hour with approximately 24 people—roughly 1 pack per hour per person. It would take one circuit pack assembler 4 hours to build the same pack the old way.

In the Offices

Computer techniques and methodologies have made many clerical tasks easier to accomplish, quicker to finish and, as office workers are quick to admit, they have made workers demonstrably more productive:

> "The way we used to do it we virtually had to sit down, get a drawing, list all the components onto a sheet of paper, put the quantities down beside it, look each cost up in the cost book, write each cost down, extend it, build the missing cost, total it, add the labour manually in each item, add the labour to the material value and come up with a standard cost. That used to take me an hour to do one item. I can build a 'standard' now in less than a minute on a terminal and it's more accurate than I used to be."

> "Standard costs for products is sort of a spreadsheet function. Everything is fed into the system, you set it up, press the button and it runs the cost. You get the cost for a telephone set out in 15 minutes where it used to take 3 days hand writing it."

Staff members in particular office departments are down. The change is especially evident in certain job groups—data processing, expediters, secretaries—where the link with computer automation is particularly strong. But the impacts of new technology are felt more generally. It seems that in every Northern office there used to be less work and more people and now there is more work and less people.

> "In purchasing there were four girls and now there are only three. When they brought in the computerized system for the buyers one wasn't needed. Now there are even two less buyers."

> "At one point we probably had 10 or 12 people looking after $25 million. Now we have 3 people looking after $125 million.

In the Technical Departments

The technical departments conform to the pattern. Here Computer Assisted Design (CAD) is the major technological innovation. At Brampton, management points to average CAD productivity ratios of 3:1 over conventional methods. At London specific CAD applications such as repetitive tool design have resulted in productivity ratios as high as 7:1.

CAD has reduced labour in two significant ways; first, through productivity improvements—improved designs, decreased design time and reduced design costs, and second, in the elimination of many clerical activities associated with design—typing, copying, filing, information retrieval, even the mailing and transmittal of designs. CAD also leads to a reduction in design errors and the need for design changes. In other words, not only is it faster to process the changes, CAD actually decreases the need to do so. As one worker expressed it:

"It was much slower with the manual drawing to lay out components. We can do a job in 8 weeks that used to take us half a year before."

FROM DIRECT TO INDIRECT LABOUR: BROADENING THE IMPACTS

○

At Northern the driving factor in automation is cost. And cost, at least initially, is most visibly represented in direct labour. Today many of the jobs directly involved in production have been automated and direct labour is a shrinking factor of production. Nowhere is direct manufacturing labour more than 10% of factory costs and in most places it is actually lower. For instance, at Belleville Sydney St. 85% of component assembly is accomplished with automated processes and direct labour is now only about 6% of the cost of production. Ten years ago it accounted for around 16% of the cost.

From Northern's initial concern with direct labour there has been a progressive broadening of the reach of automation. Like a stone thrown into a pond the waves of technological change extend in ever greater circles affecting more and more workers.

As direct manufacturing labour was reduced, indirect manufacturing jobs emerged as targets—particularly jobs in inspection, testing and material handling. As indirect manufacturing jobs were reduced the indirect jobs in the non-manufacturing functions, what management refers to as non-value-added jobs, have become the focus. The company President explains the objective.

"To begin, direct labour is a decreasing share of our value-added product cost...The implication for Northern Telecom is clear. The relatively easy productivity and quality gains—the automation of simple, repetitive tasks—has become a given...To increase our value-added and profitability, we must extend such gains and develop new disciplines that encompass the total process of product design, manufacturing, material sourcing and scheduling and customer service."

Northern's strategy for dealing with indirect jobs is a mixed one. It involves computer automation and procedural innovation; it has meant pre-automation process changes and post-automation job changes. And it proceeds on three tracks:

1) reducing the activities associated with indirect labour,
2) transforming indirect labour into direct labour, and
3) applying computer automation to indirect functions.

1) Reduce Indirect Labour Activities

Just in Time (JIT) production has provided many of the procedural innovations for reducing indirect labour activity. Flow lines, inventory reduction and KANBAN techniques have combined to reduce the 'count-move-store-expedite' pursuits and the staff engaged in those functions. Flow lines have reduced the need for kitting and those whose jobs it was putting the kits together. Less buffer stock has reduced the need for people to transfer and count parts. Smaller lot sizes and relocating production operations closer together has meant less scrap and less need for people engaged in inspection and repair. And fewer parts to build and purchase means fewer parts to track and fewer workers to do the tracking.

2) Make Indirect Labour Direct

A second aspect of Northern's strategy involves converting indirect and support functions into direct value-added production. This is accomplished when direct labour—the operators or assemblers—are given more responsibilities through additional job duties or broader job classifications. It occurs, for instance, when machine operators perform minor maintenance and repair functions or when assemblers perform inspection function.

3) Apply Computer Automation

The third element involves the direct substitution of technology for workers. It can be illustrated through the introduction of computerized equipment in Inspection and Testing.

The production of Northern's products—digital switches, PBX's, telephones, circuit boards—is testing-intensive. In certain operations up to half the total time spent producing is taken up in testing. In order to cut production time management wants to reduce the overall number of tests performed and it wants to reduce the time required by individual tests. In both cases that has meant the application of more complex computerized testing equipment. As one tester explained, a new test set introduced at Brampton performs the testing functions of three formerly separate testing jobs, and it does so in less time:

> "We have these new single stage test sets that replace five of the previous sets. It can troubleshoot everything in five minutes whereas before it would take maybe two or three hours."

For testers the pressure to eliminate tests and cut testing time with new equipment has meant layoffs. Those who remain are worried about the future. A tester offers the following prediction:

> "We have maybe 600 testers right now. I wouldn't be surprised if three or four years down the road we have 50. They're trying to eliminate them all."

INTEGRATED SYSTEMS: ELIMINATING BOTH DIRECT AND INDIRECT JOBS

o

This point relates to the preceding one but instead of focusing on the job activities the perspective here shifts to the technology.

The development of computer automation, while not an even nor pre-determined process, typically progresses through three phases. Starting with stand alone automation (i.e. robot), it develops through islands of automation to computer integrated systems. Labour displacement is much greater, even though much less apparent, in computer automated systems than in those situations of discrete task substitution. In the development of automated systems—the combination of computers and telecommunications—the impact on jobs is multiplied. In the case of the Flexible Manufacturing System (FMDC) at Brampton, for instance, not only are some of the direct jobs displaced but the co-ordination and manufacturing support requirements are substantially reduced. The staff associated with transporting workpieces, preparing schedules, recording data, accounting for parts, tracking work orders and similar activities are no longer required in an automated system. As a result, whereas a robot or another piece of automated equipment reduces the need for manufacturing staff, the impact on jobs associated with the development of automated systems crosses over into administrative and design functions.

In general the need for manufacturing support people—production schedulers, expediters, QC, clerks, kitters, fork lift operators—is reduced through the automation of decisions concerning schedules, quality, movement of parts, and product output, but it is also reduced through the integration of processing functions. Similarly the need for design support people—drafting, analysis, reproduction, documentation—is reduced through the integration and automation of design functions.

The application of computer based technologies, the introduction of procedural innovations such as JIT and the development of integrative technologies and techniques (CIM), taken together, have reduced the need for both direct and indirect labour. In all cases it is the achievement of the new "more with less" manufacturing philosophy, the corporate variant of having your cake and eating it too—more output with fewer workers, more quality with fewer QC workers, more accounting with fewer people in accounting, more production control with fewer production controllers, more information with less data processing, and so on.

But changing the demand for labour is only one of a set of changing labour requirements at Northern. The others involve the composition of Northern's workforce, its distribution and the shifting lines of job responsibilities.

THE CHANGING COMPOSITION OF LABOUR

o

Northern is in a transitional period, one reflected in the shifts from hardware-based products to software-intensive systems, from manual operations to computer automation, and in the shift of emphasis from manufacturing to product design. These shifts have not only changed Northern's need for labour, they have altered its composition.

Northern management plots its future course as one of moving steadily up the technology ladder and it associates that climb with a different type of worker—the 'knowledge' worker. Northern's Vice President of Human Resources described the change for the corporation as a whole:

> "We have had a significant change over the last decade in the number of people who are what we call management knowledge workers. These are people who contribute to the corporation and add value to its operations by manipulating data, thinking and creating things. From something like 32% of our work force back in '77 they will comprise about 60% in 1987."

The shifting composition can be seen in a variety of developments:
- Certain functions such as design, marketing and customer service are assuming greater relative importance in Northern.
- There is a shift from workers engaged in production to those engaged in information-based activities.
- There is a shift from direct to indirect labour.
- There is a shift from bargaining unit to non-bargaining unit jobs.

The changing composition is true not only for the organization as a whole but within its various locations. An example from the London office underlines the point. In 1981 the non-managerial staff was composed of 51% clerical, 26% technical (ET) and 23% professional (non-bargaining unit). By 1987 the composition had changed to the point where only 40% of the total was clerical. The ET ranks increased to 32% and the professional ranks had expanded to 28%.

The changing composition can also be seen at the level of particular job functions. Computer automation is often an occasion for management to change the technical composition of the workforce. The introduction of Computer Aided Design (CAD) to Northern design departments is precisely such a situation. Currently CAD operators—in terms of experience, background and qualifications—are a mixed group. Some operators are relatively recent new hires out of community college while others are draftspersons or tool designers of long service who have successfully made the transition to the new technology. Whatever the current occupational structure, the trend is overwhelmingly away from clerically graded drafting jobs to college trained technicians. Throughout Northern drafting workers are being replaced with ET CAD operators. As one worker described it:

"There is drafting but not draftsmen." In fact CAD, perhaps more clearly than any other computer technology, has virtually eliminated an entire occupational group.

The displacement of drafting workers is a two stage process. First, the productivity increases associated with CAD and the ability of engineers and professional designers to do more complete designs themselves at CAD terminals reduces the need for bargaining unit workers. In some locations this means an actual decrease in the 'headcount' while at other locations it means 'future staff avoidance.' Second, it gets expressed as a shift in the occupational structure, and here Northern's preference for recently graduated technicians rather than internally retrained workers is apparent.

Although each Northern location is somewhat different, the pattern is a general one; there are fewer draftspersons, and computer drafting is becoming a technical job.

CHANGING DISTRIBUTION: FEWER JOBS — HIGHER GRADES

o

When computer automation is applied to specific production operations the result is not only fewer jobs but a different distribution of jobs. Some jobs are eliminated, other jobs appear for the first time and the remaining jobs are often different in terms of skill, grade and functions than those that were there before. In a manufacturing context the changing mix of labour can be observed by comparing those areas of a plant where manual operations and automated production co-exist and/or by comparing the composition of the workforce before and after automation. Examples of each from Northern's Brampton plant illustrate the changes in labour distribution prompted by computer automation.

Line Cards

Line cards are small circuit boards used in DMS (Digital Multiplexing Systems) central office switches to assign phone lines to subscribers, route calls and to provide some enhanced telephone features. The relevant operation for comparing the pre- and post-automation composition of the workforce is component insertion. In the production of line cards both automated and manual operations co-exist. The high volume card is run on the automated line, the low volume and more complicated cards are assembled on the manual slide line.

The distribution of the workforce is quite different on the two operations. The automated insertion line is a 10 station integrated line that includes nine robot insertion cells and a pre-wave inspection station. It is staffed by two grade 6 set-up/troubleshoot operators, one on each side of the line. In addition the area has two dedicated electronic technicians—a cross between electrician and machine repair—who look after the robots in the automated insertion and in the line card test room.

On the manual side of the operation assembly is conducted on a slide line staffed by eight grade 2 assemblers (June 1987) with one grade 6 lay out worker. Both the manual and the automated line has a pre-wave inspector, formerly a grade 5 repair operator but now a grade 2 inspector.

FMDC (Flexible Manufacturing Development Centre)

The introduction of computer automation in the FMDC area changed the mix of the workforce and increased the proportion of higher graded jobs associated with circuit pack assembly. In a traditional manual assembly department at Northern upwards of 80% of workers are typically in the grade 3 or 4 categories. In the FMDC over half the workers are grade 6 and 7 (over 90% are grade 5 and up). In addition there are two dedicated electronic technicians (so-called 'supertrades') assigned to the area and a number of excluded salaried workers (computer programmers) and engineers spend some or all of their time working in the department.

While the application of new technology in specific departments or particular operations might lead to higher graded jobs, that finding cannot be generalized to the operation as a whole. Instead computer automation can result in a polarized workforce with a gulf between the limited number of higher graded positions and the majority of lower graded positions. At Northern the evidence to date is not overwhelming either in one direction or the other. There are pockets of upgrading and downgrading but the general trend to date points to a larger proportion of the workforce in higher graded jobs.

BLURRING THE JOB LINES

○

In office automation formerly clear divisions between jobs get blurred and duties flow both horizontally and vertically over job boundaries. What were formerly different tasks—i.e. data entry, buying and expediting—are automated into the same job. Technology consolidates tasks and provides opportunities for redefining jobs and for changing relations.

At times this has resulted in lower graded workers in the offices taking on some of the functions previously associated with higher graded jobs. More often it has meant higher graded workers assuming the data entry and related tasks formerly done by lower graded workers. As one worker points out:

"In scheduling we used to have one individual who 90% of their work was keying the information we had collated on a daily basis. Today that person does zero. Less than three years ago we did no keying at all. Now we do it all."

Another worker expresses some of the consequences:

"Before data inputting was exclusive, now everybody does it. Everybody in the department can do my job. Before my job was an essential position. Nothing would move without my job. Not so now."

Blurring job lines extends beyond particular departments and beyond the traditional distinctions between administration and production, as can be seen in the growing overlap of previously distinct office and plant jobs. Plant workers on computer terminals are performing duties done exclusively by office workers in the past and office workers at terminals are doing work traditionally performed by plant workers. Since one of the explicit goals of management is to use the new information technologies to integrate different stages of production, situations of job overlaps and duplications will arise more often in the future.

EROSION OF THE BARGAINING UNIT

○

New information and computer technologies change jobs within the bargaining unit. They also provide opportunities to shift work outside the bargaining unit. As there is a discretionary aspect in the creation of jobs, so is there in their elimination. In various office locations workers point to managers who will surplus a bargaining unit employee and bring in a specialist, hire an engineer but not replace an ET (technician) or hire someone for a confidential position, declare a surplus and then not backfill the unionized jobs. Some workers see in this a conscious attempt to get rid of the union and most acknowledge that with computer automation the trend has accelerated.

Managerial or other excluded personnel are performing work that is the responsibility of bargaining unit members. In the clerical fields computers have made it easier to shift work and have made it harder for workers to respond:

"(In the past) no manager would sit behind a typewriter. Now we are all keyboarders. It's fashionable."

"Engineers coming out of school all type fast, so if the secretary is busy they'll just sit down and type up their own memo. And chances are the secretary will be busy because they've been cut so much."

"This morning my manager sat at the terminal and sent out a four page memo on COCUS (Electronic mail). If he didn't do that somebody else would have been."

"Managers don't manage anymore. Instead they try to do everybody's work. We would be a lot better off if they just managed."

The threat to bargaining unit work is also evident within the technical ranks, most prevalently with the transfer of numbers. Between 1980 and 1985 in Brampton only 20 ETs were hired by Northern. In the two years 1986-7 125 engineers were hired.

While the numbers indicate a shift in the balance of ETs to engineers, the actual transfer of duties is often more direct; shifting current ET work to engineers and giving new work—jobs and tasks that previously were considered ET functions—to engineers. One technician describes the process as follows:

"First the engineer is brought in to help the ET. Then part of the job is given to the engineer. Then the engineer is given the job and the ET is moved out."

THE FUTURE — MORE OF THE SAME

o

The company expects—*if* it achieves its projected 15% annual sales growth—its total population to be roughly constant through 1992. In other words the company anticipates doubling its sales over the five years 1988-1992 without increasing its workforce. In addition to this pattern of jobless growth there will be more internal shifts. According to senior managers, hourly ranks are expected to decrease slightly and salaried ranks will increase slightly. Within the latter category the company anticipates a slight decrease in managers, a decrease in the clerical and ET ranks and a growth of the professional ranks. Behind these slight shifts in composition are dramatic changes for individual and particular groups of workers.

A Vice President of the company reveals the trauma in store for workers as the company uses technological change to increase sales and productivity and to transform the composition of its workforce:

"I find myself grappling with layoffs involving 20-year employees, and as we break it to the individuals, and as they are going out the door, I almost find myself saying 'by the way, you have a son at Waterloo in computer engineering, can you send me his resume, because I'm short of those kind of people'."

Given these attitudes it is hardly surprising when people report that technological change has increased their sense of vulnerability. "My job", reports one worker, "has never been more insecure." And the threat holds little regard for what workers view as their most important protection—seniority:

"What's the future? Scary. I don't think I'll have a job. I've got 15 years seniority and I'll never retire from Northern Telecom, guaranteed."

Peripheralizing Core Labour Markets?: The Case of the Canadian Meat Packing Industry[*]

Joel Novek

Recent debates have focussed on the future of the leading mass production industries in the advanced nations (Thompson 1987; Zysman and Cohen 1987). These industries, which include autos, steel and food processing, are major employers of highly paid workers in core labour markets sheltered by high wages, rule-governed job classification systems and unionization (Beck 1978: 707) from the vagaries of lower wages and poorer working conditions in highly competitive or peripheral labour markets. It has been contended that stagnant demand for mass produced items, increasingly unstable product markets and technological transformations are placing the leading mass production industries at risk (Piore and Sabel 1984: 183–191). The strongest claim has been that the mass production or 'Fordist' paradigm itself is rigid and obsolete and on the verge of being replaced by more flexible forms of production (*Ibid*: 265) better able to adapt changing technology to the new highly competitive economic environment.

Any threat to the dominant mass production industries will have important implications for the distribution of inequality in advanced societies. By linking mass production to mass consumption through high wages, these industries have helped maintain the 'virtuous circle' (Mahon 1987: 23) of economic growth in the postwar period by transferring economic resources to a considerable section of the working class. With the mass production industries at risk, the 'mode of regulation' linking production to consumption is also at risk. A number of authors foresee greater class polarization as core labour markets shrink while competitive labour markets expand. Gordon, Edwards and Reich (1982) anticipate the survival of

[*] Abridged from Joel Novek, "Peripheralizing Core Labour Markets?: The Case of the Canadian Meat Packing Industry," *Work, Employment and Society* 3, no. 2 (June 1989): 157–78. Reprinted by permission of the publisher and the author.

the dominant mass production industries but at the cost of a major assault on the wages and working conditions of their workers; in effect, an erosion of the postwar labour-management consensus (Gordon, Edwards and Reich 1982: 243). Similarly, Burawoy (1985: 150) and Littler and Salaman (1984: 34) expect intensified managerial efforts to restore profitability by subordinating labour while Shostak (1987: 7–18) argues that workers will experience these efforts in the form of reduced wages and job security and a more hazardous working environment.

This paper will examine the Canadian meat packing industry as a case study of a leading mass production industry and a core labour market under the stress of recessionary restructuring. The meat packing industry has been selected for its importance within the Canadian context and for the fact that it was one of the earliest in North America to be organized along mass production lines. Much of Canadian industrialization has been based on the secondary transformation of domestically produced raw materials, notably agricultural, mineral and forestry products. Meat packing clearly falls into this category and is the third largest Canadian manufacturing industry in revenues and the sixth largest in employment. Until recently, relative wage levels in meat packing were significantly above the Canadian average for production workers. However, in recent years employment and relative wages in the industry have fallen bringing the long term future of the industry and its workers into question....

H I S T O R I C A L   B A C K G R O U N D

o

Meat packing in North America has been organized along mass production lines since the development of the hog slaughter industry in Cincinnati, Ohio, in the mid nineteenth century (Giedion 1948: 90). The essentials of mass production—specialized machinery, an extensive division of labour, the use of semiskilled workers and the production of a relatively homogeneous commodity for a mass market—were in place in the packinghouses of Cincinnati and later Chicago at about the same time that similar principles developed in the textile industries of New England. Indeed, it has been contended that the design of continuous flow 'disassembly lines' (Edwards 1979: 117) in the packinghouse industry was an important precursor to later developments in the fledgling auto industry. . . .

By mid century the industry had become highly concentrated. Three leading national 'full line' packers, Canada Packers, Burns Meats and Swift Canadian—a subsidiary of Chicago-based Swift & Co.—had managed through internal growth and acquisitions to dominate the Canadian market for red meat (Restrictive Trade Practices Commission 1961: Ch. 4). It is estimated that the top three were responsible for slaughtering 63% of the cattle and 61% of the hogs in Canada during the 1950s with Canada Packers enjoying the lion's share at about 35% and 29%, respectively (*Ibid*: 115).

Between them, they operated 27 packing plants in major metropolitan areas. Their large, vertically integrated plants gave them economies of scale in the production of fresh and processed meats. By locating plants and cold storage warehouses in big cities to supply wholesale and retail markets, they were able to control the distribution of their product (Kujovich 1970). In sum, meat packing, similar to autos or steel, had become a concentrated and vertically integrated industry.

Meat packing was also known as an industry which paid its employees high wages. Between 1939–49, hourly wage levels at Canada Packers' main plant in Toronto never varied by more than 2 cents from hourly wages at leading integrated steel producers nearby (United Packinghouse Workers of America 1958: 33). The industry became firmly established as a core labour market, however, with the signing of master collective agreements between the United Packinghouse Workers of America, forerunner of today's United Food and Commercial Workers, and the three leading packers in 1946 (Robertson 1984: 20). The Packinghouse Workers were responsible for bringing C.I.O. style industrial unionism to the meat packing industry. . . .

As in other mass production industries, the postwar period was a time of prosperity and expansion. Economic concentration and labour market stability were supported by stable growth in consumer markets. Between 1960–80, red meat shipments increased from 2.5 to 4.2 billion lbs. (Canadian Meat Council 1987: 2) and in dollar value from $1.0 to $6.9 billion. Per capita consumption of red meat increased from 136 lbs. in 1960 to 179 lbs. in 1976 before dropping off to 167 lbs. in 1980 (Statistics Canada 1986). Employment of production workers rose from 20,000 to 26,600 in that period while total employment increased from 26,000 to 35,000 (Statistics Canada 1985). Meat packing rose to third place among Canadian manufacturing industries in the value of shipments and from twelfth to sixth place in employment. Growth was good for labour. During the 1970s, wage rates in meat packing were 110% of the manufacturing average (*Ibid*).

By the late 1970s and early 1980s, however, the situation worsened considerably. Between 1980–86, red meat shipments increased by only 5% and per capita consumption dropped to 157 lbs. (Statistics Canada 1986). After tax profit margins dropped to below 1% on sales (Statistics Canada 1984) and capacity utilization rates reached as low as 55% at some large plants during the early 1980s (Kerr and Ulmer 1984: 28). The industry has undergone significant consolidation and restructuring. Employment fell sharply. Between 1980–86, the number of production workers fell from 26,600 to 22,900 while total employment dropped from 35,000 to 31,000 (Canadian Meat Council 1987: 2). Employee compensation also suffered as collective agreements reached in 1984 froze wages for a two year period. Clearly meat packing is in trouble as both a leading mass production industry and a core labour market.

The most visible symbol of decline has been the closure of many of the giant multistory packinghouses which used to dominate the industry. Canada Packers has closed eleven such plants. The latest example is the shutdown of Canada Packers' Winnipeg operations with the loss of 900 jobs. Swift Canadian closed plants in Calgary and Winnipeg with the loss of 1,100 jobs and then sold its remaining operations to Alberta-based Gainers in 1981. Burns Meats has closed five plants nationwide. Some estimates place total plant closures at 30 nationwide since 1975 with 8,000 jobs lost (Robertson 1984: 21). Why is an industry which at one time appeared stable and secure in such obvious turmoil? A number of important trends involving organization, technology and markets have radically transformed the industry's operating environment. These changes, in turn, have had a destablizing impact on labour markets and working conditions. . . .

INTENSIFICATION OF PRODUCTION

o

A number of writers have interpreted the 1980s round of recessionary restructuring and concession bargaining in leading North American and European industries as part of a general managerial strategy to raise profit margins by tilting the balance between labour and capital in favour of the latter (Littler and Salaman 1984; Burawoy 1985; Gordon, Edwards and Reich 1982). Lower labour costs and greater managerial control of the shop floor would translate into increased surplus value and thus a way out of economic stagnation. This analysis runs the risk of generalizing across a wide variety of industrial sectors in vastly different economic circumstances facing distinct short term and long term problems. For Piore and Sabel, however, an assault on wages is a particular response of mass producers unable or unwilling to innovate: 'When product and production technology freeze . . . the firm is likely to respond to competition from other mass producers by pressing down wages' (Piore and Sabel 1984: 264). Furthermore, wage cuts are often linked to speedups on the factory floor: 'The speedup is to mass production what the cut in piece rates is to customized production' (Ibid).

The linkage between wage cuts and speedups is underscored when we consider that meatpackers have not only reacted to rigidities in labour costs by pressuring wage rates down; they have also reacted to rigidities on the packinghouse floor by intensifying the labour process and speeding up the pace of production: '(Meat) industry direction is toward higher speed kills and automation (sic) is being examined both for expected labor savings and for its potential to increase those speeds' (Supinsky 1985:20). What must be explained is the fact that the combination of lower wages and higher production speeds is not only being imposed at the older less efficient plants, as Piore and Sabel suggest, but also at some of the newest and potentially most efficient plants in the industry.

The core of the problem lies in the failure of the industry to move beyond simple mechanization to more sophisticated strategies based on automation (Zysman and Cohen 1987:164). Because no two animals are alike, much of the work is still butcher's work to be done by hand, even in the most modern plants.[1] About 50% or more of packing plant employees work with knives or with hand held power tools.[2] Unlike other industries such as oil refining or steel making where automation has drastically reduced the number of workers directly involved in processing, accurate dismemberment of carcasses and precise cuts of meat still require extensive manual labour by workers wielding knives and power tools. The labour-intensive nature of meat packing can be illustrated by the fact that both value-added per production worker and value-added per person hour are significantly below the manufacturing average[3] while wages, at least until recently, were higher. Packers have responded to this situation by simultaneously attempting to cut wages and to step up output.

The shop floor organization of labour also promoted rigidities. The division of labour is highly fragmented and a complex system of job classifications, work rules and labour grades has evolved through the process of collective bargaining. One mid-size packing plant with around 600 employees which is not untypical has 26 major job classifications, 406 subclassifications and 41 pay scale related labour grades in its collective agreement.[4] Other regulations govern work rules and hours of work.[5] These regulations represent an 'institution of the truce' (Rex 1961) between labour and management and cannot be altered without extensive negotiations. Since the major focus of often bitter labour-management negotiations has been wage levels and job security, speedy progress in this area is unlikely.[6]

A third factor affecting shop floor relations is the commodity nature of much of the meat packing industry with almost 75% of revenues coming from sales of unbranded fresh meat. The opportunities for firms to gain market share by differentiating their product from their competitors are restricted to the upper end of the market for processed meats. For most meatpackers success continues to mean, as it has meant in the past, the ability to produce large volumes of a standard commodity at the lowest possible cost. In sum, there is little alternative to high volume mass production.

As the labour process cannot be quickly transformed either by automation or by wholesale changes in the pattern of work rules and job classifications, the solution the industry has seized on is for workers to do the things they have always done on the packinghouse floor but to do them much faster. Workers are increasingly called upon to perform tasks which are machine paced, repetitive and technically controlled (Edwards 1979: 116–117). According to a former packinghouse employee: 'The rise in productivity has been made simply by increasing the speed the cattle go down the line and yelling at everyone to keep up' (Pettit 1987).

Mechanization has had a major impact on the labour process. Overall output per person hour has risen from 83.6 lbs. in 1980 to 102.8 lbs. in 1986 (United Food and Commercial Workers 1987: Table 5), double the rate of increase for the previous six year period. In the new mechanized single storey plants, carcasses are shackled and hung from high speed overhead rails which whisk them along the kill floor while butchers skin and dress them on the go. Conveyer belts carry shoulders, loins or bellies along rapid 'disassembly lines' where workers chop, carve and trim them into consumer ready cuts. Motorized 'jiggers' pull trains of one ton vats loaded with product from one work site to the next where they are mechanically unloaded to feed the waiting knives and machines. During an eight hour shift the continuous production does not stop except for a half hour lunch break and two ten minute coffee breaks.

At 'Plant C', a unit of 'Lowery Packers', there was a virtual doubling of the hog kill between 1984–7 in order to make up for capacity reductions due to the closing of three of the company's older plants.[7] In 1984 the plant was killing between 1200–1500 hogs per day. By 1987 the hog kill rate was up to 2700 per day and is projected to rise to 3300 which is the current maximum capacity of the kill floor. Behind the big jump in the hog kill was an increase in the speed of the overhead rail moving carcasses along the kill floor. The rail has a variable speed drive allowing managers to 'crank up' the pace.[8] Four years ago it ran at 240–300 hogs per hour depending on the size of the kill. In 1987 the rate was up to 400 and by the latter part of the year was running at 440 per hour.[9]

Current plans call for the rate to rise to 500. At 400 hogs per hour, workers on the line have a 'cycle time' (Smith 1987:53–4) of 9 seconds to make their cut and get ready for the next carcass. If the rate rises to 500, they will have only 7 seconds. Furthermore, the speedup on the kill floor has occurred without any increase in staff. The number of workers operating knives, saws or power tools on the kill floor has held steady at 75.[10] Since machines have not taken over their work, the inescapable conclusion is that they are working faster—much faster.

Not only is the work faster, it is also more repetitive and monotonous. Older plants varied between hog and cattle slaughter with the larger beef carcasses processed at a rate one-third to one-quarter the pace for hogs. Workers often divided their time between the kill floor and cutting and processing operations. Today, specialized plants are designed to simultaneously kill, cut, trim and package a single species throughout an entire shift. Workers, positioned only a few feet apart, thrust and wield their knives or sharp tools, making similar cuts over and over again at a pace set by the chain or conveyer. The cuts have been simplified in order to speed production and the chief skill appears to be the ability to keep up the pace. If a worker cannot keep up the others on the line must work harder in order to maintain the rate of output.

This is evident in the ham boning section of 'Plant C' where the work of removing skin, fat and bone from pork hind legs in preparation for curing has been fully reorganized into a high speed disassembly line. The reorganization started in the early 1980s. Prior to reorganization 16 relatively skilled butchers called 'ham boners' were responsible for trimming, dressing and boning entire hind legs into half their weight in processable meat.[11] They worked over a stationary table and threw the finished product into vats. They were largely self paced. The work required strength, skill and perseverance. A good ham boner could dress a ham every 4 minutes or at a rate of about 15 per hour.[12]

The stationary table was replaced by a conveyer belt fed by a hydraulic lift.[13] The work was simplified and broken down into a variety of detailed cuts performed by 15 workers on a continuously moving line. Power tools were introduced but they did not replace the manual use of knives; rather they stepped up the pace of the knifework. The line is fed by a powerlift operator who dumps vats of hind legs onto a stainless steel table. Two 'wizard' knife (knives with power-driven revolving blades) operators then remove the balance of the external fat. The hams travel down the conveyer where 10 knifemen either remove a specific bone or trim internal fat and gristle on the go.[14] The line ran at a speed of 280–300 hams per hour; today it runs at 360 hams per hour giving each knifeman a 'cycle time' of approximately 9–10 seconds to perform his task.

In 1986 a second conveyer was added. Two lines run during the day and one on the night shift. The pace is maintained by the skinning machine operators who place the hams with skins removed on the conveyer.[15] Workers holding razor-sharp knives are forced to match the pace of machine operators. If a worker cannot keep up the others down the line must work faster just to maintain the pace. Arguments occur among workers accusing one another of going too fast or too slow.[16] The sense of stress is heightened by congestion as workers are sandwiched between the moving table and large vats for waste and trim located two feet away. From management's perspective, however, the changes are viewed positively for workers put pressure on each other to keep up production speeds.[17]

The use of high speed machine pacing, repetition and technical controls to address productivity problems has seriously affected working conditions on the packinghouse floor. This contributes to a further erosion of meat packing's status as a core labour market. Perhaps the most dramatic evidence of this deterioration has been a rising injury rate for meat plant workers. Meat packing has always been hazardous owing to its reliance on manual knife work and the need to lift heavy loads. The Quebec Commission de la Santé et de la Securité du Travail (Commission 1985:158), for example, found that the injury rate among slaughterhouse workers was higher than for any other food and beverage industry. However, there are indications that in recent years a bad situation has been getting worse.

Information supplied by the Workers' Compensation Board of Ontario[18] shows that in Ontario which is responsible for 40% of total meat industry employment there has been a rising trend for injury claims in meat packing, especially since 1983. The rate for settled claims in meat packing has risen from 13.76 to 16.08 injuries per 100 employees between 1983–86 and has consistently been almost double the average for all manufacturing industries. The number of days lost due to accident or injury is up substantially since 1983. In that year there were 438.58 days lost per 100 employees in meat packing versus 210.65 in manufacturing but by 1986 the rate had risen to 643.29 in meat packing and 287.10 in manufacturing. The rate of days lost in meat packing has risen by 47% over a four year period.

At 'Plant C' the accident rate[19] has risen in tandem with the rise in output. The number of lost time accidents at the plant was 25.8 per 100 production workers in 1983 and 26.7 in 1984. In 1985 with the intensification of production well underway the rate rose dramatically to 39.4 per 100 production workers, almost 40% of the bargaining unit. The rate levelled off somewhat to 36.1 in 1986 but then rose again to 38.8 in 1987. Recent reports show more than 20 lost time accidents per month. Most injuries are either to the hands and wrists (35%) or to the upper body, especially the back and shoulders (25%). These injuries are usually indicative of repetitive trauma.

In addition to higher production speeds, other factors related to industrial restructuring also contribute to a high accident rate. The lower starting wage for new employees encourages meatpackers to turn over their labour force. As older workers quit, retire or are laid off due to plant closures, a new cohort of young and relatively unskilled workers has been hired at the lower rate. At 'Plant C', one third of the 650 production workers on the job in 1987 had been hired since late 1984. Since many companies have only the most limited training procedures, this new cohort may be subject to a high accident rate. Poor labour relations at many plants resulting from conflict over wage rates, job security and technological change hamper the effectiveness of joint union–management safety committees. All these factors can be indicative of falling labour market status.

CONCLUSIONS

o

Over the past decade the Canadian red meat packing industry has undergone significant restructuring. Capacity has been reduced due to a large number of plant closings usually involving multistorey vertically integrated facilities built before World War 2. The industry has become more specialized and deconcentrated while the market for meat products has become more competitive and unstable. The largest integrated producers have lost market share to a growing number of specialized slaughterers, fabricators or processors who can produce a product more cheaply or of higher quality than the full line packers. These findings provide partial confirmation of the Piore and Sabel hypothesis that in situations of high competition and unstable markets integrated mass production is giving way to more specialized forms of industrial organization.

The trend toward specialization in meat packing does not, however, point to the end of the mass production paradigm (Williams 1987:435) in favour of 'flexible specialization'. Specialization in meat packing has meant the intensification of mass production principles, not their abandonment. The new specialized slaughter or processing plants are based on economies of scale that go beyond the capabilities of the older integrated plants. The commodity nature of the business means that successful firms will have the lowest unit costs. The fragmented division of labour and de-emphasis on workers' skills also remain intact. Since meat packing is at bottom stubbornly labour-intensive, packers have responded to shop floor rigidities by intensifying the labour process through mechanization rather than by transforming it through automation. Indeed, the construction of specialized beef, pork or processing plants and the continued deskilling of the labour force indicate a trend toward inflexible rather than flexible specialization.

Alongside efforts to step up the pace of output, packers have attempted to cheapen the cost of labour in order to counteract stagnant demand and production inefficiencies. With the master agreements no longer in force competitive pressures, including the threat and the reality of plant closures, have caused relative wages to fall. At the same time, independent packers have established themselves in the rural, non-union labour market periphery placing additional pressure on wage rates in the red meat industry. A tougher environment in the packinghouse industry has been transferred to the labour force in the form of reduced relative wages and job security and, in some cases, deteriorating shop floor conditions and higher injury rates. Clearly, the status of the red meat industry as a core labour market has been significantly diminished.

Whether this experience is generalizable to other industries remains to be seen. Global theories of capitalist restructuring featuring pervasive managerial attacks on the status of labour, for example, cannot fully explain a situation where meat packing wages have fallen relative to other mass production industries, notably autos and steel. The possibility raised here is of further fracturing of core labour markets as some industries recover strongly from the recession of the early 1980s with employment and wage levels on the rise while others remain mired in stagnation and decline. In the Canadian context, the prosperous automobile industry exemplifies the former condition while meat packing represents the latter. This divergence in the fortunes of some leading industries and their employees suggests that rigid dualisms such as core and peripheral industries or primary and secondary labour markets ought to be modified to better reflect the dynamics of industrial rise and decline.

Finally, the problems faced by packinghouse workers raise questions about the role of unions in the process of industrial restructuring. The

United Food and Commercial Workers, similar to other industrial unions in the mass production sector, appeared better adapted to the concentrated and stable industry of the past than to current conditions. There was a symmetry between the master agreements on the one hand and a concentrated and vertically integrated industrial structure on the other. Indeed, the master agreements aided industrial stability by discouraging efforts by individual firms to lower wages to secure competitive advantage. Whether the union can adapt to today's more regionalized and competitive structure remains to be seen.

NOTES

o

1. At the new Springhill Farms hog slaughter plant, for example, an innovative 'hot skinning' process for dressing hog carcasses was introduced which dispensed with the traditional dipping and scalding. The quality and cost performance of the new system proved disappointing and the plant has reverted to older and more labour-intensive technology (Toronto Globe and Mail 1988: B11).

2. Interview with the Manager of Human Resources, 'Lowery Packers', 3 February 1988.

3. Value-added per production worker was $61,000 in meat packing versus $71,450 in manufacturing and value-added per person hour was $21.69 in meat packing versus $34.32 in manufacturing (Statistics Canada 1985).

4. Agreement between 'Lowery Packers' and United Food and Commercial Workers International Union (Agreement 1986).

5. One contentious rule in most collective agreements guarantees 37 hours of work per week, despite seasonal fluctuations in the industry.

6. Interview with representative, Local 111, United Food and Commercial Workers, 16 February 1987.

7. Interview with Plant Superintendent, 'Lowery Packers', 29 January 1988.

8. Interview with Manager of Technical Services, 'Lowery Packers', 7 December 1987.

9. Interview with Plant Superintendent.

10. Interview with Manager of Human Resources.

11. Interviews with former employees in ham boning at 'Lowery Packers', 4 November 1987.

12. *Ibid.*

13. Plant tour, 'Lowery Packers', 7 December 1987. Author's observations.

14. The process is described in a student paper written by a former ham boner at 'Lowery Packers' (Hidlebaugh 1986: 8–10).

15. Interview with worker on ham boning line, 25 January 1988.

16. *Ibid.*

17. Interview with Manager of Technical Services.

18. Data provided through the assistance of the Canadian Centre for Occupational Health and Safety, Hamilton, Ontario. Calculations performed by the author.

19. All data on accident rates are calculated from the monthly accident reports of the joint labour-management safety committee at 'Lowery Packers'.

BIBLIOGRAPHY

o

Beck, E.J. *et al.*
(1978) Stratification in a dual economy: a sectoral model of earnings determination', *American Sociological Review,* (October) 43, 704–720.

Burawoy, M.
(1985) *The Politics of Production,* London: Verso.

Canadian Meat Council
(1987) *Canada's Meat Processing Industry: Background Information,* Islington: Ontario (June).

Commission de la Santé et de la Securité du Travail
(1985) *Aliments et Boissoins au Quebec: monographie sectorelle,* Quebec.

Edwards, R.
(1979) *Contested Terrain,* New York: Basic Books.

Giedion, S.
(1948) *Mechanization Takes Command,* New York: Oxford.

Gordon, D.M., Edwards, R. and Reich, M.
(1982) *Segmented Work, Divided Workers,* Cambridge: Cambridge University Press.

Kerr, W. and Ulmer, M.
(1984) *The Importance of the Livestock and Meat Processing Industries to Western Growth,* Ottawa: Economic Council of Canada (March).

Kujovich, M.
(1970) 'The refrigerator car and the growth of the American dressed beef industry', *Business History Review,* 44, 4 (winter), 461–482.

Littler, C. and Salaman, G.
(1984) *Class at Work,* London: Batsford Academic and Educational, Ltd.

Mahon, R.
(1987) 'From Fordism to?: new technology, labour markets and unions', *Economic and Industrial Democracy,* 8, 5–60.

Pettit, L.
(1987) Letter to the *New York Times* (July 12) op-ed page.

Piore, M.J. and Sabel, C.
(1984) *The Second Industrial Divide,* New York: Basic Books.

Restrictive Trade Practices Commission (1961) *Report Concerning the Meat Packing Industry and the Acquisition of Wilsil Limited and Calgary Packers Limited by Canada Packers Limited,* Ottawa: Department of Justice.

Rex, J.
(1961) *Key Problems of Sociological Theory,* London: Routledge and Kegan Paul.

Robertson, J.
(1984) 'Packing up jobs in the meat industry', *Our Times* (November), 20–22.

Shostak, A.
   (1987) 'Blue collar worker alienation' in Cary Cooper and Michael J. Smith (eds.) *Job Stress and Blue Collar Work*, New York: John Wiley, 7–18.
Smith, M.J.
   (1987) 'Machine-paced work and stress' in Cary Cooper and Michael J. Smith (eds.) *Job Stress and Blue Collar Work*, New York: John Wiley, 51–62.
Statistics Canada
   (1985) *Manufacturing Industries of Canada: National and Provincial Areas* (31–203), annual.
Statistics Canada
   (1985) *Manufacturing Industries of Canada: National and Provincial Areas* (31–203), annual.
Statistics Canada
   (1984) *Corporation Financial Statistics* (61–207), annual.
Supinski, K.
   (1985) 'Kill floor automation: Fact or fantasy?', *Meat Industry* (May), 20–22.
Thompson, G.
   (1987) 'The American industrial policy debate: any lessons for the U.K.?, *Economy and Society*, 16, 1 (February), 1–74.
United Packinghouse Workers of America
   (1943) 'Submission of Local 216, U.P.W.A., to Board of Conciliation Appointed Under the Industrial Disputes Act to Inquire into the Dispute between Canada Packers, St. Boniface, Manitoba and Local 216, U.P.W.A.'
Williams, K. *et al.*
   (1987) 'The end of mass production?' *Economy and Society*, 16, 3 (August), 405–438.
Zysman, J. and Cohen, S.
   (1987) *Manufacturing Matters*, New York: Basic Books.

Workers' Use and Knowledge of the 'Internal Responsibility System': Limits to Participation in Occupational Health and Safety*

Vivienne Walters and Ted Haines

Worker participation regarding occupational health and safety can assume various forms. Strong workers' movements may press their claims, workers may exercise control over the organization of their work, or provision for worker involvement may be contained in health and safety legislation. In each of its forms, it is argued, participation improves health and safety by broadening definitions of occupational disease, changing policy, extending compensation, or reducing accidents and illness.[1] In this paper we focus on legislative provision for worker participation. Canadian legislation does allow for worker involvement—though it is limited when compared with a country such as Sweden (Elling, 1986; Navarro, 1983)—and here we will look at the extent to which workers use the resources available under health and safety policy in Ontario.

Ontario's occupational health and safety legislation is founded on the principles of 'internal responsibility' which assumes some worker input into health and safety issues. External regulation is downplayed and workers and employers are encouraged to resolve their problems at the plant level through a willingness to co-operate and work towards a consensus. In their review of occupational health and safety for the MacDonald Commission, Digby and Riddell have argued that the 'expansion and fine-tuning of the internal responsibility system' is one of the main policy issues which merit 'detailed scrutiny' (1986:313). "The strengthening of the internal responsibility system is one way to increase the costs to employers of an

✠ Abridged from Vivienne Walters and Ted Haines, "Workers' Use and Knowledge of the 'Internal Responsibility System': Limits to Participation in Occupational Health and Safety," *Canadian Public Policy* 14, no. 4 (1988): 411–23. Reprinted by permission of the publisher and the authors.

unsafe work environment, as well as raise the level of awareness of safety issues for both management and labour' (Digby and Riddell, 1986:314).

Central to the internal responsibility system are joint health and safety committees (JHSC) with equal representation of workers and management. Bolstering these committees are workers' health and safety representatives who can play an important role in conveying workers' concerns to committee members as well as transmitting information back to the workforce.[2] These representatives can also inspect the workplace and investigate accidents. In these respects they are important links in the structure established to represent workers' interests and to facilitate the expression of their concerns. To some extent short-circuiting these more time consuming mechanisms for dealing with problems is workers' legal right to refuse work they believe to be unsafe. Here, there is the possibility for a worker to deal immediately with more pressing issues by initiating procedures of investigation established under the Act. JHSCs, workers' representatives, as well as workers' right to refuse work are, then, key elements enabling worker participation, though management retains control of decision making.[3] Despite potential problems arising from the 'uncomfortable' relationship between workers and management at the plant level, it has been argued that there is greater potential for direct worker participation at this level than when decisions are removed from the workplace (Gevers, 1985).

Recent criticisms and evaluations of the existing legislation have been preoccupied with the administration and enforcement of *The Occupational Health and Safety Act* (McKenzie and Laskin, 1987) and with workers' access to information on substances with which they work (Grossman, 1986). What has received considerably less attention is the extent to which the internal responsibility system is used by workers to deal with their health and safety concerns. . . .

M E T H O D S
o

The sample was drawn from six workplaces in a highly industrialized area in southern Ontario. They include unionized and non-unionized, and large and small workplaces. The employer co-operated with us in establishing the sampling frame in one of the companies. We sampled from union records in three instances and used snowball samples in two.[4] The questionnaire was structured but also included many open-ended questions. The shortest interviews were 45 minutes long while some lasted for over four hours. Interviewing started in the Spring of 1984 and was completed almost a year later. . . .

PATHS OF ACTION
o

Eighty-five per cent of the sample felt that their work might harm their health and of the 434 symptoms they mentioned, 57 per cent had been experienced by them or observed in their fellow workers. Sixty-three per cent of the sample reported time lost from their job due to a work related problem. Asked to rate the magnitude of the anticipated health effects of their work, 31 per cent said that it would be small, 39 per cent said that it would be moderate and 25 per cent felt that it would be substantial. Clearly, the bulk of the sample recognized hazards in the workplace.

We looked at three different types of actions respondents might take to deal with their health and safety concerns. We wanted to know whether they had asked for information on some health and safety matter during the past year and, if so, who they had approached. They were also asked whether some aspect of their health and safety at work had worried them and, if this was the case, we explored how they had dealt with it. If no work refusals had been mentioned, we asked respondents whether they had ever refused to work because they felt it might be a danger to their health or to someone else. It is striking that despite beliefs about the damaging effects of work on health, relatively few respondents took these various actions. And of those who did pursue issues, few made use of their rights and resources under the legislation; they communicated primarily with their supervisor.

Only 22 per cent of the sample had asked for information during the previous 12 months—in one workplace as few as 7 per cent of respondents had done so. Of the 164 workers who identified and discussed a health and safety concern, 29 per cent had taken no action and had not discussed it with anyone, while a further 9 per cent had only discussed it with co-workers. Among those who did raise the issue—even if only with co-workers—51 per cent said the problem was fixed or that it was an ongoing issue, whereas 38 per cent said they had not pursued it any further. As far as refusals were concerned, 41 per cent said they had refused to work for health and safety reasons, though the vast majority of these appear to have been informal refusals, not under the legislation.[5]

These data alone suggest that many respondents did not articulate their concerns and that there was limited use of the resources provided under current health and safety policy. This is also true if we look at the paths of action followed by those workers who did pursue their concerns. Their descriptions of their refusals to work and their worries about their health and safety contained relatively few references to the elements of the internal responsibility system embodied in the Act.[6] There were only scattered references to 'Bill 70' and to JHSCs. Twenty two per cent of respondents did not know the identity of their health and safety representative, and of those who followed through on a concern about their health and safety only 25 per cent said that they had spoken with him or her. Of those who had asked for information during the past year, only 33 per cent had approached their representative. By these yardsticks, workers' health and safety representatives do not appear as a strong, familiar and well used link in the system established for dealing with occupational health and safety problems.

With respect to workers' right to refuse work believed to be unsafe, there are more obvious constraints which would render this a right not to be lightly used.[7] Indeed, only four respondents had exercised it—all the other descriptions of refusals appear to refer to informal protests or negotiations about some aspect of a job. In some cases informal refusals were effective and the problem was fixed.

> The wrappers on the wheels were in bad need of repairs. It's jute and all fraying. When it's whipping around you're afraid of getting your fingers caught. I reported it before I went on and they fixed it, but I told them I refused to run it like that.

One respondent suggested that, paradoxically, with a legal right to refuse, there often was no need to do so. The legislation empowered workers and gave added weight to their informal refusals.

> We're not given too much argument these days, with Bill 70. I never pull it though. You just say you won't work there until they get something fixed and then they will correct it.

In other examples, the worker was not required to work (this was not always so) and the supervisor or a co-worker did the job instead, though, as the second quotation indicates, there are problems with this approach.

> There was iron in the trough. Molten iron. If you slip and fall, you don't get back up. The supervisor did the job. They didn't want to remove the iron. Would have been too expensive.

> An overhead hoist fell and hit me. I was off for three months. When I went back it had been put back and fallen again so I refused to work under it. They gave me another job and found someone else to do it. It fell on him. Now someone else works under it.

The main health and safety contact which respondents reported was with their supervisor, not their health and safety representative. Supervisors were asked questions and told about problems, though they were seldom reported to be the source of respondents' knowledge. Of those who had asked for information during the past year, 61 per cent had asked their supervisor—almost twice as many as had approached their representatives. And 47 per cent of the respondents who pursued a concern they had about some aspect of their health and safety had raised it with their supervisor while just 25 per cent had discussed it with their representative. Among the 201 respondents who said their employer had provided them with information on possible hazards in their work, 48 per cent said it was provided by their supervisor. . . .

These data prompt questions about the efficacy of the internal responsibility system which underlies current occupational health and safety policy. The apparent weakness of respondents' ties with their health and safety representatives suggests weak links in the system. And insofar as this is structured to facilitate expression of workers' concerns by means of representatives and joint committees, the heavy reliance on supervisors may short circuit this system of representation and serve workers' interests less well. We move now to consider why workers do not pursue their health and safety worries and use resources provided under existing policy more fully, for it is not the case that they place a very low priority on these issues. Asked to pick their three main health concerns from a list of seven, 64 per cent ranked work related health hazards, and 47 per cent accidents at work, among the top three.[8] And in terms of bargaining priorities of workers who were unionized, health and safety was generally ranked fourth, after wages, job security and pensions.

EXTENT AND NATURE OF KNOWLEDGE

○

Here we focus on two main themes—respondents' lack of knowledge of their rights and the different types of knowledge of workers and management. Both may contribute to respondents' lack of action and infrequent use of the various elements of the internal responsibility system. Asked about their rights under existing occupational health and safety legislation, 31 per cent of the sample said they did not know them or else gave an answer which indicated they were not aware of the contents of the Act. (There were some substantial differences between workplaces; in one small unionized plant 71 per cent did not know and among the non-unionized workers, 62 per cent were not familiar with the legislation. The comparable figures in the other four workplaces ranged from 16 to 22 per cent.) When workers did mention a right under the legislation, it was the right to refuse that was most frequently recalled—by 61 per cent. . . .

Respondents were asked to comment on whether they thought there were health effects associated with any of the chemicals, gases or fumes, dusts, or metals with which they worked and with noise, shift work and piecework (of which they might have no experience). If they made a statement about the presence or absence of health effects, they were asked how they learned about this. The responses varied little across the items and here we focus on the first chemical mentioned by those who said they worked with chemicals. We have already noted that only 7 per cent said that their supervisor was the source of their opinion and 7 per cent referred to their health and safety representative. Two per cent mentioned their union and 1 per cent attributed their opinion to a training course. The main sources for statements were respondents' own experience (49 per cent) and their observation of their co-workers (30 per cent) as well as the claim that it was their own personal feeling (20 per cent). Some of this latter category was made up of statements that they 'think' a substance must have certain effects, or inference of harm because 'breathing all that stuff can't do you any good.'

What these data suggest is that workers employ a different complex of experience-based knowledge than is embodied in technical expertise. Certainly they appear to draw little on the more accepted, 'objective' sources of information—training courses, studies, material safety data sheets, and various other scientific sources. These represent two often conflicting approaches to the accumulation of knowledge (both of which are open to criticism). One respondent alluded to such differences:

> Every chemical affects every individual differently. When they do medical studies they find an overall picture, but they don't examine how it affects an individual. Sure, the government has safety data sheets, but they're based on inadequate research. With the chemicals at work I know exactly how they will affect me. I know my body and I can tell the different effects of each one at the end of the day.

Several writers (Doern, 1977; Navarro, 1980; Hauss and Rosenbrock, 1984; Mergler, 1987) have drawn attention to these types of knowledge and have shown how that of workers is accorded much less legitimacy. This too may represent a barrier to the use of procedures under the legislation. The concerns of workers do not flow from and are not expressed in terms of the dominant medical-technical paradigm and as such are less likely to be 'heard'. Because of this they may also be less frequently expressed.

Mergler (1987) has suggested that workers' experience should be more fully recognized, for even if it is not evidence of the early stages of clinical disease, it does represent expressions of impairment. Others too have noted that these views arise from experience, even though their lack of scientific base allows them to be dismissed as 'housewife data' (Smith, 1981). But while some argue they must be taken into account in educating workers (Cohen, Colligan and Berger, 1985) they are typically seen as neither legitimate nor objective and, at best, people are uncomfortable with them. Most extreme are those who dismiss workers' perceptions as emotional, unfounded and no more than 'fashions' (Walters, 1982). These observations prompt questions. Is the challenge to provide better training and education for workers and to increase their familiarity with the dominant paradigm? Or should we be educating workers about their rights and mechanisms to express their concerns, thereby facilitating the articulation of workers' definitions and allowing these to be more readily debated?

OTHER CONSTRAINTS

o

While our research was not designed to explain why relatively few respondents pursued health and safety issues, our data do provide some additional clues to why this is so. Here, we touch on the dominant ideology regarding occupational health and safety as well as some of the constraints which are structured into workers' experience.

One theme that has been emphasized by management is that of individual responsibility—stressing the role of workers in protecting their health and safety. It is the positive expression of a "blame the victim' ideology, in which responsibility and blame are vested primarily in the worker (Sass and Crook 1981). This theme was echoed by our respondents. Asked about how they could control their health and safety at work, 51 per cent of the responses mentioned strategies that clearly emphasized individual responsibility—'be careful,' 'wear protective equipment,' 'don't cut corners,' 'clean up spills'. Other responses such as 'make yourself aware of hazards,' 'educate yourself,' were ambiguous in that they could be seen as a prelude to different types of action, but many of these probably could also be classified as individual responsibility themes. Only 12 per cent of responses mentioned what we have called collective strategies, in that they referred to mechanisms beyond the workers themselves—for example, a refusal to work by 'pulling a Bill 70,' making use of health and safety representatives or joint committees, or relying on procedures established by the union. The problem with the very strong emphasis on individual responsibility is that it presents workers with a fairly narrow repertoire of responses, one which does not reflect limits to workers' personal control of their working environment. Furthermore, individual responsibility may be more applicable to safety hazards than to health hazards. Certainly this is what respondents implied, for they saw themselves as having more control over their safety than over their health. They were asked to rate their degree of control over each on a scale from 1 to 5 with 1 representing no control, and 5, complete control. Thirty-nine per cent circled 1 or 2 for health hazards and 15 per cent did so for accidents.

Indeed there was a paradox, for despite the emphasis on control, albeit in individual terms, interviews were also marked by a sense of fatalism. A fatalism which seems to be matched with inaction.

> They aren't going to pay any attention to what you say. They might say, if you don't like it, go find a job someplace else. If you mention it to other people, they just pretend they didn't hear you. I'm sure they're concerned, they just don't want to rock the boat. I could have mentioned it to personnel, but I guess I figured they wouldn't do anything about it anyway. Why put my job in jeopardy.

If you want the job, you take what you've got.

No, I wouldn't refuse. If you don't want your job, someone else will.

I'm afraid to complain too much or I may lose my job altogether.

I need a pay cheque. They could make life miserable for you for complaining.

Sometimes it's so cold and I can't move around. I've been tempted to refuse but haven't. They'd tell me to go home and it would be a day's pay lost.

It is as if the theme of individual responsibility is almost learned by rote, but pervading everything is a less well defined and less frequently endorsed sense of lack of control. Several writers have shown how workers must balance their dependence on a wage against their desire for health (Elling, 1986; Nelkin and Brown, 1984; Walters, 1985; Navarro, 1980; Doyal, 1979) and it is such contradictions which are reflected in the comments of many respondents. Given the day to day realities of coping with hazards, individual strategies may represent a realistic appraisal of what is possible (Crawford, 1984). However, the two themes of responsibility and lack of control clearly co-exist, highlighting the conflicts faced by workers.

Other constraints were not mentioned so frequently. Twenty five per cent said they or their co-workers had been hassled for raising a health and safety problem. (In one workplace 38 per cent said that this was so and in another, 33 per cent.)

At first the foreman said 'You can't refuse to work, I'll suspend you'. But he didn't.

If you want to go directly by the book, they can make life miserable for you. They can pull or change your days off, put you on shifts. You know they can schedule you however they want.

If I do everything by the book, it takes time to get the proper people, or set up the scaffold and all that. It can take you hours. Or you can just do it. It may be unsafe, but you make do with what you've got. If you want to go by the book you get screwed around.

But other possible fears were far from widely reported—constraints were phrased in the more general and fatalistic terms cited earlier. Asked if they had anticipated various sanctions if they complained about health and safety at work, 10 per cent said they had feared they would lose their job; 9 per cent of those working shifts had feared bad shifts; 7 per cent of those working overtime had worried they would not get this; and 14 per cent had feared that they would lose a better job. A related issue is supervisors' enforcement of health and safety rules. Forty nine per cent of respondents said their supervisor always did so. Others reported varying degrees of enforcement and 24 per cent reported that rules were enforced sometimes or never. In many of these cases it was said that infractions were tolerated or encouraged.

> Every day you ignore a rule—they only bug you if they want to get you. They just look the other way. A lot is left because the job has to be done. You couldn't do the job 100% safely in the time they give you.

> The foreman will tell you health and safety before production, but he means exactly the opposite.

> When I was at ——— you would be suspended right away if you didn't look out. Not here. All they're worried about is production. They will suspend you for being late, but they won't bother if you're ignoring safety rules.

CONCLUDING COMMENTS

○

We started with the theme that worker participation can help to improve health and safety in the workplace, yet our data suggest that, even though Ontario's legislation makes some modest provision for such participation, many of workers' health and safety concerns are not given expression and they make relatively little use of the internal responsibility system. Their main tie is typically with their supervisor and that with their health and safety representative is often weak or non-existent. Despite respondents' perceptions of the harmful effects of their work, they often did not pursue their worries—at least not in the ways we have studied.

We have suggested that this lack of action may be explained partly by the narrow range of options contained within the dominant ideology regarding occupational health and safety—that of individual responsibility. Moreover, workers face contradictions between their desire for health and their need for a wage and these priorities must be balanced. It is understandable that health and safety appears after wages, job security and pensions in respondents' priorities. At times, supervisors or others may capitalize on workers' fears by hassling them for raising health and safety issues or else by allowing or encouraging rule breaking. Indeed, respondents' strong ties with their supervisors are cause for concern, since responsibility for both productivity and health and safety are thereby vested in this one figure. Yet these are often incompatible and the appropriate balancing of priorities in any given situation is by no means readily apparent (Walters, 1985). It is for this reason that workers may benefit from having an alternative channel through which to express their concerns, one such alternative being workers' health and safety representatives. Frenkel and Priest (1979:21) have suggested that ways should be investigated to make it easier for workers to raise problems with someone other than management. For though it may be appropriate for potential hazards to be reported first to management, they argue that this may be a deterrent for some, and in other cases workers should know there are alternatives if management is unresponsive. We would advocate that problems be reported to both management and worker representatives from the outset and that attention be devoted to strengthening the apparently weak role of workers' health and safety representatives.

Apart from the broader ideological and structural constraints which workers face, one of the more disturbing findings of this research is respondents' unfamiliarity with existing policy and their rights under this. Knowledge of the legislation was linked with the three indices of action we have used; those who did not know anything about the Act were those least likely to ask for information, to pursue a health and safety worry, and to refuse (informally) some potentially hazardous aspect of their job. Our own data, added to the suspicions voiced by JHSC members (Advisory Council on Occupational Health and Occupational Safety, 1986), suggest the need for greater attention to the education of workers about their rights. In settings more conducive to workers placing the highest priority on their health and safety they would be more aware of institutionalized supports and would have a greater range of options at their disposal for expressing their perceptions, definitions and interests.

NOTES

o

1. Such arguments concerning the role of worker participation can be found in: Dwyer, 1983; Elling, 1986; Gardell, 1982; Gevers, 1985; Karasek *et al.*, 1981; Navarro, 1980; 1983; Sass, 1986; Smith, 1981.

2. JHSCs can vary greatly—in size, frequency of meetings, frequency of inspection of the workplace, and whether they are advisory or decision making bodies (Advisory Council on Occupational Health and Occupational Safety, 1986). For example, in one study (Walters, 1985), workers' health and safety representatives reported committee structures ranging from companies with an extensive network of area committees which fed issues to a JHSC of six or eight members, to workplaces which met the minimum requirement of a single committee with two members from each of management and labour. Meetings might be quarterly or as often as biweekly. One workers' representative was allocated three days a week for his health and safety responsibilities, while another struggled to represent 3,000 workers in just three hours a week. There were also differences in the information to which representatives had access.

3. Digby and Riddell have argued that the efficacy of committees may be limited if their role is purely advisory (1986:313). They advocate an extension of the authority of JHSCs and a strengthening of their role as a channel of information.

4. Snowball samples were developed by identifying a small number of workers in each plant and then asking each respondent to provide the names of other workers who might be eligible to be included in the sample.

5. Refusals under the legislation follow set procedures of investigation and there are safeguards for workers so that they will not be penalized. Informal refusals, where the worker does not invoke the legislation, carry no such protection or

guarantee of investigation. Workers' protests may be ignored or work simply assigned to someone else. The problems with such informal approaches are illustrated below in quotations from workers. Such examples suggest that the internal responsibility system has to be used to be effective.

6. One employer in the study has been exempted from the requirements for JHSCs and worker representatives, but workers were covered by other aspects of the legislation. Workers at this company have been excluded in all calculations concerning health and safety representatives.

7. Even though there are protections for workers there are deterrants to work refusals. A production process may be disrupted at a substantial cost to the employer and other workers. Although the worker who refused should not lose pay, he or she may be hassled in other ways in the future and labelled a troublemaker.

8. These were followed in declining priority by tobacco use, being overweight, water pollution, lack of exercise and alcohol consumption.

REFERENCES

Advisory Council on Occupational Health and Occupational Safety
   (1986) *Eighth Annual Report. April 1985 to March 31 1986. Volume 2* (Toronto: Advisory Council on Occupational Health and Occupational Safety).

Cohen, Alexander, Michael J. Colligan and Philip Berger
   (1985) 'Psychology in Health Risk Messages for Workers,' *Journal of Occupational Medicine*, 27:8:543-51.

Digby, Caroline and W. Craig Riddell
   (1986) 'Occupational Health and Safety in Canada.' In W. Craig Riddell (ed.), *Canadian Labour Relations* (Toronto: University of Toronto Press).

Doern, G. Bruce
   (1977) 'The Political Economy of Regulating Occupational Health: The Ham and Beaudry Reports,' *Canadian Public Administration*, 20:1-35.

Dwyer, Tom
   (1983) 'A New Concept in the Production of Industrial Accidents: A Sociological Approach,' *New Zealand Journal of Industrial Relations*, 8:147-60.

Elling, Ray H.
   (1986) *The Struggle for Workers' Health: A Study of Six Industrialized Countries* (Farmingdale, New York: Baywood).

Frenkel, Richard L. and W. Curtiss Priest
   (1979) *Health Safety and the Worker: An In-depth Consideration of Hazards and Effects as Revealed in Survey Data, Report Summary* (Cambridge, Mass.: MIT, Centre for Policy Alternatives).

Gardell, Bertil
   (1982) 'Scandinavian Research on Stress in Working Life,' *International Journal of Health Services*, 12:1:31-41.

Gevers, J.K.M.
   (1985) 'Worker Control Over Occupational Health Services: The Development of Legal Rights in the E.E.C'., *International Journal of Health Services*, 15:2:217-29.

Grossman, Michael
    (1986) 'A Worker's Right to Know About Workplace Chemicals,' *At the Centre*,
    September, pp. 8-11.
Hauss, Friedrich O. and Rolf D. Rosenbrock
    (1984) 'Occupational Health and Safety in the Federal Republic of Germany: A
    Case Study of Co-Determination and Health Politics,' *International Journal of
    Health Services*, 14:2:279-87.
McKenzie, G.G. and J.I. Laskin
    (1987) *Report on the Administration of the Occupational Health and Safety Act. Volumes
    I and II* (Toronto: Ministry of Labour).
Mergler, Donna
    (1987) 'Worker Participation in Occupational Health Research: Theory and Prac-
    tice,' *International Journal of Health Services*, 17:1:151-67.
Navarro, Vicente
    (1983) 'The Determinants of Social Policy: A Case Study: Regulating Health and
    Safety at the Workplace in Sweden,' *International Journal of Health Services*,
    12:4:517-61.
Sass, Robert
    (1986) 'Workplace Health and Safety: Report from Canada,' *International Journal
    of Health Services*, 16:4:565-82.
_____ and Glen Crook
    (1981) 'Accident Proneness: Science or Non-Science?' *International Journal of
    Health Services*, 11:2:175-90.
Smith, Barbara Ellen
    (1981) 'Black Lung: The Social Production of Disease,' *International Journal of
    Health Services*, 11:3:343-59.
Walters, Vivienne
    (1982) 'Company Doctors' Perceptions of and Responses to Conflicting Pressures
    from Labour and Management,' *Social Problems*, 30:1:1-12.

Experiencing Work

EDITORS' INTRODUCTION

o

Individuals' reactions to work in general, and to their specific jobs, received attention in a number of the previous readings. But there are many topics that could be usefully considered in depth, including society-wide work values, the strength of the "work ethic," whether individuals work mainly for money or for personal fulfilment, the intersection of work, family, and community values, job satisfaction, and work-related stress. Reactions to unemployment are also relevant since they underline the central role that work plays in the lives of most people. The five articles that follow offer an in-depth look at some of these crucial issues.

Rona Maynard presents findings from a 1987 Environics survey of employed Canadians which, like many previous studies, reveals that a large majority of workers report themselves to be somewhat or very satisfied with their jobs. However, general job satisfaction measures fail to pick up the discontent that exists in the work force. When asked whether they would choose the same job again, given the opportunity to start over, almost half of the survey respondents stated that they would choose another line of work. A large minority reported that they were dissatisfied with their promotion and career prospects. Maynard also reports that women were considerably less satisfied than were men with their career opportunities. Furthermore, job satisfaction was lower among young workers, compared to their counterparts a decade earlier.

Some of the observations made in earlier readings can help account for these findings. Discontent about career options might result because many middle-aged workers have "plateaued" in their careers, due to a mismatch between the demographic profile of the work force and hierarchical organizational structures. Since women face more barriers to promotion, their greater concerns about career prospects would be expected. And given the difficulties they face in finding satisfactory employment, greater dissatisfaction among today's young job-seekers is not surprising. Maynard concludes by suggesting that employers who are worried about productivity should take seriously the dissatisfactions of their employees, thus linking the discussion to the debates addressed in Part 3.

In a more critical article, James Rinehart asks why blue-collar workers in routinized assembly-line jobs would report that they are satisfied with their jobs. Some sociologists have answered that many workers have "instrumental" orientations to work, viewing a job as nothing more than a means to obtain other goals. So long as such workers are well paid, it is argued, they will remain satisfied, even in boring and meaningless jobs. But Rinehart argues that instrumental work attitudes are typically not brought to the workplace; instead, they are shaped on the job. Since most blue-collar workers have little option but to remain in their jobs, unless they are willing to accept a reduced standard of living, their expectations are adjusted downward to match the rewards offered by their jobs.

The implication of this argument is that the job satisfaction expressed by many blue-collar workers may be rather superficial. Rinehart suggests that work stoppages, absenteeism, and other behavioural indicators of dissatisfaction more accurately reflect the discontent beneath the surface. This poses a paradox that has captured the attention of social analysts since the time of Karl Marx: discontent seldom fuels working-class collective action aimed at transforming the economic system. In Rinehart's words, the behaviour of blue-collar workers remains a "curious blend of acquiescence and defiance."

While Rinehart focuses on the male-dominated manufacturing sector, Ester Reiter describes her personal experiences of working in the lower-tier service sector where women and youth make up the majority of the work force. In many ways, the low-skill, standardized jobs in the fast-food industry remind us of the repetitious assembly-line jobs in manufacturing. But there are some important differences: few jobs in the lower-tier services are unionized, and many pay close to the minimum wage.

Teenagers fill a large portion of the positions in fast-food restaurants. For them, low-pay and part-time jobs may not present a major problem given that such positions complement school activities, and that most teenagers still live at home with their parents. Immigrant workers and women with young children make up the remainder of the fast-food work force. Fast-food jobs may be the only options available to many immigrants. Women with children may choose these part-time positions so that they can continue to maintain their domestic and child care responsibilities. But as Duffy and Pupo observed in Part 2, in an earlier reading about women in part-time jobs, women's labour market choices are made within the context of larger structural constraints. If other better-paying part-time jobs were available, or if full-time positions were more flexible with respect to working hours, we would no doubt see fewer women working in fast-food jobs.

Judith MacBride-King and Hélène Paris continue the discussion of work–family conflicts. They report results from a recent Conference Board of Canada survey of over 11,000 public and private sector workers in 1,600 work organizations. This research clearly documents the extent to which Canadian workers have difficulty balancing their work and family responsibilities. The consequences for workers include stress, absenteeism, turnover, and blocked careers.

The authors are obviously concerned about the personal costs to employees, but their real audience is Canadian employers and managers. MacBride-King and Paris list a number of critical demographic changes affecting the work force: female labour force participation, including the participation of mothers of young children, continues to rise; dual-earner families have become the norm; and the number of single-parent families is growing. At the same time, the traditional supply of young (typically single and childless) entry-level workers is declining because of low birth rates.

Once again we encounter the "C" word. MacBride and King warn that if firms and government departments wish to remain "competitive," they will have to address concerns about work–family conflict; otherwise they will not be able to maintain a skilled and committed work force. The authors recommend that, among other things, employers offer more flexible work arrangements, provide assistance with child care, begin to address employees' concerns about elder care (the population is aging and the number of elderly dependents is growing), and institute programs to provide counselling and relocation assistance.

In the last reading, an extract from a book on the experiences of unemployment, Patrick Burman discusses the impact of prolonged joblessness on individuals' self-identity. Work is obviously important for making a living, but it also fulfils many other human needs. People desire to be productive and creative, and, to a large extent, paid employment is the arena in which these desires can be met. Work provides structure to daily life and social interactions with co-workers. Hence, unemployment, particularly when it lasts for many months, can be extremely distressful and undermining to one's self-identity.

Because of these deep-seated personal effects, the unemployed are more likely to lose a sense of efficacy, and to blame themselves for their own predicament, rather than acting collectively to try to change the political and economic system. In a sense, Burman's description of this accommodation to unemployment reminds us of Rinehart's arguments about how instrumental work attitudes are formed in work settings that offer few personal satisfactions.

DISCUSSION QUESTIONS

o

1. Given that a large majority of workers report that they are at least some-what satisfied with their jobs, why should we worry about the "quality of work life"?

2. In your opinion, which has a larger effect on job satisfaction—the aspirations and expectations of workers, or the work rewards they receive?

3. Do individuals' work attitudes change as they get older?

4. Which type of job do you think would be least satisfying—an assembly-line factory job or a job in a fast-food restaurant? What type of job would you expect to find most satisfying?

5. Are satisfied workers also more productive workers?

6. Individuals choose to have children, so why should employers have to worry about how their employees balance work and family responsibilities?

7. Why is it that the unemployed seldom become militant or politically active in an effort to improve their situation?

SUGGESTED READINGS

o

Anthony, P.D. *The Ideology of Work.* London: Tavistock, 1977.

Hamilton, Richard, F., and James D. Wright. *The State of the Masses.* New York: Aldine, 1986.

Hayes, John, and Peter Nutman. *Understanding the Unemployed: The Psychological Effects of Unemployment.* London: Tavistock, 1981.

Kamerman, Sheila B., and Alfred J. Kahn. *The Responsive Workplace: Employers and a Changing Labor Force.* New York: Columbia University Press, 1987.

Karasek, Robert, and Tores Theorell. *Healthy Work: Stress, Productivity, and the Reconstruction of Working Life.* New York: Basic Books, 1990.

Rose, Michael. *Re-Working the Work Ethic: Economic Values and Socio-Cultural Politics.* London: Batsford, 1985.

How Do You Like Your Job?[*]

Rona Maynard

At this time of economic tumult, few subjects provoke more passionate debate than jobs: creating them, protecting them, wringing more competitive clout from them. But the arguments of the economists and the politicians have long obscured the views of those whose paycheques and prospects are at issue—working Canadians. How satisfied are they with their jobs, and what demands are they likely to make of employers in the coming years?

Report on Business Magazine asked Environics Research Group Limited, a Toronto firm specializing in opinion polls, to probe the feelings of Canadian employees nationwide. The answers look encouraging at first glance. A commanding 89% of Canadians claim to be very or somewhat satisfied with their jobs, a figure consistent with other Environics findings over the past decade.

But employers cannot afford to be complacent, for the survey reveals simmering discontent in two of the fastest-growing segments of the workforce. Among workers under 30, the dissatisfaction rate has doubled to 16% today from 8% in 1977. And professional women as less satisfied than professional men with major aspects of their jobs—particularly their opportunities for advancement and promotion.

Moreover, many Canadians who say they are happy with their work in general express reservations about various aspects of their jobs or their chances for promotion. Nearly half admit that if they had it to do over again, they would choose another occupation, and only a slim majority, 56%, are satisfied with the odds for moving up. These answers suggest an underly-

[*] Abridged from Rona Maynard, "How Do You Like Your Job?" *Report on Business Magazine*, November 1987, 120–25. Reprinted by permission of the publisher and the author.

355

ing frustration among segments of the workforce. The result is a new tough-mindedness that will challenge business for years to come.

Unlike their parents, who trustingly devoted 40-odd years to a single employer, today's workers keep a close eye on their options. As companies cut costs by slashing jobs and boost production with new equipment, 59% of Canadians expect to spend time on work-related training. Half expect to go job-hunting; 43% plan to switch careers. This rejection of old-fashioned corporate loyalty is even more pronounced among employees under age 30.

While Canadians will hit the books and pound the pavement for fulfilling careers, they are reluctant to neglect their personal lives. A family-first attitude, while most evident among women, is gaining among men. Forty-two per cent of Canadians say they would not give up leisure or family time to advance their careers, and only 36% would consider a transfer. More than half plan to retire before age 65.

Jean Marc Morassutti[1], a 26-year-old technologist for Boeing in Winnipeg, typifies this growing insistence on personal pleasure. Not about to work overtime, he leaves work promptly each summer day to "put on my shorts, take the dog out for a walk, put the boat on the water and have fun with my wife." He wants to retire no later than age 55 "because I've seen my father work till he turned 65 and not live long enough to enjoy it." Meanwhile, he is seizing all the after-hours enjoyment he can. "I like toys, and to pay for those toys I have to work. But if I could have four days of work and three of leisure, I'd take it."

The survey's message is clear. Today, employees expect not only the traditional rewards of job-holding, a steady paycheque and a secure future, but emotional rewards that are more difficult to quantify. "We spend half to a third of our waking hours at work, commuting there, or thinking about our jobs," comments Pamela Ennis, a Toronto industrial psychologist who has conducted employee-satisfaction surveys for more than 60 corporate clients including Via Rail, General Foods and Four Seasons Hotels. "We don't think of it as a place to earn money, but as a place to grow and develop—like an extended family."

What fosters job satisfaction? A growing number of employers, intent on stretching productivity, are betting on glossy new programs: big-ticket performance appraisals, employee-of-the-month contests and fitness centres. But managing employees well, like raising children, depends more on consistently communicated values than on hit-and-miss morale boosting. "Programs can actually lead to open ridicule," says John Young, senior vice-president of human resources for Four Seasons Hotels in Toronto. "My boss can wear a button proclaiming we're the greatest, but unless he or she has created a good work climate, I'm not going to believe it."

Whether they are janitors or general managers, most Canadians want appreciation for their skills, interest in their aspirations and information on the corporate goals their efforts promote. They want to be treated like fully rounded human beings, not names on the payroll. Modest as their hopes may sound, too few employers are fulfilling them.

Judy Stucka, 38, grosses $500 or $600 a week supervising the cashiers in an Edmonton supermarket. She is highly complimentary of her boss, who shows his appreciation of the store's senior staff by taking them out to occasional dinners. "Something that simple can really make you work harder," she says. "But the boss I had before was not that kind of person. You did your job, and that's it. He had a hard time saying thank you." That attitude eventually prompted her to move on. Such restlessness does not surprise Ennis, who calls lack of recognition "the number one dissatisfier."

Few forms of recognition matter more to employees than constructive criticism. Although many companies have annual performance appraisals that purport to keep them informed of their progress, workers often view the procedure as just another bureaucratic ritual. "Ninety-nine per cent of the people here are getting the same range of salary increase," says a 45-year-old Montreal engineer. "Sometimes it looks like people working very hard are not getting any more appreciation or pay than someone who isn't working at all."

No matter how fair the performance appraisal, it is no substitute for a manager's steady attention. Beth McEwen of Bedford, N.S., has found that personal touch at Digital Equipment of Canada, where she is a contract administrator. "I've worked for employers who couldn't care if you were gone tomorrow—who let you think your job could be done by anyone because 100,000 people out there are looking for work," says McEwen, 28. "But here, there's always someone to help you if you need assistance, and they're open to letting you set out your own job plan that suits what they're after and what you want to accomplish. They know every person goes about a job in a different way."

If employees expect to help set their own agendas, they are equally intent on pride in the results. Clarence Towndrow, 52, of Edmonton has been a heavy-equipment operator for 36 years because every job gives him a sense of accomplishment. "It's sort of like painting a picture—you have to visualize the results before you start," he explains. "People don't see our work because it's covered up, but if you're going by a tank farm and you see the containment dikes in nice straight lines, you know someone worked very hard to get them picture perfect."

Unlike Towndrow, who oversees a job from proposal to completion, many employees are responsible for a tiny corner of a task whose overall shape they do not understand. They crunch numbers for a head-office honcho or make widgets for machinery they have never seen. The resulting alienation plagues not only unskilled high-school graduates, but technical stars with PhDs. The Montreal engineer worries that his company lacks a sound business plan: if one exists, management hasn't bothered to tell the staff.

To prevent this kind of disaffection, forward-looking employers strive to keep staff informed of their goals and operations. John DeShano, president of Great Northern Apparel, for example, holds informal meetings with small groups of employees at plants across the country.

But many other employers don't take the time to do this or don't know how. "When I ask employees what information they would like about their company, even hourly workers mention profits, strategic plans and advertising," remarks Ennis. "I tell employers to communicate absolutely everything, except for extremely confidential plans, until the employee says, 'Enough is enough.'"

Providing information is a snap compared to providing the career opportunities that many employees demand. In-house training and promote-from-within policies cannot always compensate for cutbacks in management jobs or competition among ambitious baby boomers.

Just ask Stephen Parenteau, a 30-year-old engineering technologist aiming to become a director of his firm in Kanata, Ont. "I've been offered jobs at other firms, and my bosses have always told me, 'Don't go. We'd like to get you into management,'" he says. "But statistically, I've got a one in 12 chance at what I'm shooting for. Naturally, they can't guarantee me a position on the board."

Relatively speaking, Parenteau has it easy. Professional men take a more optimistic view of their prospects for advancement than any other group in the labor force. By almost every measure, they are Canada's happiest employees, and their edge over everyone else increases with age. Others feel less privileged.

Take union members, whose leaders have fought doggedly for pay and benefits. More content than nonunionized workers with these bread-and-butter features of their jobs, they are also less pleased with their chances for promotion and access to decision-making—a pattern that persists among both skilled and semiskilled unionists.

What's behind their complaints? It depends on whom you ask. Donna Dasko, senior associate of Environics, points to the unions' chosen role as the intermediaries between workers and management. "The structures are more rigid," she suggests. "That's good for many people, but frustrating for others as the workforce in general becomes more educated and more interested in decision-making." But at the Canadian Labor Congress, vice-president Dick Martin blames management for excluding the employees who hire and fire—the very people closest to the reins of power—from bargaining units. "There is some trade-off involved," he admits, "but the lines are drawn by management."

If unionists seem conflicted, women appear even more so—especially professional women. On the one hand, they are the country's most committed workers: 65% would choose the same career again, compared with 56% of professional men. "Women going into business have had to get their focus very clear," comments Phillip Daniels, an industrial psychologist and a partner at Stevenson Kellogg Ernst & Whinney in Toronto. "They may get a later start than men in order to have children, but by their 30s and 40s, they're really getting their careers in stride. They're a little more mature than the men."

On the other hand, they are a lot less pleased than men with their treatment by employers. When professional women size up their odds for getting ahead, the gender gap becomes a chasm. Only 49% express optimism compared with 62% of men.

The obvious culprit is discrimination. "I've seen a few job applications come in from women, and everybody made snide remarks about them," confides a young male engineer. "These guys are from the '50s, and our firm is no different from anyone else's. We've had female draftspersons and when they cry a little on a bad day, management will say, 'Typical woman.'" A guy will come in with a hangover and they say, 'He just had a few drinks.' Asked whether the attitudes of younger staffers like him will eventually improve women's prospects, the engineer responds, "It's hard to keep your ideals. We tend to learn from the people that we work under."

Most Canadians believe that old-line attitudes hold women back, to judge from similar previous surveys by Environics. But ask them about their own workplaces and few share the concerns of the young engineer. Only 20% think that their employers give women fewer opportunities than men, and a mere 14% believe that women earn less than men for similar jobs. While professional women detect unfairness more frequently than almost anyone else, such women are clearly a minority. Comments Elaine Todres, assistant deputy minister of the Ontario Women's Directorate in Toronto and a prime mover behind the province's new pay equity legislation: "It's extremely difficult for an individual who's very well trained to accept the fact that she may be a victim of discrimination."

Dianne Palovcik certainly rejects that notion. At 40, the Edmonton special education instructor is nothing if not career-minded: She networks through volunteer activities, devotes some of her evenings to work-related meetings and has taken a course in administration to help qualify for an administrative post. And she insists that women themselves must accept responsibility for their own advancement. "We must be prepared to make some changes in how we think about ourselves—to believe that we ruddy well can do the job and take a crack at trying," she argues. "We have to make sacrifices—work late to stay organized and pursue education."

Although employers would surely be quick to agree, they have never raced so hard to fatten women's paycheques and groom them for promotions. They are playing a numbers game that has been forced upon them by federal and provincial legislators, and their belated efforts raise a troubling question: If employees don't perceive discrimination around them, will they resist campaigns to push women up the ladder?

Not if top executives demand their support, argues Lynda White, equal employment opportunity co-ordinator for the Royal Bank in Montreal. The percentage of women in the Royal's management ranks has climbed from 8% a decade ago, when the equal opportunity program started, to 24% today (a figure that excludes junior managers). Numerical targets for women's recruitment and promotion have motivated managers since 1982, and White's office checks up on them quarterly. "If you're making someone accountable, it doesn't matter whether he believes in a program or not," says White. But she adds that with 35,000 employees across Canada, the bank cannot keep an eye on them all. "Individual biases inevitably come into play, much as you hope they won't."

Employers struggling to keep up with women's will to advance face an equally tough challenge from the most restless and critical young workers ever to comb the classifieds. Even young professionals express more dissatisfaction across the board than the workforce as a whole, and those with high-school education or less are more vocal yet. Forty-five per cent of this relatively unskilled group take a dim view of their chances for advancement, compared with about a third of Canadians generally, while 31% have complaints about job security compared with the overall rate of 24%.

Because the survey excluded the unemployed, it only hints at the disaffection among Canada's least skilled and least desirable workers: high-school dropouts. Still, the evidence it offers is already grim enough that Dasko of Environics speculates about a "lost generation."

Krys Przybylski, 25, of Toronto was working in a health-food store at the time of the survey, but has since quit because "the wages were disgusting, $4.50 an hour." It was only the latest in a string of jobs, from survey taker to security guard, that have never paid more than $5.50 an hour. Now collecting unemployment, the grade 12 graduate dreams of opening a health-food restaurant or learning psychotherapy at a holistic health centre. "There might be job opportunities, but a lot don't stimulate your human dignity," she says. "There are a lot of worthless dippy things to do like fold boxes. How does that make somebody feel?"

Employers understandably accuse young people like Przybylski of expecting too much money for too little effort. "That's the nature of youth," counters Ken Dryden, former Ontario youth commissioner. He adds that youth absorb their expectations from the environment—notably from TV fantasies of the good life. Dreaming of what Dryden calls "designer lives," they can't buy the right cars and clothes with the work they find in a tight job market.

"Employers invest where they feel the investment will pay off, in those with university and graduate degrees," says Dryden. "Those who are filling the other jobs are very much interchangeable people. There is such a thing as a dead-end job. Though all of us like to think that no job is without value and that every job will prepare you for the next one, if you don't see some tomorrow as better than today, it's hard not to feel psychologically cut off at the neck."

To combat this malaise, a few companies are working to educate youth about workaday realities before they leave school. Adopt-a-school programs, pioneered in the United States during the early '70s, match employers with nearby schools so that students can follow workers through a typical day or hear talks by managers about corporate behavior. In return, the school might share its sports facilities or language classes with the company. A year-old program in North York, Ont., has the support of seven corporations including Petro-Canada and Manufacturers Life Insurance Co. "Business has a role to play in mentoring and motivating students," explains Fern Stimpson, director of employment policy in Manulife's corporate human resources department. "We hope we'll encourage students to stay in school longer."

Because even high-school graduates can end up punching rivets, a growing number of companies strive to give hourly employees more pride in their jobs. For example, General Foods turns teams of workers loose to solve production problems in its Cambridge, Ont., plant. "We pushed the authority down the line to the people who actually know what makes a machine run faster," says Greg Cox, vice-president of human resources. Star brainstormers are rewarded with cash prizes. Such moves have clearly paid off for General Foods. Although the company has cut 300 blue-collar jobs over the past three years, productivity is up.

Keeping Canadians happy has never been business' job. But employers after better results from a leaner workforce will have to revise their thinking. As the survey demonstrates, it is a chance to shine that gets Canadians up in the morning. And results-minded employers have their work cut out for them.

NOTE
o

1. Employees quoted throughout were selected from those surveyed.

Contradictions of Work-Related Attitudes and Behaviour: An Interpretation*

James W. Rinehart

Are manual workers discontented with their jobs, or is the idea of alienated labour merely a creation of embittered intellectuals? Years of discussion and research have yielded no unequivocal answers to this question, and the nature of the relationship between workers and their jobs remains a contentious issue. One basis of the controversy can be located in the two distinct methods employed to generate data on the working class. The sanguine view of the world of work is derived mainly from attitude surveys, which depict jobs as tolerable and wage-earners as contented. In contrast, behavioural analysis is more likely to furnish evidence of industrial conflict and disenchantment with work. In this paper I shall evaluate these two approaches to the study of work and provide a conceptual framework to interpret and reconcile their divergent images. . . .

THE MEANING OF INSTRUMENTALISM AND JOB SATISFACTION

o

It is because variations in the intrinsic characteristics of most blue-collar jobs are not large and because such differences as do exist are situated in authority relationships in which the process and purposes of production are not governed by workers that we are justified in raising questions about the

* Abridged from James W. Rinehart, "Contradictions of Work-Related Attitudes and Behaviour: An Interpretation," *The Canadian Review of Sociology and Anthropology* 15, no. 1 (1978): 1–15. Also published in Graham S. Lowe and Harvey J. Krahn, eds., *Working Canadians: Readings in the Sociology of Work and Industry* (Toronto: Methuen, 1984), pp. 19–30 [reprinted by Nelson Canada in 1991]. Reprinted by permission of the publisher and the author.

meaning of "satisfied" and "instrumental" reactions to work. To argue, as Goldthorpe and his associates (1969) have, that the dilemma of the working class is a choice between high wages and gratifying work is to suggest a degree of variation in job complexity and control which simply does not exist. As Fox (1974: 161) remarks, "men who have never experienced intrinsically satisfying work can hardly be said to have 'chosen' intrinsically unsatisfying work." Consider the following statement of an "instrumental worker": "You don't achieve anything here. A robot could do it. The line here is made for morons. It doesn't need any thought. They tell you that. 'We don't pay you for thinking,' they say. Everyone comes to realize that they're not doing a worthwhile job. They're just on the line. For the money. Nobody likes to think that they're a little cog. You just look at your pay packet—you look at what it does for your wife and kids. That's the only answer" (Beynon, 1973: 114).

Instrumental orientations should be understood as rational adaptations to jobs that are characterized by extreme specialization, subordination, and inequalities of prestige and treatment. If jobs are selected on the basis of economic criteria, this only reveals the flatness of the world of blue collar work and not an absence of (abstract) desires for gratifying jobs. *Workers opt for jobs with relatively high wages in exchange for what can only be minor losses in intrinsic work satisfaction.*

Instrumentalism is shaped by objective realities. So too are "satisfied" responses to work, which should not be construed as statements of preference. They are no more than pragmatic judgments of one's position *vis-à-vis* the narrow range of available jobs. Also relevant to understanding the significance of job satisfaction is the permanent existence of the reserve army of the unemployed and the constant threat of redundancies, lay-offs, and plant shutdowns, all of which are responsible for pervasive feelings of insecurity among the working class. The "choice" that is presented to most workers is that between work which is intrinsically unsatisfying and no work. A job, any job, is preferable to none at all, and this necessarily affects evaluations of work. . . .

The prevalence of abstract yearnings for decent work is also shown by a tendency of manual wage-earners who report job satisfaction to state they would select a line of work different from their own if they could start their lives over again. A national survey of Canadians found that 85 per cent of blue-collar workers were satisfied with their jobs. When these same persons were asked what type of work they would seek if they were to re-enter the labour market, 52 per cent of the skilled and 64 per cent of the unskilled chose an occupation different from the one in which they were then employed (Canada Department of Manpower and Immigration, 1974).[1] Coburn's (1973) study of Victoria residents revealed an equally large disparity in manual workers' expressions of job satisfaction and the jobs they would choose in hypothetical circumstances.[2]

It is not conceptions of *ideal* work that serve as the basis of job orientations, expectations, and choices. Rather, it is logical to conclude from the evidence that *the comparative frame of reference used by workers to select and evaluate their jobs is mainly a negative one.*

WORKING-CLASS ACTIVITY: CONFLICT AND ALIENATION

o

The argument I am advancing is that workers' attachments to jobs are in fact limited, pragmatic, and instrumental. But in contrast to the position taken by most observers—even the majority of those who view instrumentalism and job satisfaction as rational responses to limited job choice—my thesis is that such job orientations neither imply nor factually entail indifference to or acceptance of the nature of work.

High wages cannot neutralize the impact of what earners are obliged to do for over one-third of their waking hours, year in and year out. To argue that workers select jobs on economic grounds is not tantamount to saying that non-economic working conditions are a matter of indifference. It is unrealistic to believe that even the most calculating workers can effectively ignore and insulate themselves from daily workplace experiences. The validity of this argument is not shown by workers' attitudes, especially as they are expressed in survey analyses. Rather, it is most forcibly revealed by workers' actions.

Class conflict is endemic to capitalist societies. The outlines of Canada's turbulent history of industrial relations have been drawn by Jamieson (1971). Strikes are a persistent feature of the industrial system, and they periodically erupt to involve massive numbers of workers. This country has experienced five major strike waves in the twentieth century, the latest one occurring in 1974-5, when there was an all-time high in the number of man-days lost from strikes and lock-outs. While many observers claim that this record is proof of workers' overriding concern with wages, the reality of work stoppages is more complex.

Without denying the salience of pecuniary interests, it is important to realize that strikes are a complex phenomenon. Work stoppages ordinarily arise out of a multiplicity of contentious issues, and during the course of a strike it is not unusual to find shifts in the importance workers attribute to the issues (cf. Hyman, 1972; Knowles, 1952). Even if we assume (along with government agencies) that the major causes of a strike can be classified and ranked in terms of salience, it is clear that a substantial number of work stoppages (now as in the past) are not rooted in economics per se, but are the result of grievances arising from working conditions broadly defined— job allocation and transfer, forced overtime, work loads and work speeds, safety and health problems, disciplinary measures and dismissals, etc....

Strikes are only the most obvious expressions of working-class discontent, the tip of the iceberg as it were. Less visible workplace struggles are continuously waged overworking conditions and managerial prerogatives. While organized labour has fought for economic gains, struggles over the organization and control of the workplace have been waged primarily by rank and file workers on the shop floor, independent (and sometimes in defiance) of the union.

Class relations are sharply etched in the daily encounter between bosses and workers, resulting in antagonisms which take various forms—slow downs and sit ins, restriction of output, wildcat strikes, working to rule, absenteeism and tardiness, personnel turnover, insubordination, and sabotage. In this constant "war of the workplace" workers not only resist managerial authority but at times collectively act to take over some part of management's role. What must be stressed is the routine character of factory conflicts. While ordinarily hidden to all but insiders, they are not an episodic phenomenon but a permanent feature of social relationships within capitalist enterprise (cf. Faber, 1976; Glaberman, 1975; Johnson, 1975; Rinehart, 1975; Roy, 1967; 1969; Watson, 1972).

ATTITUDE-BEHAVIOUR INCONSISTENCIES

o

If workers were really satisfied with or indifferent to their jobs, conflict and struggle would not be such a prominent feature of the world of work. But the disparity between job attitudes and on-the-job behaviour is only partly resolved by a re-interpretation of the meaning of attitudes. We are still left with an irreducible residue of uncertainty about such interpretations. How are we to treat the fact that workers do say they are satisfied with work, however minimal and qualified these assessments may be? There is no complete answer to this question. In fact, it would be surprising if attitude-behaviour discrepancies could be neatly reconciled, because what astute observations of the working class reveal is that such contradictions are not at all unusual. Consider the following examples of the striking inconsistency of values and behaviour.

Goldthorpe and his associates (1969) found that workers held privatized values; they were oriented to their immediate families and were not deeply involved with other workers or working-class institutions. Moreover, these workers tended to view their relationship to the company as a cooperative one rather than one of opposition and conflict. Yet, it is now well known that shortly after the publication of the final volume of the study these same cooperative, privatized workers engaged in a militant strike that included threatening the life of the company director, running up the red flag, and singing the "Internationale."

A similar phenomenon has been described by Glaberman (1975) in his study of World War II no-strike pledges among the United Auto Workers. Prior to being presented with a secret ballot on the no-strike issue, workers were beseiged by patriotic proclamations of the media as well as their own union leaders. The message was clear—uninterrupted production was necessary for the effective pursuit of the war effort. The UAW membership voted two-to-one in favour of banning strikes. Nevertheless, "before the vote, during the vote, and after the vote, a majority of auto workers were on strike" (Glaberman, 1975: 29).

The disparity between consciousness and action is also emphasized in Mann's (1973: 51) discussion of a study of the turbulent 1960-61 general strike in Belgium. Workers interviewed just prior to the strike were described as "apathetic trade unionists, hostile to political strikes and completely ignorant of radical reform programs." Mann reported that the author of the study was surprised to learn that these same "apathetic" workers had assumed active, leading roles in the general strike.

The above cases are dramatic illustrations of an ordinary phenomenon. It is not unusual to find lip service being paid by workers to hegemonic values, with a corresponding behavioural denial of them. Wage-earners generally adhere to the notion that improvements in one's socio-economic position are dependent on individual efforts. In practice, however, they rely on their union—a collective means—for such advancement. Workers have been known to condemn organized labour for holding too much power and yet evince fierce loyalty to their own union. They may oppose strikes in general and actively support a work stoppage at their own plant. Workers can endorse private enterprise one day and the next day occupy a factory and demand that it be taken over by workers, the community, or the government. And workers usually express some degree of job satisfaction at the same time as they are struggling against the way in which work is organized. . . .

C O N C L U S I O N S

Industrial conflict is a manifestation of antagonisms deriving from the unequal distribution of power. Because the purposes of production are determined by employers and their managerial minions, the needs and interests of workers are secondary to and often interfere with the central capitalist need of profitability. However, the immediate problem as perceived by workers is not capitalism or capitalist authority relations. Rather, their daily dilemma is how to exist within this system with the greatest amount of ease, security, and autonomy. To make life on (and off) the job more tolerable workers are forced to resist capitalist authority, to defend customary prerogatives, and to extend their own control over work routines.

This is not to imply that working-class struggles ordinarily are the result of a well-formulated philosophy of workers' control and socialism. In fact, resistance occurs despite workers' adherence (however inconsistent and superficial) to dominant values which justify and legitimize integral elements of capitalist production. But when workers react to specific irritants as they arise on the shop floor, the underlying cause of these conditions generally remains unchallenged.[3] The fundamental issue is not time clocks, wage rates, autocratic foremen, or repetitive jobs, but power, and each specific workplace deprivation is merely a manifestation of prevailing authority relations.

In the final analysis, struggles of instrumental and "satisfied" workers can only be described as a curious blend of acquiescence and defiance—an accommodation to the structure of capitalist authority and resistance to the actual exercise of this authority whenever it adversely affects working people. It is in the melange of tensions and contradictions arising from capitalist domination and the subordinate position of workers that one finds the dynamic of progressive social change.

NOTES
o

1. Data from the Department of Manpower and Immigration's "Work Ethic Survey" as re-analyzed by Peter Archibald, John Gartrell, and Owen Adams.

2. Such large response differences are not typical of groups such as professionals, managers, and proprietors. For example, Coburn (1973) found that 82.9 per cent of professionals were satisfied with their jobs, and 73.8 per cent would choose the same occupation if they could start again.

3. It is important to emphasize that "in trying to solve the problems of their daily lives, people sometimes find they must act in ways which also challenge the whole organization of society" (Brecher, 1972: ix). Canadian workers have periodically threatened constituted authority, most notably in the Winnipeg general strike and in the more recent general strike in Quebec. Outside Canada the most clearcut challenges to bourgeois authority have arisen recently in Italy through the formation of democratic worker committees and factory occupations and in the French events of 1968, where factories were occupied and "General Assemblies" of workers raised demands for workers' control of industry.

REFERENCES
o

Beynon, Huw
    1973 *Working for Ford*. London: Penguin.
Brecher, Jeremy
    1972 *Strike!* San Francisco: Straight Arrow Books.
Canada Department of Manpower and Immigration
    1974 "Work Ethic Survey." Ottawa.

Coburn, David
1973   *Work and Society: The Social Correlates of Job Control and Job Complexity.* Ph.D. Dissertation, University of Toronto.
Faber, Seymour
1976   "Working class organization." *Our Generation* 11: 13-26.
Fox, Alan
1974   *Man Mismanagement.* London: Hutchinson.
Glaberman, Martin
1975   *The Working Class and Social Change.* Toronto: New Hogtown Press.
Goldthorpe, J.H., D. Lockwood, F. Bechhofer, J. Platt
1969   *The Affluent Worker in the Class Structure.* Cambridge: Cambridge University Press.
Hyman, Richard
1972   *Strikes.* London: Fontana/Collins.
Jamieson, Stuart M.
1971   *Times of Trouble: Labour Unrest and Industrial Conflict in Canada, 1900-66.* Ottawa: Information Canada.
Johnson, Walter
1975   *Working in Canada.* Montreal: Black Rose Books.
Knowles, K.G.J.
1952   *Strikes: A Study of Industrial Conflict.* Oxford: Blackwell.
Mann, Michael
1973   *Consciousness and Action Among the Western Working Class.* London: Macmillan.
Rinehart, James W.
1975   *The Tyranny of Work.* Don Mills: Longman Canada.
Roy, Donald
1967   "Quota restriction and goldbricking in a machine shop." In *Readings in Industrial Sociology.* ed., W. Faunce, pp. 311-34. New York: Appleton-Century-Crofts.
1969   "Making-out: a counter-system of workers' control of work situation and relationships." In *Industrial Man*, ed., T. Burns, pp. 359-79. Harmondsworth: Penguin.
Watson, Bill
1972   *Counterplanning on the Shop Floor.* Boston: New England Free Press.

Working in a Burger King Outlet*

Ester Reiter

The growth of the restaurant business and the expanded market for eating out can be viewed as the successful realization of the liberal vision of the good society. Business prospers, jobs are available for whomever wants them, and women need no longer be tied to the stove. Eating out is affordable and thought to be an enjoyable experience. Yet while the marketplace flourishes, and individual freedom reigns in that arena, the constraints that exist behind the scenes at work tell a less cheery story. For many people, in particular women and young workers, the kind of jobs available to them and the ability to use their creative abilities at work are very restricted.

Theodore Levitt, writing in the *Harvard Business Review*, describes how many jobs are now essentially "machine tending." From a business point of view, this is a brilliant innovation—applying the methods of the assembly line to the service industry. Thus, a McDonald's retail outlet is admired as "a machine that produces, with the help of totally unskilled machine tenders, a highly polished product. Through painstaking attention to total design and facilities planning, everything is built integrally into the machine itself, into the technology of the system. The only choice available to the attendant is to operate it exactly as the designers intended."[1] Karl Marx, in the *Communist Manifesto*, written over one hundred and twenty years earlier, described essentially the same process. "Owing to the extensive use of machinery and to division of labor, the work of the proletarians has lost all individual character, and consequently, all charm for the workman. He becomes an appendage of the machine, and it is only the most sim-

* Abridged from Ester Reiter, *Making Fast Food: From the Frying Pan into the Fryer* (Montreal and Kingston: McGill–Queen's University Press, 1991), chapter 5, "Working in a Burger King Outlet." Reprinted by permission of the publisher and the author.

ple, most monotonous, and most easily acquired knack, that is required of him."[2]

What businesspeople celebrate as an advance, and the embodiment of freedom, others describe as the precise opposite. The conditions for freedom, from a socialist or Marxist perspective, are not free selling and buying in the marketplace, but the abolition of the ability of one group of people—capitalists—to appropriate the work of others in order to make a profit.

Machine tenders are people with hearts and minds. How do they feel about the work that they do? I wanted to explore what this job felt like from the inside. What is it like to be a machine tender?

Getting first-hand experience in order to do a study is a particular kind of fieldwork in sociology—called participant observation. It has certain advantages. Rather than deciding in advance what the important questions are, involvement in the situation allows researchers the opportunity to learn something they didn't know before. In other methods, such as surveys, findings are limited to confirming or disproving previously decided upon hypotheses. Yet reducing phenomena to measurable operationalized variables, necessary with more quantitative approaches, often oversimplifies and distorts what we want to study. Reality is complicated and changing. The ongoing process that can be experienced when one actually goes into a setting more accurately captures what goes on than the static snapshots gathered through quantitative methods. . . .

When I decided to study work in the fast food industry, I realized that the most suitable approach was to enter the setting and interact as normally as I would in any situation. Sure, my presence would make things a little different, but not substantially so. A fast food restaurant would not reorganize the work because I was observing it. Observing in a setting, without engaging in interaction with the people around me, seemed to me to be deluding myself. I couldn't be invisible, and so I would stand out even more. Besides, acting as the removed observer would not only limit the information I would have access to, but would give off the message that I thought I was somehow "better than" or "above" the people I was studying. I know I am luckier than many of the adult workers who have fast food jobs but I certainly don't consider myself "better." . . .

O R G A N I Z I N G   T H E   C U S T O M E R
" E X P E R I E N C E "
o

The Burger King restaurant in which I worked, which I'll call Briarwood, was a company-owned outlet, located within a shopping mall in a suburb of Toronto. The mall is set at the intersection of a highway and a main thoroughfare; the Burger King sign is quite visible as one approaches from either road. The store is surrounded on three sides by a large parking lot, with space for several hundred cars. A "drive-thru" window occupies the fourth side, where customers may be served without leaving their cars. Approximately 35 percent of the store's business uses the "drive-thru."

A large porch, with round stone picnic tables for the use of customers in mild weather, fronts the brick and glass Burger King building. A small, professionally landscaped garden borders the store. Cement receptacles lined with garbage bags are liberally provided to handle the debris of the meals, which are completely packaged with disposable materials. Crew members are sent outside periodically to make sure that there is no garbage strewn about; keeping the parking lot clean is considered important for business. This company is convinced that if customers see a clean lot, well-maintained landscape and building, and sparkling glass, they will have a positive mental image of the food and service. . . .

The customer's order is taken by a "counter hostess," or cashier who, like the menu, follows a standardized format. First, a smile and the greeting. She says, "Hello, welcome to Burger King. May I take your order, sir?" or a minor variant of the above. Chances are this greeting will be offered by a young pretty teenager. If it is lunchtime on a school day, adult women in their twenties or thirties or older women and men in their fifties and sixties can usually be seen working at the various work stations.

If a customer orders only two items, the cashier will suggest a third to fill out "the food triangle." What the company calls "the food triangle" consists of a sandwich (or hamburger), fries, and a drink. The profits on fries and drinks are largest, so cashiers are trained to gently convince customers to include these items with their order.

Profitability in menu items varies. Drinks, particularly soft drinks, tea, and coffee are the most lucrative. They are sold at about 600 percent of their cost, excluding the price of the cup. Fries are the next most profitable item, with a 400 percent markup. The lowest margin markup is the chicken sandwich, at 100 percent. . . .

In Burger King's training manual for employees, the emphasis on smiling is explained. The attitude of the crew people and the management creates what is called an "atmosphere" or "personality" in each Burger King restaurant. Since the "counter hostess" has the most contact with the customers, she in particular needs to present a "good attitude." This attitude reflects not only her positive feelings for the job and for fellow workers, but for superiors as well.

> Smile with a greeting and make a positive first impression. Show them you are GLAD TO SEE THEM. Include eye contact with the cheerful greeting.

If a customer is eating her meal at Burger King, she is handed her order on a tray. Each part of the meal comes wrapped in its own disposable package, to be separately used and consumed. The condiments—salt, vinegar, ketchup—are also provided in their own individual, disposable packages. Only the tray, covered with a disposable tray liner, is not to be discarded.

Tray liner designs are changed periodically as they are used for advertising purposes. They are decorated with slogans such as "Hop on the Whopper Wagon," featuring smiling young people in and near a jeep, holding hamburgers. The captions explain why these young people seem to be having such a good time: "The best tasting Burger that ever filled a bun."

A maximum of three minutes elapses from the time the customer enters the restaurant, decides what to order, and leaves the counter with the meal.[3] During busy times, when each cash register is staffed by both a counter hostess and an "expeditor" who helps the cashier by collecting the orders, it is not uncommon for the meal to be ready for the customer before she has had a chance to pay for it and receive her change. Quickness of service is known as SOS (speed of service), and is stressed as one of the most important elements in restaurant profitability. . . .

Eating at Burger King is referred to by the company as a "dining experience." It is constantly stressed how important it is that the restaurant be a pleasant place so that customers will want to return. A sign in the crew room downstairs framed and enclosed in glass reminds employees of this:

Why Customers Quit

- 1 % die
- 2% move away
- 5% develop other friendships
- 9% competitive reasons
- 14% product dissatisfactions
- 68% quit because of *attitude of indifference towards customer by restaurant management or service personnel*

"Counter hostesses" or cashiers are impressed with the importance of making the market setting resemble as much as possible life outside the cash nexus. Customers are called "guests" and doing a good job means not just serving them the food they ordered but making them "happy." Employees are told, "Your job is a sort of social occasion. You meet people—you want these people to like you, to like visiting your restaurant." The first and last duty of the counter person is to make the customer feel that they are not just paying cash for a service but that they are genuinely welcomed. . . .

RECRUITING WORKERS AT BURGER KING

Finding new workers is a perennial problem in the fast food industry. "Kids today just don't want to work," said one manager in his early twenties who was wearied by the constant search for new workers. The front-page headline for a May 1989 issue of *Restaurant News* is the same as forty years previously—"The Labor Crisis." The industry is on the lookout for creative solutions to this crisis—hiring retirees, the handicapped, and in the United States, visible minorities. One Burger King in Michigan is helping with day care—paying $1.50 an hour to local day care providers for employees with young children.[4]

The need for workers is constant enough so that even the paper placemats on each tray are sometimes used to recruit workers. Invitations to become part of the "Burger King family" are offered: "If you're enthusiastic and like to learn, this is the opportunity for you. Just complete the application and return it to the counter." The application form is on the right-hand side of the placemat.

In the fall, when there had been unusually high turnover because of the beginning of school, a sign placed in the Briarwood crew room asked,

---

Wanna make $20?

It's easy! All you have to do is refer a friend to me for employment. Your friend must be able to work over lunch (Monday-Friday). If your friend works here for at least one month, you get $20.

Availability is the most important criterion for being hired by Burger King. Second to availability is something called "good attitude." The head manager defined this as displaying an eagerness to work, enjoyment of the work, and appearance. "Some people," Helen, the assistant manager, informed me, "are turned down because they are overqualified, or want too much money. Sometimes they want too many hours, and we just can't give it to them."

Burger King successfully uses young people in its advertisements. Handsome, wholesome smiling teenagers are pictured serving food that we are all encouraged to buy. I assumed that there were particular reasons for finding teenagers desirable workers. However, what I found was the industry's capacity for making a virtue out of necessity. When teenagers are in plentiful supply then their youthful, healthy appearance can be used to market the product as well as serve it. The main concern is with finding a labour force that is plentiful and will work for minimum wage. Linda, the head manager of the store I worked in, professed a preference for the adult women workers. They were thought to be steadier, and more reliable. "They come in. They have a certain pride in the job. They like things to run smoothly and well, whereas the part-timers don't care as much. They are young kids, and they keep a job maybe three to eight months."

Nevertheless, she would never station older workers at the cash register when younger ones were available. "Our customers expect a certain image, and the older people wouldn't look right," she explained. She used "older" as a term relative to the high school students. These women were not teenagers, but many of them were still in their twenties and thirties. All managers agreed that for Burger King's requirements, teenagers are the most available labour force at the lowest cost.

The industry is increasingly looking to much older workers, people of retirement age, as the supply of young people seems to be running out. There are fewer young people in the population and more job opportunities available to them. At the time I worked in the store, Burger King head office personnel in Miami were interested in hiring retirees, because of the high percentage of older people in that area. Now, this trend has come to Canada. McDonald's has a program called "McMasters" — geared toward hiring retirement age workers. Burger King too advertised for older workers at a job fair for seniors in Toronto and also has an arrangement with a school for the retarded to hire workers with special needs.

Fast food has also been a place where new immigrants with limited command of English can find jobs. Some of the most reliable workers at the Burger King in which I worked were young people newly arrived in Canada. Most of the workers in the second Burger King I worked in briefly years later spoke Spanish.

Just as Burger King's hiring criteria have to do with availability rather than the job itself, people take jobs at Burger King because it fits in with their other obligations. For young people, the reasons are straightforward. The only kind of work they can do is outside school hours. For many, it is a first and they start work feeling excited to be holding down a job. One young fifteen-year-old said, "it's prestigious to be working." The work at Burger King is for many young people the best of the limited alternatives available. It pays better than babysitting. The hours (although inconvenient) are preferable to those of a paper route and the work is less isolating than a job in a donut shop or a convenience store. There is a larger workforce of young people at Burger King, and thus more socializing than at most alternative work sites.

There are special difficulties to contend with in relying on a teenage labour force. Manager, acting in Burger King's interests, often find they must deal with parents who are acting in their children's interest. Interfering parents plagued the head manager.

> We have a lot of interfering parents now. When kids are hired, they are read the riot act with respect to being available for closings. (This means staying till 12 on weekdays, or 1 on weekends.) Then mothers call to complain. They call head office, the labour board.

> If they are responsible enough to have a job, they have to do the hours too. There is a communication problem between the kids and their parents.

We get the silliest calls. I got one this afternoon from Karen's mother saying she was up late last night and couldn't work tonight's shift. What does one have to do with the other? She didn't even go to school today. She had exams for one hour. Or Joanne, who's quitting because school is ending in two months and she has to stop work because of her marks. It's more likely too many late nights with her boyfriend.

The women with families who worked in the daytime also took the job for reasons that had little to do with the actual work. As one woman put it, "It was a job, and it was steady, and it was close. I could ride my bike to work. They were actually fairly good with me about the hours they would give me." Another woman explained, "With this job, I could be home when the kids returned from school. Babysitting is so expensive that it really doesn't pay to get a full-time job."

Adult women need the money but are restricted to jobs that still allow them to meet their family obligations. One pregnant worker was hoping to hold on to her job long enough so that she could afford a crib, carriage, and playpen for her new baby. The younger daytime workers are unskilled, school dropouts. One young girl said, "This is the only job I can do."

Thus people take jobs at Burger King for a number of reasons. Jobs are hard to come by, particularly for those people with limited skills and training; they don't have many options. Pressures from other spheres of life restrict students and women with families to certain kinds of jobs. While these other obligations make work at Burger King one of the few options they have, they also serve to limit Burger King's power over them. The job at Burger King does not encroach too much on their responsibilities to their families or their schoolwork. . . .

A PROFILE OF THE WORKERS

o

During the day, the Briarwood Burger King was staffed by "full timers" or employees who worked a few hours every day. There were, on average, twenty-five such workers during the time I was there. (As the workforce was shifting constantly, I must rely on averages.) Most of these workers were women. Approximately one half of them were married. While most had limited education, a few had completed high school and some had even acquired some additional training. One woman had a nursing degree, another was a college graduate, and a third had started training for nursing. Other daytime workers were women under eighteen years of age who had not completed high school. Only one or two young men worked during the day. One was a high school graduate who couldn't find a better job, while the other had dropped out of school in grade nine to help support his family.

In my restaurant, most of the daytime workers were white. Some of them were new Canadians. One of the most efficient workers in the kitchen was a young woman named Lydia who had recently emigrated from Hong

Kong with her parents. When she first started working she knew very little English, but learned her job quickly. She was hoping that she would soon begin school part time. Her family could not afford for her to go full time.

At the beginning of the fieldwork, approximately half of the daytime workers were working more than four-hour shifts. Four worked an eight-hour shift almost every day. These daytime workers, particularly the married women, worked for a variety of reasons. Most of them needed the money badly to help make ends meet. Helen, the assistant manager, and I discussed the impact of a new scheduling system that would do away with any shifts longer than four hours. Her comments were as follows:

> Julie is saving up for a fancy wedding, she will be fine. However, Sylvia's a single parent, and is badly off financially, Jeanette's on welfare. Darlene lives at home, but her father's sick. Ginnie has saved up and is moving out on her own. She'll be paying almost as much for a month's rent on an apartment as she makes at Burger King. Judith's husband works for a company that is not doing very well and he keeps getting laid off. She has two school-age children, and has been trying to supplement her Burger King hours with another job on Saturdays.[5]

Judith was later promoted to swing manager, and worked all night long till 6 AM. She had two children to look after in the day. As it turned out, she was pregnant at the time. Her baby was born prematurely, and weighed less than two pounds. Ida, another worker, miscarried just after a long weekend of hard work in the restaurant. She felt that the arduous work on her feet at Burger King had contributed to losing her baby. Both of these women needed to work to pay the rent.

Some of the younger daytime workers also had difficult lives. Ann was a few months short of sixteen and had left home because she said her mother pretended to be an invalid to get her to stay away from school and look after her. She was staying with a friend's parents, and wanted to live with her grandmother and return to school. Cathy, who was fifteen, lived in a foster home. She soon left Burger King to attend hairdressing school. Two Portuguese–Canadian sisters, who were fifteen and sixteen, had both said they were one year older than they were because they were afraid Burger King wouldn't hire a fifteen-year-old. Their father, a restaurant manager, had lost a lot of money. The two girls had dropped out of school to work, and their mother had also found a job. Their father was currently waiting on tables.

Despite the difficult circumstances of their lives, and the pressure to earn money, a number of women said that they liked coming to work. One woman who worked three-hour shifts said that it was a nice break in the day and she was grateful to pick up a bit of extra money. Another said, "At least when I come here, I'm recognized. If I do a good job, a manager will say something to me. Here I feel like a person. I'm sociable and I like being among people. At home I'm always cleaning up after everybody and nobody ever notices." Another woman explained that she felt very depressed at home, and would complain if there was anything she had to do. She enjoyed working. "I go home, and I come here. It's not just the money because the money is not enough. It's like living in two worlds."

When the full complement of staff was on the payroll, about seventy-five workers were hired for evening and weekend work. They were called "part-timers." The average age of these workers was about sixteen and they were more varied in sex, racial backgrounds, and socioeconomic circumstances. About half of this group was male, about one-fourth of the workers were black, and there were a number of youngsters of Portuguese, Italian, and East European descent.[6]

A number of the black youngsters in my Burger King store were college bound; three brothers originally from Jamaica and another brother and sister who subsequently found better jobs elsewhere all expected to go on beyond high school. Most of the other youngsters were just expecting to finish high school, and maybe enter a training course in a community college. Seventeen-year-old Eileen, one of a pair of Scottish sisters, was one of the few workers in Burger King who expressed an interest in pursuing a career with Burger King. She wanted to enter management.

The workers at Briarwood came from varying economic circumstances. Some of the high school students had parents who were quite well off and had encouraged their children to work, hoping they would develop a good work ethic. One head manager thought that class background did not make much of a difference in the ability to recruit and hold on to workers. From his experience at Burger King he felt that while a youngster is in school, she or he did not feel much pressure to stay at a job they did not like, even if the parents were not well off. They would just quit. On the other hand, the *Nation's Restaurant News* reported bussing inner city teenagers to staff fast food outlets in wealthy suburban locations. Presumably, some restaurant managers have found that economic background is relevant in recruiting workers.[7]

QUALITY, SERVICE, AND FRIENDLINESS

○

When workers take a job at Burger King, they are asked to place their responsibilities to Burger King above everything else in their lives: school, family, friends. They are expected to come to work with little advance notice, at irregular hours, and to work as hard as possible for Burger King and Burger King's customers. They are to obey whatever manager happens to be ordering them about, and not make a fuss if they are told to do two contradictory things at once. In contrast, customers are offered consistency and convenience. They and their children will be cared for at Burger King by contented workers.

In *The Cultural Contradictions of Capitalism,* Daniel Bell identifies this phenomenon as a contradiction of values between the ethics of consumption and those of work. In Burger King, the quality of self-discipline required of workers is directly in opposition to the appeal to self-indulgence with which the potential consumer is lured to the store.

Burger King, like all fast food chains, runs on the principles first pioneered by McDonald's: QSC, standing for Quality, Service, and Cleanliness. Quality is defined as standardization and predictability; service is defined as speed; and cleanliness is valued not as a means for ensuring healthfulness, but for its associations with order, which can help promote sales.

The standardization of food is presented as a virtue: the customer knows what she is going to get. However, Burger King's product is not all that different from what can be found at any other hamburger chain. Therefore the selling of the meal, the service part of the business, is crucial. Friendly, fast service in pleasant surroundings will provide the incentive to return that the food cannot. Each Burger King customer, child or adult, is treated as a separate individual. Unlike the situation in a Chinese restaurant where the casserole is shared, or in a family-run Italian restaurant where a whole family digs into one pizza, each fast food customer is given her own burger.

The emphasis on cleanliness has a double function for the restaurant. First, it keeps the customers coming in. Second, since workers are told to use any free time for cleaning, it is used to reinforce the message that workers owe full use of their labour time to their employer. Like the friendliness of the crew, cleanliness is used as a promotion for the store. The image to be conveyed is that Burger King "cares," perhaps to make up for so many other aspects of peoples' lives that are cold and indifferent.

In training workers, management must ensure that the informal work relationships are pleasant enough so that a friendly atmosphere will be created for the customer. They must also make it clear that working at Burger King is different from being a customer. Their task is a difficult one, because the teenagers and the women who work at Burger King are, in fact, both the market and the labour force for the store. Managers know that an important part of the job is to keep the crew smiling, but they must also make sure that workers don't have too good a time.

NOTES

○

1. Theodore Levitt, "Production-line Approach to Service," *Harvard Business Review* 50, no. 5 (1972): 46.

2. Karl Marx, *Communist Manifesto* [originally published in 1848].

3. Service time has been reduced to two and one-half minutes since I did my field-work.

4. *National Restaurant News,* (NRN) 22 May 1989, F48.

5. Personal communication, February 1982. The name of the store manager has been changed.

6. It was more difficult to get to know the "part-timers." There were more of them, and because of the ad hoc scheduling system, I seldom worked with the same group.

7. *NRN,* 22 May 1989, F32.

Balancing Work and Family Responsibilities*

*Judith MacBride-King
and Hélène Paris*

Major changes in the composition of the workforce coupled with changes in societal expectations regarding work and family pose fundamental challenges to Canadian organizations. More women are working outside the home for pay. There are more dual-earner families and more single-parent families in Canada than ever before. The labour force has changed; attitudes have changed.

Dana Friedman, an expert on work and family issues in the United States, has written that "demography is destiny". These words have a distinct ring of truth. Changes in the demographic face of Canada not only reflect the realities of individuals as they live out their lives, but also have major implications for employers and policy makers today and in the future.

DEMOGRAPHY IN MOTION: OUR CHANGING POPULATION

○

Since the post-war baby boom, Canada's population growth rate has steadily declined. The average annual rate of population growth fell gradually from a high of about 3 per cent in the 1950's to less than 1 per cent in 1986.[1]

In recent years, an important contributor in the slowdown of population growth has been the decline in immigration. However, a major factor has

---

* Abridged from Judith MacBride-King and Hélène Paris, "Balancing Work and Family Responsibilities," *Canadian Business Review* 16, no. 3 (Autumn 1989): 17–21. Reprinted by permission of the publisher and the author.

been the steady decline in Canada's birth rate. In the 1950's, the number of births per 1,000 Canadians was 28. By 1985, this had fallen to 15 per 1,000.

Fertility rates have also been decreasing. In 1960, Canadian women had an average of 3.9 children and by 1986, that figure had dropped to 1.7.

As a result of low fertility rates, the population of Canada is ageing. In 1986, seniors (those aged 65 years and older) represented about 10 per cent of our population. It is estimated that by 2011, this group will account for almost 16 per cent of the population, and by the year 2036 will represent almost 25 per cent.

Another important demographic change is the increasing number of Canadians seeking divorce. In 1968, when the Divorce Act was proclaimed, 11,343 divorces were granted: by 1985, the number had increased to 61,980.

Higher divorce rates have contributed to a rise in the number of single-parent families in Canada. In 1971, 11.3 per cent of all families in private households were headed by single parents. By 1986, this number had climbed to 12.7 per cent. Although there has been an increase in the number of male-headed single-parent families, the overwhelming majority (82.2 per cent) of single parents are women.

THE CANADIAN LABOUR FORCE

o

These demographic trends have had a substantial impact on the labour force. There is no question that the most significant change in the composition of the labour force over the past few years has been the dramatic increase in the participation of women. In 1951, only 23.5 per cent of Canadian women participated in the labour force. By 1987, this figure had grown to 56.2 per cent, and The Conference Board of Canada predicts that it will reach 63.1 per cent by 1993.

Furthermore, increasing numbers of women have chosen to remain in the labour force after marriage or the birth of their children. In 1971, 37.0 per cent of married women participated in the labour force. This figure had risen to 57.4 per cent by 1987. In 1975, 41.6 per cent of women with children under 16 years of age worked outside the home. This figure climbed to 56.8 per cent in 1983. The participation rate of married women with children under 6 years of age has taken an even more dramatic leap—from 49.4 per cent in 1981 to 62.1 per cent in 1986.

The effect of women's increased participation has been a rise in the number of dual-earner families in Canada. In 1961, only 20 per cent of all two-parent families reported that both spouses worked outside the home. By 1981, this had increased to almost 40 per cent. In 1986, the census revealed that more than half (53 per cent) of husband-and-wife families were dual-earner.

High levels of divorce have contributed to an increase in the number of single-parent families in the labour force. In 1984, there were 163,000 more single parents in the labour force than there had been just seven years earlier in 1977. By 1986, 61.2 per cent of single parents participated in the labour force.

A T T I T U D I N A L   C H A N G E S
o

In addition to demographic changes, there has been a marked shift in the attitudes of Canadians toward their work and their employers. As well, there has been a redefinition of what constitutes appropriate roles for men and women both at home and in the workplace. Many women today are unwilling or unable, financially, to forego their jobs or careers for homemaking responsibilities. Many men are taking a larger role in the care and nurturing of their children. Increasingly, when given a choice between more involvement with a career or more involvement with their families, more men choose the family.

Consequently, men are being called upon to provide more support at home. Clearly, the "organization man" is being replaced by women and men with new sets of values.

In recent years, many organizations have downsized, and in some firms whole layers of the organizational hierarchy have been removed. This has created insecurity, and a situation where employees can no longer assume that they are "lifers" in their organizations. With fewer opportunities to advance and faced with plateauing, some employees are reacting by shifting their career goals to family and leisure activities. A Conference Board of Canada study found that in 1985, 35 per cent of employed Canadians in the 25 to 44 year-old age group would forego some of their salary for more time off. Of those who preferred to work fewer hours, 42 per cent of the women and 20 per cent of the men cited personal and family responsibilities as the main reason.

I M P L I C A T I O N S   F O R   C A N A D I A N   O R G A N I Z A T I O N S
o

These demographic, social and attitudinal changes have important implications for Canadian organizations. Trade barriers are being removed and companies are manoeuvring to gain from increased trade with the United States, with the integrated European market, and with Pacific Rim countries. At the same time, the pool of workers that employers traditionally had relied upon has changed dramatically. For many years employers had the pick of a very large crop of mostly male employees. Today, employers are competing for fewer skilled employees and many of these employees increasingly are women.

As women continue to have fewer children or decide not to have children at all, these trends are the harbingers of labour shortages in the future. Labour shortages already exist, particularly in Central Canada and in the hospitality and service industries and in health care.

Those companies that respond to and anticipate changes in the workforce will gain a competitive advantage in the marketplace of the 1990's. Today's successful organization places a premium on attracting, retaining and motivating qualified staff.

RESEARCHING WORK AND FAMILY

o

In order to gain a better understanding of the impact of these demographic and social changes on Canadian organizations and their employees, The Conference Board of Canada embarked on a major research program to explore work-family dynamics. During 1988 and 1989, the Conference Board surveyed 1,600 organizations and over 11,000 public- and private-sector employees. The Conference Board's research explores how Canadians cope with balancing their responsibilities at home and at work, and examines the Canadian corporate response to workers with family responsibilities.

SURVEY OF CANADIAN EMPLOYEES

o

The Conference Board of Canada's survey of employees was designed to examine the changing family and to explore the extent to which family responsibilities affect persons at work both in terms of their own well-being and in terms of their advancement opportunities within their jobs or organizations. Of central importance to this research was the relationship between employees' responsibilities outside of work and their performance at work, as well as the relationship between the difficulties in balancing work and home and employee absenteeism.

Employee Stress

Preliminary data indicate that 66 per cent of the surveyed employees have experienced at least some degree of difficulty balancing their responsibilities at work and at home. For 20 per cent of employees, juggling various demands is "very difficult" or "difficult" to accomplish.

Almost 80 per cent of those surveyed reported experiencing some degree of stress or anxiety as a result of attempting to cope with conflicting demands. Over 25 per cent indicated experiencing "a lot" to a "moderate degree" of stress.

Employee Absenteeism

The productivity and efficiency of organizations can be affected when employees are absent from work or when employees spend time at work dealing with family matters. Almost half of the employees surveyed indicated that they had experienced interruptions in their work or that their workload had increased because colleagues were absent from work due to family responsibilities.

Respondents reported that they missed an average of 3.0 full days and 1.5 part days during the six-month period prior to the survey. They were late for work and left work early on almost two occasions each. Many of those who missed work gave family responsibilities as the reason for their absence. Over a six-month period, respondents missed an average of 1.0 full day and 1.5 partial days of work for family reasons. In addition, they were late 2.0 times and left work early an average of 1.6 times in order to deal with family matters.

Results from the Conference Board's survey suggest a strong link between the level of employees' difficulties in balancing work and family, the associated stresses, and average rate of absenteeism. For example, those employees who reported it was "very difficult" to juggle their various demands missed an average of 4.5 full days from work, whereas those reporting no difficulty missed only 2.5 days. A similar relationship was found between reported stress levels and absenteeism. Those indicating that they experienced "a lot" of stress missed an average of 4.9 days during the six-month period prior to the survey, whereas those reporting no stress missed 2.5 days.

Retention and Turnover

Over 10 per cent of those surveyed reported that they had left a position or job in the past because of work and family conflicts, and over 14 per cent said they were considering leaving their current employers for these reasons.

Organizational efficiency can be affected when employees refuse transfer or promotional opportunities. Organizations rely on transfers as a means to enhance corporate effectiveness, and relocations and transfers have traditionally been seen as cost-efficient methods of deploying resources for increased productivity. Consequently, an employee's refusal to move may have a detrimental effect on the organization.

In the Conference Board's survey, slightly over 17 per cent of employees who had been offered promotions reported having turned them down for family reasons, and almost 25 per cent had refused transfer opportunities.

Advancement Opportunities

Slightly over 30 per cent of the respondents perceived that their child care or "other" dependant care responsibilities have in some way limited their opportunities for advancement in their jobs or organizations. Respondents indicated that their home obligations created situations where they were unable (without considerable difficulty) to put in extra time at work or to relocate or transfer when required.

The survey shows that some employees (7 per cent) have reduced their work time or changed from full-time to part-time work in order to better accommodate their family's needs. In addition, although over one-half of the respondents indicated their willingness to work longer hours in order to advance in their organizations, 51.7 per cent said that their responsibilities at home made it difficult.

Who's Responsible?

The survey also asked employees who they thought had the most responsibility for finding solutions to work and family conflicts—employees themselves, employers, governments or unions.

The majority of employees believed that dependant care issues were primarily an individual responsibility, and 44 per cent said they were satisfied that their employers were doing "enough" in this area. However, almost one-third indicated that they would like to see their employers more involved, and a considerable number looked for increased government involvement in work and family issues. Respondents were less likely to seek direct assistance from their unions but rather saw their unions as playing an advocate role.

Employer-provided on-site child care facilities or employer-subsidized child care were at the top of the list for those employees who sought further involvement from their employer. In addition, respondents indicated that some form of personal or family-related leave would assist them in meeting their various demands. Many employees simply requested more understanding from their employers and looked for more flexibility in their everyday working lives.

Bottom-line Concerns

As the survey results indicate, the difficulties faced by individual employees in managing their personal and work lives can result in reduced performance caused by stress, increased absenteeism, high turnover, a lack of available employees for full-time work, and inequities in workloads. As all of these factors contribute to efficiency and productivity, the survey findings suggest that work and family conflicts can have an impact on the bottom line of an organization.

For instance, a recent survey of U.S. companies revealed an average annual turnover rate of 12 per cent. The authors of the study estimate that in an organization of 500 employees, this translates into a cost of U.S. $600,000 per year. In addition, the Warner-Lambert Company in the United States has estimated the costs of absences and tardiness due to child care and dependant care needs at $250,000 a year in one location alone.

In response to the changes in society and the desire to attract and retain qualified employees, some organizations have developed a variety of policies and benefits for workers with family responsibilities.

Child care benefits, flexible work schedules, family-related leave, and counselling and referral services are some of the programs that companies are using today to assist their employees which, in turn, benefit the organization.

SURVEY OF CANADIAN ORGANIZATIONS

o

In order to explore the prevalence of family-supportive programs in Canadian organizations, The Conference Board of Canada undertook a major survey.

In terms of the more visible form of program or benefit, employers in the Conference Board's survey tended to opt for information or referral programs for parents or for "caregivers" (those who provide care to an elderly, disabled or infirm family member).

The most frequently mentioned forms of employer support for employees with children were child care information and referral services (8.4 per cent), assistance to employees with sick children (7.8 per cent), child care centres—either on-site or support for child care centres (4.8 per cent), and parent education seminars (4.6 per cent). In addition, a small number of companies in the Board's survey were considering the future implementation of some form of support for working parents.

Some organizations have responded to the needs of employees who provide care or assistance to elderly or infirm family members. Six per cent of the surveyed companies have elder care information and referral programs, and 2 per cent provide some form of assistance to employees whose elderly relatives either live at home or who are institutionalized.

Organizations surveyed also offer assistance to employees who provide care to disabled relatives. Again, the support offered primarily took the form of information regarding the care of persons with special needs. Ten per cent offered such support.

A significant number of employers offer a variety of services to employees through Employee Assistance Programs (EAPs), and many also extend at least some of the services to the families of employees.

Chief among the types of supports offered to employees through their Employee Assistance Programs were counselling for alcohol and drug abuse, retirement counselling, financial counselling, and physical fitness programs. In addition, and important from the work and family perspective, some companies offer employees counselling for marital or stress-related problems.

Programs most often available to the family members of employees consisted of retirement counselling, financial counselling and assistance regarding alcoholism and drug abuse.

In those companies that offer relocation assistance, the most common service was real estate services (62 per cent). A small proportion (16 per cent) offer employment placement for spouses of transferred employees.

Another way in which organizations have responded is by implementing various alternative working arrangements and leaves for workers with family responsibilities.

Almost half of the employers surveyed indicated that they have instituted flexible working hours in their organizations. Almost 30 per cent offered the option of part-time work with prorated benefits. Over 25 per cent have compressed workweek schedules, and almost 20 per cent offered some employees the option of job sharing. In addition, 11 per cent of the companies have implemented work-at-home arrangements.

With respect to leaves or time off for family or personal reasons, over half of the employers reported that their organizations have some form of family-related leave. Almost 50 per cent indicated they permit employees to use their personal sick leave for family reasons, and slighty over 8 per cent offer "other parental leave" (i.e., child nurturing leave).

With respect to parental leaves, the Board's survey found that 50 per cent of the organizations offer mothers extended maternity leaves, and 25 per cent, prematernity leaves. Almost 37 per cent of the respondents offer an adoption leave and 17 per cent offer fathers time off upon the birth of a child.

Although there were some deviations from the pattern, the survey revealed that the larger, more affluent organizations or public-sector organizations were more likely to offer the various benefits, leaves and alternative working arrangements noted above.

Most organizations reported that family-responsive programs have been effective in assisting them in managing their human resources more effectively. That is, generally the majority of those employers who offered child care supports, alternative working arrangements, and a variety of leaves perceived them to be particularly effective tools in the recruitment and retention of employees, in reducing employee stress, in maintaining employee morale, and in reducing the rates of absenteeism in their organizations. These organizations perceived clear advantages in these programs.

FUTURE PROSPECTS

o

The Conference Board of Canada's survey of organizations suggests that employers who are aware of the need for family-related benefits and working arrangements, and those who do believe that they have a role to play in work-family dynamics, are more likely to introduce family-responsive supports in their organizations.

The future implementation of family-related benefits and supports will be in large part contingent upon companies' assessments of three factors: their employees' needs; the cost associated with these supports; and the impact of these supports on such human resource areas as recruitment, retention and productivity. However, there is much debate about whether the effects of family-related supports on organizational effectiveness can, in fact, be quantified.

Clearly, the demographic profile of Canada is changing—there has been a dramatic increase in women in the labour force, employee attitudes toward work and leisure are shifting, and employers are faced with current and projected labour shortages. To remain competitive, organizations need to acknowledge all these changes. The implementation of family-related benefits is one way to do this.

NOTE

o

1. The demographic data in this article were obtained from the following sources:

    Canada's Population from Ocean to Ocean, Catalogue no. 98-120 (Ottawa: Statistics Canada, January 1989).

    Current Demographic Analysis: Report on the Demographic Situation in Canada 1986, Catalogue no. 91-209 (Ottawa: Statistics Canada, May 1987).

    Sandi Orlik, *Handbook of Canadian Consumer Markets,* 4th edition (Ottawa: The Conference Board of Canada, 1989).

    National Economic Forecast (Ottawa: The Conference Board of Canada, Spring 1989).

    The Nation: Labour Force Activity, Catalogue no. 93-111 (Ottawa: Statistics Canada, March 1989).

    The Nation: Families: Part 2, Catalogue no. 93-107 (Ottawa: Statistics Canada, March 1989).

    Women in Canada: A Statistical Report, Catalogue no. 89-503 (Ottawa: Statistics Canada, March 1985).

    Workers With Family Responsibilities in a Changing Society: Who Cares? (Ottawa: Canada Employment and Immigration Advisory Council, June 1987).

Coping with Unemployment Over Time[*]

Patrick Burman

Any generalizations about the temporal patterning of the self's experience throughout the jobless spell are risky because of the latter's sheer variety. The literature suggests that the first stage is often shock and immobilization. Shortly thereafter, there may be some optimism and minimization of the problem, as the person defines the inactivity as a kind of holiday. Then, as the months draw on with no success finding a job, there is a second broad stage characterized by emotional turmoil, depression, and withdrawal. Here the belief that "things will be all right" is undermined and one's identity comes under strain. With prolonged unemployment, a third stage emerges, involving the scaling down or readjustment of hopes. The individual starts to accept the fact that the standards of the employed past are not going to be reliable basis for evaluating achievements in the present. There is less active distress at this stage, with the emotional trajectory slightly rising and stabilizing.

Our treatment here will look at the *initial reaction* to the termination of employment, and then the *later phases* of the lengthening unemployment spell. The pivotal figure is the unemployed self, and how the generally changed social identity following job loss affects *personal* identity.

INITIAL REACTION
o

Of the 41 "job losers" in my sample, 10 informants expressed shock when their employment was terminated. NORMA, 24, had been working for five

[*] Abridged from Patrick Burman, *Killing Time, Losing Ground: Experiences of Unemployment* (Toronto: Wall & Thompson, 1988), chapter 10, "The Self." Reprinted by permission of the publisher and the author.

months as a bus driver at the London Transit. Late one night, in an act of horseplay, she had climbed through the window of her parked bus into the bus driven by a friend of hers which had pulled up alongside. A passenger spotted it and reported her. After being asked for an explanation by management, she was fired three days later. She was in her fifth month of a six-month probationary period within which management could dismiss employees more easily. At a time when women L.T.C. bus drivers formed only 1% of its work-force, NORMA was thinking of challenging the dismissal on grounds of sexual discrimination. Similar horseplay by men—she knew a man who drove occasionally with his foot out of the window—had resulted in only a fine or suspension.

When asked how she felt at the time: *"I was in shock, I couldn't believe it.... He asked, 'Do you have anything to say for yourself? and I said 'No'. Like, I couldn't believe what happened.... I went out of there laughing."* She went over to some other drivers and told them and they laughed, hardly believing anything so ridiculous. *"But the day after, it hit me. And I was crying like anything."* She staying inside away from her friends, and had little motivation to look for a job. The only thing she had ever wanted to do was drive a bus.

BERNARD, waiting for a good job which would let him fly his fiancée to Canada to begin their family was laid off from his labourer's job at a tree farm. *"I was so set back.... I kept in bed, slept the whole day. Then watched television through the night....I got into serious drinking, trying to drown my problems."* A similar reaction was expressed by LORNE, fired from a dishwashing job: *"I didn't want to be talked to, didn't want to be seen.... It's like I lost my best friend."* He had been called on the phone by the employer and told not to bother to come in that day, that his work had been too slow. *"I was in shock; I didn't say anything, just OK."*

Being suddenly banished from a familiar environment left the self feeling wounded and out of place. MONICA had been given a poor evaluation as a receptionist by a supervisor who allegedly did not know her work, which had been praised by others who did. The oral report of the evaluation was made to her in about four minutes:

> She told me everything on it [the three-page evaluation] *in about four seconds flat. Her mouth was going a mile a minute. She gave an evaluation. And I remember being so shaken up by it that I couldn't talk....*
>
> And then she said "Do you have any questions?" *Well, I couldn't speak.... I was so shocked. And then she said, OK, then, that's it." And she stood up to walk out, and I felt like saying "Don't open the door." Because I was crying, and there were all counsellors outside.... Like, we were in there a good four minutes. That was the evaluation, four minutes. Rather a rushed thing, because she had other things to do. As if my job.... It was my job that was on the line. And then, she had left.*

She sat there and took some deep breaths. Others had gone into a meeting and she was supposed to answer the phones. *"I was so upset that I couldn't work anymore, I couldn't think. If the phone rang, I didn't even know it was the phone. You know, all I could think about was my child.... You know, I had done this for two years. It was my routine, and I enjoyed it. I enjoyed the students."* While the counsellors were in a meeting, she sat typing, not really knowing what she was doing. Yet she must have looked stricken, because when a couple asked where a room was, they took one look at her face, apologized and left.

The worker, as a factor in the productive process, worked. But the worker's *self* on the job wanted to do more than work. It wanted to "appropriate" the job into its identity-formation, to use it as a vehicle for communicative and craftlike purposes. So offices, machines, and work areas, while nominally owned by the company, were often felt by the workers to be their own personal possessions and territories—a kind of ownership-by-involvement. Being laid off, then, for some, was to be deported from a fellowship and a personal territory. Not surprisingly, a few of the informants compared being laid off to losing a best friend.

WARREN's last job, sponsored by the Welfare Department, had been with a demolition company. Every dollar earned was a dollar taken off benefits. Thought the work was dirty, involving cleaning and wrecking, and the pay insufficient, WARREN valued it:

> *Dirty, tough, but I tell you, I felt a hell of a lot good. I came home, I could sleep good at night, the wife and I got along really great,... We had a little bit of money to go out, wasn't much, maybe she'd go to Bingo, I'd go to a movie...and we had a little bit of money to spend for the kids.*

With every expectation of continued employment, WARREN was quietly handed an envelope containing holiday and severance pay; the boss had not said a word. He described his reaction as *"nauseous,"* as though someone had dropped a twenty-pound weight on his stomach.

> *I just kinda felt like, like there was a void in your stomach.... Like, wow, you had work and all of a sudden, it's not there. Like a friend, you know, like a real close friend, and he moves away and you feel, wow man, that's gone.*

Back in the home, he was fighting with his wife again. While employed, his marriage had been *"great"*; now, *"we just live, that's it."*

The initial phase of shock experienced in a sudden layoff was not undergone by all the job losers in the sample. Some experienced anger, some saw the layoff coming and were resigned to it. Another reaction, reported by about seven informants, was a feeling of *relief* at having been set free from the previous job. In a few cases, the job had involved working nights, which disrupted normal family routines. SIMON, fired from his job, felt that the night work was dead-end and poorly paid anyway. BRENDA, a waitress at a donut shop, quit, partly because she was required to work at night and partly because of the refusal of the boss to put her on full-time rotation. For a time she briefly experienced that sense of being on a holiday (*"I was having a ball"*) which was sometimes associated with the early phase of unemployment. But now, jobless and on Mother's Allowance for a year, she was bored and restless and wanted full-time employment.

Some people reported being glad to be free of the constraining aspects of the job. FRAN quit her job as office manager and secretary-receptionist at an office rental agency. She had become dissatisfied: the original owners were not involved anymore, there was too much pressure, and she wanted to do less typing and more headwork. While upset at quitting, she quickly felt much better at the widening of options. She did some job searching, then went back to school, and was using her intelligence more actively. Knowing that she did not have to stay where she was excited her. She was not as tired as when working and had a more energetic and pleasant social life. She was on Unemployment benefits, and had the whole-hearted support of her family. (*"I'm very lucky."*)

If the job was hated, unemployment could come as a relief. Some of the younger men, supported by parents and their peer group, were glad they were not doing kitchen work. As HERB remarked:

Why should I have a job doing something I don't want to do? Because that would definitely lower self-esteem, as far as I'm concerned.... There's too many people working and all they do is complain about, "I hate my job." So why don't you quit, do something else?

In some cases, however, the relief could be short-lived. GAIL had stood up to an emotionally abusive boss who screamed at the top of his lungs for her to sit down as he prepared to tongue-lash her, unjustly in her view. She simply turned heel and left his office. That act gave her *"one half second of satisfaction and a lot of woe after."* She was relieved to be out from under his authority, but, as a 50-year-old divorcee living alone, with few prospects after five months of unemployment, she wondered about the wisdom of her act. Chain-smoking, anxious, she bitterly contemplated the high price she had paid for the exercise of her autonomy.

The comparisons between the "shocked" and the "relieved" were instructive. The "relieved" more often had quit their jobs, hence had controlled the timing and prepared emotionally for the event. Except for GAIL (above), the other "relieved" persons had some financial and social support, such as an employed spouse or a parental home and income to draw on. These people had options and resources.

By contrast, the "shocked" and immobilized were more likely to have been involuntarily deprived of paid employment, and thus lacked emotional preparedness or control over timing. Their job loss shattered their time frames rather than being integrated into them. More of them were unattached individuals, or single parents, possessing fewer resources of financial or social support. Four of the ten were from out of town, having extended kin in Exeter (60 miles away), other parts of Canada, the United States, and Kenya.

To sum up, those with financial and social (especially familial) support could choose a living situation which enabled them to pursue personal goals. People without such resources also lacked the accompanying free-doms—for them the job's enabling characteristics were desperately clung to. The job was more pivotal in their search for community, for self-esteem, and for an income. Being deprived of that job involuntarily, suddenly, was a profoundly threatening experience.

LATER   PHASES
o

The cross-sectional rather than longitudinal design of the study makes gen-eralizations about temporal effects on job search rather tentative. It may still be possible, however, to determine effects over time by grouping the sample into segments according to *duration of unemployment.* Were there significant differences in attitude and behaviour regarding job search among the vari-ous groupings?

My findings, as in the case of the initial impact of unemployment, partly corroborated and partly complicated the pattern sketched in the literature. For the long-term unemployed, there was considerable flattening of affect and morale, with resigned hopelessness replacing more active distress. In addition, new assumptions about one's relation to the environment and to the future appeared in seminal and developed form in the long-term unem-ployed. What was unexpected were the similarities which appeared across the board.

For those *unemployed three months or less,* there was some buoyancy expressed about the job search. BRENDA, with her small retarded child, was energized, even possessed, by the job search. It served as a welcome contrast to being in the home. For married TONY, the job search was, for now, a relaxed and self-fulfilling adventure. His wife supported him finan-cially and emotionally in his desire to find exactly what he wanted, and he had not yet been rejected that often. But in some of the accounts by those unemployed three months or less, there appeared a pessimism, a defeated-ness, an attitude of coasting—which were usually associated with more prolonged unemployed spells. What explained it? This "premature" sense of defeatism seemed to possess those who had experienced unemployment and the frustrations of the job search in the past, often more than once. Their past employment had been sporadic; as they began their latest job search their attitude was part dread and part resignation—"Here we go again."

In those *unemployed four to six months,* the theme of *"being dragged down,"* of experiencing a loss of enthusiasm and confidence, was more pronounced. There was still an alternation of emotional "highs" and "lows." But the "lows" were starting to have a cumulative, qualitative impact on the job search. This was expressed by SIMON, unemployed five months:

Every letter of rejection hurts in a sense, you know, it's one more disappointment, and [I] feel kind of, almost used to it,...like you kind of expect it, and so the next time I do a letter of application, I kind of feel, well, I'm just going through the process, I'm really not going to get the job.

The longer I'm without work, the more letters of rejection I get, the less likely I am to apply for the next job and the less confident I feel about it. And I'm sure that that colours the interview that I have, if I'm lucky enough to get an interview.

Over time the job search was becoming an empty ritual, devoid of meaning and personal implication. The self recoiled from it, partly out of protection, partly because, *as work*, repeated job-hunting offered no consummation, no result.

In the group *unemployed seven to twelve months*, we notice a number of patterns, some of which will appear in mature form in the long-term unemployed. One of them was *dread and anxiety* about the future, with an accompanying desperate sense that one must hold on. This was particularly evident among those in a disadvantaged market position, especially older women. The end of work seemed to bring home thoughts of one's mortality. GAIL talked of clinging to life: you simply could not allow yourself to die, or crawl into a shell. JOANNE had an almost paralyzing vision of her own contingency:

There are times when I am so scared that I'm not going to find a job, I think, "What the hell is wrong with me?" Even if I can't find a job in the field that I want, I can always work as a temp, and stay busy. My head knows this, OK?—but my guts go like that, and they just start wringing and I can get scared to death .... I'll have periods of insomnia. I'll get very short-tempered with my husband and with the children.

As she continued, notice how JOANNE's realistic anxiety about her market position veered into self-disparagement and a fear that her life would unravel: *"Sometimes I think there is something wrong with me. I ask myself, 'Why are you permitting this anxiety to come into your life?' And yet I seem powerless to stop it."*

As the job search lengthened, the sense of oneself as a worker—which is central to our social identity—tended to weaken. FRAN, unemployed for 10 months, remarked:

I don't think I've ever been unemployed as long before. So it's getting used to seeing yourself as unemployed too. Like you always looked at yourself as a worker.

One women said that one looked over the jobs on offer and began thinking, "I can't do that, I can't do that." People started settling for less, hence their talents came to be under-used even if they did find work. DEBBIE put it clearly:

I think you tend to have a defeatist attitude about yourself and about the kind of jobs you can do so you start looking for things that aren't as demanding. And also if you haven't been working, employers are less likely to hire you, if you haven't been involved with some kind of job.

"*At the beginning,*" commented BETH, "*I was feeling so good about myself that that was a lot easier.... Towards the end I was feeling like such a loser.... You portray this, it's written all over your face: 'Nobody wants me, please take me,' so that makes the communication and everything else.... You're almost begging for a job. That's humiliating.*"

In those *unemployed more than one year,* we see a kind of entrenched adjustment to unemployed conditions, both tender- and tough-minded. The "tender-minded" spoke in a resigned, muted tone when talking about the prospects of finding employment. Several could no longer believe that their unemployment would end. CONNIE, single, laid off from an advertising firm, had the attitude of "*Why bother, I'm not going to get it anyway.*" Her job-hunting had fallen off in frequency. She had also considered suicide. There was a suicidal hint in the words of AGNES, unemployed 27 months:

I'm terribly depressed. I wonder if there is anything ahead, or should I just depart? [Laughs] Really, you do get to that point. I mean there's absolutely nothing ahead for me. Remarriage—that would be the only thing that would do something for me right now. And there's not too many men my age that I could live with.... I think our whole system is in very big trouble. And I am just one of the victims.

All five informants who had hinted at suicidal intentions at one time or another were longer-term unemployed. MONICA talked of a phase when she did "*self-destructive things.*"

I'd be driving and I'd drive real fast and hope to hit a bridge or something. Then I'd say, "Come on! Your son's in the back seat."

The long-term unemployed were represented in all the categories of pathological behaviour. Of those informants who had explicitly mentioned depression as a problem, who had complained of anxiety, who had mentioned blaming self, who had admitted to excessive sleeping, who had had problems with drinking or desiring to drink as an escape—in all these distressed categories, those unemployed six months or more predominated.

Having so little leverage on their future, some long-term unemployed assumed religious postures. The question of whether they would find employment shifted to "Is there a role for me in the social order?" The responses to the question ranged from faith to agnosticism to plain existentialist waiting. MARTHA, when asked what advice she would give to a newly-unemployed person, replied: "*I guess in some cases religion. You've got to believe. A lot of people get strength from religion. I just think that better things are to come. There's got to be something out there for me.*" A few were skeptical that they will ever find decent work, adopting a certain resignation.

The *tough-minded* response was not to look to the future, but to live existentially. Faced with a future that seemed indeterminate and fateful, people relaxed their attempts to influence or anticipate it—in effect, lowering their expectations of life. Young PETER stated that he did not plan, but just looked *"forward to what might happen. I don't have specifics, but I just look forward to continued life."* GORD, unemployed for over two years, had given up the idea of a family. He had abandoned planning, figuring it would be a long haul which would not get any better, so he had best find a calm way of coping with it. The various expressions had a similar ring:

> *I take the day as it comes. No use planning because you don't got the money to plan with. (DICK)*

> *What's the sense in setting a time-table, because I'm not going anywhere. (MAT-THEW)*

> *I don't make plans. I just sit at home, waiting for a letter to arrive or a phone call that will have some good news, but it never seems to come. (ANDREW)*

COLLEEN, though not long-termed unemployed, has waited a long time for even the chance at a good job. She offered a sort of parody of planning. *"I sit down, have a cup of tea and my cigarette, and think about what I'm not going to do today."* The woman suggested, more seriously, that her life was lived within each day, not the longer time spans. *"You try to do something. Either go to the bank, make some kind of outing. Go to the store."* As the unemployment dragged out, people who used to plan veered to the opposite of the planned state and lived intuitively—as if spurning the future that had been taken from them: *"It comes and goes.... Whatever my mind swings to, I'll do that. No, I don't have any fixed periods of time."* (MATTHEW)

Some adjustments were more focused than others. NANCY, 28 and single, laid off as a sales representative, and unemployed for 18 months, was looking forward to a course for women in trades. She talked of the effect of her long-term unemployment as involving *"a total change of attitude.... Go with the flow."* She and one other long-term unemployed woman drew *radical* not quietest conclusions from this, however. Having tried so hard, taken the right courses, "paid her dues" and still not found work, she concluded that the fault was not hers and she must not blame herself. On the strength of this, she worked with the local Union of Unemployed Workers to help the unemployed to make their just claims on society. *"Go with the flow"* meant that the self should cease its lone struggle against a society which overburdened selves with undeserved blame, and join itself with forces that sought to change society.

Most were not so fortified, however. A few spoke of adjusting themselves to a new order, wherein high technology provides little full-time work. GORD felt that his underemployment was a harbinger of tough times to come. He continually made a virtue of his necessity. He compared

> *sitting and reading for four hours, and doing some job that's useless, that there's no need for, that's not helping anyone, or not helping yourself either. Just the idea of keeping your hands busy, to me it's senseless. I'd rather sit down and read. You're not screwing up the environment, making a mess.*

His defense of his odd-jobs way of life seemed partly genuine, but also fueled by resentment. GORD resented the fact that his unemployment and poverty made him unattractive to women—so he criticized the women of today as shallow (as though *he* were rejecting *them*). Having been rejected by his family during some drinking years, he posited the view that one should never get close to one's family.

His ambivalence at being on the margin was caught in this passage:

Well, I've resigned myself to the fact that I'll never meet anyone and have a family....And I have a kind of resentment against that....Maybe my feeling of self-worth has gone down.... I probably wouldn't meet anyone and have one or two children. I've resigned myself that will never happen.

To be honest, I don't really give a shit.... It doesn't really matter.

Plainly it did matter, but he had to find some way to live with his unsheltered position in the marginal work world, as well as social rejection. GORD's "coming to terms" with those probabilities which hedged him in was chiefly the consequence of his marginalization but also partial contributor to his predicament....

To the owner of this book

We hope that you have enjoyed *Work in Canada: Readings in the Sociology of Work and Industry* and we would like to know as much about your experiences as you would care to offer. Only through your comments and those of others can we learn how to make this a better text for future readers.

School _____ Your instructor's name _____

Course _____ Was the text required? _____ Recommended? _____

1. What did you like the most about *Work in Canada?*

_____

_____

_____

2. How useful was this text for your course?

_____

_____

_____

3. Do you have any recommendations for ways to improve the next edition of this text?

_____

_____

_____

4. In the space below or in a separate letter, please write any other comments you have about the book. (For example, please feel free to comment on reading level, writing style, terminology, design features, and learning aids.)

_____

_____

_____

_____

Optional

Your
name _____ Date _____

May Nelson Canada quote you, either in promotion for *Work in Canada* or in future publishing ventures?

Yes _____ No _____

Thanks!

FOLD HERE

MAIL ➤POSTE

Canada Post Corporation / Société canadienne des postes

Postage paid
if mailed in Canada

Port payé
si posté au Canada

**Business
Reply**

**Réponse
d'affaires**

0107077099   01

TAPE SHUT

TAPE SHUT

Nelson

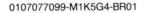

0107077099-M1K5G4-BR01

Nelson Canada
College Editorial Department
1120 Birchmount Rd.
Scarborough, ON M1K 9Z9

PLEASE TAPE SHUT. DO NOT STAPLE.